Women, Money and Markets (1770–1914)

Women, Money and Markets (1770–1914)

Representing the Invisible Hands of the Economy

Edited by

Emma Newport and Joyce Goggin

THE BOYDELL PRESS

First published 2026
The Boydell Press, Woodbridge

ISBN 978-1-83765-210-5

The Boydell Press is an imprint of Boydell & Brewer Ltd
and of Boydell & Brewer Inc.
website: www.boydellandbrewer.com

Our Authorised Representative for product safety in the EU is Easy Access System
Europe - Mustamäe tee 50, 10621 Tallinn, Estonia, gpsr.requests@easproject.com

A CIP catalogue record for this book is available
from the British Library

To Isabelle Alexandra,
a little invisible being who was expected to become visible,
and did so during the birth of this book.

Contents

Illustrations

The editors, contributors and publisher are grateful to all the institutions and persons listed for permission to reproduce the materials in which they hold copyright. Every effort has been made to trace the copyright holders; apologies are offered for any omission, and the publisher will be pleased to add any necessary acknowledgement in subsequent editions.

Abbreviations

DRO	Derbyshire Record Office
EIC	East India Company
EMH	Efficient Market Hypothesis
H.M	His/Her Majesty
HM	Edith Wharton, *House of Mirth*
LLM	Large Language Models
MS	manuscript
ODNB	*Oxford Dictionary of National Biography*
OED	*Oxford English Dictionary*
PROB	probate
RLF	Royal Literary Fund
SRO	Staffordshire Record Office
TMS	*The Theory of Moral Sentiments*
TNA	The National Archives
UCLA	University of California, Los Angeles
WN	*An Inquiry in the Nature and Causes of the Wealth of Nations*
WOC	*The Woman of Colour*
Wonderful Adventures	*The Wonderful Adventures of Mrs. Seacole in Many Lands*

Contributors

Olivia Biber, University of Bern

Olivia Biber is a doctoral researcher working on her PhD project situated at the intersection of literature, gender and queer studies, and economics. Before joining the team at the University of Bern, she was a research and teaching assistant at the University of Zurich. Olivia's current research explores how textual reticence in the Victorian novel responds to shifting gendered social and economic environments.

Peter Collinge, Keele University

Peter Collinge is a historian, researcher, writer and public speaker and a Fellow of the Royal Historical Society. His research interests include eighteenth- and nineteenth-century businesses, the Old Poor Law, workhouse gardens, food and drink, and health, leisure and tourism. He is the co-contributing editor of *Providing for the Poor: The Old Poor Law 1750–1834* (2022) and the author of numerous articles on business, markets, labour and the economy in the eighteenth and nineteenth centuries. Following the completion of his PhD on businesswomen in Georgian Derbyshire, Peter worked as a postdoctoral researcher on an AHRC-funded project, *Small Bills and Petty Finance 1700–1834: Co-creating the History of the Old Poor Law*. This was a collaboration between academics at the Universities of Keele and Sussex, archive services and volunteers.

Lana L. Dalley, California State University, Fullerton

Lana Dalley is a professor and department vice chair who works on women writers, economic theory, feminist and gender theory. With Jill Rappoport, she is the co-editor of the book *Economic Women: Essays on Desire and Dispossession in Nineteenth-Century British Culture* (2013). Lana's work on Victorian women's writing and economics has appeared in *Victorian Literature and Culture*, *Women's Writing*, *Victorians Institute Journal*, *Victorian Poetry*, *Nineteenth-Century Gender Studies* and *The Routledge Companion to Literature and Economics* (2018), among others. Most recently, she edited a four-volume anthology of primary sources *Women's Economic Writing in the Nineteenth Century* (2023).

Sarah Dredge, Sheffield Hallam University

Sarah Dredge is a senior lecturer whose research focuses on nineteenth-century women's fictional writing as political discourse, which has lately led to an interest in women writers' engagement with political economy. She has published various pieces within these areas. Sarah's most recent publication has been on Mary Seacole: '"Rice Puddings Made Without Milk": Mother Seacole Reforms "Home Habits" in the Crimea', in *The Routledge Companion to Literature and Feminism*. Before that, Sarah has published on Jane Austen and political economy, including '"Within View of His Own Warehouses": Sites of Change in *Pride and Prejudice* and *North and South*', in *After Austen*, edited by Lisa Hopkins (Springer International Publishing, 2018), and contributed '"I Have Tried to Write Truthfully": Fictions of Science in Women's Writing of Nineteenth-Century Political Economy', to *Political Economy, Literature & the Formation of Knowledge, 1720–1850*, edited by Richard Adelman and Catherine Packham (Routledge, 2018). She has previously published 'Negotiating "A Woman's Work": Philanthropy to Social Science in Gaskell's *North and South*', *Victorian Literature and Culture*, 40:1 (2012), 83–97.

Joyce Goggin, University of Amsterdam

Joyce Goggin is a senior lecturer in literature at the University of Amsterdam, where she also teaches film and media studies. The co-founder of the interdisciplinary research network 'Women, Money, and Markets: 1600–1950', Joyce has published widely on gambling and finance in literature, painting, comic books, film, TV and computer games. She has recently edited *Aegean Sponge Fishing and the Island of Kalymnos: An Ethnography and Industrial History*, from the Greek (Brill, 2024). Other recent publications include 'Framing John Law: G(u)ilt, Fiction, and Finance', in *Moralizing Commerce in a Globalizing World Multidisciplinary Approaches to a History of Economic Conscience, 1600–1900* (Oxford, University Press 2022), and *Comedy and Crisis: Pieter Langendijk, the Dutch and the Speculative Bubbles of 1720* (Liverpool University Press, 2020).

Emma Newport, University of Sussex

Emma Newport is an associate professor in English literature whose research interests include eighteenth-century literature, material culture and gender studies. She has published a range of works, including 'The Fictility of Porcelain: Making and Shaping Meaning in Lady Dorothea Banks's "Dairy Book"', in *Eighteenth-Century Fiction* (2018). She is also contributing a chapter to the volume *Encountering Tea: Histories and Objects, 1650–1850*, (UCL Press, 2026). She is the co-founder of the network 'Women, Money, and Markets: 1600–1950', which brings together scholars from various fields to explore economic history and literary studies.

Catherine Packham, University of Sussex

Catherine Packham is professor of eighteenth-century literature and thought in the department of English at the University of Sussex. Her research addresses the interrelations of philosophy, natural philosophy and political economy in the eighteenth century, together with their connections with literary culture. Catherine has worked extensively on the writings of the eighteenth-century moral philosopher and political economist, Adam Smith, as well as on Mary Wollstonecraft. In addition to numerous journal articles, her books include: *Eighteenth-Century Vitalism: Bodies, Culture, Politics* (Palgrave, 2012) and a recent monograph, *Mary Wollstonecraft and Political Economy: The Feminist Critique of Commercial Modernity* (Cambridge University Press, 2024). She has also co-edited *Political Economy, Literature & the Formation of Knowledge, 1720–1850* (Routledge, 2018) with her colleague Richard Adelman. *Why Read Wollstonecraft?* is forthcoming from Routledge in 2026.

Janelle Pötzsch, Ruhr-Universität Bochum

Janelle Pötzsch is a philosopher and literary scholar and teaches academic writing at Ruhr-Universität Bochum, Germany. Her research interests include political philosophy, applied ethics, history of ideas, and eighteenth- and nineteenth-century philosophy and literature. Janelle has edited *Jonathan Swift and Philosophy* (Rowman & Littlefield, 2016) and published journal articles in *Philosophy and Literature*, *Women's Studies* and *Critique: Studies in Contemporary Fiction*, among others. She has previously published 'Marriage, Morals, and Progress: J. S. Mill and the Early Feminists', *History of European Ideas*, 48:6 (2022), 795–810.

Janette Rutterford, The Open University

Janette Rutterford is professor emerita of finance and financial history. Her research centres on corporate finance, investment management and the history of finance. She has authored several texts, including *Corporate Finance & Capital Markets*, *Financial Strategy* and *An Introduction to Stock Exchange Investment*. She was involved in a major Economic and Social Research Council research grant investigating women's wealth and investment from 1870 to 1930. Her latest publications concern the history of investment trusts, the history of shareholder activism and the importance of women as retail investors in the history of the London Stock Exchange.

Tim Sommer, University of Munich

Tim Sommer is a lecturer in English literature and culture at Ludwig-Maximilians-Universität Munich. His research is located at the intersection of literary studies, book history and cultural sociology, with a specific focus on authorship and the literary marketplace. He has published widely on these and related topics in venues such as *Romanticism*, *Book History*, the *Harvard Library Bulletin* and the *Journal of World Literature*. He is the author of *Carlyle, Emerson and the Transatlantic Uses of Authority: Literature, Print, Performance* (Edinburgh University Press, 2021) and the editor of *Cultural Heritage and the Literary Archive: Objects, Institutions, and Practices between the Analogue and the Digital* (Routledge, 2025).

Camille Stallings, The American University, Dubai

Camille L. Stallings is assistant professor of English at the American University in Dubai. Her doctoral thesis, 'The Ethics of Friendship in the Victorian Novel', investigates theories of friendship in the Victorian novel, newspaper press and periodicals. The *Victorian Periodical Review* published her essay, 'Seriality and Characterisation in the Press: Death Club Sensationalism, the 1848 Revolutions, and Reviews of Mary Barton' in its autumn 2024 issue. She has also contributed several entries to *The Palgrave Encyclopedia of Victorian Women's Writing*, as well as the annual economic review chapter for *The Year's Work in Critical and Cultural Theory*. She earned her DPhil at the University of Oxford. Her current research considers transnational friendship and British social clubs in the British Empire.

Hazel Vosper, University of Lancaster

Hazel Vosper's doctoral research focused on the experiences of female investors in England from the mid-nineteenth century until the early twentieth century. An active contributor to the Women's History Network, Hazel's key areas of research are the influences on women's engagement with financial securities, particularly the impact of both the domestication and commercialisation of investing, and the representation of female investors in print culture.

Foreword

Alexandra Buchan-Heelas

Growing up in Hong Kong as the daughter of an investment banker, finance has always fascinated me. After graduating with a degree in history, I chose to pursue a career in investment management, joining a graduate scheme in 2010 in the aftermath of the Global Financial Crisis. I was the only woman in my graduate intake, and only about 10 per cent of candidates at the assessment day were female. Today, despite some progress, women still make up only 12 per cent of UK fund managers, and fewer than one in five senior investment roles are held by women.

My own career has been hugely rewarding, but not without challenge. Returning to work twice after maternity leave was one of the hardest things I've ever done. Handing over my clients to other portfolio managers felt like surrendering my entire career's work. Returning meant rebuilding confidence while struggling with the very real juggle of young children at home. I was lucky to have a great employer, a supportive husband and excellent childcare, but often women don't. It is at this point that talented women can end up leaving the industry altogether. Every year in the UK, tens of thousands of women lose or step back from jobs after having children and, in finance, an already small pipeline shrinks long before board level.

It was these experiences that led me to co-found *Women Who Work*, a network supporting ambitious women returning to work in finance and professional services after maternity leave. Much of the existing support is focused on part-time or flexible arrangements, but the women that we see want something different; they want to return full time, to be promoted, to become partners and directors. Our aim is to provide the mentorship and peer support that is otherwise lacking, and to create an environment to talk about everything from childcare to bonus negotiations. Alongside this, I have volunteered for a charity called *GAIN (Girls Are Investors)*, which seeks to change perceptions of finance among female school and university students. The 'Wolf of Wall Street' stereotype still puts many young women off applying. In reality, investment management is varied, purposeful and can offer the chance to do good – from running charity portfolios to promoting financial education. *GAIN* has already reached thousands of students and placed hundreds into internships, showing what is possible when we take action.

That is why this book, *Women, Money and Markets,* is so important. It reminds us that women have always been part of the economic story, even when they were rendered invisible. From entrepreneurs and landowners to investors and writers, the women in these pages were exercising financial power in ways that shaped households, markets and empires. Their names may not have made it into the pages of economic history, but their influence was real. For women in finance today, that legacy matters. It counters the idea that we are 'new arrivals' in the marketplace or that our presence needs justification. It shows that women's economic contribution is not an innovation but a continuation.

Looking ahead, the importance of women in wealth and investment has never been greater. Over the next two decades, trillions will change hands in one of the largest intergenerational wealth transfers in history. Women will inherit, manage and grow that wealth, and they will rightly expect to be heard and understood. Historically, in my industry, we often dealt primarily with husbands, while wives attended meetings but did not engage. With younger clients, that is no longer the case. Decisions are made jointly, financial literacy is high, and diverse family structures are commonplace. Women's perspectives on risk and long-term planning often differ from men's, and in certain market environments those differences can be particularly valuable. This is not about one gender being 'better' at investing than the other; it is vital to recognise that diversity of thought leads to stronger outcomes. Multiple studies have shown that teams with a wider range of voices make better decisions – and investment is no exception.

The benefits also extend beyond the boardroom. When women are economically visible, the impact is felt across generations. Research shows that daughters of working mothers go on to earn more and are more likely to reach leadership positions themselves. Sons raised in households where mothers work are more likely to share childcare and household responsibilities as adults. In other words, women's participation in the economy shapes the future of families, workplaces and society.

This book offers us both a reminder and a challenge. A reminder that invisibility does not mean absence: women's hands have always been at work in the economy; and a challenge to make sure those hands are now recognised, valued and visible – in boardrooms, investment decisions, and the financial lives of families around the world. The invisible hand has always been there, and it is high time we saw it clearly.

Alexandra Buchan-Heelas
Co-founder of *Women Who Work*

Editors' Preface

The chapters in this collection are united by their focus on women as economic agents and theorists. From their presence in shareholder lists and business records to their literary representations as investors, artists, writers and entrepreneurs, women's contributions to the economy have often been overlooked, misunderstood or misrepresented. This volume continues the work of those who have sought to redress the public perception of women's inconsequence and invisibility in the formation of the modern economy, including that of Amy Erickson, Jill Rappoport and Nancy Henry. *Women, Money and Markets* provides a study of the ways in which women leveraged sentiment, education and capital to navigate the constraints of their time and to develop their agency and autonomy.

In addition to examining the diverse ways in which women participated in economic life, this book addresses the broader theoretical implications of their actions. Contributors consider the interplay between affect and economics, challenging the conventional narrative of the market as a space of rationality and control. By revealing the market's susceptibility to human emotions, relationships and desires, these essays invite readers to reconsider the historical foundations of modern capitalism and the enduring role of sentiment in shaping economic systems.

The women in these pages are not mere subjects of history but architects of change. Through archival recovery and literary analysis, *Women, Money and Markets* reveals the ways that women negotiated, contested and redefined the boundaries of economic life. This volume invites readers to recognise women's influence in these spheres and, in doing so, this collection contributes to a growing understanding of economic history that recognises the visible hands of women in the financialisation of the economy in the long nineteenth century.

The Structure of the Book

This edited volume is divided into three parts, each of which addresses different kinds of female economic agency and the value of paying attention to it: 'Risky Women'; 'Economies of Feeling'; and 'Professional Conduct'. The four chapters in each part are arranged chronologically to provide periodisation of the three themes, prefaced by a short introduction to the conceptual framework of the section. There were many possible schemas for arranging this volume, such are the surprising, as well as the expected, connections that emerge between chapters; accordingly, the editors have indicated in the footnotes when a specific notion or reference in a chapter complements that of another. Readers of this volume will undoubtedly find many more such instances of their own. Indeed, a more useful heurism to describe the relations between the twelve chapters might be a marketplace of interlocking ideas, with cross-references and returns to ideas that are put to work in different periods and conditions. Concepts such as sympathy, the interaction of public and private spaces, and references to Adam Smith and David Hume, circulate the pages of this edited collection, as do subjects of female education, protection and conduct, bourgeois ambition and aristocratic privilege, and the invitation to *follow the money*.

The study opens with Janette Rutterford's set of methods that serve the recovery of hard-to-see women, and discusses how the markets responded to a surfeit of women in the nineteenth and early twentieth centuries; Peter Collinge demonstrates the strategies that an individual woman of means might deploy to evade the restrictions meted by coverture; and Hazel Vosper provides evidence that a significant number of women were studying and participating in diverse markets and disseminating advice to encourage others to do the same. Joyce Goggin provides a concluding chapter that looks at representations of women without fortunes, at risk of becoming a surplus woman, and the gambles that they are willing to take to address that precipitous condition.

Part Two, 'Economies of Feeling', addresses women's contribution to progress in the evolution of the modern economy and the ways in which they might offer alternative models, seen in Catherine Packham's study of Mary Wollstonecraft's fiction to interrogate the role of credit and belief as well as passion and prudence in the market, to the work of Emma Newport and Olivia Biber, who look at the tensions that arose between progress and maintaining the status quo, and how women might respond to, or intervene, in economic and industrial crises of the nineteenth century. Sarah

Dredge considers the difficulty of professionalising care, especially when those expert hands belonged to Mary Seacole, who was neither white nor English. As such, 'Economies of Feeling' addresses the variance found in the hands of women, which move from the gestural to a more explicit manipulation of active sympathy, and how this shift is at least partially informed by concepts of moral, ethical, or sympathetic conduct, and how these were gendered and racialised.

In Part Three, 'Professional Conduct', contributors consider how women fashioned careers as artists, economists and writers, and how they participated in the professionalisation of these fields. Despite the popular perception that writing was the last resort of the abandoned, widowed, single or otherwise unwanted or surplus woman, or that writing was either contradictorily a hobby for pin money or one small step removed from sex work.[1] Tim Sommer, Janelle Pötzsche, Lana L. Dalley and Camille Stallings, take a female writer from a different point in the nineteenth century in order to offer case studies of the ways in which women forged a professional relationship to writing and navigated the pressures on, and barriers faced by, female writers, thinkers and artists.

Each chapter variously demonstrates how the publications of women writers served as interventions on the topic of the female artist and intellectual at work. Tim Sommer and Camille Stallings look at female creators and their approaches to professionalisation, as well as the domestic and professional hurdles that women had to tackle during this period. Janelle Pötzsche's study of Harriet Taylor Mill, for whom economic laws were operating in the private sphere and resulted in her vigorous refutation of the wage-fund doctrine. Lana L. Dalley addresses head on the dearth of female political economists in the present day and makes the case for where and how to find women economists in the nineteenth century, especially by addressing their role in writing popular texts on political economy that reached and impacted on broad audiences.

[1] See also the representation of a gin-drinking, cat-loving, dishevelled and half-disrobed writer Elizabeth Inchbald, in the throes of a literary struggle with pen and paper in the satirical print *I'll tell you what! That 'such things are' we must allow, but such things never were till now*, H. Wigstead (delineator), printed by E. Jackson, *c.*1790. Stipple print, *c.*20.6 × 23.6 cm. Laura J. Rosenthal, *Infamous Commerce: Prostitution in Eighteenth-Century British Literature and Culture* (Ithaca NY: Cornell University Press, 2006); Nancy Armstrong, *Desire and Domestic Fiction: A Political History of the Novel* (New York: Oxford University Press, 1987).

Acknowledgements

This volume owes its existence to the many contributors to the *Women, Money and Markets* network, whose scholarship and collaboration have shaped the vibrant community it has become. Since its inception in 2017, more than 100 scholars have helped to expand our collective understanding of the complex intersections of women, finance and the marketplace. While twelve contributors are represented in this volume, the work of many others continues to inform and expand the field in meaningful ways.

Peter Collinge has been unfailingly supportive and has shared his wealth of knowledge of the archive, and contributed to the indexing process. The contents herein are improved immeasurably by his influence. Peter Collinge and Sarah Dredge have contributed their leadership over many hours each year to the growth of our network from 2017 to the present day, as has Barbara Straumann, who took on the especial challenge of running our annual conference at the University of Zurich during the pandemic.

At the University of Sussex, I am fortunate to work with an inspiring group of scholars specialising in the eighteenth and nineteenth centuries, including Bethan Stevens, Hannah Field, Andrea Haslanger and Richard Adelman. I extend my deep gratitude to my colleague Catherine Packham for her guidance on matters of economic theory and political economy, which have shaped the development of this edited collection significantly. I am also grateful to the Media, Arts and Humanities Research Institute for the support received in twice hosting the network of scholars affiliated with *Women, Money and Markets* at the University of Sussex. My thanks also go to Helen Newport for her invaluable proofreading.

I extend my greatest thanks to my co-editor, Joyce Goggin, whose vision and dedication have been integral to the success of the network and the creation of this book. Her friendship, and the many other friends made throughout the network's existence, has been the greatest joy of undertaking this research. Her contributions have been invaluable, and this project could not have been realised without her collaborative spirit and unwavering commitment to its completion.

Editorial Conventions

Citations are provided in footnotes, except in the instance of chapters that have a primary text under discussion, for which page numbers are given in parentheses within the body of the text.

Unless otherwise noted, all references are to Adam Smith's *An Inquiry into the Nature and Causes of the Wealth of Nations*, edited by Kathryn Sutherland (Oxford: Oxford University Press, 2008; originally published in 1776).

Note on spelling

Original spellings have been retained wherever possible.

Introduction

EMMA NEWPORT AND JOYCE GOGGIN

In the satirical print 'An Holland Smock to be Won' (1770, cover), a lady's cotton smock hangs empty from a tree to advertise to all, including the illiterate, the prize to be won in a women's footrace.[1] Yet this undergarment possesses a shapeliness, and is so titillatingly low-cut, that one can easily imagine the breasts and legs that might be there when the race is won. A young man has climbed the tree to which the garment is staked, suspended by the sleeves as though the invisible woman is at the pillory, in order to lift the underskirt and peek lasciviously at the riches beneath – the branch standing in for his own erection.

Much as this print satirises the marriage market, it also raises the spectre of women in the marketplace more broadly. For women, the stakes of a competitive market are different from those for men. In this image, the female runner's body is involved as both agent and prize, whereas a notice nailed to the tree below the smock announces a contest for men in which they will compete for 'a flitch of bacon'. In other words, while women compete for an intimate and sexualised item of clothing, men compete for edible commodities. The prize for men is represented by a paper notice in a manner analogous to marriage banns, while reminding the viewer of the way in which bills of exchange could stand in for goods and property. Men are bringing home the bacon; women, in this instance, are a spectacle to be feasted upon. Accordingly, the image leaves viewers with the impression that a woman's position in competition is tainted: improper and inviting her own exploitation, and bringing her into the purview of illegality. At the base of the tree in the print, a woman is wielding a hand that goes unseen as she picks a man's pocket; hence, prostitution and theft are clearly foregrounded in 'An Holland Smock'. If a woman's hand is involved in the market, the print suggests, then it works only in the murkier realms of commerce.

It is worth noting that this print was published just six years before Adam Smith's *The Wealth of Nations* (1776), in which he refers to the invisible hand

1 See cover. John Collet, *An Holland Smock to be Run for by Any Woman Born in This County: The Best Woman in Three Heats*. Published by Robert Sayer and John Smith, 1770. Copy held by the editor of this volume.

of the economy; a metaphor that receives brief mention in both *The Theory of Moral Sentiments* (1759) and *The History of Astronomy* (1795), but otherwise represents a small part of Smith's political economy. Yet the invisible hand has since become a catechesis that has captured the imaginations and analyses of Western economists.[2] The theory of the invisible hand, in which the outcome of individual behaviour is an orderly and, above all, rational socio-economic system, remains an appealing metaphor, though one that has travelled very far from its original sense.

Smith's literary metaphor emerged from a moral philosophy that saw human self-interest tempered by sympathy, justice and the limits of human reason. In the twentieth century, the invisible hand was excised from the rest and became instead a general principle of market fundamentalism and market infallibility for the economists of the Chicago School, including Milton Friedman and George Stigler; for libertarians like Friedrich Hayek, Smith's metaphor of the invisible hand served as proof of the epistemic superiority of markets, which could resist or correct human error. While more recent economic historians have addressed the problem of the discorporate hand and the departure made from the original sentiments of Adam Smith, the pursuit of rationality, and the related and misplaced confidence that mathematics and markets can erase emotion and error, arguably reached its zenith in Eugene Fama's Efficient Market Hypothesis (EMH). Fama's EMH posits that market prices at any given time reflect fully all available information; in this framework, the market functions as if guided by an 'invisible hand' of information that is incorporated into prices, which in turn guides the allocation of resources.[3]

An inclination towards faith in the EMH informs current belief in algorithms, as algorithms might be assumed to be the ultimate invisible hand: it appears that 'algorithms do not think, but they communicate; they establish connections, they create expectations, and they make society possible

[2] Frédéric Bastiat, *Economic Harmonies*, translated from the French, with a Notice of the Life and Writings of the Author by Patrick James Stirling (orig. 1850; Edinburgh: Oliver and Boyd; London: Simpkin, Marshall & Co., 1860); Alfred Marshall, *Principles of Economics*, 8th edn (London: Macmillan, 1920); John Maynard Keynes, *The General Theory of Employment, Interest, and Money* (London: Macmillan, 1936); Paul A. Samuelson, *Economics: An Introductory Analysis*, 1st edn (New York: McGraw-Hill, 1948); Milton Friedman, *Capitalism and Freedom* (Chicago IL: University of Chicago Press, 1962); Joan Robinson, *Economic Philosophy* (Harmondsworth: Penguin, 1962); Kenneth J. Arrow, *Essays in the Theory of Risk-Bearing* (Amsterdam: North-Holland, 1971); Joseph E. Stiglitz, *Whither Socialism?* (Cambridge MA: MIT Press, 1994); Kaushik Basu, *Beyond the Invisible Hand: Groundwork for a New Economics* (Princeton NJ: Princeton University Press, 2010).

[3] Eugene F. Fama, 'Efficient Capital Markets: A Review of Theory and Empirical Work', *Journal of Finance*, 25:2 (1970), 383–417.

in a way comparable to money or markets'.[4] Accordingly, the credulous might be persuaded that algorithms could eventually capture and harvest complete sets of data, which they cannot, and that algorithms might therefore offer the apex of rationalisation – the true invisible hand – excised from human emotion, which they are not. With the ascendancy of the algorithm comes an equally troubling conviction that artificial intelligence will provide the next step in achieving omniscience in the market. Modern financial markets, and those who operate in them, have been inclined to assume that the invisible hand of algorithmic trading and large language models has given, or will give, rise to the ultimate rational and interconnected market.[5] Large language models (LLMs) are already impacting on the speed of US equity markets – but they have also increased their volatility, indicating that LLMs are not going to move markets beyond the cycles of boom and bust, which have been blamed on such contagious sentiments as greed, hope, credulity, irrational exuberance and fear, all of which infect markets.[6]

Consequently, recent work by economists reinforces the concern that there is no successful mechanism by which to extract and cordon off the market from human emotions and behaviour.[7] It is increasingly clear that markets fail to be rational and instead respond to and reveal the desires and limitations of the people who participate in them. There is, therefore, a pressing need to historicise the relationship between affect and the economy in order to challenge the faith placed in technology in modern financial markets. The reality is, however, that the increasing complexity of the technologised modern financial system of algorithmic trading 'undermines the self-correcting virtues attributed to the market by the invisible hand metaphor and the efficient market hypothesis', and that 'far from guaranteeing

4 Elena Esposito, *Artificial Communication: How Algorithms Produce Social Intelligence* (Cambridge MA: MIT Press, 2022), p. 18.

5 Adam Hayes, 'Enacting a Rational Actor: Roboadvisors and the Algorithmic Performance of Ideal Types', *Economy and Society*, 49:4 (2020), 562–95. https://doi.org/10.1080/03085147.2020.1782054.

6 Eric Budish, Peter Cramton, and John Shim, 'The High-Frequency Trading Arms Race: Frequent Batch Auctions as a Market Design Response', *Quarterly Journal of Economics*, 130:4 (2015), 1547–621; Donald MacKenzie, *Trading at the Speed of Light: How Ultrafast Algorithms Are Transforming Financial Markets* (Princeton NJ: Princeton University Press, 2021), accessed via ResearchGate; International Monetary Fund (IMF), 'Artificial Intelligence Can Make Markets More Efficient – and More Volatile', *IMF Blog*, 15 October 2024, www.imf.org/en/Blogs/Articles/2024/10/15/artificial-intelligence-can-make-markets-more-efficient-and-more-volatile. See also, Robert J. Shiller, *Narrative Economics: How Stories Go Viral and Drive Major Economic Events* (Princeton NJ: Princeton University Press, 2019).

7 Gerald Nestler, 'The Derivative Condition: A Present Inquiry into the History of Futures' (unpublished doctoral thesis, Goldsmiths, University of London, 2017); Robert Wosnitzer, '*Desk, Firm, God, Country: Proprietary Trading and the Speculative Ethos of Financialism*' (unpublished doctoral thesis, New York University, 2014).

stability, financial markets have often amplified instability, which suggests that the alleged invisible hand is, at best, an unreliable guide'.[8] Furthermore, any algorithm put to work in trading has been designed by human hands and comes into contact with human behaviour. As Donald MacKenzie suggests, algorithmic markets function as 'engineered ecologies' that are prone to glitches, latency races and flash crashes, challenging the notion that the algorithm represents the ultimate form of disembodied rationality.[9]

In light of these recent economic trends, the contribution of *Women, Money and Markets* to theory lies in its re-examination of sentiment and the market, especially the relationship between *affect* and *effect*: of feeling and doing, in which sympathy and affect are not passive ontological states but active forces in the teleology of the economy. This volume provides consideration of the invisible, misunderstood or misrepresented history of affect and sympathy in the economy, whereby feeling serves as one of the invisible engineers of market ecologies. Such notions of the influence of 'gut-feeling' or 'financial intuition' in trading has only recently begun to be understood as a function of neurobiology rather than mere whimsy or anecdote, with a new understanding emerging of how interoceptive ability, or the capacity to sense internal bodily states such as the heartbeat, correlates with trading success, challenging the notion that algorithmic trading is purely cognitive.[10] Emotions and bodily signals are integral to rational decision-making, not its antithesis.

Rather than taking for granted the imagined rational hand of the market, a major concern of this book centres on the relationship between affect and the economy, taking the reader back to the original Smithian hand in a number of ways. The work of Catherine Packham and Sarah Dredge reconsiders the role that Smith found for affect and sympathy in the market. Their work, and that of others in this collection, takes apart the fallacy of rationality governing exchange, demonstrating in different ways how the circulation of care and benevolence, belief, credit, and feeling informs progress towards a modern market system. More broadly across this volume, with a return to the invisible hand as an agile metonym rather than serving as a metaphoric universal law governing the economy, the chapters herein ask: what kind of hand occupies the imagination? Is the assumed hand of the capitalist white and male? What does it mean for the formation of the

8 Alessandro Vercelli, *Crisis and Sustainability: The Delusion of Free Markets* (London: Palgrave Macmillan, 2017), p. 87; Alessandro Vercelli, *Finance and Democracy: Towards a Sustainable Financial System* (Cham: Palgrave Macmillan, 2019), p. 72.

9 MacKenzie, *Trading at the Speed of Light* ; see also Andrew W. Lo, *Adaptive Markets: Financial Evolution at the Speed of Thought* (Princeton NJ: Princeton University Press, 2017).

10 Peter Bossaerts, 'What Can Neurobiology Teach Us About Emotion and Rationality in Financial Decision-Making?', *Frontiers in Psychology*, 12 (2021), 667541.

modern political economy when the hands in the market fits neither of these descriptions? Do those hands behave in the same way, with the same consequences, unintended or otherwise, or do the hands move differently? This collection uncovers and pays attention to the hands that serve as a recurring motif across many of the chapters. There are labouring hands, gentle hands, sympathetic hands, serving hands, nurturing hands, controlling hands, and especially *writing* hands; above all, they are hands that move in complicated and surprising ways between nation, community, business, family and the individual to whom they belong. The essays in this collection make the case that women's role in the economy could be as consequential as Adam Smith's invisible hands.

Throughout this volume, the turn to the didactic is frequent: women are found shaping economic behaviours as authors and educators, two roles frequently indistinguishable from one another during this period. For historians as much as literary critics, fiction can serve as both cultural artefact and 'cultural instrument'.[11] Writing possesses a constitutive power. Fiction offers a means of historicising individual and mass acculturation, as well as the transition to modernity. Print cultures operate at the interstices of the public and private, circulating ideas between different hands.[12]

Throughout the twentieth and twenty-first centuries, cultural and literary theorists have grappled with the idea that fiction possesses a disciplining function that reinforces a dominant or hegemonic position.[13] However, long before Foucault suggested that the mind might be shaped by 'a kind of moral orthopaedics: a set of techniques for straightening the soul', Mary Wollstonecraft made the link between pedagogy, children's literature and the writer's ability to intervene in and shape national concerns.[14] To her

[11] On the novel as cultural instrument, see Michael McKeon, *The Origins of the English Novel, 1600–1740*, 15th anniversary edn (Baltimore MD: Johns Hopkins University Press, 2002).

[12] A popular idea since Habermas's pioneering work on the public sphere was published in 1969, Leonore Davidoff and Catherine Hall use 'separate spheres' as an analytical framework, linking gender roles to middle-class economic formation in Leonore Davidoff and Catherine Hall, *Family Fortunes: Men and Women of the English Middle Class, 1780–1850*, rev. edn (London: Routledge, 2002); among others, Amanda Vickery provides criticism of the over-simplification of the 'separate spheres' argument in 'Golden Age to Separate Spheres? A Review of the Categories and Chronology of English Women's History', *The Historical Journal*, 36:2 (1993), 383–414.

[13] See, for example, Edward Said, who describes 'the enormously systematic discipline by which European culture was able to manage – and even produce – the Orient politically, sociologically, militarily, ideologically, scientifically, and imaginatively during the post-Enlightenment period', it is a reminder that Western fiction does the same to the Occident – and that *economically* might be added to Said's familiar list. Edward W. Said, *Orientalism* (London: Routledge & Kegan Paul, 1978; repr. 1980), p. 11.

[14] Michel Foucault, *Discipline and Punish: The Birth of the Prison*, trans. Alan Sheridan (New York: Vintage Books, 1977), part 3, pp. 179–80.

Original Stories from Real Life; with Conversations Calculated to Regulate the Affections, and Form the Mind to Truth and Goodness (1788), Wollstonecraft attaches a preface:

> These conversations and tales are accommodated to the present state of society; which obliges the author to attempt to cure those faults by reason, which might never to have taken root in the infant mind. Good habits, imperceptibly fixed, are far preferable to the precepts of reason; but, as this task requires more judgment than generally falls to the lot of parents, substitutes must be sought for, and medicines given, when regimen would have answered the purpose much better.[15]

Wollstonecraft pathologises the national condition, while asserting the natural authority of mothers as well as fathers to participate in determining the progress of society, and of narratives – written by men *and* women – to facilitate its advancement, and to supply the shortfall in any inadequate parenting of the next generation.

Staking her claim about the importance of and the need to attend to the novel, Wollstonecraft's contemporary, and her intellectual counterpoint, Anna Laetitia Barbauld, provides a pioneering account of how novels 'have been moulded upon the manners of the age, – and, in return, have influenced the manners of the succeeding generation by the sentiments they have infused and the sensibilities they have excited'.[16] Barbauld writes about the ways in which the British novel might be handled in 'the war of systems', as she considers the ways in which novels could interrogate 'those systems of philosophy or politics which have raised so much ferment of late years'.[17]

15 Mary Wollstonecraft, 'Preface', in *Original Stories from Real Life; with Conversations Calculated to Regulate the Affections, and Form the Mind to Truth and Goodness* (London: J. Johnson, 1796).

16 Anna Laetitia Barbauld, *The British Novelists; with an Essay, and Prefaces Biographical and Critical, by Mrs. Barbauld*, 50 vols (London: Printed for F. C. and J. Rivington; W. Otridge and Son; A. Strahan; T. Payne; G. Robinson; W. Lowndes; Wilkie and Robinson; Scatcherd and Letterman; J. Walker; J. Cuthell; Vernor, Hood, and Sharpe; R. Lea; J. Nunn; Lackington and Co.; Clarke and Son; C. Law; Longman, Hurst, Rees, and Orme; Cadell and Davies; E. Jeffery; J. K. Newman; Crosby and Co.; J. Carpenter; S. Bagster; T. Booth; J. Mobray; J. and J. Richardson; Black, Parry, and Kingsbury; J. Harding; R. Phillips; J. Mawman; J. Booker; J. Asperne; R. Baldwin; Mathews and Leigh; J. Faulder; Johnson and Co.; Sherwood and Co.; J. Miller; W. Creech, Edinburgh; and Wilson and Son, York, 1810), pp. 1–2.

17 Anna Laetitia Barbauld, 'On the Origin and Progress of Novel-Writing', in *The British Novelists; with an Essay, and Prefaces Biographical and Critical, by Mrs. Barbauld*, 50 vols (London: Printed for F. C. and J. Rivington; W. Otridge and Son; A. Strahan; T. Payne; G. Robinson; W. Lowndes; Wilkie and Robinson; Scatcherd and Letterman; J. Walker; J. Cuthell; Vernor, Hood, and Sharpe; R. Lea; J. Nunn; Lackington and Co.; Clarke and Son; C. Law; Longman, Hurst, Rees, and Orme; Cadell and Davies; E. Jeffery; J. K. Newman; Crosby and Co.; J. Carpenter; S. Bagster; T. Booth; J. Mobray; J. and J. Richardson; Black, Parry, and Kingsbury; J. Harding; R. Phillips; J. Mawman;

At the same time, Barbauld found that other novels might not be 'written to favour any particular system; the whole is the play of a fine imagination delighting itself with images of perfection and happiness, which it cannot find in any existing form of things', as in her description of *Gaudentio di Lucca* (1725).[18] The extensive publication history of Anna Laetitia Barbauld's *The British Novelists* (1810), with its fifty-volume scope and a remarkable list of booksellers and publishers, represents a significant print run and high expectations for commercial success and cultural impact. Though any classificatory enterprise of this period, including those applied to the novel, reflects a drive to impose order rather than provides evidence of coherent or absolute systems, Barbauld's discursive engagement with systematisation nonetheless reveals women's active role in shaping prescriptive taxonomies. Barbauld is contributing to the formation of an early literary canon of the novel, showing how women might be adept users of contemporary critical vocabulary, and could participate in public intellectual discourse.

The nature of women's participation in early public discourse is an example of Michael McKeon's argument in action: that literature resists simplistic division into hegemonic and counterhegemonic categories. Rather, 'the social function of literature', he writes, 'consists less either in regulation or in deregulation than in an investigative inquiry into their interpenetration'.[19] By writing a discourse on the novel attentive to systemic patterns and interdependencies, and to the potential for variance and instability, and by equipping readers with enduring conceptual tools for literary analysis, Barbauld encourages her readers to embrace women's participation in investigative inquiry, particularly through novel reading and writing. At the same time, she is inviting her readers to engage with the novel's diverse and often contradictory functions, as do her contemporaries such as Mary Wollstonecraft. Accordingly, the women discussed in this volume are not violently resisting the systems that they observed, participated in, decried, or imagined, including those systems that produced female poverty and economic dependence; nor are they straightforwardly reinforcing systems, behaviours and practices that could benefit them, as educated and often wealthy women, in ways largely unavailable to other categories of women.

J. Booker; J. Asperne; R. Baldwin; Mathews and Leigh; J. Faulder; Johnson and Co.; Sherwood and Co.; J. Miller; W. Creech, Edinburgh; and Wilson and Son, York, 1810), Vol. 1, pp. 1–62; at pp. 23, 26, 59.

18 Barbauld, *The British Novelists*, pp. 59, 39–40.

19 McKeon, *The Origins of the English Novel*, p. x. See also Clifford Siskin, *The Work of Writing: Literature and Social Change in Britain, 1700–1830* (Baltimore MD: Johns Hopkins University Press, 1999).

While the eighteenth-century mania for classification reflected a desire for, rather than the achievement of, comprehensive knowledge, it is the case that many interlocking and complex systems emerged or evolved during the financialisation of the British economy during this period. As Catherine Packham discusses in her chapter, credit operates at the interstices of individual interpersonal social relations and in economic activity taking place at a regional, national or international level, 'lubricating' a system of credit that became more complicated as new financial mechanisms were introduced to the market, such as paper money. Emma Newport pays attention to the ways in which global economic crises metastasise through trade, exchange and speculation: risk, which is mutually constitutive of credit, exposes the interdependence and causal relationships between individuals, institutions and corporations that are mediated by the connective tissue of markets. For Lana L. Dalley and Janelle Pötzsch, women like Harriet Taylor Mill, Harriet Martineau and Millicent Garrett Fawcett, were participating in forms of investigative inquiry that test and advance ideas on the role of women in markets and the broader economy, while also exploring the scope and potential of women's participation in the modern political economy as theorists and enfranchised citizens.

Because our focus is on women who have actively entered public discourse at pivotal moments in economic history, and although *Women, Money and Markets* includes stories from across the social spectrum, readers will most frequently encounter voices from, or accounts concerning, the British middling sort and elite. The work herein serves to emphasise and extend the point that Nancy Henry has made; namely, that women during this period were in possession of or acquired significant amounts of money and capital assets; capital, of course, could include emotional, cultural and intellectual capital, as well as financial capital. These women put their capital to work in ways that demonstrated their sophistication, their desire for professionalisation, and their boldness in the response to risk – and, at times, their complicity in the legal and social structures that protected their class position.[20] Nonetheless, when we consider women as an investing class, it encompasses a more diverse group than the modern reader might suppose. As Rutterford reminds the reader, the group includes the skilled working classes; furthermore, non-white citizens could inherit wealth and make investments.[21]

[20] Nancy Henry, *Women, Literature and Finance in Victorian Britain*, ed. by Nancy Henry (Cham: Palgrave Macmillan, 2018). Henry shared an early version of her chapter 'Charlotte Riddell's Financial Life and Fiction', (pp. 179–224) as a paper at the inaugural Women, Money and Markets Conference (King's College London, 2017).

[21] The orphaned Sarah Forbes Bonetta, who was born in Oke-Odan, in present-day Ogun State, southwestern Nigeria, in 1843, became a ward of Queen Victoria; an annuity was later secured for Forbes Bonetta's daughter. See Helen Rappaport, 'Sarah Forbes

The women discussed across all twelve chapters examine – robustly or more circumspectly – the systems that create, maintain and animate the modernising economy during the late eighteenth, nineteenth and early twentieth centuries; in some cases, women imagine alternative systems or offer correctives. These women, real and fictional, contribute to literature's biotic entanglements with the economy, ideology, epistemology, belief, culture and the imagination – entanglements that are not merely exchanges but dynamic, reciprocal processes through which literature and these domains co-evolve. Women are not mere consumers in the market, and the novel is not just a product to be consumed. Women and their writing, investing and work, vitalise the market ecosystem, inflecting its moral, intellectual and aesthetic dimensions, and reshaping the ways in which knowledge, value and meaning circulate.

By building on the work of Amy Erickson, Mary Poovey and Nancy Henry, this volume turns on its head the notion that women were merely managing household finances or earning their living by their pen or paint as a proscribed and isolated solution to being abandoned by their husbands – or failing to find one. Several chapters in this book, including those of Sarah Dredge, Tim Sommer and Camille Stallings, offer an interpretation of the ambition and profit-seeking that went hand in hand with the gendered professionalisation of women in these fields, as they consider how caregiving, wiving and mothering intersected with this process. The challenge of balancing work and domestic responsibilities while securing fair remuneration has long been central to women's economic lives. Yet, as Lana Dalley reminds us, these are not the only issues women face, nor are they concerns exclusive to women. Framing them as such risks siloing women's engagement with economic and political discourse, marginalising their contributions as economists and reducing their role to mere appendages to central debates, which in turn makes them easier to ignore, disparage or excise.

Played out in an exchange of essays published in *The North American Review* between 1879 and 1894, the problem of the 'Woman Question' emerged in popular discourse during the *Fin de Siècle* – though the 'querelles des femmes' has a much longer history, which is addressed this volume.[22]

Bonetta: The Captive African Princess Gifted to Queen Victoria', *HelenRappaport.com*, https://helenrappaport.com/queen-victoria/sarah-forbes-bonetta/ (accessed 8 September 2025); see also Daniel Livesay, *Children of Uncertain Fortune: Mixed-Race Jamaicans in Britain and the Atlantic Family, 1733–1833* (Williamsburg VA: Omohundro Institute of Early American History and Culture; Chapel Hill NC: University of North Carolina Press, 2018).

22 On the 'Woman Question': Francis Parkman, 'The Woman Question', *The North American Review*, 129:275 (October 1879), 303–21. Parkman is otherwise best known for his support for early eugenicist and anti-immigration policies. See also Julia Ward Howe, Lucy Stone, Thomas Wentworth Higginson, Elizabeth Cady Stanton and Wendell Phillips, 'The Other Side of the Woman Question', *The North American Review*, 129:276

Dalley takes up the 'Woman Question' when discussing Millicent Garrett Fawcett's participation in the Suffrage Movement; Sommer uses it to frame the professionalisation of art and writing in the work of Anne Brontë; Stallings invokes it in her call to rethink critical uses of household manuals in studying women's participation in the economy.[23] Moreover, several chapters in this book reveal how women found ways to circumvent the social and legal restrictions that they encountered. Peter Collinge, for example, looks at how ecclesiastical law, wills and probate, local customs and litigation provided profitable mechanisms by which literate and numerate women of means might participate in financial and legal decisions, their hand firmly on the tiller. Lana Dalley tackles what she describes as the 'epistemic discrimination' faced by women economists, whose ability to produce knowledge of economics was doubted, even if they were seen as capable of teaching the subject.

In paying attention to women who made, lost, inherited and put to work significant sums of capital, this edited collection shares examples of women as theorists, investors, wives, mothers, writers, businesswomen and industrialists, brought together in a single volume – and sometimes in a single person – in order to capture the complexity and dynamism of female roles in the economy. At times, pictures of the women in this collection are necessarily drawn from the fictional and the ephemeral: pocketbooks, trade bills, paintings, literary works, life writing, manuals – but also wills and testaments, chancery records, contracts, financial portfolios and bankruptcy proceedings. By juxtaposing case studies of real women with fictional representations of women and the economy, a more detailed picture emerges of how women's contributions were described and prescribed.

Women, Money and Markets picks up and expands the view of Hannah Barker and Elaine Chalus that, where historians had previously read conduct literature as simply descriptive, in truth, literary works serve both to prescribe and describe.[24] To this end, a number of the chapters in this

(November 1879), 413–46; Francis Parkman, 'The Woman Question Again', *The North American Review*, 130:278 (January 1880), 16–30; Lydia Lvovna Pimenoff, 'Science and the Woman's Question', *The North American Review*, 156:435 (February 1893), 248–51; Sarah Grand, 'The New Aspect of the Woman Question', *The North American Review*, 158:448 (March 1894), 270–6; Ouida (Maria Louisa Ramé), 'The New Woman', *The North American Review*, 158:450 (May 1894), 610–19.

23 See also Elizabeth K. Helsinger and William Veeder, *The Woman Question: Society and Literature in Britain and America, 1837–83* (Chicago IL: University of Chicago Press, 1983); Nicola Diane Thompson, *Victorian Women Writers and the Woman Question* (Cambridge: Cambridge University Press, 1999).

24 Hannah Barker and Elaine Chalus, 'Introduction', in *Gender in Eighteenth-Century England: Roles, Representations and Responsibilities*, ed. by Hannah Barker and Elaine Chalus (London: Routledge, 1997), pp. 1–28. Barker was the keynote speaker at an early Women, Money and Markets Conference.

volume explicitly or implicitly read novels as a form of critical fabulation, in which the novel itself stands as a method of reconstruction of lives that otherwise only exist as archival fragments. While Saidiya Hartman's work on fabulation has helped interdisciplinary practitioners to embrace creative practice as an essential tool in the process of making the invisible visible, it is Hartman's idea of 'foraging' and her model of 'raiding' archives 'for fragments upon which other narratives can be spun' could describe some of the methodologies adopted in this volume. Janette Rutterford, who pioneered research in this area, and Peter Collinge, might be of service to the literary critic or historian working in this field.[25]

In addition to offering economic, cultural and literary historians a set of methodologies for recovering and re-examining women's contributions to economic development, this collection of essays advances the economic study of narrative at the specific intersection of gender and finance – both in theory and in praxis – throughout the long nineteenth century. In so doing, the essays help readers to find female apparitions in the archive and give form to their presence through interdisciplinary research methods. Consequently, when thinking about finding women in the archive, *Women, Money, and Markets* asks some difficult questions: to what extent did some women participate in their own obscuration in the archive – and what role did their methods of disguising their participation play in women's wider invisibility in the economy? While Lana Dalley shows how writers like Martineau, Marcet and Garrett Fawcett refused to 'smuggle' in topics under the guise of fiction, choosing instead to use fiction as a deliberate pedagogic tool in the belief that political economy and financial matters are best communicated representationally, Olivia Biber and Camille Stallings show how other women writers, like Elizabeth Gaskell and Annie Thomas, took a more cautious approach, avoiding such overt and revealing interventions in their use of fiction.

How seriously should the modern reader take women's public and even private disavowals of their agency and engagement in discussions of markets, the circulation of money, risk and credit, and their socio-economic and political consequences – especially when their printed works, or financial history, reveal their thoughtful and thorough reflection on these subjects, though that reflection may be framed by apology, prevarication or hesitancy? Other strategies available to women seeking to obscure their engagement with economic discourse included, but were not limited to, concealing their identities through anonymity or pseudonymity when investing or publishing, and exploiting the plausible deniability afforded by fiction. This latter approach was often accompanied by modes of allusiveness or indirection, allowing

25 Saidiya Hartman, *Scenes of Subjection: Terror, Slavery, and Self-Making in Nineteenth-Century America* (New York: Oxford University Press, 1997), p. 12.

women to comment on economic matters without overt declaration. In the case of female investors and writers seeking publication, women could have recourse to trusts, agents, brokers and advisers acting on their behalf in order to conceal their own agentic position. When Hazel Vosper writes about how women learned financial self-protection, the spectre of how women might choose to hide their economic agency arises, along with how their financial dexterity served as another means of protecting themselves. This practice results in difficulties when researchers look for archival evidence of women's involvement in the markets as well as readers of fiction, especially where narratives penned by female authors are concerned.

Conclusion

This volume has emerged from the decade-long collaboration between an international network of scholars who are specialists in the literature and economic history of the eighteenth, nineteenth and early twentieth centuries. The work herein provides accounts of women engaged in different kinds of economic activity across the long nineteenth century, in order to increase the visibility of women who have hitherto either been unseen or have not been considered in relation to the market and the economy. Spanning over a century, this collection challenges the popular belief that, prior to the Married Women's Property Act of 1882, women lacked economic agency and were wholly dependent on the kindness of male relatives until widowhood – or, conversely, that the Act ensured that women arrived at full and equal economic agency alongside men.

While much work has been undertaken by Amy Erickson and her successors in economic history, in the fields of cultural studies and literary criticism, it is remarkable how entrenched the perception of female non-participation in the economy remains, despite the successes of scholars such as Nancy Henry, Jill Rappoport and Lana Dalley. This commonly held and persistent misapprehension speaks to the continued value and necessity of examining fictional and real representations of heiresses and other women of property and means, and of studying the 'portionless' as well as the 'surplus' women of the period. Our work brings together discussions of a range of women in British and colonial economies in order to demonstrate the extent, as well as the complexity, of female participation in and changes to modern economic development, especially in relation to the emergence of the novel, beginning with Mary Wollstonecraft's *Maria; or, The Wrongs of Woman* (1798), to the Brontës' and Elizabeth Gaskell's mid-nineteenth-century novels, and Edith Wharton's turn-of-the-century *The House of Mirth* (1905).

Across the volume, many contributors have set out different ways in which women directed or received a financial education, through both formal and informal means. In turn, the book charts the development across this period from women's individual agitation for emancipation in the works of women like Wollstonecraft, into the popular political and social movements of the *Fin de Siècle* that underpinned the transatlantic suffrage movement. The 'Woman Question', which manages to be as nebulous as it is all-encompassing in its embrace of the moral, social, political, public and private positions of women, unfortunately remains as contentious in the twenty-first century. Recent political discourse has reproduced well-worn, even exhausted, points of debate about women's participation in public and private life: family and family planning, maternal health, breadwinning, and even the right to vote.[26]

The chapters herein demonstrate how different kinds of women managed their own fortunes and finances; how they sought to educate others and to become educated about their money and about markets that extended beyond the local, and beyond the realm of marriage; and how women invested, managed and dispersed their money by taking advantage of, and shaping, increasingly sophisticated financial instruments. This book examines the clear evidence of women's active engagement in matters of finance, and with it provides an alternative history of the marketplace that is neither masculine nor unfeeling, thus negating the presumption that the ultimate goal of capitalism is the erasure of sentiment by the rational and invisible hand of the market.

The editors of this volume wish to make clear that any emphases on the importance of feeling to economic performance, or assertions of market irrationality or fallibility, are not the consequence of women's long history of participation in the economy. Women do not introduce emotion to the marketplace. The marketplace is founded on, is flooded with, and feeds on, feeling. By looking again at the long history of emotion, and by paying attention to the women who made inquiries into the nature and function of feeling, any residual faith in a self-regulating and rational market, intended ultimately to arrive at social cohesion, evaporates. If anything, it is the presence of the different kinds of hands in the market – sympathetic, gestural, disciplining, nurturing, writing – that does much to expose and

[26] On the ways in which women's rights are under attack and how that assault has spread globally, see Siân Norris, *Bodies Under Siege: How the Far-Right Attack on Reproductive Rights Went Global* (London: Verso, 2023). In *The Perils of Populism*, Tobias and Stein have demonstrated that American far-right, twenty-first century populist movements have renewed efforts to present 'women as producers of the nation whose role is conceived largely in terms of maintaining traditional households [and] raising children'. Such modern populist positions echo remarkably closely the words of Francis Parkman, the anti-suffrage essayist who argued that 'women, and not men, are of necessity the guardians of the integrity of the family and the truth of succession', and that women are therefore unsuited to public and economic life ('The Woman Question', p. 307). See Sarah Tobias and Arlene Stein (eds), *The Perils of Populism* (New Brunswick NJ: Rutgers University Press, 2022), p. 4.

ameliorate the abuses and exploitation of capitalism. What is significant in this volume is the ways in which different kinds of affect in the economy might be recognised and put to work in theory and in practice, including to address systemic issues. This collection considers how affect and sentiment could provide a mechanism by which to critique the inequities and harms that are the other surplus of a capitalised system. Accounts are given of the suffering that increasing financialisation could wreak on those whose lives it affected, as well as of those who sought to profit from the continuation of that same system. As such, this volume also contains examples of women who wielded hands that participated in the worst features of the formation of the modern British economy: ones built on enslaved labour, or that relied on extractive and ecologically as well as socially harmful commerce and industry. In making women's economic lives visible, and in drawing attention to the gestural as well as the more explicit moves of women to intervene in the history of economic thought and behaviour, *Women, Money and Markets* provides examples of real and fictional women and their position as economic agents and where to find them – especially if one does as Catherine Packham and Joyce Goggin instruct: *follow the money*.

No longer the empty Holland smock, vulnerable to penetration, the prize to consume and be consumed, the women studied in this collection are presented as embodied subjects who articulate various agential positions in the market.

Part One

Risky Women

What kinds of women were investing during the eighteenth and nineteenth centuries? What were they investing in and with what attitudes to investment, and where might these women be found? What are the risks and rewards of searching for them? In this first section, Janette Rutterford, Peter Collinge, Hazel Vosper and Joyce Goggin each offer their own methodology for recovering and discussing women investing in different kinds of market and industry across the late eighteenth to early twentieth centuries.

In the opening chapter, one of the leading scholars in the field of the history of finance, Janette Rutterford, sets out her methods for recovering hitherto invisible female investors. Rutterford offers an account of her archival searches through which she was able to sketch a portrait of 'lady investors' in the late nineteenth and early twentieth centuries, including their presence and their preferences at annual general meetings as active stockholders.

Following this chapter, Peter Collinge provides a case study in which he expands Rutterford's methods for recovering women's stories in 'Art, Industry and Estate Management: Ellen Morewood (1741–1824) of Alfreton Park'. In the case of Morewood, a female industrialist, Collinge asks historians to look again at her actual portrait and the landscape against which she is set, and to read this with her wider archival record of business practices in order to give colour and shape to her wide-ranging interests and vagaries of fortune. Ushering in the nineteenth century, coal-mine owner, railway builder, landowner and fiercely litigious, Ellen Morewood is an exemplar of the ways in which women recognised and circumvented the legal fiction of coverture.

In the third chapter, 'Protection and Education: Investment Advice for Female Investors in *Fin de Siècle* England', Vosper attends to a distinctive sub-genre of print culture that arose in the mid-nineteenth century and that focused on financial advice for a small but growing number of female investors. Here, Vosper shows how the proposed education for women was aligned with the type offered to men, and provides evidence of the ways in which discussions about women's investments were not confined to low-risk, conservative options. Education, rather than reliance on a prudent and trustworthy male companion, was increasingly seen as a more dependable source of guidance and protection for women entering the financial sphere.

Advising readers to 'follow the money', Joyce Goggin analyses Lily Bart's rise to the bottom in the closing chapter of this section, 'For the Love of Money: Desire and Economy in *The House of Mirth* (1905)'. Here, Goggin deploys 'following the money' as a hermeneutic exercise. Through the figure of a gilded-age socialite, single and without a fortune at the age of twenty-nine, Wharton presents the reader with a brutal picture of a woman negotiating the marriage market as it intersects with the stock market in turn-of-the-century New York. Goggin's chapter reminds the reader that the marriage market serves as a microcosm of the greater market of stocks and investments within which it functions, as well as a reflection of the larger economic concerns of trade and exchange that extended far beyond the domestic for women.

Taking the four chapters of this part together, a picture of female management and investment emerges that is sophisticated and largely efficacious, revealing women who took on risk while finding ways of working in the service of their own autonomy, with or against, in the vernacular of Hazel Vosper's essay, male 'protectors'.

1

Invisible Women: Uncovering the Female Economy and Marketplace

JANETTE RUTTERFORD

This chapter will describe the conventional as well as the more unusual sources that have, over the past two decades, allowed researchers to quantify the significant presence of women in Victorian and Edwardian financial markets. Reflecting on a career spanning over 100 single and co-authored publications, the contents herein will highlight the pitfalls of using the various archives: for example, explaining how, in the case of share registers, the role of trustees can bias estimates of how many shareholders held how much of which security over time.[1]

There are several reasons for the delay in making these important discoveries. One reason was that social historians were side-tracked by the debate relating to Davidoff and Hall's influential separate spheres argument in their book, *Family Fortunes: Men and Women of the English Middle Class, 1780 to 1850*, published in 1987 – at a time when there was limited data available to support or refute it.[2] Literary and cultural historians, on the other hand, were constrained by a perceived need to critique Victorian capitalists, using tropes such as the 'greedy capitalist' and the 'exploited poor', rather than

[1] The editors note that the number of publications authored and co-authored total 177. At time of publication, Janette Rutterford's research has been cited 2,101 times, with 858 of those citations occurring since 2020. It is a clear measure of the growing investment by scholars in this field and the importance of Rutterford's contributions have made to investigating women and finance.

[2] Kathryn Gleadle, 'Revisiting Family Fortunes: Reflections on the Twentieth Anniversary of the Publication of L. Davidoff and C. Hall's '*Family Fortunes: Men and Women of the English Middle Class, 1780–1850*', *Women's History Review*, 16:5 (2007), 773–82.

discuss, in neutral terms, the seminal importance of finance, in particular of investment, in the novels of the period.[3]

Business and finance historians adopted a top-down approach for their studies of the Victorian and Edwardian marketplaces, producing biographies of bankers and of banks, of railway barons and railway companies, of companies and their promoters or founders, while choosing to ignore the more than a million small investors who funded them.[4] And, even if these barriers were crossed, the so-called democratisation of investment, noted by contemporaries – if not by their historians – was attributed as late as 2001 to the man, *not* the woman, on the street. Only a handful of articles reported information from shareholder lists before the mid-2000s.[5] Much more evidence was therefore needed on both the importance of investors in general, and of women investors in particular. This was no easy task, as the National Archives had only a sample of registers for companies no longer in existence.

Share registers listed male occupations and female marital status, highlighting the importance of women's legal status for investment choice. This was not the only factor taken into consideration. Women, it emerged, liked to buy shares in companies that were household names and with which they were familiar. This discovery led to links to the substantial suffragette movement literature, which provided evidence of women shareholders receiving dividend income, consuming these household products and obtaining advertising income for the suffragette press from these companies. Further newspaper and magazine archives highlight the difference between women shareholders' right to vote on company matters since before the South Sea Bubble, and the failure to obtain women's partial parliamentary suffrage until 1918. Newspaper archives also provide evidence of women intervening at shareholder meetings, mostly relating to company performance and corporate governance, but occasionally on ethical or philanthropic issues.

3 See Catherine Gallagher, *The Industrial Reformation of English Fiction: Social Discourse and Narrative Form, 1832–1867* (Chicago IL: University of Chicago Press, 1985); Mary Poovey, *Uneven Developments: The Ideological Work of Gender in Mid-Victorian England* (Chicago IL: University of Chicago Press, 1988); Nancy Armstrong, *Desire and Domestic Fiction: A Political History of the Novel* (New York: Oxford University Press, 1987).

4 See Youssef Cassis, *City Bankers, 1890–1914* (Cambridge: Cambridge University Press, 1994); Geoffrey Jones, *British Multinational Banking, 1830–1990* (Oxford: Clarendon Press, 1993); Ranald Michie, *The City of London: Continuity and Change, 1850–1990* (London: Macmillan, 1992); Philip L. Cottrell, *Industrial Finance, 1830–1914: The Finance and Organization of English Manufacturing Industry* (London: Methuen, 1979); S. G. Checkland, *The Rise of the Industrial Society in England, 1815–1885* (London: Longman, 1964).

5 For example, 'The Shareholder and His Capital', in Wendy N. Munyon, 'Shareholders' Rights in the Common Market: A Comparative Study', *Cornell International Law Journal*, 9:2 (May 1976), 191–238, p. 194.

Other aspects of women investor research include the role of women as family members, from supporting a bankrupt husband to relying on an annuity as the 'surplus' unmarried and bereaved daughter, and as the widows 'and orphans' vulnerable to fraud. Numerous government select committees have shed light on the fate of widows, spinsters and other uninformed investors. Many investment texts and pamphlets aimed at countering this ignorance, to be found in the British Library and often also in the US university libraries. Individual portfolios and share transactions relating to women can also be found housed in the archives of advisers as well as in wills, probate and philanthropic institutional archives.

Perhaps most relevant to this collection is the link between female authors and their investment portfolios, two of the few areas of female activity that were socially sanctioned. This involves, in some cases, a re-reading of the texts and, in others, personal correspondence, memorandum books and accounts, together with details relating to family finances from wills, probate, court cases, inheritances and earnings. The methodology and links between various, perhaps unexpected, aspects of women investors will continue to develop over time in this most interdisciplinary of topics. There has been much less discussion of who these investors were and especially the role played by women as investors: that is, the 'feminisation of investors'. For example, Preda's comment on Victorians' understanding of investment: 'women are always excluded from financial discussions, on the explicit grounds that they cannot understand investments', may be taken as representative of the general underlying assumption that women were neither interested in nor capable of appreciating financial matters.[6] Cheffins's 400-page book, *Corporate Ownership and Control* (2008), which looks at demand and supply for stock market investment from the eighteenth century to the present day, makes no mention at all of women investors.[7] Additionally, until recently, literary and cultural critics of Victorian novels preferred to concentrate on a Marxist-inspired view of industrial capitalism. Women's role in industrial capitalism was approached by literary critics from the perspective of women as exploited workers rather than as capitalist *rentières*, despite examples such as *North and South* (1855) by Elizabeth Gaskell and *Anna of the Five Towns* (1902) by Arnold Bennett.[8]

6 Alex Preda, 'The Rise of the Popular Investor: Financial Knowledge and Investing in England and France, 1840–1880', *The Sociological Quarterly*, 42:2 (2001), 205–321, p. 216.

7 Brian R. Cheffins, *Corporate Ownership and Control* (Oxford: Oxford University Press, 2008), pp. 123–7, 293–6.

8 See 'Introduction', in *Women and Their Money 1700 to 1950: Essays on Women and Finance*, ed. by Anne Laurence, Josephine Maltby and Janette Rutterford (London: Routledge, 2009), p. 7. See also Nancy Henry's Women, *Literature and Finance in Victorian Britain: Cultures of Investment* (London: Palgrave Macmillan, 2018).

Biographies of female authors such as Elizabeth Gaskell, George Eliot and Charlotte Riddell have until very recently ignored the financial aspects of their private lives, as if their handwritten lists of portfolio holdings, their correspondence with their financial advisers, and the impact on their finances of missing a dividend, were not relevant to their writing. Charlotte Brontë lost money on York and Midland Railway shares in the 1840s railway mania. Indeed, Virginia Woolf believed that having sufficient unearned income was a prerequisite to good novel writing, arguing that lack of money severely affected the quality of an author's output, so that 'one could not but play for a moment with the thought of what might have happened if Charlotte Brontë had possessed say three hundred a year'.[9] More dramatically, both Mrs Henry Wood and Ellen Marshall, who wrote novels about domestic bliss threatened by financial crises – including bank failures – were married to men whose own banks had failed. Catherine Gore, author of *The Banker's Wife*, which was published in 1846, lost £20,000 twenty years later from a bank fraud. It was a febrile period for male and female investors, which threatened enormous risk as much as it promised rich reward.

Discovering Women's Agency: The Composition of the Female Investor Community

Women in particular were significant investors due to the legal system and demographics. Single women – spinsters and widows – had the same legal rights as men, including attendance and voting at annual general meetings; significantly, single women represented around half the female population. The number of unmarried middle- and upper-class women was high due to the primogeniture system that favoured the eldest son at the expense of daughters and younger sons. These so-called 'redundant' or 'surplus' women needed investments to provide unearned income from which to live.

Consequently, there were numerous spinsters and widows with unfettered access to investing in stock market securities. The 'surplus woman' was a feature of the nineteenth-century census.[10] The 1871 census gave totals of 11,190,000 males and 11,664,000 females. Women over the age of fifteen comprised 3,945,000 wives, 2,731,000 spinsters and 879,000 widows: a total of some 3.6 million unmarried women, or 48 per cent.[11] In 1871, there were 600,600 more women than men over the age of nineteen. This figure rose

[9] Virginia Woolf, *A Room of One's Own* (London: Hogarth Press, 1929), p. 65.

[10] See www.visionofbritain.org.uk/census/ (accessed 28 November 2024).

[11] Janette Rutterford, David Green, Josephine Maltby and Alistair Owens, 'Who Comprised the Nation of Shareholders? Gender and Investment in Great Britain c. 1870–1935', *Economic History Review*, 16:1 (2011), 157–87.

to 1,147,700 in 1911 and, after the First World War, to 1,849,000 in 1931.[12] During this period, life expectancy rose from being thirty-nine for men and forty-two for women, for those born in 1841, to fifty-one for men and fifty-eight for women born in 1901: a seven-year gap that lasted for decades. That gap implied the existence of a large number of relatively young widows who needed an assured income for a longer life. More had to be set aside for pensions as the nineteenth century came to a close because life expectancy was increasing rapidly. This was exacerbated for widows with children, although the average number of children per household plummeted from 4.9 children on average in 1871, to 2.4 in 1924. Middle-class children were educated for a longer period, with school-leaving age rising from ten to fourteen years old between 1870 and 1918; middle-class children were becoming more expensive to educate if they wished to enter a profession. Saving for old age was made easier by the increase in real growth in the economy by 1.7 per cent per year from the 1870s to the 1890s, enabling a new middle class to pay for their living costs in retirement, for their children's education, and to provide for their family after their own death. Many of these so-called surplus women had an incentive to look for income from their investments to supplement low wages, or no earned income at all. Spinsters and widows are, then, present in large numbers in the share registers and accounted for half of all female investors in the 1880s. This figure falls to 40 per cent by the 1930s, with the value of their holdings reducing from 45 per cent to under 30 per cent of the total value of women's holdings by the 1930s.

Part of the explanation for the decline in the proportion of spinsters may be explained by changes in the law regarding married women, which included the Married Women's Property Acts (1870, 1882, 1893), of which the Act of 1882 was especially transformative. The 1882 Act granted married women the right to own, control and manage property, including wages, investments and inheritances, independently of their husbands. The Act formally overturned the doctrine of coverture, which had previously merged a woman's legal identity with her husband's on marriage, although, as Peter Collinge shows in this volume and Amy Erickson and others have demonstrated elsewhere, women had long found ways to evade, overcome or ignore the restrictions of coverture, which might reasonably be called a 'legal fiction', or what Lon Fuller describes as that 'awkward patch applied to a rent in the law's fabric of theory. Lifting the patch we may trace out the patterns of tension that tore the fabric and at the same time discern elements in the fabric itself that were previously obscured from view'.[13] In other words, a legal fiction is an acknowledged falsehood maintained as true for the sake

[12] Ibid.

[13] Lon L. Fuller, *Legal Fictions* (Stanford CA: Stanford University Press, 1967), originally published in *Illinois Law Review*, 25 (1930–1).

of legal or theoretical coherence; in the case of coverture, *male convenience* rather than legal coherence might best describe coverture.

Despite successive acts addressing married women's legal position, the privations that continued in relation to property ownership were substantive enough to require a further Law of Property Act (1925), which simplified and modernised British property law, including inheritance rules, making it easier to transfer and register property; it also abolished primogeniture in intestate succession, allowing daughters to inherit real property more equitably. These successive acts between the 1880s and 1930s clearly helped to move the dial on women's investment portfolios and their distribution of asset classes, as the change in the share registers for the same period reflect the changing legal status of women.

Turning back to the issue of the 'surplus woman', however, Bessie Rayner Parkes claims that the literary subject of the 'woman struggling alone', whether 'a fox-like Becky Sharpe or a passionate and yet austere Jane Eyre' was new to the nineteenth century; while literary history may contest her position, Parkes is attempting to frame the contemporary urgency of her publication in 1856.[14] Parkes argues that the surplus women were some of the 'thousands and thousands of destitute educated women' of the age.[15] She described the work of the Governesses' Benevolent Institution that provided annuities of £15 for retired teachers who were otherwise without means.[16] The demand was enormous. The Deakin Institute was founded in 1852 with £3,000 to pay annuities to unmarried Protestant women living in England. In 1880, the Chairman reported 'a sad tale of disappointment' – some women had 'applied for the fourth, fifth, sixth or seventh time' for an annuity of £20 or £25 and been turned down.[17] The single woman 'struggling alone' and anxious to avoid a wretched retirement was a potential investor, but one who was seen as far likelier to make hazardous decisions and suffer accordingly. However, not all single women were in dire financial straits. At the other end of the spectrum were women of means. The 1871 census, for instance, identified a group of 141,000 women 'of rank and property' out of the total of 6,463,000 women over the age of twenty-one. Some of these women were the super-wealthy: members of aristocratic families, such as the Rothschilds, but others were from more modest backgrounds who, typically through inheritance, acquired significant investments.

Married women were also potential investors in financial securities, either directly, in the case of single women, or indirectly in the case of married

14 Bessie Rayner Parkes, *Remarks on the Education of Girls, with Reference to the Social, Legal, and Industrial Position of Women in the Present Day* (London: John Chapman, 1856), p. 54.

15 Ibid.

16 Ibid. p. 192.

17 Sheffield City Archive: LD 2189.

women until 1870. Married women, who under common law had no legal identity other than that of their husband were able, under equity law, to have a marriage settlement in the form of a trust that was managed by trustees. Trustees were often family members but not usually the husband, and on the woman's behalf would provide 'pin money' and, later, a 'widow's jointure'. Trustees were responsible for the capital in the trust, which was typically invested in long-term, fixed interest, low-risk stock exchange securities which were most often used to fund the marriage settlement. In the share register, securities in trusts were entered in the name of the trustees and not the ultimate beneficiary.[18] Since trustees were overwhelmingly male, this method of accounting for share ownership increased the apparent importance of male as opposed to female investors as the share record would usually show the names of two men, rather than, perhaps, a widow and her children.

Trusts were not confined only to the wealthy. A contributor to the *Cornhill Magazine* described marriage settlements as 'common, indeed ... nearly universal among the comfortable and moderately wealthy classes'.[19] In a study of the Victorian trustee, Stebbings finds that 'all sections of the middle classes, and some of the skilled working classes employed the trust'.[20] Gentlemen, clerks in holy orders, butchers, printers, merchants and yeomen were typical of 'middle-class settlers'.[21] Morris cites the use of trusts in 77 per cent of male wills in a sample of middle-class wills in Leeds from 1830 to 1834 to transmit wealth to widows, daughters, sisters and nieces.[22] However, not all women had access to trusts and it led to extreme hardship for women whose husbands could and did deprive them of all their property and leave them destitute. In one case quoted by Lee Holcombe, an abandoned wife retrieved her position by setting up a school. Her husband returned from Australia, took the school's assets that were his under common law, and left her again penniless.[23]

As a result of this and similar injustices, the early Victorian campaign to give property rights to married women can be found in Brougham's Bill of 1857, which was somewhat entwined with the attempt to improve the financial position of divorced and separated women; it proved partially successful in the form of a Married Women's Property Act of 1870, which

18 This was not the case in Scotland.

19 *Cornhill Magazine* (1863), p. 668.

20 Chantal Stebbings, *The Private Trustee in Victorian England* (Cambridge: Cambridge University Press, 2002), p. 6.

21 Ibid.

22 Richard J. Morris, *Men, Women and Property in England, 1780–1870. A Social and Economic History of Family Strategies amongst the Leeds Middle Class* (Cambridge: Cambridge University Press, 2005), p. 121.

23 Lee Holcombe, *Wives and Property: Reform of the Married Women's Property Law in Nineteenth-Century England* (London: Wiley-Blackwell, 1985), p. 66.

gave women ownership rights over property acquired after marriage. The act covered earnings from employment or skill, investments and earnings from investments of special types, and inherited property, and included government annuities; savings banks; public funds or stocks; shares in limited companies; industrial, provident, friendly, building and loan societies; and life insurance policies. The Act of 1870 meant that it was important for women to demonstrate their creative activities were producing income and were a proper form of employment, not a hobbyist's occupation.[24] The Act was, however, unsatisfactory in a number of respects: it did not cover assets brought into the marriage, and it required husband and wife to make an agreement as to the ownership of those acquired later by the wife. A wife whose husband did not agree to separate ownership was, therefore, no better off after 1870. It was not until the 1882 Married Women's Property Act that wives acquired the same rights as single women and men to own all property irrespective of its date of acquisition. After the passing of these Acts, it became much easier for married women to invest both indirectly directly and in the stock market, and so the proportion of spinsters and widows in the share registers fell.

Supporting Evidence

In conducting the research for this chapter, we used a database of more than 30,000 shareholders in forty-seven different domestic, colonial and foreign company share registers between 1870 and 1935, spread across seven different industry sectors in order to examine women shareholder preferences. The Companies Acts made it a requirement that companies should produce detailed annual returns of their shareholders that were to be submitted to the Registrar of Companies (now Companies House) and were available for public consultation. This was an onerous requirement, as was bemoaned by the chairman of the *Judische Colonialbank* in 1900:

> To give you only one example, I may refer you to the fact that according to English law it is necessary to supply Somerset House within fourteen days of the General Meeting with an accurate list of all shareholders, their names, addresses, and occupations, and with any changes in the amount of their holdings. Imagine, Ladies and Gentlemen, what that means with over 120,000 shareholders![25]

[24] The move to retain earnings from skill or employment informs the accounts of gendered professionalisation found in the final section of this volume.

[25] Guildhall accounts file of *Judische Colonialbank* for 1900. For more details, see Janette Rutterford, Josephine Maltby, David Green and Alastair Owens, 'Researching Shareholding and Investment in England and Wales: Approaches, Sources and Methods', *Accounting History*, 14:3 (2009), 269–92. See also TNA Kew J 107/57/229 ('Jewish

The record referred to by the Chairman of the *Judische Colonialbank* was the Form E, a document issued by the Registrar of Companies to be completed and returned annually.[26] This was made a statutory requirement by the Companies Acts of 1856 and 1862 under which it was mandatory for companies to file an annual statement detailing their equity capital structure (authorised and issued) and a list of their shareholders, both ordinary and preferred. Names, addresses and occupations of shareholders were also required. Changes in the number of holdings during the year were also given.[27]

Records of shareholders were kept by companies for a variety of purposes. For example, the *share register* was a list produced by a company which it transcribed into a Form E annually. It commonly took the form of a list of names and addresses and the number and type of shares held, but it was up to the individual company to decide how to arrange it and what further information, if any, to include. It was normally updated annually. The *share ledger* was a collection of accounts showing movements in each shareholder's investment, such as purchases, disposals and bonus issues. It was updated when alterations occurred in the account. The *subscription list* applied in the case of early limited companies where a small number of individuals agreed to subscribe to the shares of a new company. The *allotment list* was the list of subscribers to new capital, either of a new company or of new shares of an existing company.[28] All companies were required to produce the Form E, and they might choose to maintain some or all of the other items listed, depending on their needs.

Share records for English and Welsh companies exist in a variety of archives. Company archives, to be found in local record offices and private or corporate collections, are the best source of share registers, share ledgers or subscription and allotment lists. The Access to Archives website describes itself as containing 'company archives held locally in England and Wales and dating from the eighteenth century to the present day', and is an excellent starting point.[29] For a relative sample of companies in England and Wales, including some railways, that no longer exist, Form Es are to be found at

Colonial Trust (Juedische Colonial Bank) Ltd'); Jewish Colonial Trust, *Memorandum and Articles of Association*, registered 20 March 1899, National Library of Israel Digital Collections; *Geschäftsbericht nebst Bilanz und Gewinn- und Verlustrechnung für die Jahre 1899–1922*; Jewish Colonial Trust Share Clubs, *Statuten des Jewish Colonial Trust Share Clubs*, June 1900, National Library of Israel Digital Collections.

26 This is a particularly useful source of data produced in the UK. In other countries, such as the United States, there was no such national requirement for listing shareholdings at a particular point in time, on an annual basis.

27 Rutterford et al. 'Who comprised the nation of shareholders?', 174.

28 Ibid. 173–4.

29 See www.nationalarchives.gov.uk/a2a (accessed 27 November 2024). A similar function is served for Scotland by the National Archives of Scotland and for Northern Ireland by the Public Record Office of Northern Ireland.

the National Archives in the BT31 series. Companies still in existence have lodged their records, including Form Es, with Companies House. The Bank of England has its own archive of ledgers of government securities holders (included in our study alongside corporate shareholdings). There are some industry archives with share record collections: for example, the National Gas Archive has a number of share registers of gas companies.[30]

Although the quality of individual records will vary – some may be less detailed than others, or different secretaries of the same company may be more or less likely to add helpful notes – they still represent a rich source of data about investors, which allowed us to explore gender differences in investment, as well as marital status and occupation. Our research group found that, for example, women in our sample represented 15 per cent of investors in the 1870s compared with 45 per cent in the 1930s, and grew from 5 per cent to 33 per cent by nominal value of shares held over the same period. The challenge was to identify a diverse selection of companies – both large and small – spanning seven sectors and seven decades. These included a mix of publicly listed ('quoted') and private ('not quoted') firms, and covered a range of financial instruments such as debentures, preference shares and ordinary shares. We included companies operating in the domestic, colonial and foreign context, and companies registered in England and Wales, but with operations elsewhere.[31] To do this, we explored not only Companies House and the National Archives, but also individual company archives such as Cunard, and company new issue files held at the Guildhall Library.

The results of this research demonstrate that women in the sample preferred certain types of security and companies in certain sectors. They liked low-risk securities such as fixed interest debentures or preference shares, which had fixed interest payments or fixed dividends, respectively; by the 1930s, women represented 60 per cent of debenture holders, 50 percent of preference shareholders and 40 per cent of ordinary shareholders.[32] They liked railway securities, especially those guaranteed by the state such as Southern Mahratta Railway Indian railway stock; and banks and utilities – such as London Electric Supply Corporation – which offered high, regular income.[33] These investors were able to choose the level of risk by type of sector and type of security but could also choose to spread the risks of investment by holding several securities in a portfolio of shares.[34]

[30] See ww.gasarchive.org (accessed 25 November 2024).

[31] For more details, Rutterford et al., 'Researching Shareholding and Investment in England and Wales', 269–92.

[32] Rutterford et al., 'Who Comprised the Nation of Shareholders?', 157–87.

[33] Ibid.

[34] Ibid.

Women also liked to invest in shares which were household names, such as Boots the Chemist, J. Lyons tea shops, and department stores such as Bon Marché.[35] As Henry Lowenfeld, the editor of the *Financial Review of Reviews*, complained in 1907, individual investors were buying shares in companies they could physically see were doing well. He deplored the role of the London tube and omnibuses that brought in crowds from the suburbs, who then bought shares in 'drapery stores and light-refreshment establishments', to such an extent that the yield on these investments had fallen to below that on 'first-class brewery debentures'.[36]

However, the directors of these companies were happy to have lady shareholders. In 1926, the Chairman of Bovril's, a beef-extract product, said 'half of the shareholders are ladies, showing that those who knew most about the virtues of Bovril think it good policy to be interested in it financially also'.[37] Another example of the perceived importance of women investors by the companies in which they invested is that of Spratt's Patent, the dog food company, whose Chairman, at the 1903 Annual General Meeting (AGM), noted that, of the 1,482 shareholders, there were 585 'ladies, who were generally investors and who were therefore, as a rule, preferable to those [men] who bought the shares merely as a speculation'.[38]

We also looked at 508 estates at death that include stock market investments for the period of 1870 to 1902. In both samples we found that women increase in importance as shareholders over time, in some cases, usually for lower risk securities such as preferred shares, women outnumbered men by the 1920s and 1930s. Women liked lower-risk securities, such as government bonds (domestic, colonial and foreign), brand name companies and utilities, and financial securities that had high income.

By the end of the nineteenth century, women preferred financial securities to land; they were higher yielding than land, required no maintenance, and were easier to buy and sell. Through this preference, women were significantly and directly responsible for the financialisation of the modern British economy. UK government bonds were safe, but they too became unattractive in yield terms by the turn of the century. Investors seeking a higher return were forced to invest in foreign or colonial securities, fixed income securities, or in domestic company ordinary shares, to gain higher yield. This preference for low risk is logical given that there were many single women, spinsters and widows who relied on investment income on

[35] Ibid.

[36] Henry Lowenfeld, *Financial Review of Reviews*, 25 (November 1907), 15–25.

[37] 'Bovril, Ltd', *Financial Times*, 26 February 1926, p. 22.

[38] *Economist*, 14 March 1903, p. 477. The greater predilection of male investors compared to female investors to speculate still persists today. See B. M. Barber and T. Odean, 'Boys will be Boys: Gender, Overconfidence, and Common Stock Investment', *Quarterly Journal of Economics*, 116:1 (2001), 262–92.

which to live, with many having no other sources of income or capital, and also no pension.

Financial securities were also more attractive than insurance that put obstacles in the way of women, through quarter or annual premiums unsuitable for women with fluctuating incomes, higher premia for women and unwelcome medical examinations. Insurance companies had noticed the longer life expectancy of women and paid smaller annuities to them than men. Moreover, the 1890s to the early twentieth century saw a boom in new issues of shares of companies that had a track record, such as Guinness, Alsop, Dunlop, and Schweppes, and women felt able to buy not only preference shares, but also, in some cases, ordinary shares, particularly when they understood the sector in which they were investing. They could also reduce their investment risk by diversifying their portfolios across a number of companies, so average holding size went down.

AGMs and Women Investors

Under company law, shareholders had substantial powers of corporate governance. At the AGM, the directors' report and accounts, as well as the proposed dividend, had to be approved by shareholders by a vote. Shareholders could also elect or reject directors and vote on the choice of auditors. Company law required that all shareholders be given advance notice of meetings and resolutions, allowed them to table their own resolutions or, more immediately, propose amendments to resolutions currently being discussed. In addition, shareholders with a combined holding of as little as 10 per cent of shares could call an extraordinary general meeting and, if they so desired, vote to remove the entire board of directors with a bare majority of 50 per cent of the votes.[39] Small shareholders could play a significant role as few companies had large shareholders with a controlling stake.[40] Collaboration was facilitated by public access to shareholder lists deposited with the Registrar of Companies, as well as by the concentration of head offices of companies in the West End and the City of London, which allowed for large attendances of shareholders at meetings.[41]

Until recently, the received opinion was that women were passive investors and did not contribute to annual general meetings, or corporate governance in general, however little attention has been paid to the extensive reports of AGMs that included not only the chairman's report, but also discus-

[39] Janette Rutterford, 'The Shareholder Voice: British and American Accents, 1890–1965', *Enterprise & Society*, 13:1 (March 2012), 120–53.

[40] Janette Rutterford and Leslie Hannah, 'The Unsung Activists: UK Shareholder Investigation Committees, 1888–1940', *Business History Review* (2023), 741–75.

[41] Rutterford, 'The Shareholder Voice: British and American Accents, 1890–1965'.

sions between the chairman and shareholders.[42] Reporters from newspapers such as the *Financial Times* and *The Times* diligently attended meetings and reported on events, which sometimes included heated debate. A breakthrough in our search for women's activity in the stock market and in the financial sphere, came when searching the *Financial Times* archive during Covid and showed that the term 'women shareholders' was alien to contemporaries: they preferred the term 'lady shareholders'. Using this search term made it possible to identify many occasions when women actively contributed to corporate governance for the companies in which they invested, through correspondence with the company, contributions made during the AGM, or as members of a shareholder investigation committee.

Contemporaries, on the other hand, did recognise that women could, and did, play a significant role in corporate governance. Louise Creighton, a noted author of popular history books and a social activist – and also publicly in favour of women's suffrage from 1906[43] concurred: 'It is said that where women are serious investors they are generally conscientious shareholders, attending the meetings of companies in which they are interested, taking intelligent interest in their reports, and faithful in using their votes.'[44] Even when unable to attend in person, women could appoint another shareholder as proxy or write to the chairman or secretary of the company, as many did. The author of a letter to the Editor of *The Times* relating to the forthcoming annual general meeting of the Oil Trust, which had 8,000 shareholders, was concerned that the venue, which seated 500, would not be large enough. He wished to point out that:

> We have lady shareholders in this company and they, like many of the older shareholders, will not be prepared to take the physical risks and undergo the discomforts of being crowded together in a packed meeting room for anything from one and half to three hours.[45]

The absence or presence of women shareholders at a shareholder meeting could change the outcome of a vote. This was particularly the case if the vote was by show of hands, based on one shareholder, one vote. If dissatisfied with the result of a show of hands, a poll could be requested by a small number of shareholders including members of the board (the exact number depending on the articles of association) when shareholders would be able to vote by proxy or in person and this would usually be one share one vote.[46]

[42] Ibid.

[43] Judith F. Godden, 'Creighton, Louise Hume (1850–1936)', *Oxford Dictionary of National Biography*, September 2004, https://doi.org/10.1093/ref:odnb/38640.

[44] Creighton, Louise, 'Women and Finance', *Financial Review of Reviews*, 59:20 (September 1910).

[45] 'Letter to the Editor', *The Times*, 11 December 1913, p. 16.

[46] For more on this, see Rutterford and Hannah, 'The Unsung Activists'.

Before the 1930s, many companies had preference shares with full voting rights, and women were omnipresent in the preference shareholder lists.[47] As the author of another letter to *The Times* pointed out, before a proposed reconstruction of the City of London Brewery, there were 780 holders of £500,000 of the brewery's Preference Stock – in arrears by £95,000 in interest payments – 'of whom 303 are ladies and ladies have votes'.[48] He went on to suggest an amendment to the reconstruction proposals to improve the offer for these preference shareholders. More than half of the companies in the 1911 sample noted above had preference shares with full voting rights, and women were omnipresent in the preference shareholder lists.[49]

Shareholders had to approve – by majority vote – the dividend to be paid to shareholders and, given the importance of regular income to many of the shareholders, there was usually some discussion on that topic at the meeting. Women's preference for regular dividend income was recognised as being of primary importance by company directors and male shareholders alike. The chairman of Jokam Tea referred to a letter he had received from a lady shareholder in which she had argued against a proposed dividend increase, saying that any positive change to her regular £50 twice a year, which she knew she could count on, would make her anxious that, if the dividend could go up, it was just as likely to go down.[50]

Male shareholders used women as an excuse to recommend a higher dividend than that proposed by the board, as at the Aerated Bread Company 1904 meeting, arguing that an extra 6d per share would 'be much appreciated by the large number of lady shareholders who depend on the dividend on those shares for a certain amount of their income'.[51] However, the letters from shareholders of the Prudential Assurance Company from 1915 to 1924 show that just as many men as women who wrote to the company were anxious to have a regular, predictable dividend payment. In this particular case, both men and women were confused by the fact that their dividends were lower than before the war, despite improved profits. They did not understand that dividends were typically paid net of income tax and the reduction was due to higher income tax rates rather than lower dividends before tax.[52] Company directors were well aware of the key role that dividends played as a source of income – especially for women who had no earned income – preferring to maintain the dividend, even if this meant

47 Rutterford et al., 'Who Comprised the Nation of Shareholders?'.

48 'Letter to the Editor', *The Times*, 27 April 1914, p. 20.

49 G. Acheson, G. Campbell and J. D. Turner, 'Active Controllers or Wealthy Rentiers? Large Shareholders in Victorian Public Companies', *Business History Review*, 89:4 (winter 2015), 661–91.

50 'Jokam (Assam) Tea', *The Financial Times*, 17 June 1891, p. 2.

51 'Aerated Bread', *The Financial Times*, 8 November 1904, p. 2.

52 Rutterford and Maltby, 'The Widow'.

paying for some of the dividend out of reserves, 'in view of the fact that many shareholders were ladies and others who were dependent on their investment for their livelihood'.[53]

When unhappy with the performance of a particular share, often linked to low or non-existent dividends over a number of years, shareholders were not shy in suggesting that a shareholder Committee of Investigation be set up.[54] This could be proposed and voted on at a shareholder meeting: by not approving the report and accounts, and instead adding a resolution to set up such a committee, when its remit could be established and a number of shareholders – typically from three to eight – elected to form the Committee. If approved by majority vote, the Committee would be allowed full access to company documents and be able to employ lawyers or accountants to help the committee establish the facts behind the poor performance. The Committee's report was presented to the shareholders at a later meeting, and the recommendations were typically approved. In some cases, the Committee came too late for the company not to be liquidated. In a random sample of fifty Committees of Investigation which were reported in the *Financial Times* between 1888 and 1940, thirteen (26 per cent) went into liquidation within two years of the setting up of the committee of investigation; eight (4 per cent) were acquired or merged; and thirty-three (66 per cent) remained as going concerns.[55] Either way, the outcome often involved the resignation of some or all of the directors.

Committees were also used for more specific issues. Unable to reach agreement over the method of recruiting four new departmental directors at the William Whiteley department store, an amendment was carried that the meeting be adjourned and a small committee of named shareholders – in this case three women and two men – would consult with the directors and report at a later date to the adjourned meeting.[56] The proportion of women on this committee was unusually high. On only a handful of occasions did the financial press report the election of a woman to a shareholder committee of investigation.[57] However, women did speak out at meetings in support of Committees of Investigation as well as on topics other than share price performance. These included requests that a Welsh mining company should introduce an employee share scheme; concern about overcrowding in third class for an Indian railway company; and treatment of the 'natives' by Cecil Rhodes, Chairman of the British South Africa Company.[58] Such

53 'Fore Street Warehouse Company', *The Financial Times*, 13 January 1904, p. 10.

54 Also called Committee of Inspection or Committee of Inquiry. For more detail on these committees, see Rutterford and Hannah, 'The Unsung Activists'.

55 Ibid.

56 'William Whiteley', *The Financial Times*, 27 March 1918, p. 2.

57 Rutterford and Hannah, 'The Unsung Activists'.

58 Rutterford, 'The Shareholder Voice: British and American Accents, 1890–1965'.

interventions reveal women adopting an ethical position, underpinned by sympathy, in advocating for improvements to corporate governance.[59] Importantly, it provides evidence that women adopted an agentic position when investing, as well as maintaining an overt, demonstrable interest in protecting their capital investment.

A Virtuous Circle: Women Shareholders as Customers and Activists

Some of the lady shareholders that I identified were not just activists on corporate governance issues. Following the trail of women active in the investment sphere led me to discover that several influential women in the suffragette movement were also investors and customers. Suffragette publications such as *The Vote*, the house journal of Women's Freedom League, featured many advertisements by companies such as department stores like Selfridges and Swan and Edgar; tearooms such as J. Lyons; hotels such as the Hotel Cecile, leading to a virtuous circle of women shareholders, customers and activists. These companies benefited from increased sales, whilst the Women's Freedom League gained income for its activities as well as better dividends from the companies concerned.

When invested for the long term in household-name companies, women shareholders felt able to make helpful suggestions in person or in writing to the directors of the firm – particularly for those companies whose products or services they understood, such as recommending that the company appoint lady inspectors to oversee the quality of service at the annual general meeting of Slaters' restaurants.[60] Women commented on companies that they knew well as customers as well as shareholders. It was in the common interest of both company directors and women shareholders to increase sales. The Edwardian era saw the rise of mass marketing, aimed at the 'spending sex', and the growth of hotels, restaurants, tea shops, milliners and department stores, as well as mass advertising on billboards, in newspapers, magazines and through mail shots.[61] Advertisements for household products such as Lipton's Tea, Spratt's Patent, Sanitas disinfectant, Viyella artificial silk and Bovril beef extract, were omnipresent.

59 For further discussion of women and ethical or sympathetic behaviour, see Part Two of the present volume.

60 See *Daily Chronicle in Financial Review of Reviews*, 63 (January 1911), 58–9.

61 See also Ellen Furlough, *Consumer Cooperation in France: The Politics of Consumption, 1834–1930* (Ithaca NY: Cornell University Press, 1991); and Pauline Maclaran, 'Marketing and Feminism in Historic Perspective', *Journal of Historical Research in Marketing*, 4:3 (2012), 462–76; Bess Norden, 'The Suffrage at Selfridge's', *New Statesman & Society*, 5:220 (1992), 34–5; Erika Rappaport, *Shopping for Pleasure: Women and the Making of London's West End* (Princeton NJ: Princeton University Press, 2001).

Company directors were well aware of the customer shareholder overlap and sought to benefit from it. For example, the chairman of a London department store, Waterloo House and Swan and Edgar, encouraged women shareholders attending the AGM to 'do their utmost, by themselves, and by influencing their friends, to increase our business. It seems to me that this is the truest form of cooperation. You take your money out of one pocket only to put it into the other by way of dividend'.[62] The chairman of Wardle and Davenport, retailers of artificial silk garments, made the same request.[63] At the close of the meeting of William Hollins, makers of Viyella, 'the Chairman observed that if any of the lady shareholders cared to go round the company's garments factory at any time, he would be only too pleased to arrange for the visit.'[64]

At other meetings, it was the women themselves who spoke out and made the plea for fellow women shareholders to be customers. A female shareholder at the Home and Colonial meeting:

> wished also to say a word, as an old customer, as to the excellent quality of the goods supplied by the co[mpany]. She had dealt with the Home and Colonial Stores for fifteen or sixteen years and not only had she received at all times the greatest courtesy from the staff and from headquarters, but the quality of the goods had been excellent. She made this statement because if there were any lady shareholders present who did not deal with the company, she hoped they would at once begin to do so.[65]

This was a frequent topic at AGMs of companies whose main customer base was female, highlighting the symbiotic relationship between women customers and women shareholders, as at the AGM of the milliners Madame Louise in 1911:

> I consider that every lady ought to buy her hats at Louise; I buy all mine there – Applause – and I believe that if every one of our lady shareholders bought their hats at Louise, our dividend possibly might be 10 per cent, instead of 7 per cent.[66]

Women's Portfolios

In my search for women's involvement, I have frequently turned to correspondence and company archives: for example, the Prudential Archive yielded share registers for 1908, and the evolution of a private company to a

62 'Waterloo House and Swan and Edgar', *Financial Times*, 17 March 1891, p. 4.

63 'Wardle and Davenport', *Financial Times*, 19 September 1925, p. 2.

64 'Large increase in the sales of Viyella', *Financial Times*, 27 March 1926, p. 2.

65 'Home and Colonial Stores', *Financial Times*, 5 April 1916, p. 4.

66 'Louise & Co', *Financial Times*, 2 March 1911, p. 5.

publicly owned company. Early investors were directors and family members and the shareholder correspondence files revealed that many investors – men as well as women – held on to their shares for many years, feeling a personal connection with their investment. Where shares did change hands, it was often from aunt to niece, or father to daughter, since Prudential shares were a very safe investment.

Other archives that I visited included the Rothschild Archive and the Barings Archive, both of which I found to hold correspondence concerning women's investment portfolios, as well as personal correspondence between the bankers and their wealthy female clients. In the case of the Rothschild Archive, I found useful examples of portfolios held directly by women, as well as portfolios held indirectly through trustees. This enabled me to understand the impact on women of holding shares in trust and how this affected the returns of their portfolios. The Barings Archive, on the other hand, yielded a large number of letters from wives and widows begging for help, as their husbands, current or retired employees of Barings, had either died or absconded, leaving these women destitute.

The other major find in the Barings Archive was a voluminous file of correspondence between Joshua Bates, a partner of the bank, and Elizabeth Caton, an unmarried American heiress, from the mid-1830s to the mid-1840s. Bess, as she was known, was a speculator all her life. She bought foreign government bonds, railway shares and even shares in start-up companies in railway-related industries. On this latter point, it is evidence of a bold risk profile. Intriguingly, there is a letter in the files referring to a friend of Bess who can only visit Joshua Bates in secret. It turns out that this friend was Emily, Lady Westmeath, the second daughter of the Marquis of Salisbury, and the separated wife of George, Marquis of Westmeath and an Irish peer. The secrecy can be explained by her ambiguous marital status: legally separated since 1827, Lady Emily Westmeath was halfway between married and divorced, in the years before the Married Women's Property Act came into effect. Anxious to prevent her husband George from taking her assets, Emily invested in secret through Barings. Emily was also an activist who published pamphlets, which denounced the behaviour of her husband, while urging the government to legislate to protect separated and divorced women from such a fate, referring to her friend Caroline Norton who was also campaigning on the same topic. The legislation to do this, the 1857 Matrimonial Causes Act, was passed a year before Lady Westmeath's death in 1858. This led me to explore the Will and Testament of Lady Westmeath in which, interestingly, she did not bequeath money but shares. She left her individual shareholdings to various female friends and their daughters to counteract the effects of primogeniture. She could not resist a final opportunity to rail at her brother, who had very reluctantly been a trustee.

Litigation between Lord and Lady Westmeath lasted until 1837 in a number of different courts – relating to ecclesiastical, equity and common law – and revealed the financial ramifications of a failed marriage for both husband and wife. The cases involved deeds of separation, child custody and maintenance, and non-payment of court costs. Ultimately, this led to a prison sentence for Lord Westmeath and some of the witnesses for the case; steep payments for all parties involved; and the longest running marital dispute of nineteenth-century England, thus shedding light on women's agency and financial independence at that time.

The protagonists used every court in the land including the House of Lords, Chancery and the Ecclesiastical court, and some of the litigation took place in Ireland. Conducting this research required visits to a variety of archives: Emily was not afraid of the limelight and viewed it as natural to expose her struggle to the public gaze. In this case, I was presented with an *embarras de richesses* in archives such as the Salisbury archives at Hatfield House, where I found correspondence between Emily, her family, and family friend the Duke of Wellington; Lambeth Palace for the Ecclesiastical court cases dealing with the separation, in which Emily's mother opposed the separation because of the scandal; the London Metropolitan Archives in which I found additional correspondence, written in French, between Emily and George during the early years of their marriage; and the National Archives looking for deeds of settlement. So neglected were these documents that when I asked for some deeds of settlement, they appeared on a trolley as a huge roll of velum, which was handed over to me and then fell apart at the first touch, shedding plumes of dust that had gathered since the Second World War.

Conclusion

This chapter has shown how a topic such as women's historical financial involvement has been lost to public view when possible sources are ignored or remain unseen. My point is that, in the nineteenth century, company shareholders were almost exclusively individuals who did not necessarily have wealth to back them up if they lost money on the stock market. This is particularly true for female investors. In this chapter I have also attempted to show that there are numerous ways of accessing evidence of female engagement in financial matters. From the South Sea Bubble of 1720, when women were assumed to be hysterical and the likely cause of the stock market collapse, through to the 1940s when women outnumbered their male counterparts as shareholders in major UK companies, it is clear that women became increasingly active in the market.

While there is much known about the perceived role of women as avatars of Fortuna during the South Sea Bubble, and the ways in which, in the nineteenth century, women were viewed as helpless victims of financial fraud in bank collapses and railway mania, archival reports of annual general meetings and individual case studies have shown that women's importance as investors increased along with their agency over time.[67] By the twentieth century, women outnumbered men as holders of preference shares overall, and as holders of ordinary shares in several major British companies. Chairmen of these companies were forced to take the female contribution to corporate governance into account.

Currently, research into women's involvement in finance has spread globally from Australia to Canada, from Argentina to Sweden. As far as the USA is concerned, however, research has been hampered by the fact that they have no Form Es, and the list of shareholders is not publicly available. Shareholder meetings are dominated in the USA by proxy voting and retail investors are much more circumscribed with respect to corporate governance than are their UK counterparts. There remains much work to be done internationally on the role that retail investors, women in particular, played in improving company performance and stakeholder rights, compared with today's world wherein institutional investors dominate the stock market.

67 See Helen J. Paul, *The South Sea Bubble: An Economic History of its Origins and Consequences* (London: Routledge, 2011); Tamara L. Hunt, 'South Sea Speculation in Finance and Fiction', in *Speculative Enterprise: Public Theaters and Financial Markets in London and Paris, 1688–1763*, ed. by Tamara L. Hunt and Michal Jan Rozbicki (Columbus OH: Ohio State University Press, 2011), pp. 133–58.

2

Art, Industry and Estate Management: Ellen Morewood (1741–1824) of Alfreton Park

Peter Collinge

George Morewood, owner of Alfreton Park in the English county of Derbyshire and the last of an ancient family of landed gentry, died at the dinner table on 1 January 1792.[1] His obituary noted his passion for planting oak trees: 'he saw many thousands rise into shady groves and sturdy timber, which added to his rich veins in coal increased a moderate fortune to a very considerable one.'[2] George left the Alfreton estate and the rest of his real and personal property to his widow, Ellen (1741–1824), the sole executrix.[3] Over the next thirty years, and notwithstanding her marriage to the reverend Henry Case in 1793, Ellen managed Alfreton Park and oversaw the

[1] This chapter is an extensively rewritten and expanded version of a case study in Peter Collinge, 'Female Enterprise in Georgian Derbyshire, 1780–1840' (unpublished PhD thesis, Keele University, 2015), and Peter Collinge, 'Morewood [née Goodwin] (bap. 1741, d. 1824) of Alfreton, Derbyshire, Colliery Owner and Ironstone Extractor', *ODNB* (2016), https://doi.org/10.1093/ref:odnb/109611. Alan Barnes and Stephen Leach's article, 'The Painter, the Patron, the Wife and her Lover: the Portraits by Joseph Wright of Derby (1734–1787) of the Revd Henry Case and Mrs Ellen Morewood (1782)', *The British Art Journal* 22 (2021), 12–17, draws on some of this material and on Peter Collinge, '"With force and arms", Ellen Morewood (1741–1824), Rebel Queen of Alfreton', paper delivered at the British Society for Eighteenth-Century Studies, St Hugh's College, University of Oxford, 8 January 2015.

[2] *Gentleman's Magazine*, 71 (1792), pp. 90–1.

[3] Kew, The National Archives (TNA), PROB 11/1213, will of George Morewood, 26 January 1792.

exploitation of coal and ironstone deposits in the area.[4] At both local and national levels, however, her active agency in the development of England's extractive industries was not without controversy.

Like many Georgian businesswomen, there is no substantive archive for Ellen Morewood. What does survive is too fragmentary and episodic to allow for a full network analysis. In the absence of ledgers and correspondence, the net has been cast wide and creatively with decisions made about how what survives can best be incorporated into narrative and analysis. The chapter is founded on a database created from non-sequential and geographically disparate source material. The database documented each occasion, whether business or personal, when Morewood appeared in portraiture, parish records, testamentary evidence, marriage settlements, legal reports, newspapers, trade directories or company records. This approach has the advantage of eliminating over-reliance on a single source which may falsely elevate Morewood's significance within her networks. Mapping connections in a visual format has enabled an examination of Morewood through the themes of art, family, inheritance, estate management, business and legal disputes. The analysis draws attention to Morewood's complex relationships with different actors and provides tangible evidence of her active involvement in industrial development. It does not assume that her participation in different situations was equally cohesive, but it does reveal her female status to be less of a disadvantage in business than might be anticipated in Georgian England.[5] Each aspect draws attention to her determination to control and manage her life on her terms and the landscape of the local political economy. The chapter, therefore, contributes to increasing scholarship on the power and authority exercised by women over landed estates in the long-eighteenth century.

In the mid-1980s, Lawrence Stone and Jeanne Fawtier Stone established the importance of landed estate transmission to and via women: between 1760 and 1779, nearly one-third of all transfers by inheritance involved women, and between 1779 and 1840, the proportion never fell below one sixth.[6] Despite this conclusion, until recently, detailed case studies on women and estate management have been relatively slow to emerge. Often, such women are regarded as exceptional, rarities or unsuccessful, rather than integral to England's developing economy. Elizabeth Montagu's (1718–1800) manage-

4 Matlock, Derbyshire Record Office (DRO), marriage settlement, Ellen Morewood and Henry Case, 7 February 1793; Stafford, Staffordshire Record Office (SRO), B/C 11, will of Ellen Morewood, 26 February 1825.

5 For a broader discussion on networks and centrality, see Sheryllynne Haggerty and John Haggerty, 'Visual Analytics of an Eighteenth-Century Business Network', *Enterprise & Society*, 11:1 (2010), 1–25.

6 Lawrence Stone and Jeanne C. Fawtier Stone, *An Open Elite? England 1540–1880* (Oxford: Oxford University Press, 1986), p. 73.

ment of mining interests at Denton Hall, near Newcastle-upon-Tyne, led John Beckett to view her as a 'shrewd businesswoman and a careful employer who took seriously the whole business of being a substantial landowner', but ultimately regarded her activity as unusual.[7] Anne Lister's (1791–1840) development of mining at Shibden Hall, Yorkshire, remains overshadowed by the personal and public challenges she faced regarding her sexuality.[8] Women's relationship with land and property and the extent to which they were able to manage large estates, however, is a more complex and integrated story than one of exceptionality. The significance of 'terms of inheritance and personal agreements' in protecting female agency over landed estates, fundamental to Ellen Morewood's experience, accords with Emma Purcell's assessment of the strategies of Mary, duchess of Montagu (d.1775), and her daughter Elizabeth, duchess of Buccleuch (d.1827), notably, the retention of significant control over the 'management and future of their properties' and the continuation of the family name.[9] *Women and the Land, 1600–1900* foregrounds the issue of gender for shaping opportunities for women in relation to property.[10] Briony McDonagh's discussion of gender, land and estate accounting, and Shaun Evan's analysis of the accounts of Eliza Gifford (1766–1842) in north Wales, both reveal female involvement in every aspect of estate management.[11] By quantifying the scale of women's landholding across a number of English counties (though not Derbyshire), McDonagh's *Elite Women and the Agricultural Landscape* brings the complexity of female proprietorship into focus. It deals with agricultural improvement, managing change and, to a lesser extent, mining, mineral extraction and transport infrastructures. Of the seventy women surveyed, only four were directly involved in mining operations.[12] This, however, was not unusual. Except for the coal mines belonging to the Morewoods, and five other major land-

[7] J. V. Beckett, 'Elizabeth Montagu: Bluestocking turned Landlady', *Huntington Library Quarterly*, 49:2 (1986), 149–64, at p. 160.

[8] Jill Liddington, *Female Fortune, Land, Gender and Authority: the Anne Lister Diaries and Other Writings, 1833–36* (London: Rivers Oram Press, 1998); Anne Choma, *Gentleman Jack: the Real Anne Lister* (London: BBC Books, 2019).

[9] Emma Purcell, 'Inheritance and Influence: Heiresses and the Montagu Property Network, c.1749–1827', *Journal for Eighteenth-Century Studies*, 44:4 (2021), 439–52, at pp. 440–1.

[10] Briony McDonagh, Amanda L. Calpern, Jenifer Aston and Hannah Worthen, 'Introduction', in *Women and the Land, 1500–1900*, ed. by Amanda L. Calpern, B. McDonagh, and J. Aston (Woodbridge: Boydell Press, 2019), pp. 1–28, at p. 1.

[11] Briony McDonagh, 'On Being "fully and completely mistress of the whole business": Gender, Land and Estate Accounting in Georgian England', in *Women and the Land*, pp. 149–75; Shaun Evans, 'The Account Book of Eliza Gifford of Nerquis, Flintshire', paper delivered at the Power and Patriarchy Conference, University of Liverpool, 25 January 2022.

[12] Briony McDonagh, *Elite Women and the Agricultural Landscape, 1700–1830* (London: Routledge, 2018), pp. 90–3, 166–79.

owners, mines on Derbyshire's landed estates tended to be leased out rather than managed directly by owners themselves.[13]

Morewood's activities within the wider context of female-controlled property and mining operations are anchored by the experiences of two women: Liverpool property developer and mine owner, Sarah Clayton (1712–79), and Morewood's near-contemporary and near-neighbour, estate and mine owner, Elizabeth Sutton (1751–1833) of Heanor Hall. Sarah Clayton, painted by Joseph Wright in 1769, displayed an energetic capacity for managing her family's estates, finances and trusts. In 1741, she purchased Parr Hall, near St Helens, Lancashire, and its valuable coal deposits from the trustees of her father's estate.[14] In 1752, she began to lay out Clayton Square and surrounding streets in Liverpool. Her control of one trust between 1745 and 1753 resulted in Clayton becoming the *de facto* manager of collieries at Whiston, Lancashire.[15] Using this experience, Clayton exploited Parr's close proximity to the Sankey Canal, opened in 1757, to transport coal to Liverpool in partnership with her nephew, coal dealer and slave ship owner, Thomas Case. Her seeming domination of the local coal trade could infuriate fellow coal owners; in 1768, Sir Peter Legh wrote of the 'utter hatred' John Mckay 'has to Mrs Clayton'.[16] Clayton's success did not last. In the late 1760s, the Parr mines flooded and, in 1771, she borrowed £10,000, offering the Parr estate as security. She also sued her mine manager for 'neglecting the collieries' and 'misappropriating money'.[17] Her business never recovered. In 1774, she transferred her estates to Thomas Case for £17,400; yet no payment was ever received. It was subsequently determined that Clayton's action was a scurrilous attempt to outwit her creditors.[18] She and Case were declared bankrupt in 1778. Within a year Clayton was dead. Yet, in an era when many businesses failed within the first few years, Clayton's survival for more than thirty marks her out as an adept player.

In 1803, John Sutton bequeathed virtually all his real and personal estate, including Heanor Hall and mining leases in nearby Pinxton, to his widow and sole executrix.[19] Until her death in 1833, Elizabeth managed the estate and its coal, and dealt with lawyers respecting property transactions and

13 John Farey, *A General View of the Agriculture and Minerals of Derbyshire, 3 vols* (London: G. & W. Nicol, 1811–17), vol. 1, p. 182.

14 *London Evening Post*, 4–6 June 1741, p. 4, col. 4.

15 Stanley A. Harris, 'Sarah Clayton's Letter and John Wood of Bath', *Transactions of the Historic Society of Lancashire and Cheshire*, 100 (1948), 55–72, at p. 55; Theodore Barker and John Harris, *A Merseyside Town in the Industrial Revolution: St Helens 1750–1900* (London: Routledge, 1993), pp. 25–7.

16 Quoted in John Langton, 'Clayton, Sarah (1712–1779)', *ODNB* https://doi.org/10.1093/ref:odnb/48911. Sarah Clayton never married but was addressed as 'Mrs'.

17 Harris, 'Sarah Clayton's Letter', 58–9.

18 Barker and Harris, *St Helens*, p. 46.

19 TNA, PROB, 11/1409/46, will of John Sutton of Heanor, Derbyshire, 1792.

marriage settlements. She operated her own canal barges and took decisive action against a boat master following his theft of two tons of coal.[20]

Clayton and Sutton displayed conspicuous, long-term engagement in land management, the development of coal mining and the use of new transport infrastructures.[21] This did not give them equal status to men. Their actions, like those of Morewood, however, challenge the presumption of a binary male public domain and a female private one in Georgian England.

Legal Status

In the long eighteenth century, marital status and the law governed in large measure a woman's ability to act in political, social and economic capacities and had an impact on the extent to which she was able to exercise control and authority over property. Single women and widows could operate independently in business and enter into contracts as *femmes soles.* The situation for married women was different. As Amy Louise Erickson articulates, 'Under the common law fiction of coverture … an English woman upon marriage lost the great majority of her property to her husband … except by special contract – until his death'.[22] Nominally, this included her right to enter into economic contracts, but rights and privileges existing under ecclesiastical law, equity, borough and local custom, and a willing tendency for the English to litigate, tempered the fiction of many common law restrictions. Furthermore, and evident in the activities of Ellen Morewood, 'social expectations, family circumstances and women's own inclinations might act to modify legal arrangements'.[23] In addition to legal entitlements created by marriage settlements, the degree to which a married woman exerted control over her property was also reliant on the relationship she had with her spouse.[24] On occasion, the limitations of coverture were simply ignored.[25] The complex settlement drawn up before Morewood's second marriage, all

[20] *Derby Mercury*, 9 August 1810, p. 1, col. 2.

[21] For example, DRO, D255 M/F 1, Marriage settlement of John Ray to Elizabeth Sutton Inman between John Inman … Elizabeth Sutton … John Ray … Elizabeth Sutton Inman … and others, 29 April 1810; D255 M/F 5, Mrs Sutton to Mr Ray and Mr Balguy, copy conveyance and assignment of real and personal estates, 5 February 1822.

[22] Amy Louise Erickson, 'Coverture and Capitalism', *History Workshop Journal*, 59 (2005), 1–16, at pp. 3–4.

[23] McDonagh, *Elite Women*, p. 19.

[24] McDonagh, Calpern, Aston and Worthen, 'Introduction', in Calpern, McDonagh and Aston, *Women and the Land*, pp. 1–28, at p. 8.

[25] Joanne Bailey, 'Favoured or Oppressed? Married Women, Property and "Coverture" in England, 1660–1800', *Continuity and Change*, 17:3 (2002), 351–72, at pp. 351–3; Amy Louise Erickson, 'Coverture and Capitalism', 6.

but overriding coverture, enabled her to retain control of virtually every aspect of her inheritance until her death thirty years later.

Joseph Wright's Portrait of Ellen Morewood

Ellen Morewood was the daughter of a prosperous middle-ranking attorney, Richard Goodwin of Hinchley Wood, Mapleton, near Ashbourne, Derbyshire. In 1768, she married George Morewood (1719–92), a man more than twenty years her senior. Their portraits were painted by George Romney. The focus here, however, is on Ellen Morewood's portrait by Joseph Wright of Derby. Superficially, she appears to be nothing more than a fashionable woman of the landed gentry, yet her pose, attire and the subtle references to industry and land management contained in the landscape setting, move Morewood beyond contemporary notions of 'acceptable' behaviour for provincial, genteel women.[26] In this reading, her character, business interests and place in the world coalesce.

Ellen was forty-one when the portrait was commissioned in 1782.[27] For its composition, Wright drew on his drawings of classical and renaissance figures with melancholy expressions made while on the grand tour.[28] Wright also drew inspiration from Lawrence Sterne's *A Sentimental Journey*, in particular the character and pose of Maria, whom he depicted twice.[29] In terms of composition, the second version (1781) is closest to the Morewood portrait. As others have observed, although dressed in pale blue, rather than in white, Ellen Morewood sits, like Maria, under a tree 'with her elbow in her lap, and her head leaning on one side within her hand … a pale green ribband … fell across her shoulder to her waist … she had got a little dog'.[30] Amina Wright points out that the Morewood portrait shows elements of sentimentality: a solitary, contemplative, seated figure, clothed informally in a sequestered, wooded location.[31] Morewood's life did not replicate the fictional Maria's grief-induced madness: she looks inquiring

[26] Clandon Park, Surrey, National Trust, Inventory nos 1440718 and 1440719, Joseph Wright, *Ellen Morewood and Henry Case* (1782). Neither survived the 2015 Clandon Park fire. The portraits can be viewed at www.artuk.org at 'Ellen Goodwin (1740/1741–1823), Mrs Henry Case-Morewood' and 'The Reverend Henry Case (1746/1747–1825), Later The Reverend Henry Case-Morewood'.

[27] On the commissioning of the portraits see Barnes and Leach, 'The Painter, the Patron', 12–17.

[28] Amina Wright, *Joseph Wright of Derby: Bath and Beyond* (Bath: Holburne Museum, 2014), pp. 75–6, 80.

[29] The second version is in Derby Museum and Art Gallery. Judy Egerton, *Wright of Derby* (London, 1990), pp. 106–7, 115; Wright, *Joseph Wright*, p. 80.

[30] Lawrence Sterne quoted in Wright, *Joseph Wright*, p. 81.

[31] Wright, *Joseph Wright*, pp. 82, 90.

rather than melancholic, and there is no dog, yet the similarity of pose, dress, and setting, perhaps reference the death of her only child, Rowland, in 1770.[32] With her left leg crossed over her right above the knee (featured in Wright's likenesses of Nicholas Heath and Fleetwood Hesketh) and her semi-transparent attire, however, Morewood's portrait also hints at emancipation.[33] In 1760, Thomas Gainsborough's portrait of musician Ann Ford caused a sensation partly because, like Ellen Morewood, it showed a genteel woman in a masculine pose, with legs crossed above the knee.[34] Oft-quoted, but nevertheless worth repeating, when Mary Delaney saw Ford's portrait she commented: 'a most extraordinary figure, handsome and bold; but I should be very sorry to have any one I loved set forth in such a manner.'[35] Her comment reflected contemporary conduct manuals: Wettenhall Wilkes advised women never to sit cross-legged 'for such free posture unveils more of a masculine disposition than sits decent upon a modest female'.[36]

The direct gaze in Wright's portrait of Thomas Staniforth, a successful Liverpool businessman and prominent trader in enslaved people, is replicated in the Morewood portrait.[37] With her head resting in her hand, a finger points to her temple. Pointing fingers are deployed in multiple portraits by Wright, including those of Brooke Boothby and Sarah Clayton, to signify knowledge and intelligence.[38] Boothby, of Ashbourne Hall, Derbyshire, points towards his head and to a copy of Jean Jacques Rousseau's *Dialogues* indicating his knowledge and interest in new philosophical thinking.[39] Clayton's finger points to a plan of the Propylea in Athens showing her knowledge of architecture, but the portrait makes no reference to her mining activities.[40] In like manner, the finger pointing

32 A memorial to the Walker family in St Oswald's church, Ashbourne, Derbyshire, shows a similarly posed figure.

33 Susan M. Wager, 'Review of Benedict Leca, Aileen Ribeiro and Amber Ludwig, Thomas Gainsborough and the Modern Woman', *Enfilade*, 24 June 2011, https://enfilade18thc.com/2011/06/24/reviewed-thomas-gainsborough-and-the-modern-woman/ (accessed 28 June 2022); Egerton, *Wright of Derby*, pp. 41, 82.

34 Wright, *Joseph Wright*, pp. 25, 35.

35 Mary Delaney quoted in P. Holman, 'Ann Ford Revisited', *Eighteenth Century Music*, 1:2 (2004), 157–81, at p. 157; Ruth Hayden, *Mrs Delaney: Her Life and Flowers* (London: British Museum Press, 2000), p. 96.

36 Wettenhall Wilkes, *A Letter of Genteel Moral Advice to a Young Lady*, 4th edn (London: M. Cooper, 1746), p. 190. See also, Holman, 'Ann Ford Revisited', 157.

37 Tate Britain, London, T00794, Joseph Wright, *Thomas Staniforth* (1769).

38 Boothby's portrait is in Tate Britain and Clayton's in Fitchburg Art Museum, Fitchburg, MA.

39 Egerton, *Wright of Derby*, p. 117.

40 Andrew Carrington Shelton, 'Storming the Acropolis: Gender, Class and Classicism in Eighteenth-Century England', in Elise Goodman (ed.), *Art and Culture in the Eighteenth Century: New Dimensions and Multiple Perspectives* (Newark DE: University of Delaware Press, 2001), pp. 125–41, at pp. 135–6. The plan is not of Clayton Square

towards Morewood's head alludes to her intelligence, yet it is not immediately apparent that she was both a landowner and an industrialist. This is not surprising. Portraits of landowners in pastoral settings, including that of Derbyshire lead mine owner, Charles Hurt (1768–1834) by Joseph Wright, often omit overt industrial activity.[41] Wright's portraits of other Derbyshire industrialists in interior settings, however, do reference their entrepreneurial activities. The portrait of textile manufacturer Richard Arkwright includes reels of cotton, while that of fellow textile manufacturer Jedediah Strutt has ledgers and letters. The portrait of land and mine owner Francis Hurt (father of Charles) displays a lump of galena.[42]

Consideration of the landscape in Morewood's portrait casts light on her business endeavours. This enables analysis to move beyond that of simply an elite woman in a romantic landscape. Regarding the landscape as an attribute of entrepreneurial and industrial activity, achievement and position, however, is revealed only on careful observation.[43] In doing so, the setting functions in the same way, for example, as the galena in Francis Hurt's portrait. Influenced by his friend John *Whitehurst's Inquiry into the Original State of and Formation of the Earth* (1778), Wright's later landscapes and portraits often reveal closely observed topographical accuracy.[44] In the portraits of Morewood and Charles Hurt, the landscapes are recognisable; Morewood at Alfreton Park and Hurt at his Alderwasley estate.[45] In both, the landscape signifies ancient lineages, and, at a time when land meant power, the land as the source of Morewood's and Hurt's enormous wealth and authority. Perhaps most significantly, the portraits denote those responsible for its management.[46] Indeed, when John Farey compiled his *Agriculture and Minerals of Derbyshire*, he 'called on leading experts in the region'. Among very many men, Ellen Morewood and Elizabeth Sutton were the

---

as stated in Langton, 'Clayton, Sarah'; Amy Boyington, *Hidden Patrons: Women and Architectural Patronage in Georgian Britain* (London: Bloomsbury Visual Arts, 2024), pp. 82–3.

41 An exception is Philip Mercier's portrait of *Sir William and Lady Catherine Lowther*. Celia Fox, *The Arts of Industry in the Age of Enlightenment* (New Haven CT: Yale University Press for the Paul Mellon Centre for Studies in British Art, 2009), pp. 208, 324, 328.

42 Egerton, *Wright of Derby*, pp. 197, 203, 205.

43 Egerton, *Wright of Derby*, p. 22. Fox, *Arts of Industry*, p. 322.

44 Andrew Graciano, 'The Book of Nature is Open to All Men', *Huntington Library Quarterly*, 68:4 (2005), 583–600, at p. 599; Jane Wallis, *Joseph Wright of Derby, 1734–1797* (Derby: Derby Museum & Art Gallery, 1997), pp. 15, 69; Wright, *Joseph Wright*, pp. 15, 69.

45 Andrew Graciano, *Joseph Wright, Esq. Painter and Gentleman* (Newcastle-upon-Tyne: Cambridge Scholars Publishing, 2012), p. 47. The companion portrait includes Alfreton Hall on the horizon.

46 Fox, *Arts of Industry*, p. 331; Graciano, *Joseph Wright*, pp. 31, 49.

only two women consulted.[47] Moreover, as many of Wright's acquaintances, including Brooke Boothby, valued the experience to be gained from outdoors, the outdoor setting suggests further that Morewood's knowledge of estate management was acquired from practical experience, as much as it might have been from books.[48] The shady grove of trees references one aspect of her fortune, but contemporaries interested in landscape also engaged in a process of topographical deduction. From closely observed artistic interpretations of what was visible on the surface, it was believed, could be discerned what lay beneath.[49] Reading the landscape setting in this way acknowledges both the visible and the invisible sources of Morewood's fortune; namely, timber, coal and iron ore extraction, though it was coal that drew Morewood into expensive lawsuits.

Joseph Wright's companion portrait shows the reverend Henry Case.[50] When it was painted, Ellen's husband, George, was still alive. Ellen married Henry Case just over a year after George's death. The portraits, pre-dating Ellen Morewood's second marriage by eleven years, make their subject matter 'remarkable' if not something approaching scandalous, especially when taken in conjunction with the knowledge that from around 1780, Henry Case was already living at Alfreton Hall.[51] Alan Barnes and Stephen Leach surmise that the portraits give recognition to an agreement between the Morewoods and Case that should Ellen become pregnant by Case, the child would be passed off as George's.[52] Here was a woman who knew that while her position in society was nominally defined by socially constructed gender norms, she had the status, power and resources to challenge them. The absence of her first husband, the presence of her future husband in the companion picture along with a dog at Henry's feet symbolising faithfulness and fidelity, and indeed, the way in which Morewood dominates the two portraits exemplify her authority. Such 'cultural self-fashioning', whereby sitters sought to raise their own social and economic significance within their immediate communities, argues Andrew Graciano, was a common trope in eighteenth-century portraiture.[53]

[47] Cherry Lewis, 'David Mushet, John Farey and William Smith: Geologising in the Forest of Dean', *Earth Sciences History*, 35:1 (2016), 167–96, at p. 173; Farey, *Agriculture and Minerals*, 1, pp. xx, xxii, xxiv.

[48] Stephen Daniels, *Joseph Wright* (London: Tate Publishing, 1999), p. 44.

[49] Graciano, *Joseph Wright*, pp. 11, 13–14, 20; Graciano, 'Book of Nature', 586.

[50] Henry Case was rector of Ladbroke, Warwickshire and chaplain to the Prince of Wales: *Derby Mercury*, 14 February 1793, p. 2, col. 1.

[51] Wright, *Joseph Wright*, p. 91, n.36.

[52] Barnes and Leach, 'The Painter', 12, 15.

[53] Graciano, *Joseph Wright*, pp. 52–3.

Inheritance and the Alfreton Estate

George Morewood's father, Rowland, died in 1754. George inherited Alfreton Park, while his elder brother, John, inherited New Hall, Castleton.[54] John died without issue in 1758. Consequently, George inherited his brother's estate, reuniting Rowland's property. George and Ellen Morewood, however, had no children who survived infancy.[55] On George's death, with no heir, and with the exception of a few legacies to servants and money for the poor, the entire estate passed to his widow.[56] George's will lacks specifics, but some semblance of the scale of Ellen's inheritance can be determined. Alfreton Park was the Morewoods' principal seat. Sitting within an estate that eventually extended to 4,400 acres (1780.6 ha), the hall housed 'a considerable collection of paintings, some of them by the best masters'.[57] Parkland, of around 90 acres (36.4 ha) contained woodland, avenues, a temple, obelisk, grotto and a 'piece of water', perhaps that glimpsed in the middle distance of Ellen's portrait.[58] There were additional landholdings across Derbyshire, notably at Castleton, Stony Middleton, and South Wingfield, and further property in Norfolk and Staffordshire.[59]

As a very wealthy widow, Ellen Morewood had considerable freedom, but, in 1793, she remarried. The settlement made prior to her marriage to Henry Case sets out in detail her real and personal estate, the extent of her own power and authority, that of Henry Case, and that of her trustees.[60] As was standard in such settlements, Ellen Morewood's estate was transferred to trustees; in this instance to two lawyers. The settlement was not unusual in stipulating exclusions of real and personal estate for a wife's sole and separate use and benefit, nor that while married she would not be subject to, nor liable for, any of her husband's debts. Likewise, when Elizabeth Sutton conveyed her Heanor estate to trustees in 1822 for the benefit of her niece who inherited on Elizabeth's death, the agreement stipulated that Elizabeth Sutton Ray was entitled to the rents and profits of the estate 'for her sole and separate use and benefit independently of John Ray [her husband] and

54 TNA, PROB 11/810/343, will of Rowland Morewood, 27 August 1754.

55 Around 20 per cent of eighteenth-century marriages produced no children: McDonagh, Calpern, Aston and Worthen, *Women, and the Land*, p. 9.

56 SRO, B/C 11, will of Ellen Morewood, 26 February 1825.

57 T. Bateman, *A Descriptive and Historical Account of Alfreton* (printed privately, 1812), p. 20.

58 Bateman, *Alfreton*, p. 20.

59 *Derby Mercury*, 20 Jul. 1825, p. 1, cols 3–4.

60 DRO, D176M, Box 22 M, Marriage Settlement of Ellen Morewood and Henry Case, 6 February 1793.

not subject to his debts, control or engagements'.[61] What was less standard in Morewood's situation was the way in which the settlement preserved her inheritance and her authority to act in all matters by stipulating that she was to be regarded as if she was 'a femme sole and unmarried'. She was not to be subject to the 'engagements, power or coverture of the said Henry Case in any manner whatsoever'.[62] Neither Henry Case nor the trustees could dispose of any of her property (except after her death) without her specific written agreement and signature. She reserved the right to use or dispose of her household goods, jewellery, pictures and furniture in Alfreton Hall as she saw fit. Specific reference was made to her retention of coal and iron-stone rights in and around Alfreton. Henry Case made no settlement on Ellen Morewood. Instead, she paid him an annuity of £1,000 in twice-yearly instalments. In return, he was to add 'Morewood' to his own name and use it on all documents, correspondence and occasions. By her marriage, Ellen Morewood did not become Mrs Henry Case or even Mrs Henry Case Morewood, as an announcement in the *London Gazette*, repeated in the *Derby Mercury*, made clear:

> The King has been pleased to grant unto the Rev. Henry Case, clerk, Rector of Ladbroke, in the county of Warwick, his Royal Licence and authority to assume the Surname and bear the Arms of Morewood, pursuant to a settlement made on his marriage with Ellen Morewood, widow and relict of George Morewood, late of Alfreton Hall.[63]

Her memorial in St Martin's church, Alfreton, illustrates that no occasion passed without Ellen Morewood reminding people that she was, and always would be, Mrs Morewood: 'To the sacred memory of Ellen the widow of George Morewood and afterwards of the Reverend Henry Case who upon his marriage with her assumed the additional name of Morewood.'[64]

Business and Estate Management

Surviving sources are silent on the extent to which Ellen Morewood and Elizabeth Sutton were involved in estate management during their respective husbands' lifetimes, but, as Penelope Lane states, 'Widows inheriting unconditionally … is indicative of many widows continuing to engage in

[61] DRO, D255 M/F 5 Mrs Sutton … assignment of real and personal estates, 5 February 1822.

[62] SRO, B/C 11, will of Ellen Morewood, 26 February 1825.

[63] *London Gazette*, 5 February 1793, pp. 107–8; *Derby Mercury*, 14 February 1793, p. 2, col. 1.

[64] Memorial inscription, St Martin's church, Alfreton, Derbyshire.

enterprise'.[65] Anecdotally, Morewood was a 'very domineering woman ... Towards the end of his life, George had very indifferent health and his wife ... took over everything'.[66] Following George's death, a more detailed picture emerges of Ellen's business activities. Not content with her already vast fortune, she exercised the authority and power that came with her position as a significant landowner by expending considerable time, effort and money in attempts to maximise the potential of the estate.

In 1792, in a small-scale transaction, Morewood authorised the sale of 252 trees.[67] More importantly, an extension to her estate and an increase in mining operations came through the enclosure of 280 acres of common land in Alfreton.[68] The act stated that 'the Reverend Henry Case Morewood, in Right of Ellen Morewood his wife, is Lord of the Manor, and as such is entitled to the Soil of the said Commons and Waste Grounds'.[69] Moreover, all rights relating to coal and ironstone devolved to the Morewoods 'as were any other Mines within or under any of the lands' enclosed by the Act.[70] Either by the enclosure award itself, or through subsequent purchase, the majority of the commons came under the direct control of the Morewoods.[71]

Attempts to extend operations were not always successful, however. In an inquisition post mortem (*c.*1792) regarding Ellen Morewood's 'claim of coals and ironstone within Riddings in the parish Alfreton', legal counsel was unequivocal: 'I am of the opinion that ... Mrs Morewood does not appear to be entitled to the coal and ironstone deposits under Mr Rolleston's lands in Riddings and I cannot advise her to institute any proceedings for the purpose of ascertaining her rights to them.'[72] Simultaneously, Morewood fell out spectacularly with engineer and iron producer Benjamin Outram. Their dispute over mining and mineral rights under Outram's land became a landmark ruling in English trespass law. In 1793, Outram brought a case against Ellen Morewood and Henry Case Morewood alleging that on 5 May 1792 (during her widowhood), Mrs Morewood had 'with force and

65 Penelope Lane, 'Women, Property and Inheritance: Wealth Creation and Income Generation in Small English Towns', in Jon Stobart and Alastair Owens, *Urban Fortunes: Property and Inheritance in the Town, 1700–1900* (Aldershot: Ashgate, 2000), pp.172–94, at p. 180.

66 Transcription, Thomas Christmas Morewood, *Notes on the Family of Morewood (1938)*, eds, Frank Morewood and Jenny Morewood (Oakville: privately printed, 1992), p. 62.

67 *Derby Mercury*, 22 Mar. 1792, p. 1, col. 3.

68 Reginald Johnson, *A History of Alfreton* (Ripley: R. Johnson, 1968), pp. 76–8. Elizabeth Montagu made similar investments: Beckett, 'Elizabeth Montagu', p. 154.

69 Quoted in Johnson, *Alfreton*, p. 76.

70 Johnson, *Alfreton*, p. 76.

71 Ibid. pp. 77–8.

72 Derby, Local Studies Library, Derbyshire Deeds, 11103, A case on behalf of Mrs Morewood as to her claim of coals and ironstone within Riddings [1792?].

arms broke and entered a certain coal mine' belonging to Outram at Cow Close in Alfreton and had 'dug out … large quantities of coals' and carried them away.[73] In court, Mrs Morewood 'defended the force', but as for the 'breaking and entering', she pleaded that 'the plaintiff ought not to maintain his action against her'.[74] Her defence rested on her belief that the mine or vein of coals were part and parcel of land which since 1618, had by subsequent sale and release, passed eventually to George Morewood, and, after his decease, to her as his widow.[75] The *Derby Mercury* reported that at the assizes the case that:

> attracted the most attention was the long contested dispute between Mr Outram plaintiff and Mrs Morewood defendant, being an action for getting coals under Mr Outram's land which Mrs Morewood endeavoured to justify … after an hearing of thirteen hours verdict [was given] for the plaintiff. The expenses already incurred in this dispute are £1600 at the least. Mrs Morewood is a lady of very great property and … intends to bring this business forward again.[76]

Morewood did appeal, but failed to get the judgment overturned. This was not the end of the matter. In 1803, the case reached Lord Chief Justice Ellenborough in the Court of King's Bench. Although the marriage settlement stated that Ellen Morewood was to be treated as a *feme sole* as if unmarried, the action was brought jointly against Henry Case Morewood and 'Ellen his wife'.[77] It is clear, however, that Henry's involvement was in name only. Mrs Morewood's defence once again rested on the argument that the action should fail because of her established rights to Cow Close to which she could show title. Outram's counsel again countered that the land in question did not constitute part of the lands sold or transferred since the early-seventeenth century. It also pursued an argument of estoppel; that owing to a former verdict in the plaintiff's favour on the same issue of trespass, the defendants could not rely on the same evidential arguments. Ellenborough's judgment turned on whether the defendant was estopped by the earlier verdict. He found in favour of Outram.[78]

Entering a coalmine and removing coal illegally were hardly the actions expected of a genteel woman, even if Morewood believed that she was entitled to do so. Defending her action in court and exposing her business dealings to public scrutiny ran counter to widely declared norms of female

[73] Edward Hyde East, *Reports of Cases Argued and Determined in the Court of King's Bench* (London: J. Butterworth and Son, 1807), vol. 3, p. 348; R. B. Schofield, *Benjamin Outram 1764–1805: An Engineering Biography* (Cardiff: Merton Priory Press, 2000), p. 213.

[74] Hyde East, *Reports*, p. 348.

[75] Hyde East, *Reports*, pp. 346–66; Craven and Stanley, *Derbyshire Country House*, p. 16.

[76] *Derby Mercury*, 28 March 1793, p. 4, col. 2.

[77] Hyde East, *Reports*, p. 346.

[78] Hyde East, *Reports*, pp. 354, 355.

behaviour. Jean Jacques Rousseau, who lived near Ashbourne in 1766, was one who espoused the 'proper' place for women: 'Even if she possesses any genuine talents, any pretension on her part would degrade them. Her dignity depends on remaining unknown'.[79]

Were Morewood's attempts to secure mining rights under land belonging to others exceptional? In a county where the mining laws were well-known and legal disputes over rights commonplace, two illustrative examples show that they were not.[80] First, the estate of Elizabeth Sutton was also subject to disputes. In the early seventeenth century, a series of sales, leases and agreements – the wording of which, at times, was both confusing and contradictory – led to more than two centuries of litigation between subsequent owners and lessees of the land. The situation was particularly acute when disentangling surface ownership of land from subsurface mining and mineral rights.[81] Second, there was the activity of Francis Hurt.[82] Hurt's control over mineral rights in Crich included mining rights that extended beyond his own property. Providing that the surface of the land was neither damaged nor disturbed during mining operations, there was no requirement for him seek permission to tunnel beneath land he did not own, nor to compensate owners. In the 1770s, a vein of lead ore worked by Hurt's company extended under land belonging to the Trustees of the Earl of Shrewsbury Hospital in Sheffield. In order to exploit this vein, the company dug an entrance close to the hospital's lands. The Trustees protested. As Morewood attempted to do later, Hurt relied on the sale of rights and titles detailed in documents as evidence of his entitlement. By 1782, the dispute was settled in Hurt's favour. Superficially, Morewood's situation regarding coal extraction mirrored Hurt's and, therefore, a precedent existed. There was, however, a crucial difference. Since 1288, with some exceptions including churchyards, Derbyshire's lead miners had enjoyed the legal right to 'search for lead without hindrance from the landowner'.[83] As Morewood knew full well from the advice she received regarding Mr Rolleston's lands in Riddings, the same rights did not apply to coal mining and ironstone extraction.

While the dispute over mining rights dragged on, the close geographic proximity of Ellen Morewood at Alfreton to Benjamin Outram at Butterley

79 Jean-Jacques Rousseau quoted in Linda Colley, *Britons: Forging the Nation, 1707–1817* (New Haven CT: Yale University Press, 1991), p. 240.

80 Arthur Raistirck and Bernard Jennings, *A History of Lead Mining in the Pennines* (London: Longmans, 1965), pp. 115, 181.

81 The issue was resolved in 1852. DRO, D255 M/T 66, Dead of partition of coal at Heanor, 30 April 1852.

82 The section on Hurt and Crich draws on Graciano's *Joseph Wright, Esq. Painter and Gentleman*, pp. 43–4.

83 J. H. Rieuwerts, 'Introduction, part two – The History of Mining', in Trevor Ford and J. H. Rieuwerts (eds), *Lead Mining in the Peak District* (Bakewell: Peak Park Planning Board, 1968), p. 9.

Hall and their co-dependant business interests meant that they encountered one another in other situations. Almost inevitably, new disputes arose. In 1789, an Act of Parliament gave permission for the construction of Cromford Canal linking Richard Arkwright's cotton mills at Cromford to the Erewash Canal and the river Trent. It also enabled the transportation of coal, iron ore, lead and limestone from the Derwent and Amber valleys to markets beyond their immediate localities.[84] The engineers of the canal were William Jessop and Benjamin Outram, co-partners in Benjamin Outram and Co., iron founders at Butterley. Under the terms of the Act, investors in the canal, such as George Morewood, could purchase a maximum of ten shares.[85] At his death, his shares passed to his widow, although the company's list of shareholders records, 'Exor of George Morewood Esq. decd', rather than Ellen's name. In 1792, fourteen of the Cromford Canal Company's shareholders were women. Collectively, they held fifty-eight of the 460 shares. By 1798, this figure had increased to eighteen women, holding eighty shares between them. These included shares held by widows acting as executrixes of their respective husbands: Ellen Morewood (ten), Elizabeth Brough (five) and Sarah Killer (four).[86]

Despite Ellen Morewood's immense wealth, the control she exercised over her inheritance and estates and her ownership of shares, she found that she could not always act alone. Her dealings with the Cromford Canal Company were sometimes conducted through the company's agent, rather than in person. In 1795, she asked the company to construct a railway from her Hermitage Colliery to the canal. The company minuted:

> Mrs Morewood having applied to the Committee by Mr J[ames] Unwin for the Company to make a railway to communicate between her Colliery at Swanwick and the west end of the Butterley Tunnel and also for a wharf for her coals both at the east end and west end of the Tunnel. The Committee are sorry that they must decline making the proposed railway.[87]

The decision derived not from the fact that Morewood was a woman but from the company's 'General Principal which they have observed on similar applications of not making communications with Collieries or other works for the accommodation of the Proprietors of estates at the expense of the Company'.[88] Perhaps because it was keen to engage with a substantial land-

[84] Jean Lindsay, 'The Butterley Coal and Iron Works 1792–1826', *Derbyshire Archaeological Journal*, 85 (1965), 25–43, at p. 26; R. B. Schofield, 'The Promotion of the Cromford Canal Act of 1789: A Study in Canal Engineering', *Bulletin of the John Rylands Library*, 64:1 (1981), 246–78, at p. 247.

[85] Hugh Potter and Philip Riden (eds), *Minutes of the Meetings of the Cromford Canal Co., 1789–1799*, Derbyshire Record Society, 39 (Chesterfield, 2015), pp. xiv, 51.

[86] Potter and Riden, *Minutes*, p. 154.

[87] Ibid., p. 118.

[88] Potter and Riden, *Minutes*, p. 118.

owner who would use the canal to transport coal and because she held shares in the company, however, the committee was:

> desirous to accommodate Mrs Morewood with convenient wharfs and they are willing that Mrs Morewood shall use the Company's land at the East end of the Tunnel for that purpose. And that she shall have … part of the Company's land for a wharf at the West end of the Tunnel to be prepared at the Company's expense when Mrs Morewood's Coal shall be ready to be delivered upon that part of the Canal.[89]

Undeterred by the company's refusal, Morewood began constructing the railway herself. In 1796, Henry Case Morewood was involved in discussions with Benjamin Outram and Co. regarding the supply of rails.[90] Despite this, and as was the situation with the Cromford Canal Company and Alfreton Ironworks, Benjamin Outram and Co., conducted business primarily with Ellen Morewood, answering questions she raised regarding prices, guarantees and payment methods.[91] Sometimes, influenced by her agents and factors, and much to the annoyance of the Benjamin Outram and his brother Joseph, Ellen Morewood ignored their advice.[92] In 1796, Benjamin criticised the standard of work carried out by Morewood's men on the railway: 'A bungled piece of work neither profitable to Mrs Morewood nor creditable to us and if Mrs Morewood is determined to have it done in that imperfect manner I hope she will excuse us for declining to have anything to do with it.'[93]

In the early-1790s, Morewood paid for iron from Buttlerley in coal, but terminated this policy in 1797 and protested about Outram's terms of credit.[94] Benjamin Outram wrote furiously to Morewood: 'There is not another Colliery in the Kingdom but would be glad to pay their foundry bills in coal.'[95] Moreover, he pointed out that Morewood's coal was 7d per ton more expensive than that available nearby and ordered his boatmen to take 'no more Coals from Hermitage Wharf but to lead where their custom will be more acceptable'.[96] The Outrams were outraged at Morewood insisting on settlement of their account in cash, but for her part it showed a sound understanding of business and of wider economic issues. Cash flow, critical to any enterprise, was especially so in the volatile economic climate of 1797 when the Bank of England suspended the issue of cash. This

89 Ibid.

90 Schofield, *Outram*, p. 213.

91 Ibid., pp. 213, 217.

92 Ibid., pp. 213–4.

93 Benjamin Outram, 22 October 1796, quoted in Schofield, *Outram*, p. 214.

94 Benjamin Outram, 12 January 1797, quoted in P. Riden, *The Butterley Company 1790–1830*, Derbyshire Record Society, 16 (Chesterfield, 1990), p. 129.

95 Benjamin Outram quoted in Riden, *Butterley Company*, p. 129.

96 Schofield, *Outram*, p. 216.

caused widespread concern and a scramble to settle accounts. Morewood clearly understood cash flow and knew that for all his engineering abilities Benjamin Outram's capacity to manage finances was not his strongest point. In February 1797, he wrote to Morewood, 'We have depended on a remittance from you … but have not yet received, we beg to remind you that tomorrow is our pay day, and hope you will favour us … with 200 or £300'.[97] Appeals to Morewood to settle her accounts in time for the Outrams to meet their own obligations met with only partial success.[98] Morewood's insistence that those with whom she dealt settled accounts in cash was not restricted to the Outrams. She adopted the same policy with Alfreton Ironworks. In January 1806, George Mushet noted, 'Mrs Morewood stopped coals from being sent into the works, in consequence of which my brother [David, manager of the ironworks] went into Derby' to gather funds. The following day, David Mushet 'called at Alfreton Hall to settle a coal account with Mrs Morewood'.[99] Insisting on cash payments from others and delaying her own settling of accounts until it suited her reveals Morewood's capacity for the intricacies of finance and the economics of business.

Ellen Morewood's Will

Ellen Morewood's will makes specific and repeated references to her marriage settlement of 1793.[100] Legacies, bequests and annuities ranged from the thousands of pounds given to her nephews to a year's wages for each of her nine servants. Alfreton Hall, its lands, messuages, coal and other mines and minerals, and the advowson of Alfreton vicarage, were vested in Henry Case Morewood in lieu of the £1,000 annuity settled on him at the time of their marriage. He was granted the income from the rents of her several estates, instructed to keep accounts and to produce a record of the accounts and rents of Morewood's Castleton estate. Out of these, he had to pay all the housekeeping accounts, bills, wages, taxes, domestic charges and expenses.

After Henry's death, real and personal estate devolved first to Ellen's nephew William Palmer (1780–1863) and his heirs. Should his line fail, then the estates were to pass to William's brother Charles and his heirs, and if that should fail then to their sister Mary Ann and her heirs. To inherit, William Palmer had to add the Morewood name to his own, and use it on all occasions. Stipulations requiring inheritors of landed estates

97 Benjamin Outram quoted Schofield, *Outram*, pp. 185–6.

98 Lindsay, 'Butterley Coal and Iron Works', p. 32; Schofield, *Outram*, pp. 184–5, 217.

99 George Mushet, *The Diary of George Mushet, 1805–13*, ed. R. M. Healey (Chesterfield: Derbyshire Archaeological Society, 1982), pp. 18–19.

100 SRO, B/C 11, will of Ellen Morewood, 26 February 1825.

to change their surnames ensured that established family names continued, but where the testator's name was added to the surname of the inheritor it also acted as a means of perpetuating the name of the benefactor.[101] The family story that Ellen's dominance resulted in the Morewood estates being directed away from surviving (but distant) members of the Morewood line is unfounded.[102] George did not 'cut off the entail, which proceedings were apparently barred by his father'.[103] There is no mention in Rowland Morewood's will of entail or that if George had no lawful issue the estates were to revert to the Warwickshire branch of the family.[104]

Morewood's will detailed what should happen to her personal estate, her jewellery and the extensive contents of Alfreton Hall. Jenifer Aston's analysis of nineteenth-century wills – admittedly of women by no means as wealthy as Ellen Morewood – contends that such items were described for their financial value and as a means of identifying them rather than to attach to them any feminine emotional significance.[105] In terms of personal estate, therefore, the language of Morewood's will conforms to that relating to other women. Most of the will, however, detailed her business interests, especially her coal, ironstone deposits, and her collieries and quarries. The provisions and language deployed regarding the transfer of real estate were typical for the owners of landed property. They correspond closely to the stipulations in the conveyance of Heanor Hall by Elizabeth Sutton to her niece.[106] The repeated, forthright insistence in Morewood's will declaring where her authority came from and her power to act, however, were atypical. Morewood instructed her heirs to:

> use and enjoy all the buildings engines, railroads, drains, ways, implements, machinery, horses, carriages, tools, utensils, stock and all other materials and effects … in and about my collieries … and also to erect and make use of and enjoy all such buildings, engines, machinery, pits, soughs, drains, ways, roads, powers and privileges whatsoever which may be necessary for working the same mines, minerals, collieries, quarries keeping the same … in good and sufficient repair and for the stacking, coking, selling and disposing of, taking and carrying away the produce of the said mines, minerals, collieries and quarries.[107]

101 Stone and Stone, *Open Elite?*, pp. 80, 86.

102 Joseph Tilley, *The Old Halls, Manors and Families of Derbyshire: The Scarsdale Hundred*, vol. 3 (London: Simpkin, Marshall, Hamilton, Kent & Co., 1889), p. 25.

103 Morewood, *Family of Morewood*, p. 63.

104 TNA, PROB 11/810/343, will of Rowland Morewood, 27 August 1754.

105 Jennifer Aston, 'Female Business Ownership in Birmingham 1849–1901', *Midland History*, 37:2, (2012), 187–206, at p. 202.

106 DRO, D255 M/F 5, Mrs Sutton to Mr Ray and Mr Balguy, copy conveyance and assignment of real and personal estates, 5 February 1822.

107 SRO, B/C 11, will of Ellen Morewood, 26 February 1825.

The will ensured that her industrial concerns continued, and explicitly granted her heirs the right to expand operations as necessary, but forbad mining under Alfreton Hall, its gardens, pleasure grounds and any other buildings already in existence. Throughout the business aspects of her will are repetitions of 'to which I am entitled', 'of which I shall be possessed and entitled', 'I have the power to appoint', and 'over which I have the power by my said marriage settlement'. Read in conjunction with her legal entanglements, the declarations were designed to rule out disputes over ownership and rights that had dogged many of her business dealings.

Conclusion

For Ellen Morewood's eightieth birthday in December 1821, a large party gathered at Alfreton Hall to pay its dues to 'a highly respected lady'.[108] This, however, was not the occasion for her to retire. Until her death three years later, she remained deeply embedded within the world of heavy industry. Following her death, property at Castleton, Eyam and at Dronfield, all in Derbyshire, was sold. It is perhaps a sign of her importance that most of the sales notices specified that the disposals were being conducted under the will and trusts of the late Mrs Morewood, rather than under the will of the inheritor of those properties, Henry Case Morewood, who by the time of the sales, was dead too.[109]

Like Sarah Clayton, Morewood was a true entrepreneur, a risk-taker and shrewd businesswoman, alive to new investment opportunities, alighting on projects primarily advantageous to herself. Never content to be idle and live off the proceeds of her considerable inheritance, Morewood maintained and increased her landholdings and cast an opportunistic, and, at times, an avaricious eye on property held by others. Disputes over mining rights derived from centuries-old legal agreements, just as Elizabeth Sutton's did. Like Clayton and Sutton, Morewood was determined, formidable and, when necessary, ruthless, but so too were her male contemporaries. Wealth and social standing gave Morewood, Clayton and Sutton more freedom, independence, power and authority than other women in Georgian England, but as the establishment of trusts, marriage settlements and property transfers show, not equality with men. Not all elite women acted as Ellen Morewood did, but, while married, her legal encounters and contractual dealings with men reveal her desire and capacity to circumnavigate many of the restrictions imposed by couverture. What emerges most clearly about Ellen Morewood, however, is that, like Elizabeth Montagu, she had 'the confi-

108 *Derby Mercury*, 26 December 1821, p. 3, col. 2.

109 *Derby Mercury*, 20 July 1825, p. 1, cols 3–4.

dence of a landowner in her own right. She felt limited need to apologise for her power, and instead joined with her male counterparts in a shared culture of landowning'.[110]

110 Stephen Bending, 'Negotiating Men: Elizabeth Montagu, 'Capability' Brown and the Construction of Pastoral', in Calpern, McDonagh and Aston, *Women and the Land*, pp. 176–200, at p. 178.

3

Protection and Education: Investment Advice for Female Investors in *Fin de Siècle* England

Hazel Vosper

The late nineteenth century witnessed a substantial increase in the number of individual investors in shares and bonds. Many of these individuals were drawn from the expanding middle class, and for many investing was a new experience.[1] One question that arises from this trend concerns the sources of information that investors drew on to make their investment decisions. Family ties and, for male investors, professional or social networks, were potential channels of financial intelligence. A less personal option arose from the expansion of a distinctive genre of print culture in the nineteenth century offering financial advice. Printed financial information had been a feature of the nascent stock market in London during the eighteenth century and it expanded significantly in the next century; this included newspapers as well as handbills and pamphlets.[2] A dedicated financial press emerged, supplemented by widely available financial advice books and pamphlets. A limited number of financial advice documents have been used by historians to discuss specific aspects of investment, such as portfolio construction

[1] Janette Rutterford et al., 'Who Comprised the Nation of Shareholders? Gender and Investment in Great Britain, c. 1870–1935', *The Economic History Review*, 64:1 (2011), 157–87; Graeme G. Acheson, Gareth Campbell and John D. Turner, 'Who Financed the Expansion of the Equity Market? Shareholder Clienteles in Victorian Britain', *Business History*, 59:4 (2017), 607–37; Janette Rutterford and Dimitris P. Sotiropoulos, 'The Rise of the Small Investor in the United States and United Kingdom, 1895 to 1970', *Enterprise & Society*, 18:3 (2017), 485–535.

[2] Anne L. Murphy, *The Origins of English Financial Markets: Investment and Speculation before the South Sea Bubble* (Cambridge: Cambridge University Press, 2012), p. 96.

and the dubious practices of the early financial press.[3] However, financial advice documents as a distinct genre of print culture have only recently gained the attention of historians in any great depth.[4]

One aspect of the genre that remains underexplored is the evolution of printed financial advice targeted at female readers. This chapter will consider the development of this sub-genre around the *fin de siècle* period in England. It draws on letters from female correspondents sent to specialist financial newspapers, investment-focused articles for or about female investors in the national and provincial press, and financial advice books with a targeted female readership. Although printed circulars distributed by brokers were an important part of the financial advice genre, they are not covered in this chapter on the basis that the target audience was somewhat random rather than female-focused.[5] As will be shown, assumptions about female investors within this sub-genre tended to reflect two different perspectives. Initially, from the mid to late nineteenth century, women were frequently counselled to seek a male protector on investment matters. There was little expectation that women had the capacity to make their own investment decisions and a recurrent topic within the cultural discourse was the unhappy consequences that resulted when they tried. This perspective gradually changed and, by the early twentieth century, the focus was less on a gender-based assumption of incapacity and more towards the need to develop financial education for women.

Newspapers and Financial Advice

In the latter half of the nineteenth century, the number of London-based and regional newspapers expanded significantly. In part this was a result of the removal in the 1850s of paper taxes and stamp duties, the so-called 'taxes on knowledge'. There was a doubling of titles published in London from 131 to 298, and a six-fold increase in the number of provincial titles

3 Janette Rutterford and Dimitris P. Sotiropoulos, 'Financial Diversification before Modern Portfolio Theory: UK Financial Advice Documents in the Late Nineteenth and the Beginning of the Twentieth Century', *The European Journal of the History of Economic Thought*, 23:6 (2016), 919–45; James Taylor, '"Distrust All Advice … and Make No Exception in Favour of Our Advice": Financial Knowledge and Knowingness in Late Victorian Britain', *The English Historical Review*, 136 (580) (2021), 619–50.

4 Paul Crosthwaite et al., *Invested: How Three Centuries of Stock Market Advice Reshaped Our Money, Markets, and Minds* (Chicago IL: University of Chicago Press, 2022).

5 For more on broker's circulars, see James Taylor, 'Inside and Outside the London Stock Exchange: Stockbrokers and Speculation in Late Victorian Britain', *Enterprise & Society*, 22:3 (2021), 842–77.

from 224 to 1340.[6] Additionally, there was a significant growth in women's periodicals, with over 120 new women's titles between 1880 and 1900. The growth in reading matter aligned with a steady improvement in literacy levels, especially following the Education Act of 1870. By 1888, more than ninety percent of the population were estimated to be literate.[7]

Public libraries provided growing availability of reading material as well as offering readers access to a wide variety of newspapers and periodicals, which in turn advanced literacy rates. Women could venture into this public space safely, as libraries often provided separate reading spaces for men and women.[8] More significantly, the reduction in the cost of newspapers made it possible for a well-to-do household to take a daily newspaper. This was a change from previous practices, in which newspapers were shared, read in gentlemen's clubs, or hired by the hour in public houses.[9] Now the lady of the house who, according to a press trade journal, 'had much time on her hands', would have the opportunity to read a newspaper.[10] On any given day, she might find something of interest relating to the latest parliamentary debates, royalty, or reports from abroad. One such reader, Elizabeth Van der Weyer of Windsor Forest, read a small item in *The Times* in 1872 and promptly wrote to her London bank, Barings:

> Dear Sirs, I see in today's Times that the advice from Brazil being the Confirmation of the pacific adjustment of the dispute between that Empire and the Argentine Republic. If the whole of our Argentine Bonds are not already sold, do not you think that under these circumstances we might keep five or ten thousand of them?[11]

The article to which she referred had appeared in the business section of *The Times* and concerned the resumption of diplomatic relations between Brazil and Argentina after a minor dispute. Mrs Van der Weyer was an investor and she had made the connection between a general news item and the Argentinian securities she owned, recognising that the former made

6 Martin Hewitt, *The Dawn of the Cheap Press in Victorian Britain: The End of the 'Taxes on Knowledge', 1849–1869* (London: Bloomsbury Publishing, 2013); Andrew Hobbs, *A Fleet Street in Every Town: The Provincial Press in England, 1855–1900* (Cambridge: Open Book Publishers, 2018), p. 4.

7 Alan J. Lee, *The Origins of the Popular Press in England, 1855–1914* (London: Croom Helm, 1976), 33; Margaret Beetham, *A Magazine of Her Own? Domesticity and Desire in the Woman's Magazine, 1800–1914* (London: Routledge, 1996), pp. 119–23.

8 Hobbs, *Fleet Street*, p. 40.

9 Hewitt, *Dawn of the Cheap Press*, p. 124.

10 From 'The Journalist and Newspaper Proprietor of 1900' quoted in Hobbs, *Fleet Street*, p. 55.

11 Elizabeth Van de Weyer, 'Letter to Thomas Baring', 31 October 1872, HC1.153, BAR: The Baring Archive, London; 'Money-Market and City Intelligence', *The Times*, 31 October 1872.

the latter more attractive as a holding. As the century progressed, a specialised financial press replicated the same types of connection between news events and investment impact made by Mrs Van de Weyer. Newspapers had started to report on financial news in a systematic way from the early nineteenth century although initially it was indistinct from the general news coverage.[12] Following the mid-century postal reforms, the demand for financial news encouraged a wave of new specialist titles. *The Financier and Bullionist* was launched in 1870, the *Financial News* in 1884 and the *Financial Times* in 1888.[13] The growing interest of readers in financial topics was aided by the transition from the somewhat colourless money articles of the mid-century to a more accessible and often opinionated reporting style by the end of the century. Journalists would write financial articles from the first-person point of view; illustrations enlivened the presentation and easy-to-read formatting helped a reader to quickly spot something that might be of interest on a page.[14]

Dilwyn Porter has highlighted that a further innovation for readers interested in investing was the noticeable 'commitment to the role of advisor' in investment matters.[15] One manifestation of this advisory role was through what social historian Teresa Gerard identifies as a 'new publishing phenomenon'; namely, the introduction of a regular *Answers to Correspondents* column.[16] Such columns addressed all manner of topics in response to readers' letters and the *Financial News* was one of the first to recognise the potential for its readers and their financial advice needs. It launched its column in March 1884, just three months after the newspaper began. The column was immediately popular with readers, and by December 1884 it was receiving over forty readers' letters each day.[17] Other financial and mainstream newspapers followed suit. The popularity of such columns was no doubt connected to the fact that the advice was free, but another potential

[12] James Taylor, 'Financial Crises and the Birth of the Financial Press, 1825–1880', in *The Media and Financial Crises: Comparative and Historical Perspectives*, ed. by Steve Schifferes and Richard Roberts (London: Routledge, 2015), 203–14; Crosthwaite et al., *Invested*, p. 50.

[13] Amy Edwards, *Are We Rich Yet?: The Rise of Mass Investment Culture in Contemporary Britain* (Berkely CA: University of California Press, 2022), pp. 29–31.

[14] Mary Poovey, 'Writing about Finance in Victorian England: Disclosure and Secrecy in the Culture of Investment', in *Victorian Investments: New Perspectives on Finance and Culture*, ed. by Nancy Henry and Cannon Schmitt (Bloomington Is: Indiana University Press, 2009), p. 43.

[15] Dilwyn Porter, '"A Trusted Guide of the Investing Public": Harry Marks and the Financial News 1884–1916', *Business History*, 28:1 (1986), 2.

[16] Teresa Gerrard, 'New Methods in the History of Reading: "Answers to Correspondents" in the Family Herald, 1860–1900', *Publishing History* 43 (1998), 55.

[17] David Kynaston, *The Financial Times: A Centenary History* (London: Viking, 1988), pp. 8–10.

attraction was that it was anonymous. Although writers to the *Answers to Correspondents* column published by the *Financial Times* were required to provide their full name and address, this information was not shown when a response was printed. Given the volume of readers' queries, the answers tended to be short and to the point, for example:

> WEST AUSTRALIANS (Disappointed, Hull). Sell.
>
> STEAM OMNIBUS (Widow). You should not have applied. It is now too late.[18]

Here, the securities were identified using capital letters with no information concerning the security type provided, such as whether the advice referred to an issuer's ordinary shares, preference shares or debentures. This abbreviated information would have been less than helpful to the wider readership given many companies issued a variety of security types, especially over time. The letter writer was identified by a pseudonym, which was followed by a succinct response to the writer's unseen query. The pseudonyms were seemingly either constructed from personal details contained in the letter or the writer's own self-description. Some newspapers simply printed an answer which led to some intriguing responses that hopefully the letter writer would recognise as being their reply. For example, in a response to a correspondent identified only as 'Female', three terse pieces of advice were offered: '(1) A sound investment. (2) You had better not touch it. (3) About 4 per cent.'[19]

Each column would usually include responses to a small number of women, who were identifiable by a gendered pseudonym. It is likely that there were more female contributors than initially appears as they might have requested that only their initials or a generic term such as the aforementioned 'Disappointed' be used. This was the approach favoured by Mary Smith, a schoolteacher from Carlisle, who often wrote to her local newspaper on civic matters using a non-gender specific pseudonym. She explained that she 'considered that if men knew who the writer was, they would say, "What does a woman know about politics?"'[20] For a woman writing to request financial advice there might have been concerns about being dismissed for lack of knowledge or, if disclosing sensitive financial circumstances, worries about being identified in her local community. Hence the extent to which women participated in these columns is difficult to assess accurately. What

18 'Advice to Investors', *Daily Mail*, 22 July 1898. Original capitals.

19 'Answers to Correspondents', *Financial Times*, 7 August 1889.

20 Hobbs, *Fleet Street*, p. 56; the use of a pen name by female correspondents to local newspapers was not unusual, see Sarah Pedersen, 'What's in a Name? The Revealing Use of Noms de Plume in Women's Correspondence to Daily Newspapers in Edwardian Scotland', *Media History*, 10:3 (2004), 175–85.

is apparent is that some women were seeking investment advice on a regular basis from specialised financial news outlets.

Where a female advice seeker can be identified in the 'Answers to Correspondents' column the most frequent pseudonym was a variation on 'widow'. A consistent theme of the printed responses they received was the danger of speculation and the unsuitability of high-risk investments for these women. In a representative example, one widow was informed that, 'We are afraid 5 per cent is too much to expect where the safety of the capital is the first consideration. The security you mention is not a suitable one for your purpose as there is too much of the speculative element about it'.[21]An association between widows and the risks of speculation was also made by the *Financial Times* when outlining some of the issues it faced in trying to satisfy the many reader requests it received:

> A very common type of question we receive is: 'What do you recommend as the best investment—Grand Trunk Ordinary, Cedulas "P", Chathams or Mexican Railway Ordinary?' This sort of question comes generally from clergymen, who would be shocked at the suggestion they were speculating, and widow ladies of limited means are subject to the same weakness.[22]

The vulnerability of clergymen and widows to what were considered to be reckless investments was a common trope of both the press and in literature.[23] The investments mentioned in this case were seemingly chosen to emphasis this point as, for example, the 'Chathams' were dismissed elsewhere by one broker as 'rubbish'.[24]

Investment advice was not the sole domain of the London-based financial newspapers. Provincial newspapers had established The Press Association in 1868 as a co-operative news agency that provided shared content for local papers. Syndicated reports on parliamentary debates and business developments as well as serialised works of fiction were commonly printed across multiple local papers.[25] One syndicated example was *Our Ladies' Column*, which appeared weekly in a range of geographically diverse local newspapers, including the *Lichfield Times* and the *Bristol Mercury*. It was written by 'Penelope' who proudly declared at the top of her column herself to be 'One of Themselves' to her female readers. 'Penelope' was the penname

[21] 'Answers to Correspondents', *Financial Times*, 27 November 1901.

[22] 'Our Enquiry Office', *Financial Times*, 16 April 1895.

[23] Janette Rutterford and Josephine Maltby, '"The Widow, the Clergyman and the Reckless": Women Investors in England, 1830–1914', *Feminist Economics*, 12:1/2 (2006), 111–38; Nancy Henry, '"Ladies Do It?": Victorian Women Investors in Fact and Fiction', in *Victorian Literature and Finance*, ed. by Francis O'Gorman (Oxford: Oxford University Press, 2007), pp. 111–31.

[24] Shares in London, *Chatham and Dover Railway: Duncan on Investment and Speculation in Stocks and Shares*, 3rd edn (London: Effingham Wilson, 1895), p. 125.

[25] Hobbs, *Fleet Street*, p. 8.

of Phebe Lankester, who died in 1900, after which the column continued under unknown authorship.[26] Among the recipes and chatter about high-society events, Penelope occasionally shared investment tips. Mining shares were commonly considered to be high risk investments; warnings against both South African and West Australian mines were to the fore when one purveyor of advice cautioned investors against 'following the fashion of the hour in the investment of money'.[27] Regardless, Penelope had warmed to investments in South African goldmines and informed her readers that:

> I wish I had shares in some one of these successful enterprises, which, though their field may be far away, seem to me altogether a more exciting and promising investment than is found by putting a little cash into the quiet millinery and domestic home companies which are being successfully floated just now.[28]

Penelope's mention of women's hats and staid British enterprises was perhaps a mild rebuke to her female readers for being too cautious in their investment choices. What is significant is that she assumed that her provincial female readership would be faced with investment choices, or at least be interested in reading about them.

This was a different attitude from that assumed by the authors of certain financial advice books directed at a female readership published in the second half of the nineteenth century. Investment advice books can be traced back to the eighteenth century, with the period from the great Railway Boom of the 1840s and onwards witnessing a steady increase in their volume and affordability.[29] One distinct readership that was targeted was women through either advice books that mentioned women in the title or in articles that addressed female investors directly. Although these women-focused advice publications only represented a small percentage of the total, there was a noticeable split between two narratives that constructed an imagined female investor in distinctly different ways. One narrative emphasised protection while the other emphasised education.

Protection

The narrative of protection cautioned female investors to seek out the support of men in financial matter. The core assumptions were that women needed to be protected from both their own incapacity in financial matters

[26] I am indebted to Professor James Taylor for this information.

[27] A. J. Wilson, *Practical Hints to Investors: And Some Words to Speculators* (London: C. Wilson, 1897), pp. 25–6.

[28] 'Penelope' (pseud.), 'Our Ladies' Column … South African Mines', *Bristol Mercury*, 11 May 1895.

[29] Crosthwaite et al., *Invested*, pp. 64–81.

and their vulnerability to those who sought to exploit that weakness. One of the first financial advice publications aimed specifically at women was *A Guide to the Unprotected in Every-day Matters Relating to Property and Income*, which appeared in 1863. The advice book was written by an author who styled herself 'A Banker's Daughter' and it has proved to be a popular source with several historians.[30] One reason, no doubt, is due to the forthright and eminently quotable style in which it was written. In an oft-cited section, the writer advised her readership to 'seldom consult ladies in business matters: they usually know little or nothing of business. It is much like the blind leading the blind'.[31] In real life, 'A Banker's Daughter' was Emma Sophia Galton (1811–1904) and her father had indeed worked in a bank. She was related to Charles Darwin on her mother's side and her youngest brother was the eugenicist Francis Galton. Following her father's death, it was spinster Emma who managed the finances of the extended Galton family, displaying a capability in money matters that presumably excluded her from the accusation of being 'blind' to business matters.[32]

Most of the 124-page palm-sized *A Guide to the Unprotected* contains practical advice, such as how to keep account books and write cheques. In addition, investment advice was offered with one chapter covering 'leading securities' for female investors to consider that included British government bonds and railway shares, but also government securities from East India and Canada as well as some Australian railway shares.[33] From the mid-eighteenth century the British government had raised capital by issuing loans in the form of financial securities known collectively as Consols (an abbreviation of consolidated annuities). Although investors in Consols received a relatively low return, the regular interest payments were dependable given the financial resources the issuer had recourse to. The other recommendations were more diverse and represented varying levels of risk exposure.

Galton's advice was not restricted to the lowest risk securities, but it was predicated on an assumption that the female readers would only have a small amount of capital to invest and little capacity to sustain capital losses. Readers were counselled to seek the safest possible investments, which meant accepting a return of 4.5 per cent or less, regardless of their actual needs.

30 See Josephine Maltby and Janette Rutterford, '"She Possessed Her Own Fortune": Women Investors from the Late Nineteenth Century to the Early Twentieth Century', *Business History*, 48:2 (2006), 220–53; George Robb, *Ladies of the Ticker: Women and Wall Street from the Gilded Age to the Great Depression* (Urbana IL: University of Illinois Press, 2017), p. 22; Graeme G. Acheson et al., 'Independent Women: Investing in British Railways, 1870–1922', *The Economic History Review*, 74:2 (May 2021), 483.

31 A 'Banker's Daughter', *Guide to the Unprotected in Everyday Matters Relating to Property and Income*, 1st edn (London: Macmillan & Co., 1863), p. 14.

32 Crosthwaite et al., *Invested*, p. 92; D. W. Forrest, *Francis Galton: The Life and Work of a Victorian Genius* (London: Paul Elek, 1974), pp. 107–9.

33 A 'Banker's Daughter', *Guide to the Unprotected*, 1st edn, ch. 3.

More importantly, Galton's investment advice was that an unprotected woman – a spinster or a widow – should find a man to help her. Readers were urged to 'Seek a sensible and upright Friend, who is a good man of business, to consult as to what concerns are safe or unsafe for business'.[34]

Galton was not alone in her assumptions regarding female financial dependency. In the year following the publication of the first edition of *A Guide to the Unprotected*, an article titled *Ladies and Their Money* was published in a monthly magazine for women.[35] The unnamed writer of the article sought to clarify the ways 'in which a lady's income should be treated differently from a gentleman's'. The investing practices of women were contrasted with those of businessmen, and the former were found to be wanting. According to the writer, women lacked both the authority to act and the necessary networks to provide information to act on. Instead, women were steered towards 'the funds' – that is, Consols – which paid around 3 per cent. Although the returns might have been low, it was stressed that the female investor would almost inevitably be troubled by a raft of male troublemakers (itemised as family members, local agents and solicitors, and tenants that failed to pay their rent) if she chose to pursue alternative and, as such, risky investment options.

The article appeared in the *Englishwomen's Domestic Magazine,* which was published by Samuel Beeton. He also published *Beeton's Guide to Investing Money with Safety and Profit.* This advice book contained recommendations to different types of investors, including a section titled 'Investments for Women'. It was brief and made clear that women were expected to have little active involvement in their own financial affairs, with the first sentence counselling that 'such investments should be chosen for women as are most simple'.[36] It was presumed that a male member of her family or a trusted adviser would do the choosing. The inadvisability of women being involved in the management of their own money was also a theme in *The Autobiography of a Joint-Stock Company (Limited)* written by the satirical author Laurence Oliphant. In his short story, originally published in *Blackwood's Magazine*, an anthropomorphised company tells its life story from inception to its current position, 'reclining … in the arms of my official liquidator'. The character of the personified company narrates how it had been used as a vehicle to defraud investors. The company blames gullible investors, in particular clergymen, landed proprietors and:

[34] A 'Banker's Daughter', *Guide to the Unprotected,* 1st edn, p. 13.

[35] 'Ladies and Their Money', *Englishwoman's Domestic Magazine,* 8:45 (1 January 1864), pp. 112–17.

[36] Samuel Beeton, *Beeton's Guide to Investing Money with Safety and Profit, Etc.* (London: Ward, Lock & Co., 1870), p. 53.

> widows and spinsters: for however capable you may think yourselves of enjoying the franchise, I am able from my own knowledge to declare that you are utterly unfit to manage your own money-matters, and I should never have been able to enter upon my fraudulent career had it not been for the powerful support I derived from the trusting contributions of confiding or speculative female investors.[37]

Here again, credulous men, most notably clergymen, were grouped with naive female investors, particularly widows. Together they were blamed for not recognising their own financial ineptness.[38] The story itself introduced a succession of deplorable characters, each contributing in some way to the company's eventual failure. According to Mary Poovey, the story served to emphasise the difficulty in attributing responsibility for corporate wrongdoing when there were so many who were happy to wreak havoc on vulnerable investors.[39] Emma Galton might have considered women to be vulnerable when she recommended that they find a 'sensible and upright Friend' in whom to place their trust, but Oliphant's story emphasised how difficult a task that was.

Fictional storylines such as Oliphant's often reflected real-life events. Articles appeared regularly in the press decrying financial fraudsters with particular note being taken when women were involved, thereby reinforcing the notion that women needed protection. One example from a national newspaper reported the 'latest' sorry tale of a solicitor with significant debts who had absconded overseas.[40] The article recounted that he had been entrusted with the investment capital of his clients, many of whom were women. His female clients were reported as making 'excited' calls in person at his now-deserted office in the heart of the City of London. There was no indication in the article as to the response of the rogue solicitor's male clients. Rather, the emphasis on the emotional response of the women served to heighten the dramatic impact of the story while also foregrounding their vulnerability to breaches of trust. James Taylor emphasises the importance of trust-based networks as sources of information concerning investment transactions during the nineteenth century, and the bewilderment when such trust was ill-placed.

[37] L. Oliphant, 'The Autobiography of a Joint-Stock Company (Limited) 1876', in *The Financial System in Nineteenth-Century Britain*, ed. by Mary Poovey (New York: Oxford University Press, 2003), pp. 327–56.

[38] Criticism of female investors was not unusual, for example, see Anne L. Murphy, '"We Have Been Ruined by Whores": Perceptions of Female Involvement in the South Sea Scheme', in *Boom, Bust and beyond: New Perspectives on the 1720 Stock Market Bubble*, ed. by Stefano Condorelli and Daniel Menning (Berlin: De Gruyter Oldenbourg, 2019), pp. 261–84.

[39] Mary Poovey (ed.), *The Financial System in Nineteenth-Century Britain* (New York: Oxford University Press, 2003), pp. 302–3.

[40] 'A Missing Solicitor: Excited Ladies in Chancery Lane', *Daily Mail*, 21 April 1897.

Taylor suggests there was a tension between the 'mushrooming print culture' that provided somewhat impersonal financial advice for a mass audience and 'the importance of the human factor … as investors sought safety in local knowledge and individual assessments of character'.[41] This tension is exemplified in William Cotton's *Everybody's Guide to Money Matters* (1898). Cotton explained his advice book had been 'prepared chiefly for the use of women, a vast proportion of whom are brought up in utter ignorance of money matters in the simplest form, though otherwise they may be highly accomplished'.[42] Cotton introduced his readers to a fictional 'Miss Jane Smith' and her generous uncle's bequest. The legacy comprised of £500 in cash and a packet of investment documents that somewhat bemused the recipient. Her bafflement was due, as Cotton informed his readers, to the fact that Miss Smith 'has been brought up without the slightest instruction in business matters, indeed has rather plumed herself on the idea of being quite above such things'.[43] In an echo of Emma Galton, Cotton recommended to Miss Smith that she should trust the personal advice of her banker and 'rely very much upon his opinion'. Yet Cotton still provided his female readers with an overview of how stock exchanges worked and discussed the many types of global investments. The book was full of detailed investment advice for its female readership, yet those same readers were encouraged to turn to a trusted male advisor. Cotton's approach, whilst echoing Emma Galton's views on protection, was also positioned to be of interest to women who wished to expand their financial knowledge. Cotton was possibly trying to appeal to a wide potential readership, but he was also reflecting shifting expectations arising from social changes that were not to be found in Galton's advice.

Galton's *A Guide to the Unprotected* had been a success as soon as it was published and garnered positive reviews in the press. One London paper, *The Examiner*, earnestly recommended it to those ladies 'forced to manage her own affairs', and outlined the dangers that faced women in such circumstances: 'As long as sharpers, business-like and law-protected, are in the world and consider unprotected ladies fair objects of prey, there will be need of such a book as this.'[44] It eventually ran to seven editions, with the last edition being published in 1900, just four years before Emma Galton's

[41] James Taylor, 'Trust, Friends, and Investments in Late Victorian England', *The Historical Journal*, 64:5 (2021), 1314.

[42] William Cotton, *Everybody's Guide to Money Matters. With a description of the various investments chiefly dealt in on the Stock Exchange, etc.* (London: Frederick Warne & Co, 1898), p. 6.

[43] Ibid.

[44] 'Christmas Numbers (Book Review of "A Guide to the Unprotected" 1st Ed. by A Banker's Daughter)', *Examiner*, 26 December 1863.

death.[45] The period between the first and seventh editions, covering 1863 to 1900, witnessed significant social and legal changes for women. There were increased employment opportunities especially for middle-class women, growing calls for women to be allowed to vote and improved access to primary education for girls. Some women's economic agency had increased significantly with the removal of restrictions on married women's right to own property and, more widely, there were rising numbers of women who held company shares and other investment securities.[46] These changes and their repercussions were barely mentioned by Galton in later editions other than a brief reference to the Married Women's Property Act of 1882. There were some updates to reflect the growing variety of securities available to invest in, otherwise the last edition is remarkably similar in tone and scope to the first edition published thirty-seven years earlier.

Galton's diary indicated that she remained involved in the publication of the later editions and, while her advice remained the same, it seems unlikely that the needs and attitudes of many of its potential readers were similarly unchanged. An entry in Emma Galton's diary marked the publication of the first edition on 13 July 1863 with 'Unprotected came out!!'[47] The use of exclamation marks was rare in her diaries, indicating the strength of her feelings about the event. She also later records the publication dates of the second, third and fifth editions, as well as the revision of another of her finance-focused publications; the diaries are not complete, which might account for the lack of comment on other editions. By contrast, there was another strand of advice literature for women that was more aligned with these changes. Tellingly, this narrative emphasised the need for education. The narrative was premised on an assumption that the capacity of women to understand money matters was related to a lack of financial education. The need for such education was situated within arguments that emphasised the likelihood that at some stage of a woman's life she would be faced with financial responsibilities. Further, investing was positioned as an emotionally enjoyable activity for women.

45 A 'Banker's Daughter', *Guide to the Unprotected in Everyday Matters Relating to Property and Income*, 7th edn (London: Macmillan & Co., 1900).

46 Janette Rutterford, 'Votes for Women: The Role of Women Shareholders in the Campaign for Women's Suffrage in Edwardian Britain', *Entreprises et Histoire*, 107:2 (2022), 94–8.

47 'Typescript Extracts from Miss Galton's Diary', 1898, GALTON/1/1/9/3, Wellcome Collection, https://wellcomecollection.org/works/aqg2sm6k. (accessed 1 March 2024).

Financial Education

In 1906, six years after the final edition of *A Guide to the Unprotected*, a fashionable magazine for upper-class and aspirational middle-class women called *The Lady's Realm* published an article, *Women and the Money Market*. It was written by a well-known journalist and author called Olive Malvery. At first, Malvery's views seemed to echo Emma Galton's position. Malvery wrote that the 'fact of the matter is that women do not, as a rule, possess any business capacity'.[48] Yet rather than advising women to seek a male advisor, Malvery argued that women were quite capable of understanding business matters and the real problem was that they lacked financial knowledge. Although education for girls had changed significantly in the later nineteenth century, Malvery highlighted that there were many inconsistencies regarding the question of what they should be taught, and this was especially true regarding basic finance. She appealed to her readers:

> What fashionable school would teach a girl book-keeping, or the art of accountancy? What seminary for young ladies would teach a mental arithmetic class, or place on their curriculum a time for the reading of the financial notes in any daily paper?[49]

Malvery decried 'idle women' and their 'foolish personal extravagancies' and instead she suggested that they needed 'some excitement, some occupation'. Her solution was that women should follow her example and take an active involvement in investing. Malvery wrote for an imagined community of female investors who were capable of managing their own financial investments but were held back by their lack of financial education. This contrasted with Emma Galton, who wrote for an imagined community of vulnerable female investors who were dependent on male advice. Malvery was not the first to emphasise women's capability. Dinah Craik was a well-known and prolific British journalist and writer of fiction such as the popular *John Halifax, Gentleman*. Twenty years in advance of Malvery's article, reflecting similar views, Craik had published a non-fiction collection with the first piece giving its name to the collection, *About Money*. It carried an assertive message as Craik firmly stated that:

> Every woman who has any money at all, either earned or inherited, ought to keep it in her own hands, and learn to manage it herself, exactly as a man does. There is no earthly reason why she should not. A girl can learn arithmetic just as well as a boy. Ordinary business knowledge and business habits

[48] Olive Christian Malvery, 'Women and the Money Market', *The Lady's Realm*, 21 (July 1906), p. 41.

[49] Ibid.

> are just as attainable by her as by him … Everybody expects it of him – and nobody of her; and nobody attempts to teach her how to do it.[50]

Craik made the point that although women were frequently in possession of money, as beneficiaries of bequests or family trusts, many middle-class women were also increasingly in receipt of a regular income as employment opportunities for women improved. Regardless of the source of their money, Craik argued that women should be able to take responsibility for their own financial affairs. Unlike writers who stressed the need for women to rely on men in financial matters, Craik called for the opposite:

> Every girl who is not entirely dependent on her male relations – a position which considering all the ups and downs of life, the sooner she gets out of the better – ought, by the time she is old enough to possess any money, to know exactly how much she has, where it is invested, and what it ought yearly to bring in.[51]

Craik's forthright writing style was reminiscent of Emma Galton's and there were also similarities in the basic advice they offered regarding investments. The difference between the two lay in the assumed capacity of women to exercise financial agency. The positive influence of Craik's *About Money* on attitudes towards women and financial responsibilities was acknowledged by the anonymous writer of *Counsel to Ladies and Easy-going Men on Their Business Investments*, published in 1892.[52] The writer uses the pseudonym 'Senex', Latin for old man, and addresses his introductory remarks to 'My Dear' as if speaking to a much younger woman. The writer explains that women would come into contact with 'professional persons' if they wished to invest but the latter's role should be limited to those activities necessary to 'carry your decisions into effect'. Unlike those who advocated for the protection of a man drawn from the professions, the idea of relying on advice from bankers and solicitors was dismissed on the basis that their knowledge of investments was 'usually questionable'. Instead, women were encouraged to 'decide for themselves in what security their capital shall be invested'.[53]

The book itself was more than 130 pages long, and it provided substantial detail on how to invest and what securities to invest in. For example, its female readers were counselled that the securities of European government were expensive, all mining shares were to be avoided and only a select few

[50] Dinah M. M. Craik, *About Money and Other Things : A Gift-Book* (London: MacMillan & Co, 1886), 13; Dinah M. M. Craik, *John Halifax, Gentleman* (London: Hurst and Blackett, 1856).

[51] Craik, *About Money*, pp. 10–11.

[52] 'Senex' acknowledges Craik's writings in the Preface. 'Senex', *Counsel to Ladies and Easy-Going Men on Their Business Investments: And Cautions against the Lures of Wily Financiers & Unprincipled Promoters* (London: The Leadenhall Press, 1892), p. xi.

[53] 'Senex', *Counsel to Ladies*, pp. 21–6.

Argentinian railway securities were worthy of consideration.[54] The writer argued that the need for such detail was that the 'amazing ignorance of the majority of ladies as to the most elementary facts and principles of business, has induced me to go into details, and to discuss points, which will be the veriest [*sic*] A B C to persons moving in the outside world'.[55] The writer offered women an alternative way to gain some of the financial knowledge that men could easily acquire from their interactions with 'the outside world'.

One means that was available to help bridge such gaps in financial knowledge was self-education. This was consistent with the spirit of Samuel Smiles' popular and influential *Self Help* and it was the approach taken by Olive Malvery.[56] She had enrolled in a commercial college in order to study the same subjects as 'the lad who starts in a bank or a stockbroker's office'. She seemed to be speaking from personal experience when she wrote that:

> A woman who has once tasted of the sweetness of this experience will find more excitement and joy in reading the financial columns in her daily paper and her evening journal, and watching the fluctuations of money markets, than she would in gossiping with her neighbours and wasting her time looking enviously into shop windows at things which she cannot, or ought not to, afford to buy.[57]

It is notable that Malvery highlighted the ease with which women could access investment information in the financial press. Malvery also encouraged the idea that investing could be emotionally satisfying for women, even exciting. She contrasted this against a hint of the banality of the day-to-day activities of many middle-class women. However, her insinuation was rather harsh, as some women took a proactive and purposeful approach to financial education, exemplified by female societies and social groups which arranged lectures on financial subjects for their members or acquaintances. In 1896 the Home Education Society invited a Mr Bertrand Stewart to deliver a series of talks to its members. Over the course of four lectures the speaker covered the topics of keeping accounts, insurance, domestic legal questions and investments. In his introductory remarks, Mr Stewart had been keen to reassure his listeners that:

> I hope to be able to show you that there are a good many practical details of business information which it will be of advantage to you to possess, and

54 Ibid., pp. 50, 81–3.

55 Ibid., p. xiv.

56 Samuel Smiles, *Self-Help: With Illustrations of Character and Conduct* (London: Murray, 1859); Melissa Walker, 'On Their Own: The Single Woman, Feminism, and Self-Help in British Women's Print Culture (1850–1900)' (unpublished PhD, University of Guelph, 2012), pp. 27–35.

57 Malvery, 'Women and the Money Market', p. 45.

> which you can acquire and practice without any sacrifice of the elegance, gentleness, and refinement which should always be the leading characteristic of women.[58]

Given that Mr Stewart was delivering his lectures to an audience of women sitting directly in front of him, there was perhaps an element of exaggerated chivalry in his comment. The actual content of his lectures was detailed and wide-ranging in scope. He made no further reference to the gender of his audience although a note was included in the printed version of the lectures that clarified that the 'Author of these Lectures desires it to be understood that they are not intended for persons who are already well-informed on the subjects dealt with'.[59] The implicit assumption was that the people who were already 'well-informed' were men.

Men as both stores and active transmitters of financial information, particularly within their own family sphere, formed part of the discussion concerning financial education for women. This growing expectation arose less because of changes in family dynamics or the influence of suffrage sentiments; rather it was seemingly driven by a recognition of demographic realities. As the nineteenth century progressed, well-to-do men tended to marry at an older age than in earlier periods.[60] Later marriage seems to have contributed towards a decrease in average family sizes, albeit it was just one of a mixture of reasons. The likelihood of fewer children was particularly the case within middle-class and upper-class families. One impact of smaller family sizes was that overall life expectancy for women increased, again for a variety of reasons although a key factor was the decreased exposure to the dangers of childbirth.[61] Thus, the combination of men marrying at an older age and women enjoying an increased life expectancy resulted in a high likelihood that a woman would experience widowhood at some point in her life cycle. That said, if a man did outlive his wife and was left a widower, it was likely that he lived in a household with one or more of his spinster daughters or sisters, some of the so-called 'surplus women'. The 1851 Census had revealed a demographic gap: out of the British population of 17.9 million, there were 1,042 women for every 1,000 men. By 1911 the population had doubled, and the demographic gap had widened to 1,068 women for every 1,000 men.[62]

58 Bertrand Stewart, *Outlines of Business Knowledge Requisite for Women: Four Lectures … Delivered to the Home Education Society* (London: Hatchard, 1896), pp. 3–4.

59 Bertrand Stewart, *Outlines of Business Knowledge Requisite for Women*, pp. 3–4.

60 John Tosh, *A Man's Place: Masculinity and the Middle-Class Home in Victorian England* (New Haven CT: Yale University Press, 1999), p. 172.

61 Jose Harris, *Private Lives, Public Spirit: Britain, 1870–1914* (London: Penguin, 1994), pp. 49–50.

62 B. R. Mitchell and H. G. Jones, *Second Abstract of British Historical Statistics* (Cambridge: Cambridge University Press, 1971), p. 3; Judith Worsnop, 'A Reevaluation

The combined impact of these demographic trends was that it was recognised that women were likely to outlast their husbands, fathers or, in shared households, brothers. As such, it was argued that men had a duty to prepare their female dependants for this eventuality and the financial responsibilities that a woman might assume. The anonymous female writer of an article on investment advice for women urged men to treat 'his wife, or for the matter of that, his sister or other woman relative, as a financial partner'.[63] In an article from 1910, written by the social activist Louise Creighton and titled 'Women and Finance', fathers and husbands were chastised that they 'should not make a mystery of the financial position of the family'.[64] Creighton argued that their daughters and wives should 'insist' on it because in the event that they were widowed or left fatherless 'their loneliness will be aggravated by a sense of impotence to manage their own affairs'.[65] Examples of women who were left helplessly unprepared for financial responsibility after the death of a male family member were also reflected in popular works of fiction, such as Gissing's novel *The Odd Women* (1893).[66] The sense that women needed to prepare themselves was made in a 1908 advice book titled *Women as Investors*. The writer, W.B. assumed a readership of 'women who have money to invest, or who suddenly find themselves called on to undertake business responsibilities'. W.B. favourably compared women to men in terms of capacity to invest, even if the former's actual investment education was lacking, and argued that:

> It is reasonable to suppose that, at the present day, women are quite capable of looking after their own financial interests. A little instruction and experience is all that is necessary to enable them to understand the question of investments quite as well as the ordinary young man who, at the age of twenty-one, is legally considered capable of managing his own affairs.[67]

Taking a somewhat more trenchant tone, an (unnamed) writer in the *Daily Mail* bemoaned the situation where a widow was left to manage the family finances because her late husband had not shared any financial informa-

of "the Problem of Surplus Women" in 19th-Century England: The Case of the 1851 Census', *Women's Studies International Forum*, 13:1 (1990), 21; Kathrin Levitan, 'Redundancy, the "Surplus Woman" Problem, and the British Census, 1851–1861', *Women's History Review*, 17:3 (2008), 360–3.

63 'How Women May Achieve Investment Success', *The Financial Review of Reviews*, May 1911, p. 36. Although the writer was anonymous she was identified as a 'lady engaged in business'.

64 Louisa Creighton, 'Women and Finance', *The Financial Review of Reviews*, 1910, p. 20.

65 Ibid.

66 George Gissing, *The Odd Women* (London: Lawrence & Bullen, 1893).

67 W.B., *Women as Investors* (Birmingham: Cornish Bros, 1908), p. 3. No indication was given as to whether the writer was male or female.

tion with her while he was alive. The writer imagined a scenario between a husband and wife:

> 'Run away, my dear. We are going to talk business, which a woman can't understand,' he remarks kindly but firmly. Dismissing her like a baby in short frocks to play with her toys, the husband in the study swells with the superiority of a sex whose brains are big enough to grasp the complexities of business.[68]

The writer made clear that it was a failing of the husband if he did not prepare his wife for the prospect that she might outlive him. Again, the solution proposed by the writer was education, with both law and business suggested as necessary additions to the standard curriculum for girls. The argument for better financial education had echoes with the contemporaneous campaign for better overall education for women that historian Philippa Levine argues was a 'prerequisite … in the battle for middle-class women's employment'.[69]

The sense that ignorance of financial matters was an unacceptable omission from a girl's education was emphasised by Lucy Yates in *The Management of Money: A Handbook of Finance for Women*. Published in 1903, Yates highlighted that women experienced difficulties in gaining the requisite financial knowledge and suggested that it was important that 'The education of girls ought not to be considered complete until they have learnt a good deal about the management of money and of documents relating to money'.[70] Given the title of the book, such a viewpoint was not surprising, nor can it be separated from the fact the author wanted to sell a book covering exactly those topics. Notwithstanding, the need for men and women to have a similar basic grounding in financial matters gradually gained traction with newspapers playing an important role.

When it launched in 1896, the *Daily Mail* was targeted, to an extent, at women readers. It would periodically publish articles of interest to female investors that included general market advice and more gendered topics, such as recommendations that women invest in precious jewels.[71] Other periodicals would publish explanatory series about investing, again targeted at a female audience that they assumed would have an interest in such

[68] 'Feminine Finance', *Daily Mail*, 4 April 1907.

[69] Philippa Levine, *Victorian Feminism, 1850–1900* (London: Hutchinson Education, 1987), p. 126.

[70] Lucy Helen Yates, *The Management of Money: A Handbook of Finance for Women* (London: Horace Cox, 1903), p. 2.

[71] Charles Duguid, 'How Women Should Invest', *Daily Mail*, 29 May 1907; 'Jewels as Investments', *Daily Mail*, 24 October 1903; for more on the *Daily Mail* and women readers, see Beetham, *A Magazine of Her Own?*, pp. 121–2.

topics.[72] Olive Malvery provides an example to support this assumption in her 1908 novel *The Speculator*. In the novel the main protagonist, a self-taught female investor, explains that she had been 'reading with as much intelligence as my limited education will allow, some dozen or so of the financial papers'.[73] Malvery's previously discussed view that investing could be a stimulating activity for women was echoed in an article titled 'How Women May Achieve Investment Success'. The writer suggests that reading financial articles could have unexpected benefits for the well-being of the female reader, as she noted that 'to be able to read the Money Article of the newspaper might act as a mental tonic on the mind of woman *(sic)* – at any rate , it would be a wholesome set-off to the Ladies' Page such as most journals furnish for her temptation!'[74] Some financial newspapers were keen to try to capture women as regular readers. From 1910 to 1911, *The Financier and Bullionist* published a weekly column, *Finance for Women*. The column covered financial topics directly addressed at a female readership and each column always ended with five or six recommendations for securities that they should consider acquiring.[75]

Similarly, the *Financial News* published a *Marjorie and her Money* column. It appeared every Monday with a by-line stating that it was a 'weekly chat with ladies, designed to train them into looking after their own affairs'. The notion of a 'weekly chat' emphasised the friendly, inclusive tone of the column and the sense of community that was being promoted. The investment-related topics were slightly more educational in content than those in *Finance for Women*; for example, explaining the meaning of terms such as 'Guaranteed Stock'.[76] The tone of both of the columns was engaging, inclusive and spoke to a community of women who already invested or who wanted to learn how to. The tone of these early twentieth-century newspaper columns emphasised the expectation that women were quite as capable of investing as men.

Conclusion

A distinctive sub-genre of print culture arose in the mid-nineteenth century focused on financial advice for the small but growing number of female

[72] For examples of series, see 'Investment and Management of Money: Hints for Women Part I', *Women's Penny Paper*, 21 June 1890; Amy E. Bell, 'How Women May Keep Their Money 1', *The Englishwoman's Review: A Journal of Woman's Work*, 15 April 1892.

[73] Olive Christian Malvery, *The Speculator* (London: T. Werner Laurie, 1908), p. 10.

[74] 'How Women May Achieve', p. 37. Original capitals.

[75] See 'Finance for Women (36th)', *The Financier and Bullionist*, 24 July 1911.

[76] See 'Marjorie and Her Money (28-7-1913)', *Financial News*, 28 July 1913.

investors. A combination of factors had coalesced to encourage this trend including greater accessibility to newsprint materials both in public spaces such as libraries and in middle-class households, as well as improving literacy rates. An increasingly specialised financial press offered its female readers advice on different aspects of investing such as general explanations of how capital markets worked or recommendations on what to buy and sell. A small number of publishers recognised the commercial potential of a female readership seeking financial advice and they produced specialist titles for this market niche. Whether in the press or in published books and pamphlets, two different approaches emerged. One approach proposed that women needed to be protected from both their own ignorance and those people who would take advantage of them. In this vein, the reason that many women were undoubtedly ignorant of investment matters was little explored. Instead, women's incapacity to navigate the investment world was taken as a given. The emotional responses of female investors were presented in a negative sense: women were excitable rather than rational; they were susceptible to family pressures and too trusting. For those women who did venture into this foreign world, there was little surprise or sympathy when these interlopers were taken advantage of. Even in the midst of the major social and legal shifts that characterised many women's lives in the late nineteenth and early twentieth century, there was little reaction or change in the advice from those who advocated for protection. In the main, the protection perspective has been used by historians in their discussions of women's investing activities. Although this approach aligned with the experiences of some female investors, it was only one aspect of a far wider debate.

The second approach was more reflective of the period when it insisted on the importance of education as the means to develop a women's capabilities, rather than assuming an inherent gender-based incapacity. Demographic changes provided a practical incentive for women to be given the skills and knowledge to act in their own capacity as investors. In particular, the likelihood that widows or spinster daughters and sisters might be called on to manage the finances of the household, after the male head had died, was used as a common-sense rationale for better financial education for women. The type of education for women proposed did not differ from that provided to men and the discussion of investments for women was not limited to low-risk, safe investments. The emotional responses of female investors were presented in a more positive sense: investing was positioned as an exciting activity that might make a welcome contrast to other aspects of everyday lives of women. Most importantly, the expectation was established that women needed to trust themselves and their capacity to learn the basics of finance. Education, rather than a sensible and upright male friend, was increasingly considered to be more of a reliable provider of protection for the female investor.

4

For the Love of Money: Desire and Economy in *The House of Mirth* (1905)

Joyce Goggin

In her essay on *The House of Mirth*, Diana Trilling described Wharton's somewhat melodramatic novel as being 'always and passionately a money story'.[1] While this observation may seem to reside on the surface of things, for indeed there is scarcely a page on which the reader does not find the novel's troubled heroine balancing accounts, gambling or speculating, I will argue that the roots of Lily Bart's passion for money grow much deeper. The reader is presented with a complicated protagonist who must work covertly to make ends meet in the grand fashion to which she has become accustomed, while openly proclaiming that she wants: 'money—yes, *money*!'[2] Miss Bart's uncomfortable combination of necessity and desire therefore dictates that she negotiate the most profitable marriage possible with the result, as I will explain, that she herself effectively becomes a sort of currency in circulation as well as the meeting point of the libidinal and monetary economies of the text. At the same time, the interrelation of monetary and literary practices – the way in which Wharton wrote and published the novel – have a profound effect on the structure and the telling of this particular tale of woe, so that diegetic and extradiegetic factors work in unison to structure the text.

By discussing both Lily Bart's and, more briefly, Wharton's relationship to money, I will argue that much of the standard confusion with which *The House of Mirth* is often charged can be clarified by paying attention to the

1 Diana Trilling, '*The House of Mirth* Revisited', *Edith Wharton: A Collection of Critical Essays* (Englewood Cliffs NJ: Prentice-Hall, 1962), p. 111.

2 Edith Wharton, *The House of Mirth* (New York: Viking Penguin, 1985 [1905]), p. 166. Further references in the text as *HM*; page numbers are given in parentheses after the quotation.

concerns that I have just outlined. By treating these issues as two sides of the same coin I hope to dispel some of the confusion that readers and critics have expressed on the score of Lily's inexplicable and constant irresoluteness; her refusal of attractive marriage proposals when this is precisely what she seems to be after; and the novel's perplexing refusal to conform entirely to generic conventions and satisfy readers' expectations. Therefore, rather than siding with Henry James who shrewdly remarked that *The House of Mirth* is 'two novels and too confused', I will follow the money in the text as a hermeneutic exercise. This reading, both with and against the grain of the text, pays off handsomely by highlighting how Wharton's novel provides us with a narrative of women's difficult and sexualised presence in the (marriage) market.[3]

Money and Love

Lily Bart, the source of all the melodramatic complexity at the heart of *The House of Mirth*, is beset by financial worries from the opening scene. The orphan of a ruined entrepreneur and his highly ostentatious wife, Lily is a self-described '*jeune fille à marrier*' – a delicate moniker that is wearing out at an alarming rate for the twenty-nine-year-old Miss Bart (69). Lily's advancing years then set the brutal pace at which she must make the social transactions involved in what her counter-point Lawrence Selden calls 'the vocation of marriage' (9). Worse yet, Lily's profound sense of urgency is redoubled by the uncomfortable recollection that she threw 'away one or two good chances when [she] first came out', even though she is 'horribly poor—and very expensive [and] must have a great deal of money' (10).

If Lily estimates her net worth at the high end of things, other characters in the novel equally see her as pricey goods, hence Selden's opening observation that she 'must have cost a great deal to make', when he chances upon her for the first time in the opening scene at Grand Central Station (5). Unfortunately, should Lily wish to continue costing a great deal to make she must toil on an exhausting treadmill of social engagements where potential spouses might be encountered. This places Lily in an uncomfortable double

[3] Quoted in Maureen Howard, '*The House of Mirth*: The Bachelor and the Baby', in *The Cambridge Companion to Wharton* (Cambridge: Cambridge University Press, 1995), p. 141. While the accent in the present volume is on Britain, Wharton's work enjoyed a wide readership there, and the situation in the USA in the late nineteenth century was influencing women on the other side of the Atlantic. Women in Britain were looking to the US as an innovator in the market, women's emancipation and their resultant involvement in the market. On this point, see Shafquat Towheed, '"An appreciative and grateful author": Edith Wharton and the House of Macmillan', *Publishing History*, 58 (2005), 43–77; and Helen Killoran, *The Critical Reception of Edith Wharton* (London: Boydell & Brewer, 2001), pp. 25–40.

bind where she must subscribe to the notion that it takes money to make money and invest heavily in packaging. As she tells Mr Selden:

> A woman is asked out as much for her clothes as for herself. The clothes are the background, the frame, if you like … We're expected to be pretty and well-dressed till we drop—and if we can't keep it up alone, we have to go into partnership. (12)

If Lily sees herself as a commodity to be window-dressed and sold to the highest bidder – a social ornament in which the right man may some day invest his capital – she comes by this self-assessment honestly. Hence, to Lily's account of her travails, Selden encouragingly replies 'Ah, well, there must be plenty of capital on the lookout for such an investment' (Ibid.). Likewise, her aunt and benefactor, Mrs Peniston, finds it 'natural that Lily should spend all her money on dress', remarking further that she likes to 'see her well-dressed—it's only suitable' for a young lady of the class to which Lily aspires (38, 125).

This manner of regarding Lily as 'marketable goods' reaches its pinnacle of expression in the person of her own mother, the deceased Mrs Bart. After her father's financial ruin and death Lily's mother tells her that she will 'get it all back with [her] face', meaning of course, the family fortune (28). And lest the vulgarity of Lily using her face to raise money be lost on the reader, Wharton makes Mrs Bart's crass objectification of her daughter as the family's fading capital perfectly plain in the following:

> She studied [Lily's beauty] with a kind of passion … It was the last asset in their fortunes, the nucleus around which their life was to be rebuilt. She watched it jealously as though it were her own property and Lily its mere custodian and she tried to instill into the latter a sense of the responsibility that such a charge involved. (34)

It is little wonder then that Lily adopts her mother's habit of objectifying her beauty and comes to understand herself as a commodity. Left to her own resources and Mrs Peniston's support in the form of capricious but 'handsome presents', Lily learns to rely on her looks as money in the bank: 'her skill in enhancing it, the care she took of it, the use she made of it, seemed to give it a kind of permanence. She felt she could trust it to carry her through to the end' (49).

In her essay 'The Conspicuous Wasting of Lily Bart', Ruth Bernard Yeazell comments at length on the construction of Lily as a commodity for the marriage market.[4] At the centre of Yeazell's argument is the notion that women in the 'group of rich and conspicuous people' to which Lily aspires form loci of ostentatious expenditure, for which women are groomed to act

4 Ruth Bernard Yeazell, 'The Conspicuous Wasting of Lily Bart', *New Essays on* The House of Mirth (Cambridge: Cambridge University Press, 2001), pp. 15–43.

as vehicles of display (51). This argument is borrowed from Thorstein Veblen's *The Theory of the Leisure Class*, published just five years before Wharton's novel, in which we find a discussion of how upper-class women become the display windows of their husbands' wealth and power. According to Veblen, women's role in the leisure classes is to serve as an 'index of pecuniary culture' by spending enormous sums on sartorial embellishments that serve no purpose save costing a great deal of money.[5] By mobilising such enhancements as lavish gowns and jewellery women were meant to serve as the favoured method of consuming conspicuously.[6] Hence the suitable spouse is 'the chief ornament … perform[ing] conspicuous leisure and consumption' for her partner.[7] Veblen's theory of women's role in conspicuous consumption is borne out in particular by Judy Trenor in *The House of Mirth* whom, we are told, has the 'glaring good-looks of a jeweler's window lit by electricity' (55).

Veblen's observations are equally applicable to Lily who muses that 'she had been brought up to be *ornamental* [so] she could hardly blame herself for failing to serve any practical purpose' (117, my italics). And of course, this is precisely the point since Lily's purpose is to consume and display rather than to perform any useful form of labour, hence her unsuccessful brush with professional hat-trimming when marriage no longer seems an option. The distinguishing ability to ornament expenditure is also seized on by the obsequious upstart Sim Rosedale, who sees Lily 'as a possible asset for his social climb' but 'turns away, convinced she has lost her market value'.[8] In his brutally honest if preposterous marriage proposal, Rosedale assesses Lily's acceptability as an index of the 'pecuniary culture' to which he hopes to gain entry:

> It takes two things … money and the right woman to spend it … I want my wife to make all the other women feel small … I want a woman who'll hold her head higher the more diamonds I put on it … Tell you what it is though, that kind of woman costs more than all the rest of 'em put together. (175–6)

Where the marriage game is concerned, however, it is Lily herself who comes closest to the heart of matter, knowing all too well precisely what is at stake. Entertaining the possibility of a proposal of marriage from the

5 Similarly, in *A Backward Glance,* Wharton, who was doubtless familiar with Veblen's popular work, explained that the central difficulty in writing *The House of Mirth* was to inspire interest in a story about 'frivolous society [which] can acquire dramatic significance only through what its frivolity destroys' or wastes. Edith Wharton, *A Backward Glance* (London: Constable, 1972), p. 207.

6 Thorstein Veblen, *The Theory of the Leisure Class* (New York: Huebsch, 1925), pp. 167, 353.

7 Ibid., p. 180.

8 Irving Howe, 'A Reading of The House of Mirth', in *Edith Wharton: A Collection of Critical Essays* (Englewood Cliffs NJ: Prentice Hall, 1962), p. 124.

unattractive but very wealthy Percy Gryce, Lily tells herself that she will 'have smarter gowns than Judy Trenor, and far, far more jewels than Bertha Dorset … [she will be] the one possession in which he [takes] sufficient pride to spend money on it' (49).

Lady Luck

Another way to conspicuously waste both time and money is playing bridge, a game that was specially developed in an English gentleman's club in the nineteenth century to become the rich man's whist.[9] In *The House of Mirth* playing bridge is yet one more ritual of pecuniary culture that Lily must perform in order to stay in the game. So, while Bertha Dorset, Judy Trenor and the other guests at the Trenors' Bellomont estate enjoy a game of bridge, Lily thinks of it as 'one of the taxes' she has to pay for the Trenors' 'prolonged hospitality'; later, she explains the high stakes she has lost to her horrified Aunt as being part of 'paying her way', and not appearing 'priggish and superior' (26, 172). The fact that Lily loses to 'Bertha Dorset, whose husband showered money on her, [and] must have pocketed at least five hundred' while Judy Trenor 'left the table clutching such a heap of bills that she [was] unable to shake hands with her guests as they bade her good night', merely serves to heighten the dramatic irony of her situation (27). The tension is further increased when later we find Lily in her guest room feverishly balancing her cheque book and discovering that the $300 that she was keeping aside to pacify her dressmaker have vanished. Interestingly, as the vicious circle of debt and expenditure inexorably constricts around her, the equation between gambling and sartorial ostentation spurs Lily on to spend what money she does make at bridge on 'dress or jewelry … instead of keeping it against future losses' (26).

Worse still, Lily is 'afraid of discovering' that she has fallen under 'the spell of the terrible god of chance', who drives her 'to risk higher stakes at each fresh venture' (ibid.). According to Veblen once again, Lily's relationship with luck is entirely in keeping with the economic ethic of the leisure classes, which is 'more or less incompatible with the requirements of the modern industrial process'.[10] In a chapter entitled 'The Belief in Luck', Veblen writes that the 'primitive faith' in chance and an 'animistic apprehension of things' is symptomatic of that classes' notion of productivity.[11] Similarly, Panasitti and Schull have argued that 'conspicuous consumption, leisure, and games of chance were vestiges of an outdated and predatory

[9] For more on this topic, consult 'From Whist to Bridge', in David Parlett, *A History of Card Games* (Oxford: Oxford University Press, 1991), pp. 214–37.

[10] Veblen, *The Theory of the Leisure Class*, p. 277.

[11] Ibid.

Victorian aristocracy whose pecuniary standards were incompatible with the demands of industrial capitalism'.[12] Gambling, particularly in *The House of Mirth*, is very much related to the vanishing notion of aristocratic privilege, as the growing set of *nouveau riche* make their fortunes on the stock market, progressively infiltrating 'good society' in places like Monte Carlo. Hence the comic parvenu Mr Bry for example, who sports 'a business face and leisure clothes' at the casino in Monte Carlo, and is eager to be taken up by Miss Bart's set. The Brys' upward movement is then charted as they are entrusted to Lily's guidance in the finer points of conspicuously wasting money, until they become somewhat too fashionable even for her (185).

Performance, Gender and Money

The term 'to perform' arose earlier in this chapter, in reference to Veblen and his notion that the role of women in a leisure society has customarily been to perform ostentation for their wealthy spouses. Veblen's use of this term immediately brings to mind the analytic possibilities that the notion of performance and the performative have opened up through the work of J. L. Austin and Judith Butler. I would now like to segue briefly into Austin and Butler in order to consider their notions of the performative in the context of *The House of Mirth*.

The performative was first introduced by Austin as a linguistic concept in *How to do Things with Words*, as the opposing term to the constative, or discourse that 'merely' reports.[13] What distinguishes performative utterances is that they bring into being the state that they describe. An utterance such as 'I now pronounce you man and wife', performs what it signifies and, in this case, it serves to unite two people for the duration of their marriage.

Since Austin's identification of the performative function of language the term has enjoyed an impressive career in various fields of enquiry. In Judith

[12] Mike Panasitti and Natasha Schull, 'Re-articulating the Moral Economy of Gambling', in *Kroeber Anthropological Society Papers: Essays on Controlling Processes*, ed. by Laura Nader, 77 (1994), p. 66; Gillian Beer, 'The Reader's Wager: Lots, Sorts and Futures', *Essays in Criticism,* vol. 40 (1990), pp. 99–123, where she writes that 'it was probably idleness that made card games and gambling so prominent among the pleasures' of the leisure class in Victorian England (p. 107). On gambling as an anachronistic aristocratic privilege in the nineteenth-century Russian novel, see also Yuri M. Lotman, 'Theme and Plot: The Theme of Cards and the Card Game in Russian Literature of the Nineteenth Century', *PTL* 3 (1978), 455–92; on gambling in *ancien régime* France, see Thomas M. Kavanagh, *Enlightenment and the Shadows of Chance: The Novel and the Culture of Gambling in Eighteenth-Century France* (Baltimore MD: Johns Hopkins University Press, 1993), pp. 29–66.

[13] J. L. Austin, *How to do Things with Words* (Cambridge MA: Harvard University Press, 1975).

Butler's on-going investigation of gender, she defines the performative as the 'reiterative and citational practice by which discourse produces the effects that it names'.[14] Gender, as Butler sees it, is performed as a citational exercise, and reproduces discursive constructs of what gender is or needs to do at any given juncture. Gender is what our world, or the semiotic environment in which we live, work and play (including novels, films and statements such as 'I now pronounce you man and wife') compels us to perform, frequently by conforming to hetero-normative standards.

To extend the productive use of the performative as a concept, I would like to forward the notion that money also falls under the category of the performative in terms of how it functions in monetary practice. As a token or signifier of value when it is exchanged for goods, money performs the value of the transaction or, as Mark Taylor writes, '[t]he value of paper currency was created by something like a performative utterance proffered by Congress and sustained by the confidence of people who used the money'. Hence, if one buys a product for $5, it is immediately worth $5 whether or not the price seems justified, because money *performs* the designated value in the transaction.

As Jonathan Culler has pointed out, what is interesting in both Austin and Butler's formulation of the performative is the possibility of 'misfiring', where the performative would fail to bring into being the state that it names. As Culler explains, if one says 'I do' in a marriage ceremony and s/he is already married 'or if the person performing the ceremony is not authorized to perform weddings in this community' the utterance will misfire.[15] By extension, a misfiring performance of gender, in which, to quote Butler, a girl would fail to be normatively 'girled', would result in a person or character failing to conform entirely to her cultural and ideological context.[16] What Butler is referring to more specifically is that period over which a baby ceases to be seen as an 'it' and comes to be known as a 'he' or 'she'. On a good day, this might raise the possibility of subversive, transgressive and hopefully empowering performances of gender. On a bad day, the result might be something like Lily Bart. As Lynne Tillman has pointed out, Lily's misfiring is unfortunately put to no subversive or innovative purpose: she

[14] Judith Butler, *Bodies that Matter: On the Discursive Limits of Sex* (New York: Routledge, 1993), p. 2.

[15] Mark C. Taylor, *Confidence Games: Money and Markets in a World without Redemption* (Chicago IL: University of Chicago Press, 2008), p. 22; Jonathan Culler, 'Philosophy and Literature: The Fortunes of the Performative', *Poetics Today*, 24 (2002), 50.

[16] According to Butler, the entry of the child 'into the domain of language … through the interpellation of gender'; she is quick to point out that this 'girling' or 'boying' is only the 'founding interpellation' and one which will be endlessly 'reiterated by various authorities and throughout various intervals of time to reinforce or contest this naturalised [gendered] effect': Butler, *Bodies that Matter*, pp. 7–8.

is rather a 'new woman *manquée*' than a pioneer of gender politics (140).[17] And to extend the notion of the performative once again to the realm of money, one might say that counterfeit money risks misfiring because it misperforms its ascribed value in transaction.

I am suggesting then that Lily's performance of gender constantly misfires in the text and this is why her ultimate goal of finding a good match never comes to fruition. Her egregious luck is in fact at its worst on the libidinal index where gender must be performed in order to trade favourably on the marriage market and enter into the performance of leisure and consumption for a spouse. Because Lily is 'always the bridesmaid, never the bride', her sexuality remains somehow counterfeit or lacking the authentication that only marriage could provide. Moreover, as goods in trade, Lily is both 'very expensive' and a 'great risk' with no backing, while her expiry date is much closer that her youthful appearance would suggest. The combined effect of these factors is that the perennially single Lily Bart circulates through high society as a counterfeit commodity or queer money (10, 73). I do not wish to argue that Lily's flawed or counterfeit performance of female heterosexuality, nor her seeming total indifference to men, means that she should be read as gay. The argument has been made, however, that queer or counterfeit money has long been used as a metaphor for homosexuality, hence expressions such as 'queer as a three dollar bill'.[18] In borrowing Judith Butler's felicitous expression, Loebel has suggested that Lily's ambivalent or misfiring sexuality offers 'moments of ontological trouble in this text' that 'are also moments of gender trouble, in which feminine identity faces the difference of being possible for existence'.[19] This is to say that the 'queer' relationships in the text, not the least of which is Lily's addictive relationship to the 'queer-acting' drug chloral that kills her, point to the imperfect fit between Wharton's heroine and the role that society had constructed for her (288).

Bertha Dorset, on the other hand, provides an example of a successful performance of gender in the text. No 'attendant virgin', Bertha is free to carry on with a succession of young men, replacing Lawrence Selden, denizen of the 'republic of the spirit', with the younger and more reckless social gambler Silverton, and all under the watchful yet jaded eye of her husband George Dorset (87, 68). On the other hand, because Lily's sexual escapades are not legitimated by marriage, she must bear the consequence of her sustained misfiring; namely, the scrutiny, frequently under 'the glare of publicity', to which her every move is subjected (217).

17 Lynne Tillman, 'Love for Sale', in *Love for Sale: Essays on Art, Literature, and Politics* (New York: Scribner, 2006), p. 140.

18 See William Fisher, 'Queer Money', *English Literary History*, 66:1 (1999), 1–23.

19 Thomas Loebel, 'Beyond Herself', in *New Essays on* The House of Mirth, ed. by Deborah Esch (Cambridge: Cambridge University Press, 2001), pp. 107–33, at p. 125.

Paradoxically, under the watchful eye of good society, we are permitted a truly penetrating glimpse of the 'real' fictional Miss Bart when her counterfeit self is momentarily sublimated in a *tableau vivant*. For this fashionable entertainment Lily chooses to cast herself as Reynolds' rather simple portrait of Mrs Lloyd, yet manages to elicit a 'unanimous "Oh!" from all those present (134). As the narrator explains, by choosing to appear as:

> Mrs. Lloyd … she had shown her artistic intelligence in selecting a type so like her own that she could embody the person represented with out ceasing to be herself … trusting her unassisted beauty … without distracting accessories of dress and surroundings. (ibid.)

For this one brief moment Lily's fortunes tremble on the brink of change, in the liminal space between the 'real' fictional world of the text and double mimesis, as an undisguised 'portrait of Miss Bart' herself (ibid). Fittingly, this special moment inspires Gerty Farish to remark to her cousin Lawrence Selden that they have now seen the 'real Lily' (135).

But her moment of glory is short-lived, for even before the curtain goes down on Lily one onlooker exclaims 'Deuced bold thing to show herself in that get-up … there isn't a break in the lines anywhere, and I suppose she wanted us to know it' (135). This comment causes Selden to recall that this 'was not the first time that [he] had heard Lily's beauty lightly remarked on' (ibid.). Later, even her trusted friend Carry Fisher will reinforce the general opinion that Lily is 'fast', remarking that 'when a girl's as good-looking as that she'd better marry; then no questions are asked. In our imperfectly organized society there is no provision as yet for the young woman who claims the privileges of marriage without assuming its obligations' (157).

Without the safe haven of a brilliant marriage, Lily's efforts to maintain her honour are constantly misread as overtly sexual, while under the cloak of legitimacy Bertha Dorset extravagantly expends her charms in a sort of general economy of libidinal energy.[20] From within a certain, carefully regulated order then one may gamble and indulge in questionable sexual behaviours while from without it is another matter entirely.

Fortune and Finance

This same moment of revelation in the *tableau vivant* provokes the perennially crass Sim Rosedale to declare, 'If I could get Paul Morpeth to paint her like that, the picture'd appreciate a hundred percent in ten years' (158). If taken as a pun in a similar vein, Selden's rather bored musing that Lily

20 Here, I am implying Derrida's notion of unrestricted economy; that is, one of expenditures, which are not reabsorbed into a greater, more utilitarian economy. This point will be taken up in subsequent sections below.

'always roused speculation', engages in a similar kind of double-dipping into the libidinal and monetary economies of the text (3). And speculation, like gambling at the bridge table, involves the kind of faith in chance and a willingness to take risks, which, as Veblen argued, abounded in the members of Lily's set. Indeed, *The House of Mirth* is entirely structured by chance meetings and occurrences, heralded by Lily's very first line in the novel: 'Mr. Selden—what good luck!', which she immediately follows by taking 'the risk' of going to his rooms for tea (3, 6). Maureen Howard also makes this point, explaining that Lily's initial exclamation of good fortune 'launches the imagery of chance, risk, fate, gambling, calculation which runs throughout the novel'.[21] On taking her leave, however, she is treated to the supreme *mis*fortune of running into Sim Rosedale, who himself exclaims, 'this *is* luck' as he stops her just outside Selden's building (14). This compromising chance encounter will prove to be the first in a succession of such events that lead directly to Lily's final misfortunes based on ever greater gambles until she takes a fatal dose of chloral, which is to be her greatest risk of all.

As the examples that I just cited suggest, it is *bad* luck that gains the upper hand in *The House of Mirth* as we follow Lily downwards through various circles of financial hell. But if luck is a lady, as the popular song would have it, she is also the kind of woman who must be entreated to 'be a lady tonight' – in other words, lady luck can turn quickly and painfully. More importantly, the line accords with constructions of women throughout history as inconsistent, unpredictable and fickle, a notion that may arguably be traced to classical mythology and the goddess Fortuna, with her vexing habit of divvying out good luck arbitrarily along with the bad.

Unsurprisingly, moreover, the irrational goddess of fortune shares many traits with Lily Bart, as entries made by Wharton in her daybook while she was writing *The House of Mirth* bear out. Next to a line from Dante's *Inferno* about Fortuna and how her changes to have 'no respite' Wharton wrote, 'it is she who is so reviled by the very men that should give her praise, laying on her wrongful blame and ill repute'.[22] Hence as Lily Bart drifts irresolutely through her own inferno, she becomes acquainted with the cruelty of fortune both in bridge and on the stock market, as well as with the bitter consequences of being somehow associated with this classical image of irrational womanhood.

But there is another side to Lily's implicit kinship with Fortuna. Beginning in the seventeenth century the goddess became known as Lady Credit, a personification of chance pioneered by Defoe who wrote that she 'tyran-

21 Howard, Maureen. '*The House of Mirth*: The Bachelor and the Baby', in *The Cambridge Companion to Wharton*, ed. by Millicent Bell (Cambridge: Cambridge University Press, 1995), pp. 137–56, p. 141.

22 Quoted in Howard, '*The House of Mirth*: The Bachelor and the Baby', p. 151.

Figure 1. Albert Maignan, *La Fortune passe* ('*The Passage of Fortune*'), Reims, Musée des Beaux-Arts *c.*1895 (inv. 903.19.9). Photo: Christian Devleeschauwer.

nises over Youth, Beauty, Vertue, Estate; she makes honest Women Whores and Whores honest Women'.[23] As Marieke de Goede has shown, gendered incarnations of chance helped to 'articulate a new conception of morality in which … nascent credit structures would be able to flourish'.[24] At the same time, personifying Credit as a woman was naturally of a piece with the time-honoured notion that women need to be controlled and contained as a result of their supposedly unpredictable and undiscerning natures.[25] If Lady Credit were not rigorously husbanded, contained and regulated, Defoe's argument went, she would wreak havoc on the entire body politick.

I would now like to return to the issue of misfiring circuits in *The House of Mirth*, with the help of Maignan's *The Passage of Fortune* of 1895, where we see Fortuna drifting down the steps of the stock exchange leaving loss and broken financial dreams in her wake.[26]

[23] Quoted in Marieke de Goede, 'Mastering "Lady Credit": Discourses of Financial Crisis in Historical Perspective', *International Feminist Journal of Politics* (Spring 2000), 65.
[24] Ibid.
[25] See Catherine Packham's chapter in this volume, and Catherine Packham, *Mary Wollstonecraft and Political Economy: The Feminist Critique of Commercial Modernity* (Cambridge: Cambridge University Press, 2024), esp. pp. 105, 190, 191, 203, 222, 245, 258.
[26] I am grateful to Elizabeth Legge for drawing my attention to this image.

It was perhaps just one such popular depiction of Fortuna from this period of increasingly bold speculation on Wall Street that Wharton had in mind, when she described Lily Bart in neo-classical terms in the *tableau vivant* scene.[27] Indeed some of this passage seems more to describe Maignan's illustration than the simple dress of the demure (if eroticised) Mrs Lloyd, sporting 'her *pale draperies*', which 'served only to relieve the long dryad-like curves that swept upward *from her poised foot to her lifted arm*. The noble buoyancy of her attitude, its suggestion of *soaring grace* revealed the touch of poetry in her beauty' (134, my italics).

What I am suggesting then is that Lily is cast ironically given that she is rather, a misfiring Fortuna figure, hence her bad luck in cards, which does not translate into luck in love. Where the stock market is concerned, she fares no better. In an attempt to parlay what is left of her small inheritance into a greater sum on the market, she enlists the help of the lascivious Gus Trenor, because she is 'genuinely ignorant' of the 'vast mysterious Wall Street world of "tips"' (85, 82). While he makes her 'a nice little pile', Gus expects to be repaid in sexual favours – or to use Trenor's own repulsive metaphor 'the man who pays for the dinner is generally allowed to have a seat at the table' (114, 145). Gus's consultancy therefore comes with a price tag, which lands Lily in an awkward state of obligation to a financial counsellor who wishes to be repaid *en nature*. So, if the reader was in any doubt as to the stakes of the novel to this point, Wharton writes the libidinal and monetary economies together here with brutal bluntness.

Yet while Lily narrowly escapes being raped by Gus as the 'interest on one's money', what is perplexing is her decision to pay him back the full amount of what she earned on the market at the close of the novel (*HM* 146). What the reader must accept, and what readers frequently find an *un*acceptable explanation of her behaviour is the following:

> She was realizing for the first time that a woman's dignity may cost more to keep up than her carriage; and that the maintenance of a moral attribute should be dependent on dollars and cents, made the world appear a more sordid place than she had conceived it. (169)

This passage, however, hardly seems to explain the arbitrary nature of this debt, or of Lily's total self-sacrifice. In fact, readers can only puzzle at the sheer heavy-handedness of Lily dashing off a cheque to Gus Trenor in the amount of all of her supposed earnings on the stock exchange as her very last act.[28] But the reader is not alone: Carry Fisher, who is 'always getting Gus to speculate for her [… and] never pays him back when she loses' (86) extracts

27 Images of Fortuna were popular at the time. In fact, Fortuna and her wheel graced the cover of the first issue of *Fortune Magazine* in 1930, just after the stock market crash.

28 Peter Knight draws a somewhat different conclusion; namely, that Lily obtains access to the 'rewards of the instrumental friendship between Trenor and Rosedale', that being

this oddly one-sided version of the story from Lily that, 'He speculated for you, you say? Well what's the harm? He had no business to lose. He *didn't* lose? Then what on earth—but I never *could* understand you Lily' (284).

If one may believe this passage, then Lily does *not* owe Gus the money and she knows it, which makes her fastidiousness in repaying him at the close of the novel all the more unfathomable. Surely, the extra attentions she pays both Sim Rosedale and Gus in the hopes of discretion on the score of her investments would be a grand enough assurance of her gratitude? But perhaps the reasons for Lily's peculiar behaviour lie ultimately in Gus Trenor's reading of his role as broker and the weight it will carry in society, rather than her own. While Trenor makes it clear that the amount of her debt is indeterminate and that he will not accept money in payment, he also suggests that she has obtained money from men in the past and 'settled [her] other scores already' leaving him 'out in the cold' (147).

As Gillian Beer has suggested, Gus's assumptions are of a piece with:

> the social disapproval that centered on the idea of a woman taking chances, risking all, asserting the identity of eroticism and money, flouting the slow pace of that other self-defensive form of gambling: insurance—which in the marriage market must mean for women the preservation of reputation and the search for a secure husband.[29]

Similarly, Elisabeth Bronfen writes that '[t]he disturbance the beautiful Lily Bart poses in general, since she is always on display, engenders contradictory and fatal semiotic-economic speculation precisely because, having no clear social position, she is from the start in a social boundary realm, nowhere' (271).

In other words, the now old-fashioned notion that women's participation in the stock market is unseemly, is connected to the cultural assumption that women, like Fortuna, are by nature perfidious creatures and shouldn't flaunt it. Hence, any unwed woman bold enough to consider financial speculation should be prepared to pay up with erotic expenditure implicitly understood as a parallel to monetary expenditure.[30] Seen from this perspective it becomes more understandable that Lily, as a woman who gambles and speculates, circulating counterfeit sexuality without the benefit of marriage, would be perceived as a sort of over-determined allegory of chance when it misfires: a strumpet whom everyone delights in cheating and punishing.

---

inside information, Peter Knight, *Reading the Market: Genres of Financial Capitalism in Gilded Age America* (Baltimore MD: Johns Hopkins University Press, 2016), p. 180.

29 Gillian Beer, 'The Reader's Wager: Lots, Sorts and Futures', *Essays in Criticism,* vol. 40 (1990), p. 109.

30 On this point, see also Wai-Chee Dimcock, 'Debasing Exchange: Edith Wharton's *The House of Mirth*', *PMLA,* 100 (1985), 783–91.

Bigger Gambles

While book one of *The House of Mirth* opens in Grand Central Station, the logistic pulse of Wall Street, book two opens on the steps of the casino at Monte Carlo. Inside, a carnivalesque version of the stock market is underway, composed of baccarat tables where Lily's companions dismiss 'rapidly dwindling heaps of gold' with a shrug, as she finds that her 'diminished pocket-money offer[s] small scope for adventure' (194, 198). This scene is the harbinger of all of Lily's risks great and small that will culminate in that lethal overdose of chloral that closes the novel. What is most striking about her suicide is how it is framed in the text: in terms of incalculability, measured risk, and statistics such as 'one chance in a hundred' (332). Set off against her appraisal of Rosedale's second proposal of marriage if she agrees to expose Bertha Dorset as 'essentially base' because of his strategy's 'freedom from risk', her death can be read as part and parcel of her preference for the vicissitudes of fortune.

If, like Selden, one chooses to see Lily as 'a wonderful spectacle', one then might be enticed to read her exit as the ultimate expenditure of the self on the part of one prone to indulge in chance-based, prestation behaviours under the misapprehension of maintaining some measure of control. The connection I wish to make here is to the concept of ostentatious expenditure as developed by Bataille in *La part maudite*. According to Bataille, we live within a spectrum of economic behaviours from extreme utilitarianism to prestation, or expenditure with no returns and no purpose outside of itself. In this latter category Bataille includes public spectacle, gambling and non-procreative sex, all of which are practised to some extent by Miss Bart. Moreover, in Derrida's 'From Restricted to General Economics, in which he rearticulates Bataille's notion of ostentatious expenditure he writes that to 'finally be revealed to oneself, one would have to die … death itself would become self-conscious' and in the conscious knowledge of this final expenditure with no possible returns one would supposedly come to real consciousness.[31] If one interprets Lily's death as one more gamble in a series that will lead to this kind of fulfilment rather than the subdued fulfilment of the regulated economy of marriage, it might help to explain why Selden has to struggle with his certain knowledge that he is seeing the real Lily Bart for the second and last time. This is to say that the spectacle of the 'real' Lily in the *tableau vivant* was merely the dress rehearsal for this moment of supreme revelation in death as *nature morte*.[32]

[31] Jacques Derrida, 'From Restricted to General Economy: A Hegelianism without Reserve', in *Writing and Difference*, trans. by Alan Bass (Chicago IL: University of Chicago Press, 1978), pp. 66, 251–78.

[32] Cf. Elisabeth Bronfen, 'Rigor has set in—the wasted bride', *Over Her Dead Body: Death, Femininity and the Aesthetic* (New York: Routledge, 1992), pp. 278–84.

This last point might also contribute to an understanding of another case of misfiring in the text involving Bertha Dorset's love letters to Lawrence Selden. These letters coincidently fall into Lily's possession after her compromising visit to Selden's apartment at the beginning of the novel. Selden's cleaning lady, who recognises Lily from that initial visit, sells her the letters for an unstated but large sum of money. Having paid handsomely for the letters from her attenuated budget, she then fails to put them into circulation to her advantage by incriminating her enemy. Instead, Lily tosses the love letters into Selden's fire, which he lights for her when she appears on his doorstep in the pouring rain in one of the final chapters. As these signifiers of a forgotten passion go up in flames, they take with them Lily's last opportunity to buy a second chance. This spectacle, however, is one of the few in the novel that Lily keeps to herself, rendering it void, and then follows it up by wagering her life as the final spectacle at the close of the novel. My point is that, just as in the other economies in the text that involve her – libidinal, monetary – Lily is unable yet again to successfully broker returns on her investment in the love letters. Constituting an unauthentic expression of chance, mistaken for the embodiment of Fortuna herself, Lily is rather an imperfect yet spectacular screen on which capitalist culture was invited to project its desires. This screen, however, is destined to find fulfilment only in death.

Conclusion

Previously I pointed out that the subversive potential of Lily's performance is never exploited and that it therefore simply misses the mark. Because Lily is associated with many alternative gendered identities, including Lady Luck, the other characters in her fictional world perceive that she is implicitly doubly deserving of her fate. I would now like to suggest a further link between some of the confusion in Wharton's novel and Lily Bart's bizarre behaviour, which draws the text together at both the diegetic and extradiegetic levels.

As it is well known, Wharton wrote *The House of Mirth* in regular instalments for *Scribner's Magazine*. This is perhaps an unremarkable fact, yet it connects the text solidly with the economy in which it was written. To meet *Scribner's* deadlines Wharton had to learn 'how to write with economy and concentration'.[33] By internalising an economic discipline of writing Wharton 'turn[ed] from a drifting amateur into a professional' writer, that is, someone who writes for money.[34] This ultimately meant submitting to

33 Margaret B. McDowell, *Edith Wharton* (Boston MA: Twayne Publishers, 1976), p. 43.

34 Edith Wharton, *A Backward Glance* (London: Constable, 1972) p. 208.

'the discipline of the daily task' of writing in regular, controlled sessions and producing measurable results with 'nothing short of the hand of God' as an excuse for missing a deadline.[35] In other words, Wharton was forced to enter a regulated economy of writing where instalments of the product are delivered against payment. For someone who had been accustomed to pouring out her work in an unregulated economy of bursts and starts, this must have been a formidable task.

In *A Backward Glance* Wharton wrote about her struggles to fight off 'subordinate themes' and details not germane to the utilitarian regimen of her new-found professionalism that threatened to 'crowd to the front'.[36] I think it is fair to say that Wharton's battle was not entirely won, and some of the confusion of which James wrote indeed breaks through. This confusion, I believe, arises from Wharton's being at sixes and sevens with the restraints of writing marketable instalments, free of extraneous details and overly subtle conflicts, for regular advances. This struggle for balanced accounts is the kind of struggle that Lily fights throughout the text, so that even at her darkest of moments she is aware of the 'humorous coincidence that her aunt's legacy should so nearly represent the amount of her debt' (224). However, though this may imply that the double ledger of the text has been neatly balanced, I hope to have shown that Lily's head for figures, and conventions of gender in money matters, conspire to insure that not even this equation tallies.

Likewise, to have been successful in her efforts to constrain her writing Wharton would have had to conform to the economic shorthand of a familiar genre, such as melodrama, which her readers would readily recognise, hungrily anticipating the fulfilment of their generic expectations in the next episodes. Yet *The House of Mirth* is not really a melodrama given that Lily Bart, who gambles, calculates, speculates and smokes can hardly be seen as an innocent, virtuous victim. Nor is she the vapid beauty that one would expect of a comedy of manners, which *The House of Mirth* also threatens at turns to become. In this regard as well, the novel exceeds the regulating force of convention or genre, which may also be part of Wharton's grappling with the constraints of professionalism and her rebellion against its demands.[37]

At the same time, the novel as well as Wharton's own writing practice offers readers important insights into what it meant to negotiate both the

35 Ibid.

36 Ibid. p. 207.

37 The chapter on *The House of Mirth* in Hildegard Hoeller's *Edith Wharton's Dialogue with Realism and Sentimental Fiction* is devoted to a survey of reviews of Wharton's novel, showing that it was 'read both as a realist, even satirical, novel and as a sentimental story of spiritual triumph' and indeed, virtually everything in between: Hildegard Hoeller, *Edith Wharton's Dialogue with Realism and Sentimental Fiction* (Gainsville FL: University of Florida Press, 2000), p. 96.

fictional and the real market when she was writing. Moreover, Wharton was writing about old New York – her New York. The progressive serialisation of daily life that arose as a consequence is characterised by regulated repetition and reflected in the serialised novel, a development that helped to make 'culture' available for the masses in affordable, monthly packages. And while Wharton was highly critical of the society of 'irresponsible pleasure-seekers' depicted in *The House of Mirth*, she was also somewhat reticent regarding the loss of a certain kind of beauty that does not exist without class, such as the spectacle of unregulated extravagance. Such beauty is only diminished when harnessed and controlled, as when fantastic splurging is replaced with regulated expenditure. Written in that age of conformity and the waning of the old New York – the society that Wharton criticised but belonged to – the narrative voice wavers between cynicism and affection for such intangible commodities as taste, charm and beauty.

And finally, if Lily Bart comes off as a new woman *manquée*, rebelling against nothing in particular to no positive end; and if Lily's death and the absurd settling of debts long forgotten and perhaps never incurred seems to serve no good purpose, it is perhaps traceable once again to Wharton's own irresoluteness on the issue of gender. One is, I would argue, not entirely justified in reading Lily's hardships through the hindsight of feminism, since her own mercenariness and ready acceptance of the social order, as well as frequent interjections from the narrator on the sordidness of womankind ('woman-like, she accused the woman', 'the cruelty of women to their kind') make such a reading untenable (161, 219). *The House of Mirth* is rather an undecidable text on all counts in which Wharton, perhaps in spite of herself, sowed the seeds of a critique of early twentieth-century constructions of gender in the soil of the topic of an expanding futures market.

Part Two

Economies of Feeling

Public and personal virtues, like sympathy or benevolence, which might arise from shared affections and economic interdependence, open the door for women to be moral agents in public life. Moral sentiments of this kind suggest an alternative conception of economic participation: networks of mutual benefit grounded in respect, affection and reciprocity, which function according to principles beyond the pursuit of profit. Under such conditions, women's contributions might be valued not as straightforward acts of self-denial or self-sacrificing caregiving, but as part of a shared moral and economic flourishing. Yet the proliferation of the synecdochic abstraction involved in referring to people as mere 'hands' introduces the possibility of, and opportunity for, unethical and cruel behaviour in the economy. Sympathy might be, but is not always, constitutive of progress; sympathy could also be used to soften or slow change, or serve to protect the status quo, as Emma Newport and Olivia Biber argue in their chapters.

As Catherine Packham asserts in the opening chapter of this section, 'Mary Wollstonecraft and the Affective Economy', feeling lubricates circulation in interlocking markets. Feeling is imbricated into overlapping economies – sexual, political, moral and gift, to name only four – and women's emotional deftness in that other economy, the economy of affect, can usefully interpret and shape behaviours in the market and inform economic and political motivations, as well as women's progress towards personhood and enfranchisement. Packham examines the interplay between affect and the economy by focusing on how belief and credit are addressed in both economic and literary texts. Beginning with an analysis of Adam Smith's exploration of credit, Packham addresses the broader context of human credulity, which in this model can only be mitigated by the virtue of prudence, a trait that Smith predominantly associates with men. Packham makes the case that Wollstonecraft sketches the possibility of an alternative affective economy, which is defined by an unrestricted exchange of social emotions that is neither unfettered by prudence, nor constrained by credit. In so doing, Packham highlights the exchange of beliefs and feelings between individuals, which she labels the circulation of affect, who hold the potential to challenge or even redress the harms caused by an economy grounded in predatory behaviours or self-serving and disconnected emotions.

In 'Money and Morality in *The Woman of Colour* (1808)', Emma Newport argues that, while most of the scholarship on this novel so far has been interested in the fact of the ethnicity of the central character, the titular heroine exposes the thorny relationship between profit, industry and sloth, in a text that is set against the colliding crises of British colonial capitalism in the East and West Indies. In the early nineteenth century, Britain's economy was poised precipitously between systems of monopoly and free trade, and between slavery and freed labour. Though more often read in a postcolonial context as an abolitionist novel, Newport highlights how *The Woman of Colour* reproduces an eschatological nostalgia that, while offering a confident alternative to an economy based on profit and human commodification, ultimately obscures the systemic violence of slavery and plantation life.

According to Olivia Biber, in her chapter 'Suffering without Sympathy: Economic Relations and Violence in Elizabeth Gaskell's *Mary Barton* (1848)', Gaskell's politics demand attention, particularly in the ways in which she veiled her political views in her fiction. Building on the work of Nancy Henry, Biber focuses on the industrial plot and Gaskell's portrayal of class division, which emerges from the poverty and the wealth generated by industrialisation. Biber suggests that Gaskell is showcasing directly her knowledge of political economy and economic history, even as she employed a strategy of indirect remarks, allusions, and gestures. In this eighth chapter of the volume, Biber explores how *Mary Barton*, far from suggesting radical, systemic change for oppressed factory workers, offers a gentler exercise in maintaining the status quo, and obtaining gradual reform.

Sarah Dredge considers the typologies of hands at work in 'White Hands, Brown Hands and the 'Invisible Hand': The Economy of Active Sympathy in *The Wonderful Adventures of Mrs Seacole in Many Lands* (1857)'. In her essay, Dredge explores the ideological expectations placed on women, particularly regarding their roles as caregivers and self-sacrificing figures, in contrast to profit-seeking or professional ambition. In a society that idealised female care, women were recruited for nursing under the guise of service and sacrifice, as seen in the case of Mary Seacole, who defied these norms by going to the Crimean battlefield as an independent businesswoman.

While Seacole emphasised her trained expertise and justified her actions through the language of domesticity, she also had to navigate racial prejudices that inflected her work as unworthy of recognition or reward. By presenting herself as 'Mother Seacole', she sought to counteract the stereotype of a sexualised, money-driven figure by framing her actions as selfless service, despite the economic transactions involved. At the same time, Dredge addresses the ways in which the emotional labour of women is ultimately and almost inevitably sexualised, especially when money changes hands. Her chapter hereby prepares the reader for the concluding section of this edited collection, 'Professional Conduct', which explores the challenges women faced during this period to be taken seriously on the merit of their artistic and intellectual labour and achievements, separate from those of their husbands – if they had one – and removed from any suggestion of their sexual availability.

5

Mary Wollstonecraft and the Affective Economy

CATHERINE PACKHAM

The centrality of female affect to eighteenth-century attempts to understand the passions, psychology and behaviours driving emergent commercial society has long been recognised.[1] Often cast as, at best, ambivalent icons of 'early-adopter' consumer behaviour, representations of women engaging in economic activity frequently served as lightning rods for collective anxieties about an economy seemingly increasingly skewed to market-related activities of commodity production, trade and consumption; such representations provided a focus for critiques of society's apparent ethical decline and triviality. In such depictions, women's capacity for feeling – their excessive, insatiable and transient consumer appetites – was predominant. Michael McKeon has noted how, in such representations, 'women's inveterate thraldom to the artifice of appearance, ornamentation, and fashion' continued 'the tradition of the Roman goddess Fortuna', so that 'the volatile instability and corruptibility of the capitalist market were often figured as female in the eighteenth century'.[2] Even defences of commercial society

1 For a useful overview of work on, and definitions of, affect, see Katherine Ibbett, 'When I do, I call it affect', *Paragraph*, 40:2 (2017), 244–53. For an especially insightful account of the mutual imbrication of femininity and commercial passions, see Harriet Guest, *Small Change: Women, Learning, Patriotism, 1750–1810* (Chicago IL: University of Chicago Press, 2000), esp. pp. 279–81. For a classic account of eighteenth-century consumer society, see Neil McKendrick, John Brewer and J. H. Plumb, *The Birth of a Consumer Society: The Commercialization of Eighteenth-Century England* (Bloomington IN: Indiana University Press, 1982).

2 Michael McKeon, 'Pastoral Revolution', in *Refiguring Revolutions: Aesthetics and Politics from the English Revolution to the Romantic Revolution*, ed. by Kevin Sharpe and Stephen N. Zwicker (Berkeley CA: University of California Press, 1998), pp. 241–66, at p. 283. McKeon draws on accounts of female consumer desire in Bernard Mandeville

in this period often retained the link between women and the underlying passions of consumer society. In David Hume's essay 'Of the Delicacy of Taste and Passion' (1741), women are depicted as more 'delicate' in their discernment than men, especially in relation to the 'ornaments of life, of dress, equipage, and the ordinary decencies of behaviour'.[3] While this enabled Hume to depict women as presiding figures of polite sociability, and to give female feeling 'cultural prestige', they remained symbolic figures in his account, rather than economic agents or actors.[4]

Early eighteenth-century allegories of Lady Credit make clear the extent to which attempts at understanding economic behaviour in this period operated through gendered accounts of emotion from the outset, and illustrate how eighteenth-century economic writings were also always at once writings about affect. These writings by Whig propagandists Daniel Defoe, Richard Steele and Joseph Addison sought to familiarise the public with the ways in which commercial activity, of many different kinds, involved and even depended on transitory, insubstantial or otherwise elusive feelings, located somewhere between affect, knowledge and belief.[5] The figure of Lady Credit, whose extreme sensitivity to rumour and suggestion needed to be constantly and chivalrously placated, made clear how successful activity in the new world of commerce was absolutely dependent on belief: both beliefs about opportunities for trade, and the mutual beliefs of economic actors in their creditworthiness. Credit in the economic sense was thus intertwined with notions of creditability, trustworthiness or believability. Lady Credit's flighty, delicate nature indicated the ease with which the creditable conditions necessary for trade might be disrupted, but the speed with which credit might be lost in the face of rumour or suggestion also pointed to another factor that worried eighteenth-century theorists of human nature: the threat posed to belief by credulousness. The allegory puts gender difference to work to contain the dangers posed by excessive and destabilising affect: credit, a quality courted by male economic actors, is thus separated and distinguished from the credulousness figured, via Lady Credit's behaviour, as female. Appropriate

---

Fable of the Bees, vol. 1, Remark M, T; Joseph Addison, *Tatler*, no. 116, 5 January 1710; Addison, *The Spectator*, no. 69, 9 May 1711; *Female Tatler*, nos 9 and 67, 25–7 July; 7–9 Dec 1709; Samuel Johnson's *Rambler*, no. 128, 8 June 1751; no. 191, 14 January 1752. See also Daniel Defoe's *Review*, no. 5, 10 January 1706; nos 55, 57, 59, 1, 5, 10 Aug 1710; and no. 116, 21 Dec 1710.

3 David Hume, 'Of the Delicacy of Taste and Passion', in David Hume, *Essays: Moral, Political and Literary*, ed. by T. H. Green and T. H Grose (London: Longmans Green, 1882), p.92. This sentence was omitted in some late editions of the essays.

4 Adela Pinch, *Strange Fits of Passion: Epistemologies of Emotion, Hume to Austen* (Redwood City CA: Stanford University Press, 1996), p. 55.

5 For instance, see Joseph Addison, *The Spectator*, no. 3, 3 March 1711; Richard Steele, *The Spectator*, no. 218, 9 November 1711. On Defoe, see Paula R. Backscheider, 'Defoe's Lady Credit', *Huntington Library Quarterly*, 44:2 (Spring 1981), 89–100.

male behaviour can thus placate and contain the dangers of female affective excess; a distinction between affect, as female, and male economic actors, is also enacted. Considered away from the regulating work of such allegorical scenes, however, the vulnerability of credit to credulousness – the potential flimsiness or corruptibility of the forms of belief on which economic action depended – was less easily remedied, and the intertwining of the economic and affective was arguably more complex.

This chapter explores the interconnections of affect and the economy by focusing on the treatment of belief and credit in both economic and literary writing. First, I discuss Adam Smith's theorisation of credit in his foundational work, *An Inquiry into the Nature and Cause of the Wealth of Nations* (1776) and his earlier *Theory of Moral Sentiments* (1759). As in the Whig allegories of Lady Credit, belief and credit-worthiness are shown to be central to the modern economy, but Smith's account of both the personal and institutional importance of credit operates in the context of his acknowledgement of the primary credulity of human nature: a tendency to credulousness that has the potential to undermine commercial society's institutions and functions. Only prudence, a quality strongly associated with men in Smith's gendered model, can hope to counter the persistent human fault line of credulity.

Mary Wollstonecraft's final, unfinished novel, *The Wrongs of Woman: or, Maria* (1798), whose heroine is both credulous and notably economically active, offers a striking counterpoint to this. Having previously attacked prudence in her earlier *A Vindication of the Rights of Woman* (1792), Wollstonecraft's novel, which attends to many monetary transactions and economic situations in its account of the social and sexual 'wrongs' of woman, offers an alternative perspective on economic actions and economic agents, on credit and credulousness, and on the relationship between feeling and money. I argue that it contrasts an economic system and the affects it promotes and relies on, with a story about the affective economy: about the transmission of beliefs and feelings between individuals – about the circulation of affect – which has the potential to counter, perhaps remedy, the ills of an economy predicated on predatory, self-interested and asocial feeling.

Smith and the Credit Economy

The centrality of credit in eighteenth century commercial activity is evident in the attention it was given by the foremost theorist of political economy, Adam Smith, in whose *Wealth of Nations* credit could refer to monetary loans, to the reputational quality of a person or institution ('creditable', 'man of credit'), or simply to belief, which might be founded on knowledge, feeling or something in between. Credit was also materialised in paper forms that circulated as currency: credit notes, including the accommodation bills that Venables fraudulently exploits in *Wrongs of Woman*, were forms of paper money that were in extensive circulation, both between traders seeking to engage in economic transaction unencumbered by physical coinage, and by individuals to supplement an often inadequate supply of monetary currency.[6] Paper money was also issued by banks, but this in turn relied on perception of the credit-worthiness of banks, at a time when many were regional, potentially precarious enterprises: bank collapses were not at all unknown.[7] The use of credit as a financial instrument thus relied, in a variety of contexts, on a reputational judgement of the trustworthiness, or credit, of the person or institution with which transactions took place.

The double nature of credit, as economic instrument and reputational quality, is evident in Smith's discussion of the use of bank notes as a supplement or alternative to what throughout the eighteenth-century was often a limited physical coinage. Paper money, Smith asserts, can only participate in what he calls the 'great wheel' of circulation because of the credit, or investment of belief, given to bankers:

> When the people of any particular country have such confidence in the fortune, probity, and prudence of a particular banker, as to believe that he is always ready to pay upon demand such of his promissory notes as are likely to be at any time presented to him; those notes come to have the same currency as gold and silver money, from the confidence that such money can at any time be had for them.[8]

Credit given to the banker at the local level, due to his 'fortune, probity and prudence', enables circulation of paper money at a national level. The successful operation of a financial instrument is thus dependent on something potentially altogether less substantive: the 'credit' that might derive from anything from factual knowledge to belief, reputational judgement or vague feeling. Credit – or confidence, as it is termed here – operates as a hinge between a belief-based regime of character and supra-personal economic function; between the micro level of interpersonal social relations and the macro level of economic activity at regional, national or international scale. Credit, as a belief-based response to individual character, thus oils the wheels of a *system* of credit; the economic thus depends on an affective foundation, or – given affect's interstitial character, as existing or being

[6] For details, see Mary Poovey, *Genres of the Credit Economy: Mediating Value in Eighteenth- and Nineteenth-Century Britain* (Chicago IL: University of Chicago Press, 2008).

[7] See Julian Hoppit, 'Financial Crises in Eighteenth-Century England', *Economic History Review*, 39:1 (1986), 39–58.

[8] Adam Smith, *An Inquiry in the Nature and Causes of the Wealth of Nations,* ed. by R. H. Campbell and A. S. Skinner (Oxford: Oxford University Press, 1976), p. 292. Future references will be abbreviated to *WN*.

transmitted *between* people – on the generation and circulation of affect.[9] Indeed, the operation of a generalised, abstracted and depersonalised system of credit, marked by the use of paper money and other credit instruments, relied ultimately on a regime of the person: specifically of male character.

The importance given to credit as an economic function, however, presented a potential problem given the fundamental credulity of human nature, which Smith identified in his earlier work of moral philosophy, *The Theory of Moral Sentiments*. '[T]he man scarce lives who is not more credulous than he ought to be', he stated, in an uncompromising assertion of our tendency to believe too easily, to give credit too readily.[10] In this context, *Theory of Moral Sentiments*' extensive account of the formation and operation of judgement between social actors can be read as an investigation into the act of investing belief in others. The work's exhaustive elaboration of how and why one individual might give credit to another also emerges as highly gendered, constructing as it does a culturally and class-specific regime of male character. Closely linked to rank and respectability in society, as well as to the much-vaunted qualities of prudence and propriety, credit-worthiness is central to the virtues of character – such as industry, frugality, self-command and reason – on whose implications and fruits in the economic sphere *Wealth of Nations* will further elaborate.[11] Smith's references to prudence, in discussions of rank, reputation and economic actions, also make evident that what is being described here is a gender-specific regime of behaviour. *Wealth of Nations*' version of credit, as an abstracted and instrumentalised economic tool or function, can thus be seen to derive from a culturally and gender-specific regime of the person, specifically of male behaviour. It is notable that this theorisation of the 'man' of prudence, who combines various forms of behaviours that make him both trust-worthy by others, and capable himself of judging others, is the diametrical opposite of the female figure of Lady Credit, whose extreme sensitivity and flighty nature jeopardised trade. While the credit-worthy man of prudence evidences the kinds of behaviour that enable him to take effective action in the world of commerce and business, by

[9] For a detailed account of the 'credit economy', see Poovey, *Genres of the Credit Economy*; on affect as transmission, see Ibbett, 'When I do'.

[10] Adam Smith, *The Theory of Moral Sentiments*, ed. by D. D. Raphael and A. L. Macfie (Oxford: Clarendon Press, 1976), p. 335. This observation was added to the sixth edition of 1790. Later references will be abbreviated to *TMS*.

[11] See *TMS*, pp. 54–5, p. 167, p. 189; and *WN*, vol. 2, p. 697; for a longer discussion, see Catherine Packham, *Mary Wollstonecraft and Political Economy: The Feminist Critique of Commercial Modernity* (Cambridge: Cambridge University Press, 2024), pp. 194–7.

contrast women in this account are associated with unreliable passions and relegated to the home.[12]

Given the constant exhortation in *The Theory of Moral Sentiments* for individuals to view themselves through the eyes of others, this reading of the work suggests that our shared credulousness – our too-willing, too-natural capacity to believe in others – is to be regulated through a regime of self-discipline, self-repression, self-surveillance. But the work's description of the extensive apparatus designed to repress and control credulity might prompt us to ask what a moral economy of the credulous might look like, in which belief in and sympathy for others would be freely available and readily circulate. What would it mean if our powers of belief were not restrained by prudence or propriety, and what would it mean to free ourselves from the necessity of others' belief in us? These are questions that Wollstonecraft, as we will see, explored in *The Wrongs of Woman*. Given that, as we have seen in Smith, the affective economy on which political economy rests is gendered; given that the affects that are constitutive of *homo economicus* (his capacity to give and receive credit, and to extend belief in others) are narrated in a way that relegates and excludes women and female feeling; given that, by the same token, these accounts also imply that women are constitutively excluded by nature from economic activity, it is perhaps no surprise to discover that for female economic agents to be imagined, a model of human affect fundamental to the whole construction of political economy would need to be contested. Maria, Wollstonecraft's flawed heroine in *Wrongs*, is indeed economically active in many ways, as we shall see. But the novel can be read less as concerned to integrate Maria into an economic world that operates repeatedly to enact male power and oppress women, and where (as evidenced by Maria's husband Venables) individuals of considerable moral and financial questionability operate with impunity, than as exploring the mutual imbrication of gendered systems of political economy and sexual economy, of economic and sexual exchange, and of money and feeling. And it sketches too the possibility of an alternative affective economy, based on the free circulation of social feeling, unrestrained by prudence or hampered by credit.

Affects, Objects and Persons in Hume, Smith and Wollstonecraft

The political economy that Smith outlined in *Wealth of Nations* involves a story about how human behaviour is driven by affect: political economy depends on, and brings with it, an affective economy describing the genera-

[12] See *TMS*, p. 40 and pp. 190–1; Harriet Guest, *Unbounded Attachment: Sentiment and Politics in the Age of the French Revolution* (Oxford: Oxford University Press, 2013), pp. 4–5; and Packham, *Mary Wollstonecraft and Political Economy*, p. 209.

tion and circulation of feeling between individuals and objects. In this, Smith's political economy draws on his work on 'sentiments', the eighteenth-century term for the complex terrain between thought and emotion, from his earlier *Theory of Moral Sentiments*.[13] Taken together, both works describe how affect produces relations between subjects and objects; in particular, they explain how certain kinds of affect (especially desire: for an object, for self-betterment, to be well-regarded, to be an object of attention by others, and so on) promote and sustain the production and exchange of objects. The paradigmatic example of this is given in the tale of the poor man's son in *Theory of Moral Sentiments*. Over a few dense paragraphs, Smith outlines how the poor man's son, 'visited with ambition', looks at the houses and lifestyles of the rich, and wants to live like them. He spends his life in toil to achieve a betterment of his condition. While he belatedly comes to realise, late in life, that the wealth he has secured cannot guarantee him certain fundamentals of happiness ('ease of body', 'tranquillity of mind'), his labour, and that of many others like him, collectively sustains human civilisation, including the production of the very 'baubles and trinkets' employed in the 'oeconomy of greatness' that have so seduced him.[14]

We might note here that, as with the account of the 'man' of credit, Smith's story is specifically that of the poor man's son, not his daughter. Already, then, this is a gendered story, but the implications of gender difference are starker still in David Hume's *Treatise of Human Nature* (1739) from where Smith's thinking derives. In Book Two of the *Treatise*, in an example later developed in Smith's account of the poor man's son, Hume explored the manifestation of a passion akin to, if not quite the same as, sympathy: an onlooker's vicarious participation in the conveniences of a rich man's house, and his many possessions, such as 'tables, chairs, scritoires, chimneys, coaches, saddles, ploughs'.[15] The elaboration of these objects makes clear what a quick reflection on contemporary patterns of property ownership, including laws of coverture, would confirm: that this story about affect, and subjectivity, is, in fact, a tale about male passions and the objects that a male culture of property enables men to possess or aspire to.[16] By not attending to the gender-specific nature of eighteenth-century property culture – the laws and customs that regulated property ownership at the time – Hume's account of affects and objects offers what purports to be a universal theory

[13] Here one definition of 'sentiment' in the eighteenth-century usage, from *OED*, as 'A thought or reflection coloured by or proceeding from emotion' is instructive.

[14] Smith, *TMS*, pp. 181–5.

[15] David Hume, *A Treatise of Human Nature*, ed. by L. A. Selby-Bigge and P. H. Nidditch (Oxford: Clarendon Press, 1978), p. 364.

[16] On the laws of coverture that erased married women's right to property, see Amy Louise Erikson, *Women and Property in Early Modern England* (London and New York: Routledge, 1993).

of human passions, which in fact excludes half the human race. If men and women have different relations to the property through which, in Hume's account, affect is expressed, and the human personality is to be known or constructed, that difference is not attended to. Rather, Hume naturalises the desire to possess objects without reflecting on the pre-existing economic and legal contexts that might shape that desire by limiting its possible expression. He elides the gender differences expressed by and codified in that context, including in laws of property ownership, and so silently repeats existing inequalities of the genders in relation to objects, in an account that Smith then used to theorise affective drives fundamental to his political economy. In both Hume and Smith, then, accounts of the relations between subjects and the objects that they do not possess, from which narratives of economic motivations and behaviours are derived, are gender-specific, eliding gender difference to construct human personality in the shape of the male. Wollstonecraft's *Wrongs of Woman* by contrast, as we will see, explores how women fit into this world of property and exchange between men, not least as objects of transaction in a sexual economy that parallels the transactions of the economic world. Excluded from the world of property possession as they are, it investigates alternative objects for women's sympathies and outlines an alternative affective economy to that defined by property relations, to show how a story about, arguably, the corruption of sympathy into property-envy might be rewritten.

In Hume, there is a further twist to this gendered story about relations to property. Hume's *Treatise*, like Smith's *Theory of Moral Sentiments*, was part of the Scottish Enlightenment 'science of man': an attempt to make human nature the object of philosophical knowledge in the same way that Newtonian natural science inquired into the physical world. Famously, Hume's attempt to understand personal identity in Book 1 of the *Treatise* was derailed by the scepticism that made it impossible for him to understand an individual's 'bundle' of perceptions as sufficient evidence to denote or constitute a unified, self-complete human person.[17] As Adela Pinch describes, Hume solves the consequent problem of personal identity – of what, or who, a person is; of how the subject might be known – by enacting 'a kind of person-ification' that 'ties the "bundle of perceptions" into a recognizable human form'.[18] This is achieved through applying what might be termed a proprietary logic: pride in the objects with which we are associated, including and especially possessions, produces a sense of self. Hence property solves the problem of identity, as the pride it elicits reifies the subject who owns it.[19]

[17] Hume, *Treatise*, p. 252.

[18] Pinch, *Strange Fits*, p. 24.

[19] I benefit here from an excellent discussion of Hume in an unpublished doctoral thesis by Matthew McConkey, 'Nature's Consolation: Poetry, Environment, Psychoanalysis 1740–1820' (University of Sussex, 2022).

Pride in objects associated with the self, especially possessions, thus produces the subject where philosophical scepticism has failed to do so. But, in a context where, as we have seen, men and women are situated differently in relation to property ownership, the proprietary logic in play here is evidently gendered. What chance of women's 'person-ification' via property, in a world where they are excluded from significant property ownership? Jemima's tale in *Wrongs of Woman* suggests that they are more likely to be objectified as the temporary, disposable possessions of others, than to achieve their own self-possession. Further, what eighteenth-century commentators often presented as women's deplorable desire for the frivolous and trivial objects available to them in consumer culture looks, in this context, more like the attempt to enact, through compensatory acts of consumption, the very proprietary logic that, in this reading, confers or affirms personhood.[20]

As he relates at the close of Book One, the demands of Hume's sustained philosophical investigations in the *Treatise* produced a personal crisis, if not quite of identity, certainly of his mental health and personal well-being. Unable to sustain his studies to the extent that he wished, he found himself repeatedly oscillating between periods of work and melancholic, depressive retreat, a pattern that he eventually resolved by understanding the need to socialise and relax: 'I dine, I play a game of back-gammon, I converse, and am merry with my friends.'[21] The solution to Hume's crisis here is often glossed as his discovery of the crucial eighteenth-century value of sociability, but in light of the sustaining role of proprietary logic outlined above, it is also worth noting the role of property here. Hume's self-restoration is achieved at least in part through his relation to his possessions, such as the backgammon set, and it is enabled more broadly through the leisure available to him as a member of the gentry or property-owning class.[22] Hume's personal crisis might then, by his own account, be understood to be resolved through both direct and indirect possession of objects capable of bestowing a sense of self on their proprietor.

Hume's crisis could be read against the situation of Wollstonecraft's protagonist, Maria, at the very opening of *The Wrongs of Woman.* Like Hume, Maria is also in a place of darkness, confusion, melancholy and disorientation. Unlike the philosopher, however, Maria has no personal possessions with which to soothe herself, and even her daughter has been

[20] For one example among many, see Joseph Addison, *The Spectator*, no. 10, 12 March 1711. For a case study of a woman locked up in an asylum but still engaging in shopping and consumption, and what that means for her identity, see Anna Jamieson, '"Comforts in Her Calamity": Shopping and Consumption in the Late Eighteenth-Century Private Madhouse', *Eighteenth-Century Studies*, 55:1 (2021), 83–102.

[21] Hume, *Treatise*, p. 269.

[22] For Hume's class background, see Ernest Campbell Mossner, *The Life of David Hume* (Oxford: Clarendon Press, 1980).

taken from her: an act that makes evident that even motherhood is no assurance of ownership in the eyes of the law. The one possession that remains to Maria is her body, but the breastmilk that she is still producing is, in the absence of her daughter, redundant. Although Jemima, Maria's jailor, secures Maria some paper and writing instruments, as well as loans of books from her fellow prisoner Darnford, Maria's crisis will eventually be resolved not through objects or possessions but through her engagement in social relations with others: with Jemima and Darnford. Jemima is similarly restored to her own humanity, after years of hardship, abuse and neglect, in the same process. As these three take turns narrating their life stories and listening to each other, they enact communal feeling and solidarity to create a culture in which the sense of self, of identity, is recovered and defined not by property but through sympathy and social feeling – mediated, crucially, by narrative.[23] If one of the few things that Maria still owns are her feelings, putting these into circulation, to be shared with and believed by others, proves to be the means of securing her self-possession in a context where the law still regarded her as her husband's property.

Following the Money in Wollstonecraft's *Wrongs of Woman*

Mary Wollstonecraft's final novel, *The Wrongs of Woman: or, Maria*, left unfinished at her untimely death in childbirth in 1797, has long been recognised as a powerful expression of the many 'wrongs' faced by 'woman' in the late eighteenth-century.[24] Among them, the novel is deeply concerned with women's economic experience – especially in the eight-chapter narrative of her life provided by Maria, the protagonist, which makes up by far the most substantial part of this incomplete text. Offering a sustained contrast between the economic actions of George Venables, Maria's multiply deceitful husband, and those of Maria herself, and attending to many monetary transactions and financial situations, the novel offers an alternative perspective from Smithian theories of economic actions and agents, and on credit and credulousness, and the relationship between feeling and money. Concerned both with money, and with affects or sentiments, *Wrongs*

[23] Wollstonecraft repeatedly linked storytelling to the formation of social bonds. See *An Historical and Moral View of the French Revolution*, in *The Works of Mary Wollstonecraft*, ed. by Janet Todd and Marilyn Butler, 7 vols (London: Pickering & Chatto, 1989 [1794]), vol. 6, p. 146.

[24] Among many valuable discussions of the novel, see Barbara Taylor, *Mary Wollstonecraft and the Feminist Imagination* (Cambridge: Cambridge University Press, 2003); Anne K. Mellor, 'Righting the Wrongs of Woman: Mary Wollstonecraft's Maria', *Nineteenth-Century Contexts*, 19: 4 (1996), 413–24; and Claudia L. Johnson, *Equivocal Beings: Politics, Gender and Sentimentality in the 1790s* (Chicago IL: University of Chicago Press, 1995), pp. 58–69.

of Woman tells a story that at once explores the 'wrongs' that befall women in the existing economic world, and analyses the sentiments, whether excessive and mismanaged, or sympathetic and socially orientated, in play there.

Maria's narrative, written as memoirs for her daughter, are presented as an instructional tale to 'exercise' her daughter's mind.[25] They progress from an account of Maria's childhood, family and upbringing, to her marriage to George Venables and its aftermath, but embedded in this conventional-seeming structure is a story about money: specifically the 'handsome fortune' (127) acquired by Maria's unnamed uncle while in India, which is the real object of George's desire in this rewriting of the marriage plot. As so often in novels of this period, activities in Britain's overseas territories finance action at home, but Wollstonecraft gives few details as to the origin or extent of the fortune whose attractions, rather than her own, drive the plot of Maria's marriage. Initially, we are told that the money is accrued 'by good luck, rather than management' (127): the uncle, who is liberally educated, is in India as secretary to a nobleman rather than as a fortune-seeker. Later, we are later told that hard work played some part in his enrichment. Preoccupied as he is while in India with what was to become a lost love object, the uncle is clearly not a classic 'nabob'. It is less the source of the money, however, than the feelings and actions it provokes in others that are Wollstonecraft's main concern. The combination of the uncle's money, and his residual 'petrified' (137) romantic frame of mind, will have considerable ramifications for Maria's own story.

Returned from India, the uncle becomes an important influence on the young Maria, the 'instructor' (126) from whom she acquires her own romantic turn of mind, deriving an 'ideal picture of life' (128) from the books that he lends her. It doesn't take long for this to have consequences: meeting George Venables, son of a neighbouring merchant, her 'romantic' (130) thoughts give meaning to his pleasantries: the 'tenderness' of Maria's heart 'heated [her] imagination with visions of the ineffable delight of happy love' (139). Such sentiments invest Venables' donation of a guinea, given to Maria to support a local woman fallen on hard times, with deeper significance, but this is simply the first of Venables' many schemes as he manoeuvres to acquire, through Maria, the uncle's fortune, aided by what is merely a 'mask' (130) of prudence. This plot is explicitly aided by the uncle's residual romanticism: he advises Maria to marry Venables to escape domestic unhappiness following the death of her mother and her father's remarriage, and supplies a £5,000 dowry. If Maria is partly motivated by a mistaken (and short-lived) sense that marriage will secure her 'freedom' (138), she also feels

[25] *The Wrongs of Woman*, in Mary Wollstonecraft, *Mary and The Wrongs of Woman*, ed. by Gary Kelly (Oxford: Oxford University Press, 1988), p. 124. Subsequent references will be given in the text.

gratitude for her uncle's benevolence. Retrospect will soon reveal the irony, perhaps naivety, of such sentiments.

Once married, Venables' 'gambling desire to start suddenly into riches' becomes dominant; commerce both ensures that his 'generous emotions' (143) remain dormant and provides a cover for this questionable passion. While his father had been a cautious and prudent merchant, Venables is soon involved in fraud and illegality, funded directly or indirectly from Maria's uncle's fortune, on which he also 'speculates' (178). Maria repeatedly sources further monies from her uncle to 'save' her husband from 'destruction': 'At first it was to prevent bills being noted, to the injury of his credit; then to bail him; and afterwards to prevent an execution from entering the house' (147–8). She supports the household and pays tradesmen with personal presents or loans from her uncle; discovering Venables' illegitimate daughter, she supplements the miserly allowance he has supplied for her care (149–50). Venables' predations on Maria as an asset become more explicit as he uses a 'copy of a writ' (158) to extract more of her uncle's money from her and he forces the lock of her writing desk to look for banknotes. From a friend, Mr S, Maria learns that Venables is considered a 'swindler' at the Exchange: perhaps in part due to his use of suspect 'accommodation bills'.[26] The crisis comes when Maria sees her husband's letter to Mr S, asking for a £500 loan and, noting that 'every woman has her price', advising him to try his luck with Maria's 'credulous generosity' (161). Challenged by Maria, Venables uses strikingly Smithian terminology to advise her to act 'like a prudent woman' (168) and in her own self-interest. Venables' harassment of Maria continues even after she leaves him. Her uncle having died and left his fortune (in an unusual move) to Maria's baby daughter, with Maria herself as guardian, Venables' attorney threatens that Venables will take the child unless Maria makes the inheritance over to him. Maria's offer of £500 in return for being left in peace comes to nothing; she is drugged, imprisoned and her daughter is taken. Venables' lawyer promises her release if she makes over half the fortune; once escaped, she discovers that Venables has forged several bills with her signature to again access funds.

If Venables' sexual, financial and legal predations increasingly paint him as the Gothic villain in this story, Maria by contrast repeatedly attempts to circulate money for the social good, primarily by offering economic support for others: from Peggy, the original object of Venables' deceitful charity, to indebted tradesmen, the woman caring for Venables' illegitimate child, and her indebted father and her siblings. But her 'plans of usefulness' are frustrated by Venables' 'pillages' (158). Her uncle, too, attempts to put money to good use, settling £1,000 each on Maria's sisters, despite Maria's fears that

[26] On accommodation bills, see Packham, *Mary Wollstonecraft and Political Economy*, p. 203 and pp. 260–1, note 61; and Poovey, *Genres of the Credit Economy*, pp. 36ff.

this would attract fortune-hunters. But while such schemes of benevolence, or '*liberal sentiments*' (161), as Venables might put it, might ameliorate individual circumstances, Wollstonecraft's concern is broader than this, pointing as she does to the 'constitution of society' (124) and its 'partial laws' (155). Moral feeling, and charitable action, it would appear, can only be part of the answer. The larger reach of Wollstonecraft's analysis is enabled through the embedding of Maria's autobiographical tale within the story of her imprisonment by Venables in the madhouse, so that the economic circumstances that led her there can be compared with those of her co-prisoner Darnford and jailor Jemima. Darnford, dissolute son of wealthy, gambling parents, has been locked up in a scheme to prevent his inheritance of a fortune from a relative who died intestate; his tale shows how wealth drives excessive and dysregulated passions, whether it be inherited money or that available in commerce, as in the repellently 'enthusiastically enterprising' (96) America, from where he has recently returned. Jemima's narrative, consisting almost entirely of episodes of abuse, neglect, poverty and cruelty, bears comparison to a contemporary it-narrative, in which objects, bestowed with sentience and powers of narration, throw light on society through accounts of their circulatory adventures. Like them, Jemima is little more than a disregarded object in her status as 'a slave, a bastard, a common property' (109), often unable to support herself despite working 'like a machine' (116). In a world where, as she states, money is the only route to respect, she is an 'outlaw of society' (110); if, as she says, she is 'a common property', she exists outside the structures of possession that (as we have seen) also confer identity and social worth. The pervasive, all-determining drive to self-enrichment can even be read in the very structure of the madhouse that these three inhabit, acquired as it was by a workhouse official through funds accrued by exploiting the labour of workhouse inmates.

Wollstonecraft thus provides plentiful evidence of the economic conditions that are part of the 'wrongs' of woman. But she is equally concerned with affect: with the feelings that she presents alongside, and as connected to, the financial actions mapped in the novel. The porous relationship between the monetary and the affective is signalled periodically by metaphors that, as we saw above with the word 'credit', can point at once to the financial and to the emotional. Darnford's books, loaned to Maria, are thus a (perhaps ambivalent) 'mine of treasure' (85); tending to aged parents is the 'debt contracted in childhood' (136), owed by all but, in the sexual division of caring labour, rarely paid by boys; debt too is figured in the 'frozen bond of grief' (100) binding Maria's heart in her separation from her daughter. The encroachment of financial language to describe marital relations is a mark of larger personal corruption, as in the description as a 'mere affair of barter' (153), of a woman sleeping with a husband whom she does not love, or the condemnation of the husband who never valued the 'asset' of his unfaithful wife 'till he found that there was a chance of his being indemnified for the loss of it' (155). The effects of a world determined by such relations of mere transactionality are evident in Jemima, whose stony, feelingless face shows how she is denied personhood and humanity in such a system.

What hope might there be of reforming the 'wrongs' of this world? What might be mobilised against it? An answer is suggested by the persistence of Wollstonecraft's attention to feelings, of many different kinds, throughout the text, in what is not simply an economic tale but also a story of sentiments. Feelings are immediately foregrounded in the dramatic opening of the novel, which uncompromisingly depicts the costs of Maria's sufferings in psychological and affective terms, but while Wollstonecraft evokes Gothic horror and sensational excess here, the question soon becomes Maria's need to regain self-control: to 'reflect more calmly' and 'brace her mind to fortitude' (76), in order not to become like the other inhabitants of the madhouse, whose 'groans and shrieks' (75) attest to their ongoing mental disturbance. In similar vein, Maria's memoirs exhort her daughter not to lose time in meditation but to experience and act: an echo of the emphasis in *A Vindication of the Rights of Woman* on the importance of learning from experience for female self-education. Maria's characterisation of wisdom as 'too often … the owl of the goddess, who sits moping in a desolated heart' (124) perhaps glances at her uncle's lifetime of melancholy after the loss of his beloved: if the lesson Maria offers her daughter is to learn from Maria's own mistakes, her uncle, as a key influence on her, must be part of that learning. Excessive or misguided feelings, of various kinds, cause harm in this novel, and the uncle's unreformed and unworldly romantic outlook is in Wollstonecraft's sights just as much as Venables' mendacity. Darnford meanwhile, corrupted by his indulged upbringing and the dissipated lifestyle to which he returns once freed from the madhouse, stands as a warning that in some cases reform of feeling is merely superficial or temporary.

Importantly, to reform feeling, by regulating it so as not to become its 'prey' (76), and to reflect on experience so as to learn from it, is not the same as rejecting affect entirely. It is wholly significant that the escape from the madhouse is a consequence of Jemima's resocialisation. The recovery of her humane sentiments, after a lifetime of mere survival in a world experienced as unmitigated cruelty and exploitation, is achieved through Maria's attentive cultivation of her long-neglected feelings. And while Maria's uncle's romantic turn of mind is part of what leads Maria into the 'trap' (144) of her marriage, the unusual arrangements of his will, which leaves his fortune to his grandniece (overlooking the closer, male heir of his nephew, Maria's brother), show that, if belatedly, he has perceived Venables' true nature, and united his benevolence with strategy to ensure the remainder of his money stays out of Venables' hands. In both instances, the actions of Jemima and the uncle point to how sympathetic feeling united with action has the capacity to renew community and regenerate social forms, even in an imperfect world.

Conclusion

Perhaps the dominant characteristic of both Maria and her uncle is credulity: the quality defined by Samuel Johnson as 'readiness' to credit, and that Smith identified as a persistent fault line in human nature.[27] It is this quality that makes it so easy for Venables (whose name suggests the mercantile act of 'vending' or selling), to deceive them, but by the same token Venables' story shows just how easily the Smithian quality of prudence, which supposedly regulates economic acts, and is approved by other economic agents, can be counterfeited. Venables' ability to trade with the same 'mask' (130) of deception as initially takes in Maria exposes the vulnerability of the credit – the mutually interwoven economic and moral reputations – on which economic actions rely, as well as just how far and systematically credulity can be exploited, to the extent of illegality and fraud. The parallel stories of Venables' economic deceptions and his personal ones make clear that such precarious structures of credit are involved not just in economic affairs but in sexual ones too, as in the marriage transactions by which the social circulation of women is achieved. Venables' letter to Mr S, asking for £500 credit in return for Maria's 'credulous generosity' (161) makes starkly evident the equivalence of these two exchange systems, whilst also showing the extent to which Maria, who brought £5,000 on her marriage, has declined in value.

Despite their credulity, however, Wollstonecraft's instructional tale does not attempt to warn against the dangers of belief or shore up the need for self-interested prudence. The story of Maria and her uncle does not suggest that they should abandon the capacity to believe in others that, as Smith's theory of sympathy suggests, is constitutive of human nature, and that is at the heart of sociality, as Wollstonecraft's identification of story as the primary building block of community suggests. Rather, it suggests that credulity, the social glue of belief in others, when not tricked by deception, is capable of at least ameliorating the effects of some of the 'wrongs' that stem from the current 'constitution of society', including its economic aspects. Thus, Maria explicitly counsels her daughter to cultivate 'the generous emotions, which are the foundation of every true principle of virtue' and that too often 'lie dormant' (144). *Wrongs of Woman* thus rewrites political economy's story of affect to sketch a new economy of feeling, in which crediting others enacts social renewal and creates community, even in the 'desolate garden' of a ruined world that is merely 'habitable' (76–7). Maria's belief in Jemima opens the door – literally – to a renewed freedom, and to Jemima's participation in community: initially in the madhouse triad; later, perhaps, in a household with Maria and her daughter. The 'little concerns of prudence' (189) – Smith's guiding light – are rejected by Maria as she embarks on her

[27] Samuel Johnson, *A Dictionary of the English Language* (London: 1755), 'Credulity'.

affair with Darnford, but if her romantic belief in him skates too close to fantasy – the same mistake as with Venables – Wollstonecraft shows how her protagonist's 'extreme credulity' (143) itself constitutes an opportunity for experience, reflection and learning, not least in identifying this characteristic in herself. While the affair is short-lived, witnessing the growth of the couple's affections is part of Jemima's recovery of her capacity for social feeling, as well as Maria's own capacity for happiness and self-determination.

The last completed chapter of this unfinished novel is a court scene in which Maria herself takes on the defence of Darnford, as he is tried for adultery by her husband. Concluding a detailed and devastating narrative of her treatment by Venables, Maria asserts a right to 'appeal to my own sense of justice' in a situation where laws are made 'by the strong to oppress the weak', asserting that she 'deemed, and ever shall deem, myself free' (197). Appealing to the 'justice and humanity of the jury' (198), Maria stakes everything on the possibility that the reasoned and principled account that she gives of herself will be met with sympathy and credence. Although her words show that she regards herself as free, it is evident that liberty, the political right to self-determination that would enshrine such freedom, depends on being believed by others, in a court of law. The judge's ruling, pointing to the 'fallacy of letting women plead their feelings' (198), only makes clear what she is up against.

6

Money and Morality in *The Woman of Colour* (1808)

Emma Newport

You can extract good from every evil … morality from every passing occurrence.

Honeywood to Olivia, *The Woman of Colour*, p. 76

The blessing of constant employment I take to be a secret as well worth knowledge as the philosopher's stone; it is a remedy for most of the evils of life. Had I the instruction of youth, my first, my last words should be 'rational employment'; for what ills, what mischiefs spring from idleness!

The Woman of Colour, p. 198

In 1808, the recently formed publishing partnership of Black, Parry, and Kingsbury opted to print the anonymously authored epistolary novel *The Woman of Colour*, in which the heroine, Olivia Fairfield, is a mixed-race heiress – worth £60,000 – who comes to England before eventually returning to Jamaica.[1] Her primary antagonists are venal and avaricious merchants and Nabobs, the latter of whom recently returned to England from the East Indies. The novel is situated against British colonial capitalism on the brink of great change. An Act for the Abolition of the Slave Trade (1807) had been passed the year prior to the novel's publication; concurrently, the

[1] 'Notice of Partnership, Leadenhall Street, Nov. 11, 1806', in *The Literary Panorama* (London: C. Taylor, 1807), vol. 1, p. 29. The East India Company is abbreviated to 'EIC' or referred to as the 'Company'. The firm continued under various partnerships until 1827, and held registered presses variously with Thomas Plummer, William Lane, William Plummer 1804, and with C. and W. Galabin between 1788 and 1809. See Ian Maxted, *The London Book Trades 1775–1800: A Preliminary Checklist of Members* (Folkestone: Dawson, 1977), p. 257, and *The London Gazette*, 3 March 1812, issue 16580, p. 434.

Figure 2. Agostino Brunias (Italian, *c.*1730–96). *Free Women of Color with Their Children and Servants in a Landscape*, *c.*1770–96. Oil on canvas, 20 x 26 1/8 in. (50.8 x 66.4 cm). Brooklyn Museum, Gift of Mrs Carll [*sic*] H. de Silver in memory of her husband, by exchange and gift of George S. Hellman, by exchange, 2010.59.

future of the East India Company's monopolistic charter was being debated in Parliament and the press, later culminating in the first successful legislative move to end the monopoly via the Charter Act of 1813. The vices and evils of two different but entangled factors – slavery and monopoly – were thus affecting both the emerging global commercial market and domestic politics in Britain. The future of the West Indies, in thrall to London-based speculators, was as uncertain as that of the crepuscular East India Company, which was laden with debt as a black market trade in goods flourished in response to its creaking monopoly. It was a protean moment to which *The Woman of Colour* was responding, and the novel places these complexities into the 'abler hands' of a 'stranger, and mulatto', Olivia Fairfield.[2]

Publishing such a novel proved a surprising business decision, for Black, Parry, and Kingsbury, were 'booksellers, stationers, map and chart sellers'

2 Anonymous, *The Woman of Colour: A Tale*, ed. by Lyndon J. Dominique (Peterborough: Broadview Press, 2008), pp. 90, 110. Abbreviated to *WOC*.

to the East India Company.[3] Offering titles such as *The East India Directory for 1807*, their primary readership came from among those working for the Company and the Navy, to whom the publisher advertised their catalogue as being 'particularly useful for writers, cadets and Gentlemen going to the East Indies'.[4] In service of their arrangement, Black, Parry, and Kingsbury were based in Leadenhall Street, just a few doors down from the East India Company's headquarters: so strong is the association of the EIC with this street, historians use 'Leadenhall Street' to stand synecdochally for the Company itself.[5] The printing and bookselling partnership, which included Alexander and James Black's sister Hannah, alluded to their financial dependence on this particular market in their application to become the bookseller for The Commissioners for the Discovery of the Longitude at Sea, in which they boasted of their 'very considerable sale[s]' through their 'connexions [*sic*]' with the Officers of the Royal Navy, and with those of the East India Company as well as with 'professional men of eminence attached to both services'.[6] Their finances were also enmeshed with those travelling to the East Indies: Alexander Black invested in bonds for free mariners, putting up the sureties for William Huxham and Robert Gibson, who sailed to Bengal in 1816. As one of its monopoly powers, the East India Company required people visiting the Indian sub-continent to obtain authority from it, typically setting a bond at £200, unless they were traders like Huxham and Gibson, for whom the bond was set at £500. It places the publishers of *The Woman of Colour* firmly in the midst of Company activity.[7]

Yet, despite their entanglement with the EIC, in 1808, the partnership made the decision that was seemingly at odds with their financial interests and commitments: to publish *The Woman of Colour*, a novel that pays attention to British concerns in and with the West Indies, as well as to

3 *Literary Panorama*, p. 17.

4 Ibid.

5 See Tillman Nechtman, *Nabobs: Empire and Identity in Eighteenth-Century Britain* (Cambridge: Cambridge University Press, 2010; this edn 2013), pp. 82, 142; and Anthony Webster, *The Twilight of the East India Company: The Evolution of Anglo-Asian Commerce and Politics, 1790–1860* (Woodbridge: Boydell & Brewer, 2009), p. 27.

6 Royal Greenwich Observatory Archives/Papers of the Board of Longitude/RGO 14/15: 274–285, 282r. See also 'Parry, Henry, bookseller, 7, Leadenhall Street 1800-19. Partner with Alexander Black 1800-04, James Black 1800-07 and Hannah Black 1809. Imprints: (Black and Parry), Abbey: 1800: AL331; Tooley: 1800: 423' in Maxted, *The London Book Trades*, p. 257. See also 'Hannah Black, Parry, and Kingsbury', *The Women's Print History Project*, 2019, Firm ID 1583, https://womensprinthistoryproject.com/firm/1583 (accessed 10 November 2025). With thanks to Kate Moffat and Michelle Levy at *The Women's Print History Project*.

7 'Sureties: Alexander Black, Leadhell [*sic*] Street, Bookseller', British Library, India Office Records, 'Miscellaneous Bonds', Nos 1–2945, 1814–21, IOR Reference Z/O/1/8, 6 March 1816. With thanks to Peter Collinge for his additional insights into EIC bonds and sureties.

the consequences of Britain's relations with the East Indies. The anonymous novel positions itself as critical of an increasingly financialised economy – and especially of East Indian wealth returned to Britain. *The Woman of Colour* bridges two unusual departures for Black, Parry, and Kingsbury that took place between 1806 and 1814: a foray into conduct literature and novels, mostly written by women, and the printing of a pamphlet that addresses the future of the West Indies. The second, in 1805, came with publication of a pamphlet former naval captain, William Layman, who, following his court marital, was relegated to writing advisory pamphlets directed at the Admiralty, to little effect.[8] In 1807, he published *Outline of a Plan for the Better Cultivation of the … British West Indies; Being … an Effectual Substitute for the African Slave Trade* with Black, Parry, and Kingsbury, in which he discussed bringing Chinese 'coolies' to supplant African labour.[9] There is no evidence that Layman was associated with *The Woman of Colour*, yet the conclusion of his pamphlet anticipates ideas found in the novel:

> In a moral, political and commercial point of view … nearly £100,000 sterling of capital are at stake, exclusive of the danger to be apprehended to the principal source of our naval strength, and of the public revenue, and the serious loss to our manufacturers and commerce, unless effectual measures are adopted for meliorating the miserable condition of our West-India colonies.[10]

Black, Parry, and Kingsbury's publication of his *An Outline of a Plan* (1807) carried an advert for a second pamphlet, Layman's *Strictures on the Maritime Strength of Great Britain.* Intended to be 'speedily published', it did not appear until 1821, and only then under a different publisher. Indicative of the first pamphlet's lukewarm reception, perhaps Layman changed tack – or the publisher did.

During Hannah Black's tenure between 1808 and 1812, the publishers moved into printing volumes by and for women, including the conduct literature of John Gregory and Hester Chapone; a religious dissertation translated by an unknown 'lady'; and the work of Charlotte Lennox and Anna Laetitia Barbauld.[11] Hannah Black was active in the partnership

[8] John Marshall, *Royal Naval Biography*, vol. 3.2, pp. 337–43.

[9] William Layman, *Outline of a Plan for the Better Cultivation, Security & Defence, of the British West Indies; Being the Original Suggestion for Providing an Effectual Substitute for the African Slave Trade, and Preventing the Dependence [sic] of Those Colonies on America for Supplies* (London: Printed for and sold by Black, Parry, and Kingsbury, 1807).

[10] Layman, *Outline of a Plan for the Better Cultivation,* pp. 92–3. See William Layman, *The Pioneer, or Strictures on Maritime Strength and Economy* (London: E. Bridgewater, 1821).

[11] Titles include John Gregory and Hester Mulso Chapone, *Letters on the Improvement of the Mind: Addressed to a Lady. By Mrs. Chapone*; and *A Father's Legacy to His Daughters. By Dr. Gregory* (London: Hannah Black, Parry, and Kingsbury, 1808 and 1810); Sarah Green, *The Fugitive; or, Family Incidents. In Three Volumes. By the Author*

during these years under the Black, Parry, and Kingsbury imprint, before continuing under other imprints until 1822. Given the publisher's maritime and company links, the most likely readership of these and *The Woman of Colour* would have been the men of the EIC or the Navy, and especially their wives and female relations, yet the imprint published women writers with abolitionist sympathies and associations and who addressed women's role in individual and national moral self-improvement.

While the publisher of the novel is easily traced, the identity of the anonymous author of *The Woman of Colour* remains disputed. The novel is perhaps the work of Mrs E. G. Bayfield, about whom little is known. Bayfield is presented in a poetic 'Address to Subscribers' as a wife and mother awaiting the return of her military husband from overseas, for whom 'th'ungenial gale of chill misfortune blows', implying that she is yet another female writer supporting herself by her pen.[12] More recently, Kandice Sharren has concluded an attribution chain with the name Mrs E. M. Foster, who is frustratingly opaque in the archive.[13] If the authorship is uncertain, then the publications listed under 'by the author of' prove instructive. Other novels by the same, such as *The Corinna of England* (1809), focus on women and their fortune, including the importance of women participating in Christian and benevolent labour in service of education and the poor.[14]

of Private History of the Court of England … &c. (London: Hannah Black, Parry, & Co., 1814; 2nd edn 1815); Charlotte Lennox, *The Female Quixote; or, the Adventures of Arabella. By Mrs. Lennox. In Two Volumes. A New Edition* (London: Hannah Black, Parry, and Kingsbury, 1810); Anna Laetitia Barbauld, *The British Novelists; with an Essay; and Prefaces, Biographical and Critical, by Mrs. Barbauld* (London: Hannah Black, Parry, and Kingsbury, 1810); Christoph Christian Sturm, *Reflections on the Works of God; and of His Providence Throughout All Nature. Translated by a Lady, from the German of C.C. Sturm* (London: Hannah Black, Parry, and Kingsbury, 1808). See also 'Henry Parry and Hannah Black', *The Women's Print History Project*, 2019, Firm ID 4924, https://womensprinthistoryproject.com/firm/4924 (accessed 8 January 2024).

12 Paula R. Feldman, *British Women Poets of the Romantic Era: An Anthology* (London: Johns Hopkins University Press, 2001), p. 84.

13 Sharren, Kandice, '"By the Author of …"', *Women's Print History Project*, https://womensprinthistoryproject.com/blog/post/108 (accessed 8 January 2024).

14 Consider the exclamation of an elderly aunt in *The Corinna of England*: 'Talk of fortune and independence … then, let her enjoy it like a reasonable being, and like a Christian, and use it with moderation; let her visit the poor let her work for them: Anon., *The Corinna of England, and a Heroine in the Shade: A Modern Romance. By the Author of 'The Winter in Bath,' 'The Banks of the Wye,' 'The Woman of Colour,' 'Light and Shade'*, 2 vols (London: Printed for J. Ginger, 1809), vol. 1, p. 70.

The Indies on the Threshold

In 1801, Bryan Edwards offered 'a comparative view of the two greatest branches of British commerce; the East and West Indian Trades', in which he tabulated the capital employed, import sales, export value and duties paid to the government.[15] Edwards compared the value of chartered shipping of the Company in the East Indies against the free trade of 'shipping employed direct' in the West, concluding that the latter outpaced the former by 70,000 tons.[16] While the veracity of his figures are suspect and his ignorance of the East Indian economy noted by a number of historians, Edwards demonstrates the importance placed on considering the fortunes and futures of the Indies together.[17] Land 'made a West Indian planter's money make sense', as did its position outside of monopoly.[18] For a proslavery commentator like Edwards, 'the great difference arises from the circumstance that the trade to the West Indies is carried on with our own colonial possession, which the settlements in the East never were, nor even can be considered' – a position made evident throughout his contrasting study of the East and West Indian markets.[19] The value of West Indian money lay in its source: the plantation and its familiarity, which contrasted with the 'obscure origins' of East Indian riches and the capacity for individuals to become wealthy through profitable plunder.[20]

In reality, though, the West Indies was enduring a period of social and economic turbulence in the run-up to the termination of the Atlantic Slave Trade in 1807, which ended the trade in people but did not free the enslaved people working on plantations; emancipation was not realised until The Slavery Abolition Act of 1833. Even though Jamaica had avoided insurrection when other islands such as Haiti and Saint Domingue

15 Bryan Edwards, *The History, Civil and Commercial, of the British Colonies in the West Indies: In Three Volumes. Present inhabitants. Agriculture. Government and commerce. Appendix: Containing tables of West Indian exports and imports to and from Great Britain and Ireland* (London: John Stockdale, 1801), p. 477.

16 Ibid.

17 See, especially, Peter Marshall, *The Making and Unmaking of Empires: Britain, India, and America c.1750–1783* (Oxford: Oxford University Press, 2005); H. V. Bowen, *Revenue and Reform: The Indian Problem in British Politics 1757–1773* (Cambridge: Cambridge University Press, 1991); and Sugata Bose, *A Hundred Horizons: The Indian Ocean in the Age of Global Empire* (Cambridge MA: Harvard University Press, 2006).

18 Nechtman, *Nabobs*, p. 157; for discussion of the mysteriousness of Nabobian wealth, see James Mayer Holzman, *The Nabobs in England: A Study of the Returned Anglo-Indian, 1760–1785* (New York: Columbia University Press, 1926), pp. 17, 40–4.

19 Edwards, *The History, Civil and Commercial, of the British Colonies in the West Indies*, p. 477.

20 Nechtman, *Nabobs*, p. 157.

had not, the threat remained.[21] The precipitousness of Jamaica's position between peace and rebellion, and enrichment and bankruptcy, was amplified by speculators in commodities who contributed to a massive and artificial expansion of sugar estates throughout the Caribbean, followed by a sugar bubble and overproduction crisis that fomented between 1799 and 1807.[22] Coupled with labour shortages and escalating prices during the lead-up to the abolition of the Atlantic trade in 1807, and enabled by generous extensions of credit issued in London, speculators drove up the price of people, deepening the economic crisis in Jamaica ever further. Britons were being confronted with the fact that the slave economy and an 'empire of bonded labour and ill-gotten profits' were replacing Britain's empire of trade, inculcating inefficiencies, inertia and illegality into the market.[23] Furthermore, there had long been a growing recognition that enslaved labour was less productive and more expensive than other forms of labour: the inefficiency of brutality, made even more evident when the continual supply of enslaved labour was ended.[24]

As these economic and social crises were brewing, the interlocking activities of the Slave and sugar trades and the East India Company in cotton manufacturing, banking and finance, in shipping, military contracting and government funds, which spanned two hemispheres, meant that exposure to risk permeated all parts of the economy.[25] The EIC functioned as a highly profitable private venture, yet one that carried enormous debts and liabilities.[26] In the early nineteenth century, the problem of monopoly was

[21] David Geggus, 'The Enigma of Jamaica in the 1790s: New Light on the Causes of Slave Rebellions', *The William and Mary Quarterly*, 44:2 (April 1987), 274–99. See also Christer Petley, 'Slaveholders and Revolution: The Jamaican Planter Class, British Imperial Politics, and the Ending of the Slave Trade, 1775–1807', *Slavery & Abolition*, 39:1 (2017), 53–79.

[22] David Ryden, *West Indian Slavery and British Abolition, 1783–1807* (New York: Cambridge University Press, 2009).

[23] Nechtman, *Nabobs*, p. 139.

[24] See Adam Smith, *An Inquiry into the Nature and Causes of the Wealth of Nations*, 2 vols (London: W. Strahan and T. Cadell, 1776). Recent scholarship includes Barry R. Weingast, 'Persistent Inefficiency: Adam Smith's Theory of Slavery and Its Abolition in Western Europe', *The Adam Smith Review, vol. 12* (London: Routledge, 2020), pp. 290–310. See also Tom Brass, 'Capitalist Unfree Labour: A Contradiction?', *Critical Sociology*, 35:6 (2009), 743–65; and Seymour Drescher, *The Mighty Experiment: Free Labor versus Slavery in British Emancipation* (Oxford: Oxford University Press, 2004), especially at pp. 18, 25.

[25] Maxine Berg and Pat Hudson, *Slavery, Capitalism and the Industrial Revolution* (Cambridge: Polity Press, 2023), p. 19.

[26] See Philip Lawson, *The East India Company: A History* (London: Routledge, 1993), pp. 96–102; and John Keay, *The Honourable Company: A History of the English East India Company* (London: HarperCollins, 1993).

an urgent one, as the papers of the parliamentary committee tasked with addressing the EIC attest:

> That the monopoly of the East India Company has been injurious to the nation, great evils having resulted from it: that it is inadequate to an extended trade; has locked up national capital; has retarded improvement; has not advanced trade, nor carried it to many countries within the Company's limits … that all ideas of participation in the profits of a monopoly trade, by payment into the Exchequer, ever will be vain and illusory … that the reasonings in favour of the monopoly proceed from narrow partial views, have been demonstrated fallacious, and will apply equally to every other branch of British commerce: that it is humiliating to individuals, degrading to the national character, and a national grievance.[27]

One corollary of monopoly that impacted trade and industry negatively was the illegal trade spawned by the Charter. Contemporary accounts of smuggled goods seized on entry to the port of London from the East Indies between 1806 and 1808 alone list hundreds of ships with goods seized just in the port of London.[28] It is clear from these lists that portable goods that retained a high value proved popular, especially clothing: shawls, handkerchiefs, muslins, nankeen and silks were among the most frequently smuggled goods. More robust than most fabrics and papers, and eminently popular with the fashionable, ostrich feathers remained 'more prized as ornaments than those of any other bird'.[29] Unsurprisingly, the types of goods listed in seizures at ports correlate with those advertised in 1800 for sale in the Long Room of Customs House. The *London Gazette* lists silk handkerchiefs, shawls, crape, tobacco, vulture and ostrich feathers, and sundry other goods 'allotted in small Quantities', ostensibly for the 'better accommodation' of the dealers and private persons who choose to become purchasers – but really, of course, to produce artificial scarcity that works on the credulity of the consumer, driving the black market.[30]

[27] 'Copy of a Report from the Committee of Correspondence to the Court of Directors of the East India Company, Dated 9th February 1813 – On the Subject of the Trade with the East Indies and China', *Parliamentary Papers* (London: HM Stationery Office, Session 24 November 1812 to 22 July 1813), vol. 3, p. 4.

[28] 'An Account of Goods, the Produce or Manufacture of China or the East Indies, which have been seized at the Port of London, in the Six Years last past; distinguishing the Species and Quantities; the Name of the Ship; and, if seized on board, or run from: also, the total number of Seizures, and the total Value thereof, in each year', in *Parliamentary Papers* (London: HM Stationery Office, Session 24 November 1812 to 22 July 1813), vol. 8, pp. 31–48.

[29] Thomas Mortimer, 'Ostrich Feather', *A General Dictionary of Commerce, Trade, and Manufactures: Exhibiting Their Present State in Every Part of the World: and Carefully Compiled from the Latest and Best Authorities* (London: Phillips, 1810).

[30] Customs-House, London, 2 July 1800, in the *London Gazette*. United Kingdom, Tho. Newcomb, 1800, p. 762.

The lists of seized goods serve as a reminder of the trade that sat outside of Charter restrictions. An indirect evil of the East India Company's monopoly was the flourishing of trade in that which its Charter did not cover – the trade in people.[31] The ending of the trade in enslaved people in 1807 affected West Indian merchants and cotton manufacturers, who united to petition against the continuing monopoly of the EIC over the importation of a wide array of raw and manufactured goods. The move from enslavement to abolition is not a symptom of increasing imperial benevolence for those people working in bonded and enslaved labour, or rooted in sympathy for the wider good of other economic agents. Merchants and manufacturers sought to leverage the East India Company's weakened financial position and advance the case for freer trade in order to provide alternative markets and routes to substitute the trade in people.[32] Their combined efforts persuaded the government of the problem of monopoly, which was reflected in the reports emerging from the Select Committee on East Indian affairs between 1808 and 1812 that criticised the Company's commercial practices.[33] This agitation culminated in the Charter Act of 1813, expanding non-Company commercial interests, and legitimising pluralised trade between Britain and its colonial acquisitions. In the opening decade of the nineteenth century, interests emerged in identifying new markets and affordable semi-skilled and skilled labour, which, *The Woman of Colour* appears to imply, might be found in the West Indies.[34]

The novel is clearly cognisant of the economic precipice upon which the Indies are standing, for it reintroduces a cast of Nabobs who embody the corruption of the East and the worrying imbrication of India and Britain, reanimating an older concern. The problem of the Nabob, the Asiatic plunderer, was a debate that had occupied the political and literary heavyweights of the preceding century. Almost forty years earlier, Horace Walpole, novelist and son of Britain's first Prime Minister, had written a letter to a friend stating that Nabobs had starved 'millions by monopolies and plunder', and now were set to reproduce the same in England by causing 'famine at home by the luxury occasioned by their opulence raising the price of everything, till the poor could not purchase bread'.[35] The socio-economic ills imported by Nabobs had captured the public imagination on stage and page for

[31] Eric Williams, *Capitalism and Slavery* (Chapel Hill NC: University of North Carolina Press, 1944), pp. 97–102.

[32] Webster, *The Twilight of the East India Company*, p. 55.

[33] Ibid, p. 60.

[34] See J. E. Cookson, 'Political Arithmetic and War in Britain, 1793–1815', *War and Society*, 1:2 (1983) 37–60, esp. 50–1; J. E. Cookson, 'British Society and the French Wars, 1793–1815' *Australian Journal of Political and History*, 31 (1985), 192–203.

[35] Horace Walpole, *The Letters of Horace Walpole*, vol. 8, ed. by P. Toynbee (Oxford: Oxford University Press, 1905), p. 101.

decades; consequently, renewed attention to the Nabob in *The Woman of Colour* makes sense as the West Indies were newly facing rising prices and food shortages. The fortunes of two hemispheres are simultaneously interconnected as they are contrasted in the novel.[36]

Recent critics of *The Woman of Colour* have been inclined to focus on the novel's depiction of the West Indian rather than the East Indian question. Compelling readings can be found in Brigitte Fielder's analysis of the character of Dido as not simply an archetypal faithful Black servant to Olivia; and found in the invitation of Sofia Prado Huggins to use critical fabulation as a way of approaching the violent inertia and silence of the archive about the lives of enslaved women. Prado Huggins reads *The Woman of Colour* in order to provide glimpses of the experiences of an enslaved Black woman traversing the Atlantic.[37] Critical fabulation puts novels to work in service of giving shape and colour to the apparition in the archive.[38] However, in paying attention to the publisher and its intimate relationship with the East India Company, it is clear that the presence of the Nabobs in the text demands closer examination. Additionally, Hannah Black's oversight of an era of publishing tracts concerned with religious feeling and conduct reminds the reader to reflect on the ways in which the novel concerns itself with the conduct of men and women set among the moral, political and economic complexities wrought by the predominance – and interrelation – of two urgent issues of the period: the futures of the West *and* East Indies, both of which hung in the balance. In so doing, the reader might newly see women, especially a woman of colour, affecting, and being affected by, these larger concerns.

In a reading where Olivia stands in for Jamaica herself – or at least its plantations – and is defrauded out of her fortune by the 'machinations' of the 'unfeeling' Letitia Merton (181), the novel evokes the problems beset by Jamaican planters: the potential slide into bankruptcy at the hands of speculators and investors; the West Indian economic position vulnerable to dependence on either England or America; and the threat of riot and

36 See poems including Richard Clarke's *The Nabob; or Asiatic Plunderer* (1773); or plays such as Timothy Touchstone's *Tea and Sugar; or the Nabob and Creole* (1792), and A. Thomson's *The East Indian: A Comedy* (1800), translated from the German of Augustus Von Kotzebue.

37 Brigitte Fielder, '*The Woman of Colour* and the Black Atlantic Movement', in *Women's Narratives of the Early Americas and the Formation of Empire*, ed. by Mary McAleer Balkun and Susan C. Imbarrato (New York: Palgrave Macmillan, 2016), p.179; and Sofia Prado Huggins, 'Reading Slantwise: Dido in *The Woman of Colour* (1808)', *Eighteenth-Century Fiction*, 35:1 (2023), 27–42.

38 For the introduction of critical fabulation as a methodology in the study of the Black Atlantic, see Saidiya Hartman, 'Venus in Two Acts', *Small Axe*, 12:2 (2008), 1–14, https://muse.jhu.edu/article/241115 (Accessed 10 January 2024).

rebellion spreading to the Island.[39] Food scarcity is something at which Olivia hints in her remark about the diet of 'our poor slaves' who are 'kept upon rice', and how they 'would be glad to exchange it for a little of your nice wheaten bread' (91). Early in the novel, Olivia possesses a 'rebellious and repining heart' (64), which reawakens upon the termination of her marriage to Augustus as she begins once again to 'pant for independence!' (181). After discovering that her marriage to Augustus is illegitimate, Olivia recognises, with irony, that 'by a wonderful transition of fortune [she is] now, once again, likely to be dependent on the generosity of [her brother-in-law] Mr. George Merton' thanks to the 'strange tenour [*sic*] of my father's will' (181). Likewise, Jamaica herself was facing a future of economic dependence on either America or England, especially in the wake of a labour crisis, food shortages, inflation and bankruptcies that had largely spawned from speculation in London in the slave and sugar trades. The novel makes visible a woman of colour, Olivia, ready to return to Jamaica, freshly inspired to 'zealously engage' in a project of instruction and amelioration of the Black population, who will otherwise remain 'dormant' (55). As both emblem and agent, Olivia's own reformation from one who is 'disappointed in England' (105) to becoming an enthusiast for its virtues, while acquiring 'a veneration of its soil', anticipates an English remedy for Jamaica (237). Against this, the Nabobs serve as a timely reminder of what is at stake.

Profit and Plunder

The novel begins with Olivia Fairfield heading to England aboard a ship in the Atlantic Ocean; from here, she reveals that she is the orphaned illegitimate daughter of the recently deceased plantation owner Mr Fairfield and Marcia, a Guinean woman whom Fairfield had purchased, and who died giving birth. Olivia Fairfield must marry her English cousin Augustus in order to fulfil the terms of her father's will and receive her £60,000 inheritance. On arriving in England, Olivia encounters her in-laws, the mercantile Mertons, whose sociable world is formed by extraordinarily wealthy Nabobs, the Singletons and Ingots, who dance and dine at the recently completed Pagoda. George Merton, the brother of Augustus, is concerned only with the 'plodding track of cent and per cent, and addition on addition' (119); his wife Letitia, the daughter of the rapacious merchant Manby, a man who possesses a 'spirit of hoarding', has been trained from childhood to 'decorate her little person in the costliest garb' (220, 215).

[39] See Geggus, 'The Enigma of Jamaica in the 1790s'; and Petley, 'Slaveholders and Revolution'.

Even the elder Merton, Olivia's uncle, turns out to be less scrupulous than she initially assumes. Olivia first notes that Mr Merton 'appear[s]' to possess the 'principles … [and] character for probity and integrity as a merchant', but such confidence begins to be undone at her betrothal (87). On the eve of her marriage, Olivia finds that 'diamonds and pearls have been brought' to her 'for inspection' as part of her settlement, which has been deferred to her merchant father-in-law as the 'prime agent in this business', for he 'understands these affairs better than the affairs of the heart' (109). Diamonds were markers of new wealth and were used to circumvent the East India Company's remittance system entirely and its 'panopticonic surveillance'.[40] Bills of exchange were subject to public disclosure and controlled by stringent limits imposed by the Company on the sums individuals were permitted to transmit; diamonds were not.[41] Diamonds thus paved the way for corrupt merchants who could then fuel 'a supposedly new political economy of bribery, graft, despotism and corruption'.[42]

This episode more thoroughly implicates the Mertons in the illegal trade that mushroomed during the twilight years of the East India Company. The Merton's friends, who have recently returned from India, the Singletons and the Ingots, begin to reproduce the aesthetics and behaviours of the East at home in England. The successors to Warren Hastings, they import corruption and indolence along with their shawls, pearls, curries and diamonds, including Mr Singleton's ring of 'sparkling brilliants', which so delights Mrs Merton (104). Throughout the novel, the pursuit of profit and self-enrichment brings characters into the purview of corruption, in the East Indies especially. Hence, when Sir Marmaduke Ingot departs for India:

> To go to a climate where a fortune would be speedily acquired, and every luxury of life be within his reach:—a country, where the following maxim has too frequently been adopted by the youth who have set out on the career of gain—"Get money—honestly, if you can; but, whatever you do, get money". (183)

In England, Sir Marmaduke aspires 'to get an act of Parliament' to move a turnpike 2 miles further away from his newly built pagoda (136).[43] Sir Marmaduke is willing to resort to bribery of 'a few more thousands in this contest', while remarking that 'in India we manage matters more concisely; for there, we men in power have the law vested in our hands' (137). Despite

[40] Nechtman, *Nabobs*, p. 159. The Pitt family's political dynasty was founded on the Pitt Diamond wealth. See Keay, *The Honourable Company*, pp. 214–15.

[41] Michael Edwardes, *The Nabobs at Home* (London: Constable, 1991), p. 30.

[42] Nechtman, *Nabobs,* p. 228.

[43] For the moving of roads for estates during enclosure, see: Peter Collinge, 'Gloomy Inhospitality: Limiting Access to Houses and Country Estates, 1719–1838', in Terry Dooley and Christopher Ridgway (eds), *Visitors to the Country House in Ireland and Britain: Welcome and Unwelcome* (Dublin: Four Courts, 2023), pp. 137–56, p. 150. See also Edwardes, *Nabobs at Home*, p. 31.

the association of the pagoda with China, the myth of the 'pagoda-tree' arrived from India and pertained specifically to Bengal. So-called after the gold coin of the same name, the pagoda-tree could be shaken and money picked up off the ground symbolising the love of profit of Sir Marmaduke Ingot. While the purchasing of grand estates was disrupting landed hierarchies, the diamonds, shawls and feathers and the 'princely magnificence' of the Mertons, Singletons and Ingots remain indicative of their implied involvement with illegal importation and its association with political and social corruption: sexual impropriety, bribery, hoarding, market abuse, the dissemination of false information, illegal importation and evading Charter restrictions (88).

Nabobian wealth is likewise communicated through items associated with illicit trade. Olivia describes the young son of Sir Marmaduke, Mr Ingot, as 'wrapped in a shawl ... [and] ornamented by a plume of feathers' (54). This 'new species of animal' is the corollary of the total imbrication of Britain and India: the transfiguration of the English into an Indian menagerie – at once the furthest remove from the rational and educable, and the nadir of corruption.[44] Miss Singleton, dressed in her feathers, sounds as much like a dishevelled ostrich as she does a person. Olivia pities Miss Singleton's:

> Poor shrivelled and thin neck ... Feathers of the ostrich were mounted in several directions from her head, while her bared ears, and elbows, and back, and bosom, gave to her whole contour, so freezing and so forlorn an appearance, while her volatility, and frisky and girlish airs, made her person so very conspicuous ... as a species of animal which had never before fallen under my notice. (104)

Shawls, pearls, and feathers as associated with nabobery can be seen variously in works such as James Gillray's *The Leadenhall Volunteer, Drest in his Shawl* (1797), in which the uniform of militia man of the EIC has been covered by an effeminate Oriental shawl, or in Fanny Burney's *The Wanderer* (1814), in which a document that proved the protagonist's identity, and claim to her fortune, would not be foresworn for 'all the pearls and all the shawls of the nabobs of all Asia'.[45] Idle consumption is not limited to women, moving against the common image of women as the consuming subject; male and female characters in *The Woman of Colour* and elsewhere,

[44] For discussion of the menagerie held at the EIC headquarters, see Daniel Hahn, *The Tower Menagerie* (London: Simon and Schuster, 2003).

[45] Fanny Burney, *The Wanderer*, ed. by Margaret Anne Doody, Robert L. Mack and Peter Sarbor (New York: Oxford University Press, 1991), p. 840. See also James Gillray's *The Leadenhall Volunteer, Drest in his Shawl* (London: Hannah Humphry, 8 March 1797).

are depicted as equal in their love of the accoutrements of wealth and idleness, as other men and women are in their distaste for it.[46]

In *The Woman of Colour*, then, the individual pursuit of money, luxury and personal gain remains the problem, not commerce or plantation-holding itself. The uncle of the Nabob Sir Marmaduke Ingot, Mr Bellfield, is a former merchant, but one for whom 'through his whole mercantile proceedings' was 'sanctioning, countenancing, and favouring in silence, experiencing true pleasure only, while benefiting his fellow-creatures' (168). Likewise, Augustus Merton, once he becomes a Fairfield, is 'content to live on the fortune which [Olivia's] father's will bequeathed to him with his wife' while remaining 'ever anxious to be of service to his fellow-creatures … inquiring what injuries their poor tenants had sustained, in order that he might relieve them' (119, 173). In Caroline Lumley, Olivia finds someone with 'a native simplicity' and asks for 'her assistance in forwarding a little plan for establishing a School of Industry' (153). The novel thus contrasts metropolitan commercial self-interest, the profit-by-plunder and corruption supposedly found in India and imported into England by Nabobs *and* Nabobinas, with the sociable, moral and rational community of men and women of rural England that, the novel implies by the end, has the potential to be replicated in Jamaica.

Julie Murray has written persuasively about the apparent 'incoherence' of aligning the West Indian plantation with the virtues of English country living; in her briefer assessment of the representation of the Nabobs and merchant classes, Murray concludes that *The Woman of Colour* is 'firmly aligning new money, ostentation, and bad taste with a "new species of animal"'.[47] Accordingly, the novel 'carefully and strategically relocates questions about species distinction and the limits of the human from the category of race to that of commerce, fashion, and commodification'.[48] She suggests that 'the novel's sustained critique of commerce is ultimately in service of its antislavery politics, a politics predicated on an absolute rejection of commerce and its dehumanizing and deracinating tendencies'.[49] In attending to a wider cast of characters in *The Woman of Colour*, however, I argue that, despite the Nabobian 'caricatur[es]' which Olivia says that she offers the reader, the consideration of the system of mercantilism and, against it, that of commerce and free trade, is more nuanced than such broad strokes might imply (134). In particular, I am interested in the way

[46] For discussion of women as shoppers and consumers, see Elizabeth Kowaleski-Wallace, *Consuming Subjects: Women, Shopping, and Business in the Eighteenth Century* (Chichester: Columbia University Press, 1997).

[47] Julie Murray, 'The Country and the City and the Colony in *The Woman of Colour*', *Lumen: Selected Proceedings from the Canadian Society for Eighteenth-Century Studies*, 33 (2014), 87–99, at p. 95.

[48] Ibid.

[49] Ibid, p. 99.

that the novel addresses the problem of profit for profit's sake in this turbulent period for global commerce, and in the correctives that are offered for consideration in *The Woman of Colour*.

For Kristina Huang, *The Woman of Colour* is 'a progress narrative where slavery is an event that new subjects in Jamaica move away from as their lives are "improved" under colonial rule', via a process of amelioration communicated in the characterisation of the servant Dido, and Olivia as a 'figure of imperial tutelage'.[50] Huang builds directly on Lowe's argument that the narrative dialectic of liberal freedom was constituted through a 'regulative temporality in which slavery is only legible as a distant origin', which, as Lowe has demonstrated, was in keeping with emerging discourses of free trade and new forms of colonial governance.[51] Huang reads education as an instrument of reform, or amelioration, in the novel. She argues, rightly, that:

> Amelioration is aligned with the novel's pedagogical objectives, which are heightened through the conceit of a student, Olivia, writing to her former instructor, Mrs Milbanke [and through] the emphasis on instruction, moral reform, and Christian virtue [which] echoes British imperial policies to move "from absolute coercion to forms of tutelage". [52]

Reform or amelioration was, as Huang has observed, the language typical of both abolitionists and pro-slavery advocates.[53] Yet, while Huang describes this attitude towards education and reform in *The Woman of Colour* as an 'imperial tutelage' (169), the cross-cultural comparison between the educable potential of Black inhabitants of Jamaica and the ineducable, illiberal, and stunted returnees from the East Indies complicates her analysis. Anthony Bogues, on whose work Huang draws, observes the British imperial practices that informed nineteenth-century liberal thought, writing that 'it is notable that after emancipation, commerce was aligned with a civilising mission, thus making a new ground for the colonial problem of governing the black body'.[54] However, this ambition is problematised by the presence of the Nabobs in the story, who remind the reader of the failure of commerce to civilise. When profit is pruned away from land, and instead money is made from money and things in service of self, it causes its adherents to wither. Those participating in such alienated commerce become less

[50] Kristina Huang, '"Ameliorating the Situation" of Empire: Slavery and Abolition in *The Woman of Colour*', *Eighteenth-Century Fiction*, 34:2 (2022), 167–86, at p. 168.

[51] Lowe, *The Intimacies of Four Continents*, p. 50.

[52] Huang, '"Ameliorating the Situation" of Empire', pp. 180–1.

[53] Ibid. p. 169.

[54] Anthony Bogues, 'Liberalism, Colonial Power, Subjectivities, and the Technologies of Pastoral Coloniality', in *Victorian Jamaica*, ed. by Tim Barringer and Wayne Modest (Durham NC: Duke University Press, 2018), pp. 115–36, at p. 159.

vital, less feeling, resulting in either 'a stiffness' or shrivelling into 'idleness and illiberality' (87, 118).

Huang's reading is sensitive to various historical references that frame the narrative, including the larger threat that Jamaica posed to white control, as well as to smaller contexts such as the interconnection between British education and the migrations and education of children of the plantocratic elites. However, absent from this argument are two important points. First, what to make of the contrasting idleness, illegitimacy and ineducability found among the Nabobian and mercantile characters; second, how to interpret the novel's unwillingness to bear witness to any of Olivia's plans being enacted. In extending the work of Murray and Huang, I suggest that *The Woman of Colour* portrays a form of eschatological nostalgia that is concerned with the relationship between money and land, the problem of deracinated people, and of wealth converted into 'cent [and] per cent' and figures in columns in the 'compting house' (145, 87).

In reading this eschatology in the context of an economy between monopoly and free trade and between slavery and freed labour, it is worth noting that amelioration was a term used in public discourse when addressing both issues. Politicians, such as Edmund Burke, were engaged in a battle not to 'raze Empires' but 'to reform them'.[55] For Burke, the effort was in saving the 'manners and virtues' and 'national character' of the British commercial nation.[56] In his discussions of the East India Company's monopoly, Burke felt that it was 'necessary that the correctives should be uncommonly vigorous'.[57] Burke similarly reads the ills of the Slave Trade as in need of being made 'as small an evil as possible', and to 'draw out of it some collateral good', advocating for heavy regulation of the trade and conditions of enslaved people in order to stifle and slowly extinguish the trade.[58] Although the full 'Sketch' was not published until 1812, prior to that year, private manuscripts were circulated: versions of the sketch informed public speeches by abolitionists such as William Windham, who spoke in the House of Commons on 15 March 1796, with but 'small differences in wording'; the 'Sketch' also reached the hands of Thomas Pelham, French Laurence, and future Speaker of the House and Prime Minister, Henry Addington.[59] Burke saw that 'in every regulation' that he 'proposed … the

55 Nechtman, *Nabobs*, p. 103.

56 Edmund Burke, *The Works of the Right Honourable Edmund Burke*, 12 vols (London: Rivington, 1812), vol. 3, pp. 310–11.

57 Burke, 'Speech on Mr. Fox's East India Bill, December 1, 1783', in *Works* (1812), vol. 2, p. 447.

58 Burke, 'Sketch of a Negro Code', in *Works*, vol. 10, pp. 288–326, p. 305.

59 See P. J. Marshall, 'The Negro Code', *Edmund Burke and the British Empire in the West Indies: Wealth, Power, and Slavery* (Oxford: Oxford University Press, 2019; online edn, *Oxford Academic*, 18 July 2019), p. 181–2. Burke's complete collected works were

civilization and gradual manumission of Negroes in the two hemispheres'.[60] Like the character of Olivia, Burke found that the solution to these problems lay in education and moral reform: 'Religion, Order, Morality and Virtue' and the 'knowledge of Letters, Arts, and handicraft Trades' were to be the 'chief means of such civilisation and improvement' for enslaved people, a plan that followed similar demands for Schools of Industry in England, which trained working-class children in trades while teaching obedience and work as a moral obligation, and which Olivia wished to introduce as part of her benevolent duty to the same.[61] To achieve such an eschatology, the novel places acts of doing into the active hands of a woman of colour. In this way, the novel makes visible different typologies of women and their experience of, and response to, early crises of colonial capitalism. In a period that David Gerber has described as 'the battle for economic freedom' against regulated economic conduct, which went hand in hand with a demand for political rights, *The Woman of Colour* offers a gentler alternative.[62]

Money, Markets and Morals

When discussing morality in the context of *The Woman of Colour*, I am cognisant of two important contexts: the Marxist reading of a macro-economic pre-capitalist moral economy of E. P. Thompson and the moral responsibility of paternalistic capitalism as intervening at times of crises in the market, especially related to food prices; and the second, eighteenth-century deployment of moral as synonymous with vice and evil, which could describe individual, incorporated or international behaviours in the economy. For Thompson, the moral economy describes a waning traditional way of life, tied up in obsolete titles, customs, and paternalistic responsibilities, before the advent of the modern market system.[63] Yet, as Götz notes,

published in 1812. See also Parvathi Menon, who studies protection as an alliance between the abolitionists and planters who, despite contestations, found in Burke's Code a means to attain their separate ends: Parvathi Menon, 'Edmund Burke and the Ambivalence of Protection for Slaves: Between Humanity and Control', in *Politics and the Histories of International Law* (Leiden: Brill, 2021), pp. 61–83.

60 Ibid.

61 Edmund Burke, 'Sketch of a Negro Code', p. 305. See also Malcolm McKinnon Dick, 'English Conservatives and Schools for the Poor c.1780–1833: A Study of the Sunday School, School of Industry and the Philanthropic Society's School for Vagrant and Criminal Children' (PhD thesis, University of Leicester, 1979).

62 David J. Gerber, 'II Freedom, Law, and Competition: The Nineteenth Century as Prelude', *Law and Competition in Twentieth-Century Europe: Protecting Prometheus* (Oxford: Oxford University Press, 2001), p. 18.

63 Edward Palmer Thompson, 'The Moral Economy of the English Crowd in the Eighteenth Century', *Past & Present*, 50 (1971), 76–136. See also E. P. Thompson's *The Making*

there are significant limitations to Thompson's methodology, including the absence of analysis of eighteenth-century uses of the term moral economy.[64]

Informing my second context, Götz draws attention to the conception of moral economy among eighteenth-century radical reformers such as James Burgh and Percival Stockdale, the latter known for his anti-slavery engagement; for them, the human segment of the moral economy was measured variously in the virtue, benevolence, and penitence of its 'moral agents'.[65] Thus, when Edmund Burke and his contemporaries set their sights on the colonial economy, their work was invested with the language of morality: personal vice and evil could help to explain the vagaries and vicissitudes of the market, and a man like Warren Hastings could be put on trial.[66] If Company employees in India had been corrupted, it would imply that the hierarchies and teleologies of imperial power were at fault, a dangerously anti-imperial position.[67] The fault must lie with individual motives and their own susceptibility to corruption and, against that, measures might be taken to instil resilience and enhance a person's transplantability, or to weed out those susceptible to corruption.

At the same time, colonial capitalism had brought about the abruption of inherited, traditional social relations: a change caused by the ascendancy of the inherently individualist moneyed class, and of capital accumulation through commerce, issues that occupy *The Woman of Colour*.[68] For the novel, capital accumulation as hoarding, the business of getting and selling money, and profiteering are the problem. Much as her concerns about commerce are made evident, Olivia condemns not the plantation but:

---

of the English Working Class (1963), which emphasises the agency and resistance of the English working class; that their acts of rebellion were not isolated incidents but part of a broader pattern of resistance to economic exploitation, and political repression, especially related to food shortages and price hikes. This calls to mind the Jamaican slave rebellions of the late eighteenth century. See 'The Moral Economy of Jamaican Workers', in Thomas C. Holt, *The Problem of Freedom: Race, Labor, and Politics in Jamaica and Britain, 1832–1938* (Baltimore MD and London: Johns Hopkins University Press, 1999), which makes the link between Jamaican and English working-class rebellion clear.

64 Norbert Götz, 'Moral Economy: Its Conceptual History and Analytical Prospects', *Journal of Global Ethics*, 11:2 (2015), 147–62.

65 James Burgh, *The Dignity of Human Nature* (1767); and Percival Stockdale, *Six Discourses* (1777), qtd in Götz, 'Moral Economy', p. 150.

66 Modern interpretations read Hastings as an Indophile who attempted to contain and reform the worst abuses of the EIC, but his adversaries at the time held him up as the icon of Nabobery. See William Dalrymple, *The Anarchy: The Relentless Rise of the East India Company* (London: Bloomsbury Publishing, 2019).

67 See Nechtman, *Nabobs*, p. 103.

68 See Onur Ulas Ince, 'Not a Partnership in Pepper, Coffee, Callico, or Tobacco: Edmund Burke and the Vicissitudes of Colonial Capitalism', *Polity*, 44:3 (2012), 340–72.

> The genteel vulgar, meaning those important shallow-pated beings, who have but one recommendation, viz. money!—[She] saw enough of these in the West Indies, where riches are speedily amassed,—and that disgraceful traffic, which hardens the heart, and deadens the feelings, while it fills the purse, was eagerly prosecuted by such characters! (133)

Problematically for the modern reader, Olivia makes a distinction between the profit-hungry and the plantation owners like her father, who in her view had merely failed to 'give the tone of morals to an island' through fear of the retaliation of the plantocratic elite (55). This meant that the 'minds [of the enslaved] were suffered to remain in the dormant state in which he found them' (55). Much as her 'methodistical' evangelism is evident here, dormancy implies a larger potential: the possibility of a more efficient and able workforce if only they might receive the 'same blessings of education', through the acquisition of literacy and religious instruction, which will take them away from working 'like a horse' (96).[69] Like her Black servant Dido, who intends to offer active sympathy to the poor in her 'doctor[ing]', by ameliorating the condition of 'our poor blacks' in Jamaica, a moral and economic problem might be resolved through the efforts of Olivia (121; 236).[70] Contemporary anxieties about the future of the Jamaican labour force could thus be addressed; rebellion assuaged.

I contend that a model for her future intervention can be found in Olivia's earlier plans to establish with the daughter of Reverend Lumley, Caroline, a 'School of Industry' in rural England (154). Schools of industry were designed to teach the children of the labouring poor the habit of industry – the discipline of labour that would rescue the child from the conditions of idleness and ignorance instituted by his environment, which were the same conditions feared among the enslaved.[71] According to McKinnon Dick, such schools helped to reinforce traditional values associated with the morality of labour in a time of accelerated change; they were an idea that mushroomed briefly, but failed to gain traction.[72] Although William Pitt introduced bills encouraging their development, Schools of

69 *The Critical Review* (May 1810), pp. 108–9, qtd in *WOC*, p. 327.

70 The editor of the Broadview critical edition of *WOC*, Lyndon Dominique, notes the rejection of nurse in favour of doctor for both fictional Dido and real Mary Seacole (see n. 10, p. 128). See also Sarah Dredge's essay in this present volume.

71 Malcolm McKinnon Dick, on the contemporary problem of ignorance, idleness and inefficiency among the enslaved population, see Edwards, *The History, Civil and Commercial, of the British Colonies in the West Indies* (1801) and Layman, *Outline of a Plan* (1807). See also the work of historians Anthony Reid in 'Sugar, Slavery, and Productivity in Jamaica, 1750–1807', *Slavery & Abolition*, 37:1 (2015), 159–82; and Kenneth Morgan in 'Slave Women and Reproduction in Jamaica, c.1776–1834', *History*, 91:2 (2006), 231–53.

72 Ibid.

Industry, despite their name, were considered backward-looking in an age that was experiencing the industrial revolution.[73]

Even though Olivia abandons her idea for 'the little school which [she] had projected—the children which [she] had clothed—the peasants whom [she] had assisted' after her marriage to Augustus is revealed to be illegitimate, it still gives the reader an impression of what Olivia might do for Jamaica (197). In intending to 'ameliorat[e] the situation, in instructing the minds—in amending the morals of our poor blacks', by implication Olivia is ready to adopt a similar mechanism for reform in Jamaica that could address the economic as much as the social ills of the island (236). In a climate of anxiety about the future of labour in Jamaica, enslaved labour was understood to be the least productive model of labour and least adapted to industrial and commercial advancement; until 1807, the plantocracy had relied on the continued importation of replacement hands as more efficient than encouraging enslaved people to birth children. *The Woman of Colour* seems to offer an alternative solution.[74]

Eschatological Nostalgia

The novel's denunciation of the profit-seeker, and its contrasting valorisation of the benevolent capitalism of the liberally minded and rational, could be understood as a nostalgic turn in which old economic models could contain the excesses of the present. One reading might be that such nostalgia satiates a longing for a 'simple and stable past', which in turn acts as a refuge 'from the turbulent and chaotic present'.[75] Murray describes *The Woman of Colour* as 'an impossible nostalgia' for a 'lost pastoral idyll'; however, in reading the pastoralism of the novel as uncomfortably regressive and thus at odds with its abolitionist stance, she discounts the generative nature of eighteenth-century Utopian nostalgia.[76] Rather, the 'past of *passéisme*' is in itself an ideal yet to come; the object of '*passéiste* nostalgia' and the object

[73] McKinnon Dick, 'English Conservatives and Schools for the Poor', 185.

[74] Morgan, 'Slave Women and Reproduction in Jamaica', 231–2. Morgan points to the way that 'planters calculated the costs of purchasing adult and adolescent Africans as opposed to rearing children themselves and concluded they would not encourage their seasoned women slaves to breed "as thereby so much work is lost in their attendance upon their infants"', and the children take too long to mature into productive labour. William Beckford, *Remarks upon the Situation of the Negroes in Jamaica* (1788) pp. 4–5, quoted in Morgan, 'Slave Women and Reproduction in Jamaica'.

[75] David Lowenthal, 'Nostalgia Tells It Like It Wasn't', in *The Imagined Past: History and Nostalgia*, ed. by M. Chase and C. Shaw (New York: Manchester University Press, 1989), p. 21.

[76] Murray, 'The Country and the City and the Colony in *The Woman of Colour*', p. 93.

of futuristic hope come together in the same eschatology.[77] Nostalgia could be constitutive of Utopia, and all nostalgia contains a Utopian ferment.[78]

Looking back in order to look forward was a familiar stance in eighteenth-century fiction: authors 'united in their nostalgia for a past in which making money necessitated extending affect toward others', as these works 'transform the material parts of profit—labour, credit, debt, trade, and bullion itself—into agents of sociable community'.[79] Genovese lists examples from the mid-eighteenth century, including Dodsley's *Public Virtue* (1753); significantly, these are in the hands of male authors and centre the concerns of men in the act of 'constructing new, relational models of production that could reflect the communal values of a traditional "moral economy"' and that Genovese suggests imagined an ideal georgic mutuality that countervails capitalistic emphasis on private profit.[80] This earlier period of literature did not take the dominance of the capitalistic goal, profit, as necessarily desirable or inevitable, and even conservative visions of sociable labour might provide a sustained critique of capital accumulation; *The Woman of Colour* appears to share these older beliefs.[81]

Rather than taking a position that is hostile to the system of plantocracy or commerce itself, *The Woman of Colour* adopts a position that is critical of the profiteering individual and of the idle consumer, whether East Indian Nabob or Nabobina, merchant or his wife, or West Indian planter. For *The Woman of Colour*, if to the discomfiture of the modern reader, the problem is not the origin of the money, which might be derived from the Fairfield plantation, but whether the money is made moral in the virtuous service of others less fortunate – or whether it is converted to 'so much folly, ostentation, and self-conceit' of the Nabobs, or 'the credit and high reputation of the London merchant' (88, 117). The Nabobian elements of the novel attend to the problem of the individual and the illiberal behaviours that bring with it illegal trade, bribery and corruption. Therefore, the novel's alignment between the pastoral and the plantation in *The Woman of Colour* is less incoherent than it is a form of nostalgia peculiar to the period that

77 Karine Basset and Michèle Baussant, 'Utopia, Nostalgia: Intersections', *Conserveries mémorielles* [En ligne], 22 (9 July 2018), http://journals.openedition.org/cm/3048 (accessed July 2024).

78 Ibid, p. 5. See Paul Ricoeur, *Time and Narrative*, vol. 2 (Chicago IL: University of Chicago Press, 1984); on hope and moral consciousness, see Ernst Bloch, *The Principle of Hope*, trans. by Neville Plaice, Stephen Plaice and Paul Knight (Cambridge MA: MIT Press, 1959; repr. 1995), p. 3. See also Friedrich Jameson, *Marxism and Form: Twentieth-Century Dialectical Theories of Literature* (Princeton NJ: Princeton University Press. 1971), p. 82.

79 Michael Genovese, *The Problem of Profit: Finance and Feeling in Eighteenth-Century British Literature* (Charlottesville VA: University of Virginia, 2019), p. 4.

80 Genovese, *The Problem of Profit*, p. 52.

81 Ibid., p. 3.

provides critique of and alternative economic model to the burgeoning ills of colonial capitalism: to ameliorate the febrility of an economy between monopoly and free trade and between enslaved and freed labour.

Olivia possesses 'a fine Utopian scheme for domestic happiness': 'conversation … contemplation … the society of rational and well-informed friends' and 'the power of being useful to my fellow creatures—to my poorer neighbours' (120). Yet even she recognises the limits of an eschatological nostalgia, due to the present fact that modern commerce has already moved society too far beyond a return to any kind of golden age that:

> Unless we would really turn hermits, and entirely seclude ourselves from society, we must be content to pay the common levy;—for, to form a truly unvitiated and primeval neighbourhood of undisturbed truth, simplicity, and innocence, we must revert to the golden age, and to the rapt reveries of enthusiastic poets. (156)

Rather than retreating to a state of hermitude, Olivia has been 'taught … activity, both mental and bodily' (98), and it is this 'active turn' (96) that puts nostalgic feeling to work and will seed her own and others' restitution. Her 'moralising disposition' is presented as ideal for 'extract[ing] good from every evil … [and] morality from every passing occurrence' (65, 76), echoing Burke's 'Sketch of a Negro Code', but placing the corrective and reforming zeal in her productive hands.[82]

With the 'abler hand' (91) of Olivia and with – in the opinion of Letitia Merton – her 'bookish[ness]' (123), Olivia asserts to 'keep [herself] employed' in 'rational employment' (198). When walking in rural England, Olivia might see 'a retired hut of poverty, and try to do a little good' to her 'fellow beings' to obviate the 'ills' and 'mischiefs' that 'daily spring from idleness' (198–9). Against such effort sits her adversary Letitia, who 'seems to have attained the very height of *inaction*' – such that Olivia muses, ironically, whether Letitia Merton even '*had* any legs' (90, 98; author's italics). The active nature of Olivia is one of her defining characteristics, particularly set against the indolence of Letitia Merton. From their first introduction, Olivia notes her position as Letitia's foil, the plantation heiress to Letitia Merton's 'city-heiress with a large fortune' (86).[83] But it is on this point alone that they 'meet on equal terms' (87). Letitia Merton, who 'could not pretend to teach' her child, is contrasted with Olivia, who is proud of educating Letitia Merton's young son (93, 95). Letitia Merton's own education was limited to the acquisition of accomplishments and the instilling of 'the value and the consequence of money', having been 'taught to distinguish a guinea from a

[82] The racialisation of labour and active sympathy is explored in Sarah Dredge's chapter in the present volume; see pp. 161–2.

[83] Compare this with the real-world juxtaposition made between Mary Seacole and Florence Nightingale; see Dredge in this volume.

shilling, before she could articulate' (215). Her 'ideas are all centred in self, and in money, as the grand minister to all' (90).

Letitia learned this behaviour from her father, as Manby had risen from 'the very dregs of the people' (214). His principles are described as 'sordid and confined' in his contempt for the impoverished nobleman and his willingness to receive the rich, even if the rich man were 'the most worthless being in creation, a chimney sweeper' (215), a position hostile to those who get their hands *literally* dirty in semi-skilled labour. Furthermore, Manby 'would not have increased his family circle for … one who brought him no profit' (218). Introduced through 'commercial business', Manby arranges the marriage between Letitia and George Merton based on 'calculations' that Merton 'is fit to meet the prime minister for a loan!' (218). The ability of Merton to lend to the Prime Minister recalls, of course, the way capitalised individuals could finance government – and had done so in the wake of the Bank of England Crisis (1797) by purchasing government bonds and injecting liquidity into the economy.[84] Olivia remarks on the similarity between Manby and his son-in-law, George Merton, to 'accumulate thousands upon thousands', comparing George Merton's ambition unfavourably to his brother Augustus's distaste for it (119). The circle of the Mertons, formed from among the Nabobs, reproduce similar examples of ineducability, indolence and unfeeling behaviour. The young Nabob, Mr Ingot, will only 'lounge, and loll, and curvet' (147–8); his tutor, Waller, unable to form Mr Ingot's mind 'to laudable pursuits, and to plant into it just notions', finds that his 'labours are daily subverted by the false and ridiculous theories and systems of his refined mother, and the overweening and worldly maxims of Sir Marmaduke' (165). There is 'no chance of his pupil's improvement', for his tutor is the 'one feeling being' at the Pagoda; there is no affect in circulation at this residence (165, 169).

Rather than continue its hollow and volatile relationship to credit, credulity and speculation, money must be made to make sense in the active, liberal hands of women like Olivia who ought to work to 'extract good from evil' (76). *The Woman of Colour* is thus rather Burkean in this sense – a surprising ideological stance for a publisher like Black, Parry, and Kingsbury, which was so closely tied to Leadenhall Street. As Burke worked hard to avoid condemning colonialism as a system during the trial of Hastings, in *The Woman of Colour*, the plantation itself is not the problem. However, nor may, in this novel, commerce and free trade civilise. Instead, markets might be reformed: brought to hand and imbued with virtue via well-informed and feeling moral agents, willing and able to conduct themselves with benevolence towards their social and economic inferiors.

84 See Niall Ferguson, *The World's Banker: A History of the House of Rothschild* (London: Weidenfeld & Nicolson, 1998).

Rational and principled behaviours, terms that are employed throughout the novel, could thus be introduced through benevolent interventions. The remedy, then, might be found in a communitarian economic model reliant on sociable benevolence and the maintenance of existing social hierarchies, made possible by a liberal education that produced sensible, well-informed, rational people. The novel is staged against the backdrop of the precipitous future of England and the East and West Indies and so women like Olivia might be significant, integrated participants in these connected, febrile forms of commerce. As Harrington argues:

> The representation of women as compassionate and civilising agents in effect 'moralised' the private sphere and in so doing provided an ethical anchor for middle-class values and practices, including the pursuit of economic interests … Eighteenth-century, middle-class intellectuals re-wrote the historical antagonism between civic virtue and commerce, in part, by relocating virtue in the private sphere and designating middle-class women the arbiters of virtue.[85]

The novel is not only setting out the conditions under which free women of colour might participate in such an anchoring, but it adopts a position that is more complicated than merely aligning the trade in enslaved people with a wider problem with commerce. Rather, *The Woman of Colour* is hostile to the uses to which money is put and who puts it to those uses – especially when working at the expense of others and in the promotion of hoarding and idleness.

Conclusion

In previous studies of *The Woman of Colour*, the presence of the Nabobs has remained largely unaddressed; even a review from 1810 concluded that the depiction of the Nabobs in *The Woman of Colour* offered 'nothing new'.[86] Although circulating libraries were awash with Nabob-centric fiction between 1770 and 1800, by 1808, the Nabob was a tired trope of the troubling elision of Britain and India. *The Woman of Colour* is cognisant, however, of the reanimation of old concerns during the twilight of the East India Company, and as the West Indies addressed changing economic conditions now no additional enslaved people could be brought into the labour force, and while suffering from the financial chaos wrought by speculators and investors in the sugar and other trades that influenced the Jamaican economy. In *The Woman of Colour*, the reader sees socio-economic anxieties played out with some consideration of the cause and symptoms: the root of vice and evil lay in learning

[85] Dana Harrington, 'Gender, Commerce, and the Transformation of Virtue in Eighteenth-Century Britain', *Rhetoric Society Quarterly*, 31:3 (2001), 33–52, at p. 34.
[86] The Critical Review [May 1810], qtd in *WOC*, p. 258.

only to value money and the 'unwearied application to the business of getting money', as exemplified by the Mertons, Ingots and Singletons (118).

In the novel's eschatology, there cannot be a return to the immorality of that 'disgraceful traffic', but there might be a moderate remedy that balms rather than inflames the tensions faced in Jamaica. At the same time, the juxtaposition with the Nabobian malaise remains a stark reminder of what is at stake: not only the inflationary and destabilising consequences of profit-by-plunder reimported to England, but the unbearable moral, social and economic price paid for allowing disasters such as famine to take hold, as it had in Bengal in 1770, a situation that was exacerbated by the EIC's private servants and spiking rice prices, a food staple of Bengal – and Jamaica. In resurrecting the Nabobs, the novel casts a shadow over the failure to ameliorate and stabilise a febrile moment. For Jamaica, four prismatic threats were emerging: plantation failures caused by speculation and inclement weather; inflation and food shortages; the problem of productivity among unskilled enslaved labour, especially with no further arrivals after 1807; and the threat of rebellion spreading to the island. *The Woman of Colour* offers a moderate corrective that reinforces the social order even as it addresses the future of Jamaican labour, while the characters of the Nabobs signal what hangs in the balance.

By placing responsibility for amelioration in the non-white hands of Olivia, the novel embraces 'conquest over [racial] prejudice', which proves 'a labour well worth the endeavour' (94). She is both a moral agent for change as well as a vehicle for exploring the concerns of two systems under pressure: that of Company rule and that of the plantation. Yet this proves the limits of the novel's radicalism. In this novel's eschatology, existing social hierarchies ought to be maintained. The wealthy chimney sweep should not be valued above an impoverished nobleman; the displacement of the unchristian and 'disgraceful traffic' that flourished under monopoly and in service of profit must peacefully transition the enslaved into more productive forms of labour. In this, the stabilising hand of the corrective is sought to steady the abruptions and entropy of the Indies on the threshold. *The Woman of Colour* invites the reader to imagine Olivia re-exporting to Jamaica the qualities of the 'favoured isle', England; so Jamaica too, the ending implies, might become a 'happy country, where the laws are duly administered—where the arts—the sciences flourish, and where religion is to be found in all its beautiful purity' (236–7). Such principles are ready to be transplanted back to Jamaica with a belief that the plantation made such a future possible, whereas the East Indian model of profit-by-plunder, which has obscure and obscures origins, did not.[87]

[87] Other, but related, types of obscuration are found in the 'plan[s]' of the Nabobs for remedying Olivia's position after the discovery of the illegitimacy of her marriage to Augustus: to 'form an advantageous matrimonial connexion' in Bengal 'by a feigned

Though sympathetic to matters of racial prejudice, the novel nonetheless lacks sensitivity to the abuses and violence of plantocracy; the contradictions in and paradoxical stances of the novel veer between radical abolitionism and Imperial paternalism. Yet the reader is offered a happy vision for the future, carried in the hands of Olivia, who in her person brought together white male plantation owner and enslaved Black woman with an ease that erases the exploitation and suffering inherent in those relations. Keeping in mind the painting 'Free Women of Color with Their Children and Servants in a Landscape' by Agostino Brunias, and in submitting to a thoroughly Eurocentric pastoral nostalgia, the reader might imagine a postscript to the narrative that conjures genteel, harmonious relations back in Jamaica between Olivia and those whom she describes as 'our poor slaves (my brothers and sisters)' (92). In an exercise of critical fabulation, Olivia's strategic positioning is deliberate: in the space between *my* and *our*, she parenthetically positions her racial proximity while marking her economic advantage and elevated social role – just as Brunias's painting uses skin tones and dress to represent types of people that in turn allude to West Indian social, racial and economic hierarchies, set against a landscape that made these conditions make sense, even as they conceal the violence of empire and slavery.[88]

While the author of the novel remains frustratingly opaque in the archive, the visibility given to Olivia, and the importance placed on her active role in the narrative and to Jamaica's future, invites the reader to imagine a prosperous Jamaica continuing to be untouched by riot and revolution, more stable than its neighbours or the plundered East. Set among such a convenient and comforting picturesque image, any rebellious and repining heart will indeed obey Olivia's exhortation to 'lie still!' (64). In the emphasis found on maintaining the social order and landed values among a landscape that reinforces rigid if benevolent class relations, my reading of the novel makes it a disappointing one for the modern reader. However, it is a reading that addresses the incoherence otherwise found in the novel's eschatology.

The final frustration of the novel is its prevarication: the cure is never administered and the plans never seen implemented. How able and active are the hands of Olivia and, similarly, her Black servant Dido? The question remains unanswered. It is all merely a gesture. In a political and economic moment defined by its precipitousness, the reader is brought to yet another threshold: that of Olivia Fairfield on the brink of return.

---

name', or to become a sexual 'companion' to Rolando Singleton, a fact that would remain an 'inviolable secret' (188–9).

[88] For further discussion of landscape as concealing and revealing in portraiture, see Peter Collinge's essay in this volume.

7

Suffering without Sympathy: Economic Relations and Violence in Elizabeth Gaskell's *Mary Barton* (1848)

OLIVIA BIBER

'If it be an error'

'Preface', *Mary Barton*, p. 5

Considerations of class are woven deeply into the fabric of *Mary Barton; A Tale of Manchester Life*, a text that details working-class life in industrial Manchester in the 1840s. Through Elizabeth Gaskell's middle-class imagination, the novel explores class struggle, poverty, industrialisation, but also love courtship and domesticity.[1] In this chapter, I am primarily interested in the industrial plot and her representation of class division as a result of both the poverty and the wealth created by industrialisation. Concerning Gaskell's *oeuvre* more generally, Nancy Henry argues that her:

> critique of capitalism is as much covert as it is explicit ... Rather than revealing how much she knew about political economy and economic history, she developed a strategy of indirection and allusiveness'[2]

[1] The novel's two narrative foci, industrialisation and courtship, have inspired scholarly debates regarding the form and genre of *Mary Barton*. See, for example, Raymond Williams, *Culture and Society 1780–1950* (London: Chatto & Windus, 1967, orig. 1958), pp. 87–91; Elaine Freedgood, 'Coziness and its Vicissitudes: Checked Curtains and Global Cotton Markets in *Mary Barton*', in *The Ideas in Things: Fugitive Meaning in the Victorian Novel* (Chicago IL: University of Chicago Press, 2006), pp. 55–80; Kamilla Elliott, 'The Romance of Politics and the Politics of Romance in Elizabeth Gaskell's *Mary Barton*', *The Gaskell Society Journal*, 21 (2007), 21–37.

[2] Nancy Henry, *Women, Literature and Finance in Victorian Britain: Cultures of Investment* (Cham: Palgrave Macmillan, 2018), p. 89.

Indeed, vagueness and indirection are also key features of her first novel. In this chapter, I argue that in *Mary Barton*, Gaskell develops a critique of what *is*, particularly in terms of master-worker relations, and imagines what *might be* in a subtle way that often registers in indirect statements, allusions and gestures.[3] Gaskell thereby adopts a strategy of not-saying that allows her to gesture towards, but not render fully intelligible, that which she criticises; in this, I am explicitly positioning my work in conversation with D. A. Miller who, in a different context, has addressed how texts can hover between articulation and non-articulation.[4]

The 'explanatory preface', which Gaskell added after the novel's completion at her publisher's suggestion, thereby, sets the stage and the tone for the text that follows.[5] The preface not only prepares the reader for the narrative to come in terms of the topic and setting, but also provides context for her purpose in writing it. While Gaskell gestures towards the 1848 revolutionary unrests that rippled over the European continent, she is keen to set herself and her text apart from these. She writes:

> I had always felt a deep sympathy with the care-worn men, who looked as if doomed to struggle through their lives in strange alternations between work and want; tossed to and fro by circumstances … I saw that they were sore and irritable against the rich, the even tenor of whose seemingly happy lives appeared to increase the anguish caused by the lottery-like nature of their own. Whether the bitter complaints made by them, of the neglect which they experienced from the prosperous—especially from the masters whose fortunes they had helped to build up—were well-founded or no, it is not for me to judge.[6]

Acknowledging the events on the continent in oblique terms offers Gaskell a certain legitimacy as it marks her writing as both timely and pressing, not least because she completed *Mary Barton* the year prior, almost in anticipation of the current state of affairs. At the same time, Gaskell is quick to assure that she is not interested in an upheaval of the current class and economic system, merely aiming for envisaging an 'idea … of the state of feeling' among workers in Manchester (6). Thus, she frames her text as a modest contribution that seemingly rejects political engagement or opinion,

3 I use 'master' and 'worker' to reflect the language of the time, and that of the novel itself. Gaskell uses the term 'master' throughout the novel, while writers such as Friedrich Engels use the terms 'employer' and 'employed', as well as 'master' and 'man' or 'worker'.

4 D. A. Miller, *Bringing Out Roland Barthes* (Berkeley CA: University of California Press, 1992).

5 Letter from Elizabeth Gaskell to Edward Chapman, 10 July 1848, *The Letters of Mrs Gaskell*, ed. by J. A. V. Chapple and Arthur Pollard (Manchester: Manchester University Press, 1997).

6 Elizabeth Gaskell, *Mary Barton*, by ed. Thomas Recchio (New York and London: Broadview Press, 2008), pp. 5–6. All further references to this edition.

especially on matters pertaining to the economy, as she asserts that 'I know nothing of Political Economy, or the theories of trade. I have tried to write truthfully; and if my accounts agree or clash with any system, the agreement or disagreement is unintentional' (Ibid.).[7]

This strategic stance performs a double function: it acknowledges the novel's intervention even as it attempts to appease her readership, which primarily consisted of the middle class. It is clear that Gaskell is cognisant of the novel's polarising reception. In letters to Edward Chapman and Miss Lamont, respectively, Gaskell attests to the controversy caused by her novel. To the former, she writes, 'Half the masters here are bitterly angry with me—half (and the best half) are buying it to give to their work-people's libraries'.[8] In her letter to Miss Lamont a few days later, she notes, 'Some people here are very angry and say the book will do harm'.[9] Even though she has adopted a strategic modesty, Gaskell has noted that the reading public is sensitive to her critique of what *is*, particularly in the way that it addresses economic practices and conditions, a link that exists precisely because she places her novel in the context of the revolutionary upheavals on the continent. Her two letters also demonstrate what is at stake when a woman writer attends to such matters in their writing, even with her careful positioning.

Although Gaskell deliberately obscures what exactly she is criticising, the relationship between workers and masters emerges as the clearest point of critique amid the general vagueness and ambivalence of the preface. The entire passage hovers between certainty and uncertainty or clarity and vagueness, producing a disorienting effect: the result of her strategic use of not-saying, whereby Gaskell under-elaborates her position and her critique of what is taking place. Here, my use of the prefix *under-* is again informed by Miller, as well as by Laurent Berlant and Michael Warner: Miller and Berlant and Warner have used this prefix in their work to describe the interplay of presence and absence.[10] Gaskell thus fashions herself as a neutral observer, thereby hiding her own position behind what workers either told

[7] For another reading of the preface that also focuses on Gaskell's strategic use of humility and modesty to insert herself into a political debate, see Sarah Dredge, '"I have tried to Write Truthfully": Fictions of Science in Women's Writing of Nineteenth-Century Political Economy', in *Political Economy, Literature & the Formation of Knowledge, 1720–1850*, ed. by Richard Adelman and Catherine Packham (New York and Abingdon: Routledge, 2018), pp. 89–118, at pp. 100–1.

[8] Letter from Elizabeth Gaskell to Edward Chapman, 1 January 1849, *The Letters of Mrs Gaskell.*

[9] Letter from Elizabeth Gaskell to Miss Lamont, 5 January 1849, *The Letters of Mrs Gaskell.*

[10] D.A. Miller, *Jane Austen, or the Secret of Style* (Princeton NJ and Oxford: Princeton University Press, 2005), at p. 28; Lauren Berlant and Michael Warner, 'Sex in Public', *Critical Inquiry*, 24:2 (1998), 547–66.

her of their own experiences and feelings, or what she imagines their experience and feelings to be. In the preface, Gaskell speaks of her own engagement with workers and their discontent, which she acknowledges, but she simultaneously distances herself by insisting that she is presenting events without judgement.

In writing *Mary Barton*, she describes her aim to correct an apparent 'error': in other words, that the workers are – or believe themselves to be – alone in their suffering without the sympathy of their masters: 'If it be an error, that the woes … pass unregarded by all but the sufferers, it is … an error so bitter in its consequences to all parties, that whatever public effort can do … or private effort… should be done … to disabuse the work-people of so miserable a misapprehension' (5–6). This serves as a call to action, asking the manufacturing class to disabuse the workers of their seemingly wrongfully formed opinion that masters do not care about the well-being of their workers, even as it is a veiled, but direct, critique of masters who do not sympathise with the plight of their employees. Her critique is phrased as a hypothetical sentence that offers Gaskell plausible deniability – after all, she describes something that may or may not be the case – and allows her to hide behind her own ambivalent statement. At the same time, she positions herself as sympathetic to the plight of workers in their description as 'sufferers' in the face of 'the injustice and unkindness which they endure from their fellow-creatures' (Ibid.). Gaskell adopts an active sympathy, in which her role is to offer a mechanism by which she might 'give some utterance to the agony which from time to time convulses this dumb people' (Ibid.). Yet beyond the ontology of sympathy is an engagement with class relations borne from her reflections 'on this unhappy state of things between those so bound to each other by common interests, as the employers and the employed must ever be' (Ibid.). Gaskell expands on this point by arguing that:

> If it be an error, that the woes, which come with ever-returning tide-like flood to overwhelm the workmen in our manufacturing towns, pass unregarded by all but the sufferers, it is at any rate an error so bitter in its consequences to all parties, that whatever public effort can do in the way of legislation, or private effort in the way of merciful deeds … should be done … to disabuse the work-people of so miserable a misapprehension. (Ibid.)

I read 'the error' to which Gaskell refers – allowing for the 'suffering without the sympathy of the happy' – as a failure in class relations: a relationship in need of revision. Her intervention is mainly located on a relational rather than on a structural level, although one is shown to affect the other.

Mary Barton is not a text about eradicating class differences or about reducing economic inequality, nor is it about giving voice to working-class discontent, although the text includes ample instances of voicing workers' grievances. Rather, Gaskell shows the fundamental need to critique and to adjust the relationship between workers and masters instead of rejecting existing economic structures. Her critique is articulated, and given shape, in an under-elaborated manner: what she imagines in her writing often registers as a simultaneous presence and absence, as she actively works to obscure her critique and her intervention even as she sets her novel among the febrile socio-economic conditions of the mid-nineteenth century. My methodological approach thus involves the strategic use of extended quotations to demonstrate more effectively the nuanced interplay of prevarication, obfuscation and revelation within Gaskell's work. The rest of this chapter follows a two-part structure as I move from discussing Gaskell's representation of what is to what might be, both of which circle around two dangerous conditions: violence and ignorance are the states that dominate Gaskell's considerations of what *is*; while what *might be* is structured around a relational ontology of sympathy and understanding.[11]

Cottonopolis: Manchester's Cityscape and Class Division

Mary Barton is explicitly anchored in Manchester. In comparison to some of her later texts that allude to Manchester, but are set in fictional places, notably *North and South* and *Cranford*, this novel specifically evokes this city as the setting for its unfolding class conflict.[12] This setting allows Gaskell to highlight the deep rifts between workers and masters, rich and poor, while at the same time presenting a somewhat sanitised version of the actual city of Manchester.

Friedrich Engels was among those who studied the city of Manchester and its architecture, and he did so specifically through the lens of class. An important aspect of the city that remains unelaborated in Gaskell's version is how the architecture itself contributes to class division. His seminal text *The Condition of the Working Class in England* (1845) was published around the time that Gaskell was writing her first novel and it includes his account of Manchester's cityscape. Journalistic in tone, he paints a picture of a class-divided city designed to inflame potential conflict. He describes Manchester as consisting of three circular-like zones, with minimal contact areas: the

[11] One might consider to what extent these ideas are influenced, directly or indirectly, by David Hume and Adam Smith; see David Hume, *A Treatise of Human Nature*, ed. by L. A. Selby-Bigge and P. H. Nidditch (Oxford: Clarendon Press, 1978; first publ. 1739–40), Book II, Part I, Section XI, pp. 316–18; Adam Smith, *The Theory of Moral Sentiments*, ed. by Ryan Patrick Hanley (London: Penguin Books, 2009).

[12] *North and South* is mainly set in the fictional Northern town of Milton, which resembles Manchester. Cranford takes place in the rural town of Cranford, a fictional depiction of Gaskell's native Knutsford. Cranford references a city called Drumble, which can be read as a fictional depiction of Manchester. See Borislav Knezevic, 'An Ethnography of the Provincial: The Social Geography of Gentility in Elizabeth Gaskell's Cranford', *Victorian Studies*, 41:3 (1998), 405–26.

commercial part, which forms the city's centre, is surrounded by working-class areas, which are themselves surrounded by middle-class districts.[13] To make their way to the commercial centre:

> the members of this money aristocracy can take the shortest road through the middle of all the labouring districts to their places of business, without ever seeing that they are in the midst of the grimy misery that lurks to the right and the left. For the thoroughfares leading from the Exchange in all directions out of the city are lined, on both sides, with an almost unbroken series of shops, and are so kept in the hands of the middle and lower bourgeoisie.[14]

The thoroughfares, lined with shops, connect the middle-class districts with the commercial centre of Manchester, while systematically concealing the poverty-ridden areas behind this sanitised façade. As a result, these thoroughfares allowed the middle class to travel in and out of the city centre while limiting the chance to come into contact with the misery and poverty that characterised the surrounding working-class areas. The structure of the city itself thus minimises contact zones between classes to such a degree that they can co-exist but live vastly different and predominantly separate lives. Engels maps class onto the city itself, thereby connecting the architecture of Manchester to wider socio-economic and sociopolitical struggles.[15] While the depiction by Engels is far from neutral and, more importantly, serves an ideological function in his politics, what can be gleaned from his descriptions is that class division is built into the very structure of Manchester itself.

This, then, is the context in which Gaskell composes *Mary Barton* and in which she sets her tale of class struggle. Referencing Manchester in an indirect and allusive way instead of setting her tale in a completely fictional geography registers a critique, however subtle, of middle-class complicity in working-class misery. Rather than acknowledging and revealing that poverty and wealth are produced by the same mechanisms and economic structures, for Gaskell, Manchester's middle class actively work to conceal the misery on whose shoulders their capital was built. Adopting a strategy of not-saying allows Gaskell to hint at rather than explicitly state this circumstance, which in turn obfuscates her critique. Yet while the first half of the novel builds on the idea of class separation introduced by its setting – focusing on what *is* with regard to the growing antagonism and violence between workers and masters – later sections of the text ambitiously, if still in a mediated manner, imagine what *might be* by introducing sympathy as a crucial component of master-worker relations.

13 Friedrich Engels, *The Condition of the Working Class in England*, ed. by Victor Kiernan (London: Penguin Classics, 2009), pp. 85–7.

14 Engels, *The Condition of the Working Class*, p. 86.

15 Tristram Hunt, 'Introduction', in Friedrich Engels, *The Condition of the Working Class in England*, ed. by Victor Kiernan (London: Penguin Classics, 2009), pp. 1–31, at p. 21.

Worlds Apart: Workers and Masters

In the first part of the novel, Gaskell is deeply engaged in working out the different living conditions and realities of employers and employees, as well as detailing the violent tensions upon which their relationship is based. Part of what Gaskell criticises about current class relations is that their relationship is riddled with violence and ignorance. Early chapters in *Mary Barton* primarily construct the relationship between workers and masters in terms of difference and division, while later chapters are organised around commonalities. For example, early in the novel, Gaskell discusses the 'differences between the employers and the employed,—an eternal subject for agitation in the manufacturing districts' (23). On the surface, the excerpts discussed below narrate how masters and workers experience an economic crisis differently, but embedded within them is a critique of the violence workers endure due to ignorance. Less obvious than physical violence, but nonetheless pervasive, ignorance denies the existential nature of the suffering of workers because it presents the suffering of workers and masters as different, but equal.

Embedded in a longer passage that narrates the reasons for the increasing political engagement of John Barton for the working class, as he joins a trade union and becomes a Chartist, and his growing antagonism towards mill owners, is a discussion of how class differences register in the experience of an economic crisis:

> At all times it is a bewildering thing to the poor weaver to see his employer removing from house to house, each one grander than the last, till he ends in building one more magnificent than all, or withdraws his money from the concern, or sells his mill, to buy an estate in the country, while all the time the weaver, who thinks he and his fellows are the real makers of this wealth, is struggling on for bread for his children, through the vicissitudes of lowered wages, short hours, fewer hands employed, &c. (Ibid.)

Even before crisis strikes, there is an enormous economic disparity between workers and masters that is further pronounced when trade is low. While initially, 'the poor weaver' seems to refer solely to John Barton, as the overall context of this excerpt is his increasing politicisation, ultimately, the episode also seems to function as a synecdoche of sorts. A specific scenario, or perhaps rather scenarios, is described, but this is not an incident that the reader can reliably identify as having happened to John Barton. Rather, through a process of abstraction and generalisation, the narrative simultaneously considers Barton's individual perspective and the more abstract position of the 'worker'. Oscillating between making a point about an individual and discussing an entire class, the narrative suggests that while workers struggle for mere necessities in periods of depression, masters seem to be unbothered, even thriving and able to upscale their housing. Drawing out divisions between classes, this is the first set in a series of comparative statements, hence, the passage continues:

> And when he knows trade is bad, and could understand (at least partially) that there are not buyers enough in the market to purchase the goods already made, and consequently that there is no demand for more; when he would bear and endure much without complaining, could he also see that his employers were bearing their share; he is, I say, bewildered and (to use his own word) 'aggravated' to see that all goes on just as usual with the mill-owners. Large houses are still occupied, while spinners' and weavers' cottages stand empty, because the families that once filled them are obliged to live in rooms or cellars. Carriages still roll along the streets, concerts are still crowded by subscribers, the shops for expensive luxuries still find daily customers, while the workman loiters away his unemployed time in watching these things, and thinking of the pale, uncomplaining wife at home, and the wailing children asking in vain for enough of food, — of the sinking health, of the dying life of those near and dear to him. The contrast is too great. Why should he alone suffer from bad time? I know that this is not really the case; and I know what is the truth in such matters: but what I wish to impress is what the workman feels and thinks. True, that with child-like improvidence, good times will often dissipate his grumbling, and make him forget all prudence and foresight. (23–4)

Presented in a neutral, matter-of-fact tone, the narrative teases apart how workers and masters are affected quite differently during economic crises. The juxtaposition makes clear that in one case, the crisis is of an existential nature, while in the other the effects appear negligible. While workers must cut back in all areas of life, lacking money to spend on absolute necessities, employers are still able to purchase non-essential goods, items and services. The opening of the excerpt seems written largely from the perspective of the worker in a third person narration. However, it is not quite as straightforward as that. There is a slip or a shift in voice discernible in the phrase 'when he would bear and endure much without complaining, could he also see that his employers were bearing their share' (24). While the first part appears as character focalisation, albeit an abstract version as workers at large are focalised, the second part clearly shifts focalisation to the narrator. Within the same sentence, the narration marks the presence of both character and narrator. The following sentence more clearly disentangles these voices: 'he is, I say, bewildered and (to use his own word) 'aggravated'(Ibid.). The interjection clearly signals the narrator's presence in contradistinction to the character, which produces a distancing effect. The bracketed comment further underlines their different positionalities as it introduces the idea of a sociolect that is different from middle-class speech. This is significant because the rest of the paragraph formulates a critique of what is by elaborating the effects of economic disparity from the perspective of the workers, from which Gaskell, by way of explicitly adopting a different positionality, seems to have distanced herself.

However, in the question raised herein – 'Why should he alone suffer from bad times?' – this distinction is not clear cut (Ibid.). Presented as free indirect discourse, the voices of the narrator and the character blend together and can no longer be neatly distinguished. This is a question with no clear origin or addressee, which aligns the narrator simultaneously with the position of the speaker and the audience. Through this oscillation, the critique that is being voiced no longer belongs just to the worker, because the narrator is also implicated. This shared positionality is made evident in that Gaskell adds a disclaimer: 'I know that this is not really the case; and I know what is the truth in such matters: but what I wish to impress is what the workman feels and thinks' (Ibid.). In a conciliatory tone, Gaskell once more distances herself from the worker's position and feigns alliance with a middle-class position by implying that whatever the workers feel and think does not correspond to 'the truth' to which both she and the audience of her utterance seemingly have access. Instead of elaborating, however, what is 'really the case' and deemed 'the truth', the narrator justifies her exploration of the unequal effects of an economic crisis as an instance of individualised perception – from the perspective of workers at large – rather than fact. There is a curious silence here that has itself a double meaning. On the one hand, 'the truth' is deemed so self-evident that it does not warrant further commentary. On the other hand, adopting this strategy of not-saying hides an implicit critique that cannot be addressed openly; namely, that although both classes endure a period of economic crisis, they do not suffer to an equal or even comparable degree, and ignoring this fact itself functions as a form of violence that denies the worker's reality.

The passage thus serves to humanise Barton and render him sympathetic to the reader, and to show the reader that becoming politically active in the worker's movement is a seemingly logical consequence of not only the growing misery of conditions in urban England, but also of the violence wrought by the masters of industrial relations. The masters, whom Gaskell criticises, fundamentally misrecognise the nature of the suffering of workers to the degree that positing their own suffering as equal seems not simply justifiable but *just*, even though their suffering occurs along very different trajectories. Herein lies the failure that Gaskell addresses: the masters fail to acknowledge and recognise how existing economic structures affect workers differently, and how the misery of the workers is in part shaped by fundamental ignorance.

Continued ignorance finally erupts in a physically violent form, off page, somewhere between the seventeenth and eighteenth chapters of the novel. This is where the two main narrative strands of the novel – the industrial and the courtship plots – collide: Harry Carson, the son of the mill-owner Mr Carson and Mary's potential suitor, is murdered by John Barton. After a failed meeting between workers and masters, where the former were ridiculed and ignored by the latter, the workers conceive a deadly plan to unite against and attack the masters. The murderer is appointed by draw and only revealed to the reader – and the other characters – much later in the text. The murder is afforded special narrative significance: it is not explicitly narrated yet it marks the turning point and crisis of the narrative, half-way through the novel.

In addition to stylistic emphasis, the novel presents the murder, in an under-elaborated way, as the climax to a master-worker relationship steeped in violence. Gaskell implies, rather than directly addresses, that the outbreak of physical violence is the result and the logical consequence of growing class divisions due to 'suffering without the sympathy of the happy' (5). Throughout the first half of *Mary Barton*, Gaskell has been working towards this climax. The murder is both a major narrative abruption *and* a major abruption in class relations: in its aftermath, master-worker relations can be revised and adjusted. The murder, therefore, is also where Gaskell moves from considering the violence that *is*, to imagining what *might be*, however imperfect. Rather than rejecting current economic structures, Gaskell's intervention can be located in introducing sympathy – a counter-force to violence – as a key element that can revise and adjust master-worker relations.

Breaking Cycles of Violence: Shifting towards Sympathy

The concept of sympathy, key to this novel, had already accumulated a complicated and complex history by the time Gaskell was writing. Victorian discussions of sympathy harken back to eighteenth-century philosophical debates.[16] Tracing the meanings of sympathy, Talia Schaffer argues that eighteenth-century ideas were not transferred to the Victorians in any straightforward way, but rather in processes reshaped by the Romantics. While 'in the eighteenth century … writers employed sympathy as a powerful rhetorical tool to move readers toward certain political actions', the Romantic period saw an 'inward turn' to feelings.[17] In other words, the strong political impetus to provide for those in need is complicated by a shift towards individual interiority and a concern with oneself. Rachel Ablow, for instance, writes that 'in the context of the nineteenth-century turn to institutional solutions to social problems, sympathy was increasingly

[16] For critical discussions of eighteenth-century engagements with sympathy, see, for example, Jeanne Britton, *Vicarious Narratives: A Literary History of Sympathy, 1750–1850* (Oxford: Oxford University Press, 2019); Rae Greiner, *Sympathetic Realism in Nineteenth-Century British Fiction* (Baltimore MD: Johns Hopkins University Press, 2013); Audrey Jaffe, *Scenes of Sympathy: Identity and Representation in Victorian Fiction* (Ithaca NY: Cornell University Press, 2000); Talia Schaffer, *Communities of Care: The Social Ethics of Victorian Fiction* (Princeton NJ and Oxford: Princeton University Press, 2021).

[17] Schaffer, *Communities of Care*, p. 120.

identified with the private sphere'.[18] Quoting Ablow, Schaffer adds that the sympathetic human can be thought of as 'an alternative' to the model of the self-interested economic agent.[19] Thus, during the nineteenth century, sympathy became increasingly relegated to the private sphere that, in turn, limited its presence in political economic discourse and the marketplace.[20]

The earlier conception of sympathy as a political tool, however, remains pertinent to *Mary Barton* in two distinct ways: first, in terms of the novel's reception by reviewers and second, for how it informs the characters' actions.[21] My primary concern in this chapter is the practice of sympathy the novel explores through its characters.[22] Here, the assumption is that the relational sympathy, by which individual characters develop capacity to perceive their roles and responsibilities, will lead to concrete actions undertaken to alleviate suffering. Uniting earlier eighteenth-century and newer nineteenth-century notions of sympathy, Gaskell insists that sympathy can be a powerful political tool to revise and adjust master-worker relations.

In *Mary Barton*, sympathy functions as a response to violence. Imagined as a way to alleviate violence, sympathy revises and adjusts what *is*, without dismantling or rejecting existing economic structures. Sympathy is invested in keeping the overall system in place while making life more liveable within it, and thus registers as a subtle form of intervention that is itself complicit in the current economic system. A crucial shift towards sympathy occurs during and in the aftermath of a conversation between John Barton and Mr Carson close to the end of the novel. With death looming over him, John Barton confesses to the murder to his fellow worker Job Legh and the

18 Rachel Ablow, *The Marriage of Minds: Reading Sympathy in the Victorian Marriage Plot* (Stanford CA: Stanford University Press, 2007), p. 3.

19 Schaffer, *Communities of Care*, p. 119.

20 For further consideration of the relationship between affect and political economy and the politicisation of sympathy, see the chapters of Catherine Packham and Sarah Dredge in this volume.

21 The idea that this novel provokes sympathy in the reader also featured in contemporary reviews. See also Charles Kingsley, untitled, *Fraser's Magazine*, April 1849, pp. 428–32, at p. 429. Sympathy for workers at large, as a reader's response to *Mary Barton*, need not necessarily result in the desire to minimise suffering, however. See John Forster, untitled, *Examiner*, 4 November 1848, pp. 708–9; Anonymous, untitled, *The Prospective Review*, 5:17 (January 1849), pp. 36–57. For a scholarly discussion of eliciting sympathy in readers see, for example, Mary-Catherine Harrison, 'How Narrative Relationships Overcome Empathic Bias: Elizabeth Gaskell's Empathy across Social Difference', *Poetics Today*, 32:2 (2011), 255–88.

22 For other readings of sympathy in *Mary Barton*, see, Eleanor Courtemanche, 'Inappropriate Sympathies in Gaskell and Eliot', in *The 'Invisible Hand' and British Fiction, 1818–1860: Adam Smith, Political Economy, and the Genre of Realism* (Basingstoke: Palgrave Macmillan, 2011), pp. 171–94, at pp. 176–86; Jennifer MacLure, 'Diagnosing Capitalism: Vital Economics and the Structure of Sympathy in Gaskell's Industrial Novels', *Nineteenth-Century Contexts*, 38:5 (2016), 343–52.

bereaved Mr Carson. After a brief exchange with Carson, Barton realises that they share the experience of losing a son. Parental bereavement enables Barton to develop sympathy for Carson, whom he now recognises as an individual rather than uniquely as a representative of his class: 'The eyes of John Barton grew dim with tears. Rich and poor, master and men, were then brothers in the deep suffering of the heart' (316). Gaskell's specific phrasing of 'master and men' anticipates the preface Engels later attached to the English edition of *The Condition of the Working Class in England*, in which he describes how:

> much against the spirit of Free Trade and unbridled competition, but quite as much in favour of the giant capitalist in his competition with his less favoured brother ... the larger the concern, and with it the number of hands, the greater the loss and inconvenience caused by every conflict between master and men; and thus a new spirit came over the masters, especially the large ones, which taught them to avoid unnecessary squabbles, to acquiesce in the existence and power of Trades' Unions, and finally even to discover in strikes – at opportune times – a powerful means to serve their own ends. The largest manufacturers, formerly the leaders of the war against the working-class, were now the foremost to preach peace and harmony.[23]

Gaskell provides an alternative method of arriving at peace and harmony, one that substitutes violent, organised, mass protest of 'many hands' to smaller and more intimate instances of sympathy. Gaskell employs the term 'brothers' to capture a shift in Barton and Carson's relationship. Placing specific emphasis on unity, 'brothers' carries a religious connotation while also recalling Adam Smith's conception of sympathy; at the same time, the synecdoche of Engels's 'hands of many' is here envisioned differently, relying instead on the newly intimate brothers of the master and worker standing in, metonymically, for a larger sympathetic capitalist brotherhood.[24]

In his discussion of sympathy in *The Theory of Moral Sentiments* (1759), Smith draws clear boundaries between self and other that sympathy – broadly defined as 'our fellow-feeling with any passion whatever' – is able to bridge.[25] Smith famously evokes the example of the tortured brother on the rack.[26] Arguing that another person's sensations cannot be accessed directly, and thus rely on mediation through imagination, Smith writes, the senses 'never did,

[23] Friedrich Engels, 'Preface to the English Edition' (1891), Friedrich Engels, *The Condition of the Working Class in England*, ed. by Victor Kiernan (London: Penguin Classics, 2009), pp. i– ii.

[24] Jeanne Britton provides an overview of how Smith departs from earlier thinkers of sympathy and his contemporaries alike. Britton, *Vicarious Narratives*, pp. 10–11.

[25] Ibid., p. 15.

[26] As both Schaffer and Greiner explain, Smith's notion of sympathy enjoyed continued circulation in wider Victorian culture throughout the century. Greiner, *Sympathetic Realism*, p. 11; Schaffer, *Communities of Care*, p. 120.

and never can, carry us beyond our own person, and it is by the imagination only that we can form any conception of what are his [the tortured brother's] sensations'.[27] Sympathising with another is a cognitive act through which one forms an idea of what someone else might feel, hence continuing his discussion of the tortured brother on the rack, Smith elaborates:

> It is the impressions of our own senses only, not those of his, which our imaginations copy. By the imagination we place ourselves in his situation, we conceive ourselves enduring all the same torments, we enter as it were into his body, and become in some measure the same person with him, and thence form some idea of his sensations, and even feel something which ... is not altogether unlike them.[28]

Through this process of abstraction, it is not the senses of the brother that are represented in the mind of the other person, but the other's idea of what the brother might experience or feel. What results is a cognitive rendering of the brother's pain that may bear resemblance to the sensations imagined by another person. Essentially cognitive in nature, sympathy 'designates a way for minds to conceive other people and situations and make judgements about their conditions'.[29] In order to 'place ourselves in his situation', however, a degree of familiarity is required, in Smith's case with the circumstances of the brother on the rack and in Gaskell's with the experience of losing a child.[30] At the same time, in this first moment, the burden of recognition is on Barton, the already disenfranchised party. Following his sympathetic turn towards Carson, Barton asks for forgiveness, which he is denied in the moment, as Carson leaves the house vengefully.

The passage continues by elaborating the crucial shift towards sympathy – necessary to revise master-worker relations – from Carson's perspective. Almost like a didactic exercise, it closely mirrors Barton's process of introspection and functions as its counterpart. While in Barton's case, it is the recognition of parental bereavement that evokes sympathy, in Carson's, it is a series of reflective steps that centres more explicitly around a biblical theme. On his way home, he witnesses a clash between a boy and a girl. The girl, who is physically hurt, pleads with her aggravated nurse: 'He did not mean to do it. *He did not know what he was doing*' (emphasis in original) (318). The words she utters, and that linger with Carson long after he leaves the scene, were also spoken by Barton just moments before, during his confession. More crucially, however, they remind Carson of a passage in

[27] Adam Smith, *The Theory of Moral Sentiments*, p. 13. For extended discussions of how Smith's conception of sympathy relates to the form and concerns of the novel see, for example, Britton, *Vicarious Narratives*; Greiner, *Sympathetic Realism*.

[28] Ibid, pp. 13–14.

[29] Greiner, *Sympathetic Realism*, p. 16.

[30] Smith, *The Theory of Moral Sentiments*, p. 13.

the Gospel that recalls the benevolence and sympathy of Christ. The narrative implies that this incident prompts Carson to adopt similar values, to extend understanding and sympathy towards others and help those in need. This process of reflection also makes it possible for Carson to sympathise with Barton and, in the grander scheme of the novel, it forms the basis for sympathy towards workers at large.

Revising and Adjusting: Sympathy as Practice

The novel's penultimate chapter further develops the idea of sympathy as a way of revising and adjusting class relations. The chapter begins with a conversation between Jem Wilson, Job Legh and Mr Carson, who seeks to understand why Barton killed his son. Taking place a couple of hours after Barton's death, their conversation quickly turns to the question at the heart of the entire novel: in other words, what should the relationship between workers and masters ideally be like. Job explains that Barton was not looking to abolish class distinctions, but sought to evoke sympathy for their plight and provoke measures that might be undertaken by the masters to alleviate suffering. During their conversation, Carson reacts defensively, having recourse to well-established political economic principles of *laissez-faire* trade, and of the rational and independent economic agent, absolving himself and masters at large from any responsibility for workers' well-being. Job insists, however, that what workers 'all feel sharpest is the want of inclination to try and help the evils which come like blights at times over the manufacturing places' (333). He continues:

> If we [the workers] saw the masters try for our sakes to find a remedy … even if they could find no help … we'd bear up like men through bad times. No one knows till they have tried, what power of bearing lies in them, if once they believe that men are caring for their sorrows and will help if they can. (333–4)

The problem then, as described by Job, is not the lack of power to influence fluctuations in trade, but the lack of willingness to care for and sympathise with the workers' plight. Echoing the phrase 'the agony of suffering without the sympathy of the happy' from the preface, he appeals to eighteenth-century conceptions of sympathy as a political tool to provide for those in need (5). For Smith, sympathy is largely cognitive; while Gaskell follows Smith, she also seems to place greater emphasis on physicality and presence, although, once more, this is hinted at rather than elaborated. Physically coming together, she seems to suggest, whether through face-to-face conversation or touch – such as when Carson embraces Barton on his deathbed – is important to eliciting sympathy (335).

This meaning is initially lost on Carson, but, as time passes, he eventually reconsiders his positions and adopts measures designed to revise and adjust the relationship between workers and masters:

> Mr. Carson was considered hard and cold by those who only casually saw him, or superficially knew him. But those who were admitted into his confidence were aware, that the wish that lay nearest to his heart was that none might suffer from the cause from which he had suffered; that a perfect understanding, and complete confidence and love, might exist between masters and men; that the truth might be recognised that the interests of one were the interest of all, and, as such, required the consideration and deliberation of all; that hence it was most desirable to have educated workers, capable of judging, not mere machines of ignorant men; and to have them bound to their employers by the ties of respect and affection, not by mere money bargains alone; in short, to acknowledge the Spirit of Christ as the regulating law between both parties.
>
> Many of the improvements now in practice in the system of employment in Manchester, owe their origin to short earnest sentences spoken by Mr. Carson. Many and many yet to be carried into execution, take their birth from that stern, thoughtful mind, which submitted to be taught by suffering. (Ibid.)

These two paragraphs conclude the industrial plot of the novel, with the final chapter narrating Jem and Mary's wedding and eventual emigration to Canada. Not part of the original manuscript submitted to the publisher, these paragraphs seem to synthesise most succinctly, if still vaguely, how Gaskell imagines what *might be* in conversation with what *is*. The first part of this passage imagines how previously violent relations can be revised as sympathetic. This, again, makes clear that Gaskell's critique is a moderate corrective: not interested in overturning the current economic system, but in revising and adjusting existing economic structures on a local level. Imagining how these may be transformed, however imperfectly, thus is a crucial element of her critique.

In *Mary Barton*, Gaskell suggests that part of what might be are master-worker relations that rely on dialogue and mutual sympathetic understanding across class, on adopting Christian values, and on unspecified 'improvements … in the system of employment' (335). It remains unclear what the relationship is between these three elements or, indeed, whether these should be thought of as separate developments. Largely formulated as a wish, the passage is oddly smooth and devoid of any real depth. In the grander scheme of the novel, this wish registers what might be, but it does so in a way that can be described as a utopian vision. It captures what Gaskell imagines as an ideal state of relations, in complete harmony, which is neither realisable in the now, nor the future. The wish, thus, functions as a guiding principle, as a direction to move towards, but that always lies just outside of reach. After all, as part of a utopian longing, complete harmony between workers and masters cannot be achieved. Gaskell adopts a strategy of not-saying to criticise what is by gesturing towards what might be in hopes and anticipation of a different future. Through a play of presence and absence, she under-elaborates and obscures her position.

The last two sentences of the passage above shift from the character of Carson to the focalisation of the narrator, with an additional jump in time, it seems. Whatever measures have been adopted, Gaskell appears to suggest, they have contributed to an improved, though not completely harmonious, relationship between workers and masters. It is unclear to the reader what the 'improvements' entailed and to what degree they did or did not create some form of sympathetic relations. Gaskell's refusal to specify what has changed has a dissatisfying effect.[31] The adopted measures are collated imprecisely through the use of the quantifier 'many', which at the same time deliberately obscures individual improvements through imprecision. These two sentences and, indeed, the entire passage suggest that imagining what *might be* in any concrete form, ultimately, lies beyond the imagination of the novel.

Conclusion

> 'I know nothing of political economy.'
>
> 'Preface', *Mary Barton*, p. 6

In *Mary Barton*, Gaskell criticises the violence and ignorance that characterise master-worker relations in 1840s Manchester. Nodding to and locating a degree of confirmation in the developments on the continent, Gaskell deems it necessary to revise and adjust these relations, not least perhaps to prevent more radical or revolutionary interventions. Her text registers a subtle form of critique that does not reject existing economic structures and in doing so, she proves complicit in current economic structures, while her intervention at the same time provides a corrective to what is, however imperfect. Indeed, one must bear in mind that, as a beneficiary of the current capitalist system, Gaskell or, indeed, her characters of Carson and the other masters in the novel, are perhaps unlikely to have an interest in radically re-imagining either the economic system at large, or master-worker relationships in specific. Yet in reading Gaskell's own reflections in her private letters on the reception of her novel, she is clearly most concerned with the vigorous responses to her ideas. Consequently, she strategically employs tactics like under-elaboration to conceal and obscure her interventions. This creates a paradoxical effect: her critique is both present and absent, requiring

[31] In this, there are clear similarities with *The Woman of Colour* (1808), published forty years earlier, as discussed in Emma Newport's chapter in this volume.

the reader to actively engage with the text while simultaneously shielding her from direct censure through the plausible deniability afforded by the fictional form.

Such prevarication is also apparent in the preface, where she adds the early disclaimer in which she overtly renounces any responsibility for the criticism that might be detected within the pages of her novel: 'I know nothing of Political Economy, or the theories of trade … If my accounts agree or clash with any system, the agreement or disagreement is unintentional' (6). The inclusion of such a disclaimer becomes a public demonstration of her awareness that her tale has the potential to offend expressed in her private letters, even as she pretends to conceal her familiarity with theories of political economy. Adopting a strategy of not-saying means that she can deny the knowledge that she clearly had as an investor, and thereby she can open up a creative gap in which to explore political and economic conditions that were seemingly outside of her purview.[32] In other words, the gap between what she does do and say, and what she claims not to be doing, is what allows her to articulate her position on the rights of workers and on political economy, however veiled or indirect. In terms of master-worker relationships, *Mary Barton* imagines what *might be* – building bridges between classes – which is in conversation with what *is*: violence and ignorance between classes. In the narrative of this novel, failed class relations do not serve as an insurmountable ontological rift but rather function as a catalyst for societal transformation. Sympathy becomes an agent of progress, and the connective tissue between the current state of being and the potential for a new ontological order.

[32] Henry has written about Gaskell as an investor and how her financial and economic knowledge was represented in her fiction. See Nancy Henry, 'Elizabeth Gaskell: Investment Cultures and Global Contexts', in *Women, Literature and Finance in Victorian Britain*, pp. 85–137.

8

White Hands, Brown Hands and the 'Invisible Hand': The Economy of 'Active Sympathy' in *The Wonderful Adventures of Mrs Seacole in Many Lands* (1857)

SARAH DREDGE

The 'hand' is a very busy term in discussions of nineteenth-century labour and markets, as well as the cultural forms that represent them. It features as a key symbol of the beneficial operation of the economy as an 'invisible hand' in the work of Adam Smith, and in nineteenth-century parlance, 'hands' synecdochally stand in for the workers who perform the labour and make capitalists their money; workers' selfhood is reduced to a cog in the machinery. When Pip's sister in *Great Expectations* (1860–1) insists that she has raised Pip 'by hand', she means the opposite to this, that she has raised him personally and with care – ironically, because, of course, she has not.[1] Peter J. Capuano and Sue Zemka note that 'Victorian writings are saturated with references to hands'.[2] This prevalence signals the cultural significance in this period concerning *whose* hands did *what*. In class terms, the ideological division between 'manual' labour and intellectual or professional work increases in the mid-nineteenth century: this is often represented in Victorian fiction by reading characters' hands. Turning to *Great Expectations* again, young Pip learns to be ashamed of his status as an apprentice

1 Charles Dickens, *Great Expectations*, ed. by Angus Calder (London: Penguin Books, 1985), p. 39.

2 Peter J. Capuano and Sue Zemka, 'Introduction', in *Victorian Hands: The Manual Turn in Nineteenth-Century Body Studies, ed. by* Peter J. Capuano and Sue Zemka (Columbus OH: Ohio State University Press, 2020), p. 3.

blacksmith when Estella observes to Miss Haversham, 'What coarse hands he has!'[3] Pip's mode of work and hence social identity is visible in his hands. In a gendered sense, which also relies on class assumptions, there is a central distinction around whether the work that women's hands do is paid or unpaid. Dominant gender ideology presented that middle-class women's work had to be seen to be done for love, service or charity, and not for pay, even though this 'unpaid' work had financial consequences. Women's hands must not be idle, but if they acted for personal remuneration, then it changed the nature of both the work and the woman. As the title character Aurora Leigh notes in Elizabeth Barrett Browning's novel poem, published in 1856, 'the works of women are symbolical': they symbolised *not* working remuneratively. The whole passage makes more evident the non-economic, non-functional value of middle-class women's work, which in turn makes them dependent on men:

> We sew, sew, prick our fingers, dull our sight,
> Producing what? A pair of slippers, sir,
> To put on when you're weary—or a stool
> To stumble over and vex you … 'curse that stool!'
> Or else at best, a cushion, where you lean
> And sleep, and dream of something we are not,
> But would be for your sake. Alas, alas!
> This hurts most, this … that, after all, we are paid
> The worth of our work, perhaps.[4]

Leisured women doing decorative embroidery – or tending to sick relatives or giving charity to needy parishioners – signalled their 'non-productive' status.[5]

The hand is an important recurring reference in Mary Seacole's *Wonderful Adventures of Mrs Seacole in Many Lands* (1857), in ways that mirror these contrasting associations – between hands that physically work and metaphorical hands that govern, between profit-seeking hands and helping hands, between manual labour and the invisible symbolic work done by hands that conspicuously do *not* manually labour, between the white hands of the British and Americans Seacole encounters, and her own 'brown' working hands.[6] Seacole often only notes her own skin colour in terms of others' responses and then variously terms her skin as 'dusky', 'brown' (often qualified, 'a little more brown', 'a few shades deeper brown', quoting *Punch*'s 'berry brown' in their poem 'A Stir for Seacole'), 'yellow' ('black' is always other people), but comparisons between hands are often implicitly racialised in the narrative even where no colour is stated. In her biography of

3 Dickens, *Great Expectations*, p. 90.

4 Elizabeth Barrett Browning, *Aurora Leigh*, ed. by Kerry McSweeney (Oxford: Oxford University Press, 1993), Book 1, lines 457–65.

5 Barrett Browning, *Aurora Leigh*, Book 1, line 456.

6 Hereafter, given as *Wonderful Adventures*.

Mary Seacole, Helen Rappaport discusses how Seacole refers to her colour and ethnicity in *Wonderful Adventures*, noting that Seacole 'clearly sought to downplay her "blackness"—for obvious reasons of acceptance'.[7] Racial meanings are coded even when Seacole does not refer to her own skin tone.

Capuano and Zemka argue that, since the nineteenth century, 'hands wield a figurative influence so pervasive that it is actually difficult to recognise' – 'hands' have become so figuratively familiar that we no longer see them *as* literal hands.[8] In the way of the 'material turn' in nineteenth-century studies, Capuano and Zemka usefully remind us to pay attention to physical hands rather than treating the body – and thus hands – primarily 'as a linguistic and discursive construction'.[9] It is also easy to forget when we use terms like 'manipulation' or 'manual' that we are referring to hands, and that phrases such as 'open-handed', 'on the one hand …', 'sleight of hand', having something 'in hand', and so on, have – or once had – physical referents; a difficulty of writing *about* hands, is that 'hand' terms seem suddenly to be everywhere, and can no longer be used familiarly without drawing attention to themselves.

I want to follow Capuano and Zemka's reminder not to take actual hands for granted in my reading of hands in Seacole's *Wonderful Adventures*, but it is important also to see the ideological uses that these hands are put to, and to stay aware of how the figurative paradigms of 'hands' affect how the actions and appearance of physical hands could be understood. Tracing how hands, both figurative and material, signify in Seacole's narrative helps us understand the challenge that her work in the Crimea offered to the sometimes-hidden British ideological expectations. These are norms and investments of which we can still feel the effects today, when debates recur over who was the better Crimean nurse, in a needless competition between Mary Seacole and Florence Nightingale.

My chapter looks at how Seacole's references to hands make meaning in her text via nineteenth-century critical paradigms about 'hands', drawing attention to the challenge her presence and narrative offered, and apparently still offer, to gendered and racialised ideals of both economic agency and social care. For Seacole, hands are often a sign of *doing*: her hands are busy, skilled, active, and in many cases contrasted with hands that are still, or absent, and white. The very presence of a Jamaican woman of colour nursing, tending and catering to British soldiers exposed racial and gendered expectations of caring and providing when Seacole answered the call for 'daughters of England' to go to Crimea, and this is often registered by Seacole and others with references to hands, white and otherwise. The

7 Helen Rappaport, *In Search of Mary Seacole: The Making of a Black Cultural Icon and Humanitarian* (New York: Pegasus Books, 2022), p. 28.

8 Capuano and Zemka, *Victorian Hands*, pp. 3–4.

9 Ibid., p. 1.

inadvertent rivalry between Seacole and Florence Nightingale further exposed this idealising of caring both in the context of the Crimean War, and still today in comparisons of Seacole and Nightingale that flare up and reveal racial investments. For example, in a modern assessment of their comparative contributions to nursing, Lynn McDonald concludes that:

> During the Crimean War, she was not nursing, but providing food and drink, for profit, to officers. For the ordinary soldiers, there was a "canteen," but her services were unspecified (Seacole p. 114). She announced, on printed cards, the intention of starting a "mess table and comfortable quarters for sick and convalescent officers" (p. 81), but she did not do this. She proceeded instead, on the advice of chef Alexis Soyer, to furnish food and drink. (Soyer 1857, p. 233)[10]

Similarly, but with much greater hostility that is clearly and aggressively racialised, the legacy of Mary Seacole has been called into question by the historian and journalist, Guy Walters, who wrote in response to proposed changes to the then National Curriculum in British schools that:

> despite its high prices, her "hotel" (more a glorified hut) was a popular place to eat, drink … and drink some more … The idea that a single woman working alone and away from a hospital could have done anything to combat an illness as deadly as cholera is far-fetched in the extreme.[11]

As such, the hands that act to provide care are still very much in the public eye, and the 'invisible hands' that direct systems remain far from the front lines, whether of battle or ideological debate.

In a key scene in her narrative, Seacole describes meeting Florence Nightingale in the field hospital at Scutari. Seacole contrasts Nightingale's 'white hand' supporting her 'pale' 'observant' face (82), with her own uninvited and (she implies) unwelcome hands that have been replacing bandages as she awaited her audience with Nightingale. Seacole comments that 'At some slight risk of giving offence, I cannot resist the temptation of lending a helping hand here and there' (80). Seacole's text is full of such comparisons between her own busy, skilled hands in the Crimea, fulfilling her need to offer what she terms 'active sympathy' (70), and the absent or inactive hands of others for whom she stands in, which are clearly coded as white: the

[10] Lynn McDonald, 'Florence Nightingale and Mary Seacole on Nursing and Health Care', *Journal of Advanced Nursing*, 70:6 (2014), 1436–45. https://doi.org/10.1111/jan.12291.

[11] 'The black Florence Nightingale and the making of a PC myth', in the *Mail Online* (Guy Walters, 31 December 2012). He was also quoted in an article in the *Independent* in 2013 stating 'There is no doubt that, had she been white, we would not be talking about her today and I think it is disingenuous to claim otherwise'. www.independent.co.uk/news/uk/politics/coalition-set-to-clash-over-removal-of-greatest-black-briton-mary-seacole-from-national-curriculum-8471631.html (accessed 1 October 2024).

Nightingale nurses based far from the front lines, the mothers and wives in Britain whose sons and husbands she tends to and feeds, the admiral standing and observing, 'his hands behind his back' (89) while injured men are tended by Seacole on the wharf at Balaclava.

Wonderful Adventures was written for a British readership after the end of the Crimean war. It was written to capitalise on a market for eye-witness accounts of the glories and disasters of the war, and to make Seacole much-needed money after her return from the Crimea when she was declared bankrupt. But her narrative also seems driven by a need to prove – in spite of being rejected by the War Office and by Florence Nightingale – that she had been, as she says, 'the right woman in the right place' (71). Her 'experienced hands' (169) and 'practised fingers' (87) became a powerful image, both literal and figurative, of her contribution and value to the British war effort.

On Mary Seacole

To give the necessary context on her life as she represents it in *Wonderful Adventures*, Mary Seacole was a Jamaican British woman, born Mary Grant, most likely illegitimate, to a Creole woman and a Scottish soldier, probably in 1805.[12] She is (and was) most famous for the Crimean part of her book, which was the point of its publication, but the story she tells is designed to show how her life's experiences up to that time formed her to become the 'Crimean *heroine*!' that the British forces so clearly needed (71).

In *Wonderful Adventures*, Seacole credits her aptitude for medicine to her mother, who she identifies as a skilled 'doctress' (12), and who frequently treated soldiers from the nearby military camp. But Seacole also notes that her mother ran a boarding house, and the figure of the female Jamaican boarding-house keeper had a specific racial and sexual connotation, as Paulette A. Kerr describes:

> Many lodging-house keepers were established by their white lovers and their businesses maintained by the support of white men who also formed the bulk of their clientele and for whom they provided sexual favours among other services. Most of these women were bound in informal liaisons or concubinage with white men.[13]

This association appears to follow Seacole, influencing attitudes of some towards her and her establishments. Florence Nightingale, in a private letter

[12] After extensive research Helen Rappaport claims that her exact birth date cannot be verified. *In Search of Mary Seacole*, p. 22.

[13] Paulette A. Kerr, 'Victims or Strategists? Female Lodging-House Keepers in Jamaica', in *Engendering History*, ed. by V. Shepherd, B. Brereton and B. Bailey (New York: St Martin's Press, 1995), p. 198.

after the Crimean war, suggests that Seacole's Crimean 'British Hotel' was some sort of house of ill-repute. She says, 'I will not call it a "bad house" but something very much like it'.[14] So despite Seacole's experience, proven hardihood and expertise, cultural associations of sexuality, class and racial difference made her the last person Nightingale wanted in or near her troop of respectable, middle-class and lady volunteers.

Seacole described visiting Britain twice as a young woman for business purposes, and she experienced racialised treatment on the streets of London that she projects onto her companion alone, saying 'I am only a little brown—a few shades duskier than the brunettes who you all admire so much, but my companion was very dark, and a fair (if I can apply the term to her) subject for their rude wit' (13). Her presentation of this story is indicative of her attitude to British racism, in which she largely ignores systemic issues of race and instead asserts her own limited difference from a white 'British' norm. She married back in Jamaica but was soon widowed. Her courtship, marriage and widowhood are covered in a single paragraph: her personal relationships are unimportant compared to the intervention she was making in the professionalisation of nursing. As an independent woman again after the death of her husband, her 'adventures' subsequently took her to Haiti, Cuba and to Panama, and repeatedly back to Jamaica; in each place, her labours involve both providing, through selling and cooking and doctoring. The manual references that Seacole makes about her time in Panama are telling, as several uses concern white Americans and their treatment of enslaved peoples. Seacole is very capable of her own colourism, which is richly evidenced in *Wonderful Adventures* in the terms she sometimes uses of Black people, and in her racialised judgements on people from almost every country that she encounters. However, the system of chattel slavery still in place in America, and influencing American behaviours in Panama, fuels her hatred towards the white Americans that she encounters. A couple of references to hands are nicely illustrative of this attitude as she disparagingly describes serving white Americans in her 'British Hotel' at Cruces, Panama: 'It was no use giving them carving-knives and forks, for very often they laid their own down to insert a dirty hairy hand into a full dish' (41). Soon after, she describes an incident where the citizens of the town (now Gorgona) broke into a house of a 'vicious' slave-owning young American woman due to terrible cries coming from within, and 'found the chattel bound hand and foot, naked, and being severely lashed' (52). The words 'bound hand and foot' are here both a literal description, and a familiar phrase for the inhumane treatment of others that slavery represents; similarly, she uses the phrase 'an American's uplifted hand' (41) to connote

14 Florence Nightingale, letter to Sir Harry Verney, quoted in Leila Salah, *The Impossibility of Aid: Governing Development in an Age of Emergency* (London: Duke University Press, 2016), p. 180.

slave-owning control in America. The greedy grasping hand, the 'uplifted hand', and the binding of others 'hand and foot' are presented as part of the same uncivilised 'American manners' (49; 68).

To Crimea

In 1854, Seacole heard the appeal for women to go as nurses to the Crimea issued by W. H. Russell, war correspondent for *The Times*, who was witnessing the terrible conditions and death toll experienced by wounded British forces: 'Are there no devoted women amongst us, able and willing to go forth to minister to the sick and suffering soldiers of the East in the hospitals of Scutari? Are none of the daughters of England, at this extreme hour of need, ready for such a work of mercy?'[15] The terms in which Russell makes this plea do not present the help needed as a job opportunity or a business proposition: the terms are explicitly gendered and clearly coded in terms of contemporary domestic ideology. Women are not asked to work but to 'minister'; they are not required to display skill but 'devotion'; they are not demanded as professionals but as 'daughters'. Seacole felt personally called by this plea that, to her, seemed tailored to her skills and experience. She expresses this feeling in a manual allusion, saying she 'longed more than ever to carry my busy (and the reader will not hesitate to add experienced) fingers where the sword or bullet had been busiest, and pestilence most rife' (70). Though Russell becomes her great supporter, it is soon apparent that others do not think this appeal was meant for her. As a non-white, self-supporting businesswoman and Jamaican 'doctress', Seacole is not permitted to embody the role of the 'ministering angel' of domestic ideology represented by Florence Nightingale in the war reports that fixed Nightingale's image. Nightingale also took among her nurses some working-class women with extensive experience, though she privileged her middle-class nurses' moral influence over the working women's previous experience; that Seacole still was not deemed suitable supports her assumption that her skin colour was the deciding factor.[16] Seacole's failure to meet the domestic ideal of the implicitly white angel of the home meant that she was rejected.

Seacole is very careful where possible *not* to attribute racist treatment of herself to the British (often seeming to use Americans as surrogates), but in the end, when Seacole is rejected by Elizabeth Herbert on behalf of Florence Nightingale, she cannot see any other reason for being refused: 'Doubts and suspicions arose in my heart for the first and last time, thank Heaven. Was it possible that American prejudices against colour had some root here?' (73).

[15] W. H. Russell, 'The War in the East', *The Times*, 15 September 1854, p. 5.

[16] Anne Summers, 'Pride and Prejudice: Ladies and Nurses in the Crimean War', *History Workshop Journal*, 16:1 (1983), 36.

It is in response to this final rebuff that Seacole decides to go to Crimea 'in my own way' – not ministering in a hospital but running a 'hotel for invalids' (74). While aiming to perform much the same set of services, she swaps care for hospitality. The invisible hand of race and class ideology insists that while independent Jamaican business-woman Mary Seacole, born of a British father and a Creole mother, could be a sutler, boarding-house keeper, '*vivandière*', proprietress of a 'bad house', provisioner and cook, she was not the 'daughter of England' that England expected to minister to its suffering heroes.

In spite of Seacole's attempt to make racism an American problem, it is clear that the work of her hands is always understood in racial terms, sometimes by herself, generally by others. *Punch* published illustrations of both Seacole and Nightingale at the bedside of injured soldiers. Both images are designed to celebrate the woman that they represent and, in each case, the patient reaches out pitifully to touch the attending woman's hand; but whereas the Nightingale figure is tending to the soldier, holding food and reaching to him with what looks like a cloth, the Seacole figure stands upright, clutching copies of *Punch*, holding one up as if to show her wares.[17] It is captioned 'Our Own Vivandière', meaning sutler, provisioner: Nightingale tends, Seacole sells.

Critical 'Hands': The 'Invisible Hand'

The key figurative paradigm of the hand that is crucial for this volume, Adam Smith's 'invisible hand' of the market, imagines an invisible hand that operates the macro-workings of the marketplace outside of the agency of individual workers or authorities. Smith means the abstract individual by 'he' and 'man', but, as I discuss, his model of normal, even natural, behaviours reflects ideologically gendered 'male' actions and signification. While an individual makes choices for himself, the market is the agent that has prompted them, taking the ultimate decision-making power out of his hands:

> He [every individual] intends only his own gain; and he is in this, as in many other cases, led by an invisible hand to promote an end which was no part of his intention. Nor is it always the worse for the society that it was no part of it. By pursuing his own interest, he frequently promotes that of the society more effectually than when he really intends to promote it.[18]

[17] *Punch*, 'Our Own Vivianière' (30 May 1859).

[18] Adam Smith, *An Inquiry into the Nature and Causes of the Wealth of Nations*, ed. by Kathryn Sutherland (Oxford: Oxford University Press, 1998), p. 292.

In this image of a hand as disembodied power, Smith disregards personal agency and the willed actions of specific hands towards ultimate social good; he thereby makes current power-relations natural and hence unchangeable. The hand that cannot be seen is still directing what counts as a social 'interest', and what he elsewhere terms 'benevolence', is put beyond question by individuals.[19] Whether we interpret this as providence, dominant ideology, or some mystical agency of the market itself, the significance, value and interpretation of the work done by individuals *as* individuals is put out of political agency. Local decisions and intentions of economic subjects are predicated within a set idea of human nature, and pre-woven into a macro pattern of social organisation. Smith refers to a 'propensity in human nature' to 'truck, barter and exchange', which is not 'the effect of any human wisdom'. He states that this propensity 'is common to all men', placing it beyond question.[20]

Smith is aware of female workers within his marketplace, but his model of the worker follows the male ideological model. In terms of the domestic ideology that developed alongside political economy as co-dependent ways of understanding society, while men were self-interested, even if that 'self' encompassed family interest, women were idealised as selfless. I do have to emphasise that this is *ideology*, and that while such idealisations influenced actions and how they were understood, it did not *preclude* women working, or women working self-interestedly for their own gain, or to support a family. But it was a society that idealised female caring and self-sacrifice rather than profit-seeking or professional ambition that recruited nurses by asking for 'daughters' to 'minister'. Ideology does not always determine what can happen, as Mary Seacole proved by taking herself to the Crimean battlefield, but it can shape how that is seen, how it must be presented, on what terms it can be applauded, rewarded, recorded. Seacole makes clear that her hands are trained, expert and well worth her fee, but she nevertheless most often describes her actions via the domestic ideology that the British norm did not see her fitting, in order to combat the racial understandings that would see her as a sexualised boarding-house keeper, whose 'kindness' (the word of Florence Nightingale, quoted below) had a price. She calls herself 'Mother Seacole', relates numerous instances of giving away her service or stocks freely, takes pains to emphasise the 'unselfishness' of her motives to render 'service' to soldiers abroad (73). She even makes a virtue out of going bankrupt rather than profiting in the service of the war. In the 'Conclusion' to *Wonderful Adventures*, Seacole declares:

> I returned bankrupt in fortune. Whereas others in my position may have come back to England rich and prosperous, I found myself poor—beggared.

[19] Ibid., p. 22.

[20] Smith, *Wealth of Nations*, p. 21.

> So few words can tell what I have lost. But what have I gained? I should need a volume to describe that fairly… For wherever I go I am sure to meet some smiling face; every step I take in the crowded London streets may bring me in contact with some friend. (170)

Here, Seacole's ministrations in Crimea are framed as sacrifice in service of duty, esteem, and sympathy, and one in which the cultivation of friendship substitutes profit-seeking. The notion of a friend is not necessarily, in this context, straightforwardly about intimacy or friendliness, but encapsulates the social and economic dimension bound in familiarity, trust, reputation and social capital.[21]

In my present argument, I want to apply Smith's term 'invisible hand' in a wider context than his conception of the workings of the disembodied market, to refer to how the power to be invisible is what marks out dominant ideology. In this version of Smith's operating hand, the pre-determining factors are cultural norms that guide actions and decide what counts as 'public interest', 'gain', 'value'.[22] In this light, Mary Seacole's non-white hands are never invisible: she needs to keep emphasising what she *wants* her readers to see that her hands are doing – nursing, providing – to combat the way that dominant ideology interprets her actions, as a Jamaican woman of colour. But sticking closer to Smith's intended usage, including caring for others as part of the economic system of society also presents ideological difficulties, which we see in *Wealth of Nations*. For Smith, self-interest *stands in for* care, what he calls 'friendship' and 'benevolence', in a society grown too big for ties of affection to motivate others to give the 'co-operation and assistance' that everyone needs from others.[23] Smith lists workers in society (his examples are all makers), and he distances their acts from personal caring for others: 'It is not from the benevolence of the butcher, the brewer, or the baker that we expect our dinner, but from their regard to their own interest.'[24] He thus makes it harder to account for the non-economic care work expected of women; in fact, the image he uses for the desire to be simply *given* something outside of an exchange is of a dog, begging. When 'men' attempt this, he uses the terms 'servile and fawning'.[25] When Seacole is denied the chance to go to the Crimea as a ministering angel and goes instead as a businesswoman, she inadvertently exposes the rhetorical 'sleight

21 For further discussion of friendship of this nature, see Gary B. Magee and Andrew S. Thompson, *Empire and Globalisation: Networks of People, Goods and Capital in the British World, c. 1850–1914* (Cambridge: Cambridge University Press, 2010).

22 Smith, *Wealth of Nations*, p. 291.

23 Ibid., p. 22.

24 Ibid.

25 Ibid.

of hand' by which domestic ideology masks the material and economic transactions behind ideals of patriotism, service and care.

Having been turned down as a Nightingale nurse, Seacole needs to argue that she was right to go to the Crimea anyway on the grounds of professional expertise. She is going in the same way that Adam Smith's assumed economic agent ('man') would go, as she had a set of skills that were in demand in that market at that time. But this also presented her with problems: being very visibly *not* Smith's assumed agent, Seacole is susceptible to judgements based upon her racial and gendered difference from this norm. On the first page of her narrative, she declares 'I have often heard the term "lazy Creole" applied to my country people; but I am sure I do not know what it is to be indolent' (11); the admiral she meets on first landing at Balaclava grumbles about 'a parcel of women coming out to a place where they were not wanted' (87). Women around army camps, if they were not wives and daughters, were associated in various ways with hanging on or profiting from the servicemen: with boarding-house hostesses, sutlers, camp-followers or mistresses. So, while Seacole draws attention to her energy and skill, she is still susceptible to racial and sexual interpretations, and so she falls back on domestic ideology, and calls herself 'Mother Seacole' to de-sexualise her relations with British forces. As she is not the subject expected by the invisible hand of the market *or* the ministry of domestic ideology, she is forced to continually manipulate one discourse against the other. Such ambiguities frequently layer a story of selfless ministry over a different possible narrative of self-reliant adventure, or vice versa. This is apparent in Seacole's description of her first arrival point in Balaclava. I am going to give a long quotation from this episode, as it offers several examples where Seacole references hands in ways that show her negotiating gender, racial and economic discourses.

Selling and Ministering at the Balaclava 'Sick Wharf'

Seacole opens this episode presenting the business side of her endeavours, before turning to professional nursing, which then becomes ministering:

> I remained six weeks in Balaclava, spending my days on shore, and my nights on board ship. Over our stores, stacked on the shore, a few sheets of rough tarpaulin were suspended; and beneath these—my sole protection against the Crimean rain and wind—I spent some portion of each day, receiving visitors and selling stores.
>
> But my chief occupation, and one with which I never allowed any business to interfere, was helping the doctors to transfer the sick and wounded from the mules and ambulances into the transports that had to carry them to the hospitals of Scutari and Buyukdere. I did not forget the main object of my journey, to which I would have devoted myself exclusively had I been allowed; and very familiar did I become before long with the sick wharf of Balaclava.

> My acquaintance with it began very shortly after I had reached Balaclava. The very first day that I approached the wharf, a party of sick and wounded had just arrived. Here was work for me, I felt sure. With so many patients, the doctors must be glad of all the hands they could get. Indeed, so strong was the old impulse within me, that I waited for no permission, but seeing a poor artilleryman stretched upon a pallet, groaning heavily, I ran up to him at once, and eased the stiff dressings. Lightly my practised fingers ran over the familiar work, and well was I rewarded when the poor fellow's groans subsided into a restless uneasy mutter. God help him! He had been hit in the forehead, and I think his sight was gone. I stooped down, and raised some tea to his baked lips (here and there upon the wharf were rows of little pannikins containing this beverage). Then his hand touched mine, and rested there, and I heard him mutter indistinctly, as though the discovery had arrested his wandering senses—
>
> "Ha! this is surely a woman's hand."
>
> I couldn't say much, but I tried to whisper something about hope and trust in God; but all the while I think his thoughts were running on this strange discovery. Perhaps I had brought to his poor mind memories of his home, and the loving ones there, who would ask no greater favour than the privilege of helping him thus; for he continued to hold my hand in his feeble grasp, and whisper "God bless you, *woman*—whoever you are, God bless you!"— over and over again. (87–8)

Combining visits and selling, Seacole initially here seems to exhibit the social relations as mutual exchange assumed by Smith. She has previously contacted what she calls 'friends', military personnel she had known in Jamaica, she says to 'solicit their aid' (86), but this manifests itself materially in her 'selling'. Her business cards had identified herself and her business in these terms, as given in *The Wonderful Adventures*:

> BRITISH HOTEL.
> Mrs. Mary Seacole
> (*Late of Kingston, Jamaica*),
> Respectfully announces to her former kind friends, and to the Officers of the Army and Navy generally, that she has taken her passage in the screw-steamer "Hollander," to start from London on the 25th of January, intending on her arrival at Balaclava to establish a mess table and comfortable quarters for sick and convalescent officers. (74)

She is then very pointed, however, in making clear that her chief purpose on that wharf was nursing, distinguishing this as her 'occupation' from any other work as 'business'; and she distances her work looking after the sick and wounded from remunerative work by the reminder that she had wanted to go to Crimea *only* to nurse. The word she now uses is 'devoted'. She even recasts the wharf itself, calling it here the 'sick wharf' when just before this, she had been explaining her difficulties in getting her stock landed there, presenting it as an economic space (86). In talking about making 'acquaintance' with the wharf, she places it in personal relation to herself, as she does with the admiral in charge: she reminds him that she had known his son in the West Indies when he complained at her female presence in this place of manly endeavour (87). She then claims this reconfigured space and occupation for herself when the wounded arrive, declaring it to be 'work for me' (88).

Successive references to hands follow, used in different ways. First, with 'all the hands they could get' there is the suggestion of the industrial sense of 'hands' – an unindividuated factory worker – but the term is also literal, as she goes on to describe, giving plenty of detail about what her hands in particular could do: they are skilled hands, with 'practised fingers' (ibid.). The last use is also both figurative and literal when the injured artillery man touches Seacole's hand and responds that it is a 'woman's hand' (ibid.). He is at once identifying a woman's hand as a material entity that is providing him a service, and also calling up a figurative concept of 'a woman's hand' as caring and ministering. It only adds to this that in Seacole's account, she is lifting tea to his lips. She emphasises this affective and spiritual register by speaking to him of God, reenforcing the idea of her care as 'ministry', and it is in this context that she takes on the persona of 'Mother' Seacole, standing in for the female hands that remain far away in his home. It is important to note that this aspect of the encounter is Seacole's extrapolation – the scene is modified by 'I think' and 'perhaps': she is presenting this vignette in a very particular way that starts with a marketplace, turns into a 'sick wharf', and ends in an imagined home. So Seacole's hands in this passage are at once working, nursing, comforting and substituting for female loved ones; her handiwork is both professional and domestic, as well as material and spiritual.

It is surely also significant that Seacole notes that this artillery man has been blinded: her hands are literally invisible. Touch is the sense with which he relates to her, via their hands, and in this context, she can embody the implicitly white female ideal of the ministering angel. This scene is almost repeated later in the same chapter: a gravely injured man mistakes Seacole for his wife, and Seacole comments, 'I think the fancy happily caused by a woman's hand soothed his dying hour' (89). In these two episodes, she demonstrates her intrepidity, her skills and her mothering, showing that she was, in spite of every effort to insist otherwise, 'the right woman in the right place' (71). These words come from a poem in *Punch*: '… be the right man in the right place who can—The right woman was Dame Seacole'; Seacole uses versions of this phrase several times in her narrative.[26] One last 'hand' reference from this scene on the wharf is presented by the admiral: he 'stood silently by, his hands behind his back, watching the sick being lifted into the boats' (89). In a section where Seacole shows us her hands being so

[26] 'A Stir for Seacole', Punch, 6 December 1856, quoted in Mary Seacole, *Wonderful Adventures of Mrs. Seacole in Many Lands* (London: James Blackwood, 1857), p. 118.

materially and figuratively active, the hands behind the admiral's back draw clear lines between those who do, and those who direct.

On the wharf, as also in Panama, and at Spring Hill where she sets up her 'British Hotel' near the front line, Seacole must combat the *invisible* gender and racial ideology of the assumed economic agent, but also confront the fact that as a woman, and a woman of colour, she was all *too* visible, as the *Punch* cartoon 'Our Own Vivandière' ably displays. Because of her visible difference, unlocatable ideology could interpret her work differently. Whether we take Smith's term 'invisible hand' to represent these dominant ideologies that set norms and created meanings, or whether we focus on how his version of self-interest and social good reveals the price of care, it indicates a context in which the work of Seacole's hands is over-loaded with difficulties that affect what she can do and how it is understood.

Seacole and Nightingale: Selling or Nursing?

These issues of gender, race and class, benevolence or self-interest, come together in the question that still gets raised today, usually in comparison with Florence Nightingale, of whether Seacole was nursing or selling, as if the two could not co-exist. Seacole declares that, 'If the authorities had allowed me, I would willingly have given them my services as a nurse; but as they declined them, should I not open an hotel for invalids in the Crimea in my own way?' (74). Going her 'own way' followed the pattern that Seacole had been pursuing all her previous life – providing and caring for others as her livelihood. But women selling into this market so often turns into women selling *themselves* in the market, and as an independent Jamaican-born woman selling to an army camp, this applied with much greater force to Seacole. Florence Nightingale's reasons for keeping Seacole at a distance in the Crimea, which she terms 'repelling her advances', betray this connection:

> She kept - I will not call it a 'bad house' but something not very unlike it— in the Crimean War. She was very kind to the men &, what is more, to the Officers – & did some good – & made many drunk. I had the greatest difficulty in repelling Mrs Seacole's advances, & in preventing association between her and my own nurses (absolutely out of the question) when we established 2 Hospitals nursed by us between Kadikoi & the 'Seacole Establishment' … Anyone who employs Mrs Seacole will introduce much kindness - also much drunkenness and improper conduct, wherever she is. I conclude (& believe) that respectable Officers were entirely ignorant of what I … could not help knowing as a Matron & Chaperone & Mother of the Army.[27]

[27] Draft letter to Sir Harry Verney. Appendix III in Penguin edition of *Wonderful Adventures*, ed. by Sarah Salih. p. 180.

Nightingale keeps all those roles for herself, of 'Matron & Chaperone & Mother' showing the terms on which Seacole seemed to be a threat; Seacole had used a similar set of words for herself in her narrative, but does not use the word 'chaperone': 'I must solicit my readers' attention to the position I held in the camp as doctress, nurse, and "mother"' (110). In this context, Nightingale's use of 'kind' and 'kindness' seem to suggest improper familiarity at the very least. Nightingale's nursing required money no less than Seacole's, but as an upper-class woman connected to government, her 'pale hands' were kept far from the buying, selling and working that produced that money. Seacole's explanation of her desire to go to the Crimea makes clear that women's response to the call to help the injured in Crimea – expressed in terms of their 'busy fingers' – was understood in the religious terms of domestic ideology, and their 'work' was of the ministry variety:

> But directly England knew the worst, she set about repairing her past neglect. In every household busy fingers were working for the poor soldier—money flowed in golden streams wherever need was—and Christian ladies, mindful of the sublime example, "I was sick, and ye visited me," hastened to volunteer their services by those sick-beds which only women know how to soothe and bless. Need I be ashamed to confess that I shared in the general enthusiasm? (70)

The causal relation between the 'golden streams' of money and the 'busy fingers' of domestic women is cast as religious duty. Seacole's desire to share in this 'enthusiasm' takes the form of wanting to take her own 'busy … and experienced … fingers' to use as a nurse, and that she is denied on racial grounds shows that she is excluded from the category of the 'general'. Seacole's 'busy fingers' expose too clearly the economic connection between women's work and 'golden streams' of money for domestic ideology to apply.

Seacole does, in places, use gender ideology differently to justify her work, and instead of using domestic ideology, she claims the terms that applied to male professional labour – putting her back in the context of Adam Smith's 'publick [*sic*] good'[28] that derives from self-interest:

> That the officers were glad of me as a doctress and nurse may be easily understood. When a poor fellow lay sickening in his cheerless hut and sent down to me, he knew very well that I should not ride up in answer to his message empty-handed. And although I did not hesitate to charge him with the value of the necessaries I took him, still he was thankful enough to be able to *purchase* them. (111)

She invokes the term 'doctress' here, the female suffix indicating that a 'doctor' is a man; in this context though, it is noticeable that she specifies that her patient was an officer, who could therefore afford to pay. She claims in this circumstance the right to ask to be paid for the goods and service she

[28] Smith, *Wealth of Nation*, p. 292.

provides. This recalls an earlier scene in Panama during a cholera outbreak, where she notes that 'It must be understood that many of those who could afford to pay for my services did so handsomely, but the great majority of my patients had nothing better to give their doctress than thanks' (31). Though still showing that her work was often done solely for 'benevolence', in Smith's parlance, she again calls herself 'doctress' when acknowledging that she is being paid, and this serves as recognition that her skills had material value. It was not in question that male doctors should be paid, and in the nineteenth century, doctors were paid directly for their medicines, not just their professional expertise.

By insisting that her work is worth the pay, Seacole makes clear that she is doing more than expressing assumed female nature by 'soothing and blessing' sickbeds; like a doctor, her skilled work merits recompense. Seacole can admit to being paid by associating her work with the male role of doctor; if she is being paid for the female equivalence, then it sounded a lot less like a religious mission. In Nightingale's version, this is 'kindness' of a sort that necessitated a 'chaperone' to 'repel' it.

Conclusion

The work and reputation of Mary Seacole in the Crimea caused controversy in the nineteenth century, and it still does in our current time: the most recent substantial arguments arose in response to the placing of a statue of Seacole outside St Thomas' Hospital in 2016, as St Thomas' has been closely identified with Florence Nightingale since just after the Crimean War. St Thomas' was the hospital where Florence Nightingale established the first professional nursing school in 1860, using money provided by the 'Nightingale Fund' that was set up after the war to continue Nightingale's nursing reforms. Having her legacy secured for her in this way contrasts significantly with Seacole who, by comparison, was brought to penury by her time in Crimea. The resurrection of the controversy in the modern day is part of understanding the challenge represented by Seacole's active and visible hands. In *Mary Seacole's Wonderful Adventures* – a text produced in response to financial necessity after her Crimean enterprise bankrupted her – the tension is evident in all Seacole's descriptions of her busy hands, between the tending that she needs to claim to do for love alone, and the trading that, as a non-white, working woman, she *must* do to fund it.

Part Three

Professional Conduct

Writing has long been understood as literate women's primary means of supporting themselves and their children in the absence of a husband, whether that absence was the result of death, betrayal, abandonment or the inability to find one in the first place.[1] The relationship of women to writing and publishing has often been considered supplemental to the importance of their wiving and mothering, or as a barely reputable substitute for sex work. The same can be said for those other, even less reputable professions available to women, such as the seamstress, a term that has historically been used to describe both women who exchange sex for money, as well as women who work with cloth; female innkeepers and actresses are similarly considered morally dubious. The problem, it seems, is that if a woman sells anything produced by her hand, whether the hand makes a gesture on stage, makes marks on a page or canvas, brews or pours a pint, or sews and stitches, that hand stands in synecdochally not for her labour but for her body, which is then imagined as being for sale.

This section offers a long view of women's struggle to navigate systemic barriers to employment, to manage their reputations, and of their difficulty in managing the competing demands of family life and work. The chapters offer four ways of examining women's engagement with the professionalisation of writing, especially in the chapters by Tim Sommer and Camille Stallings. Writing, for women, might justly be considered their second-oldest profession, largely because of the processes of legitimisation and self-protection adopted by women who were predominantly members

[1] Laura J. Rosenthal, *Infamous Commerce: Prostitution in Eighteenth-Century British Literature and Culture* (Ithaca NY: Cornell University Press, 2006); Nancy Armstrong, *Desire and Domestic Fiction: A Political History of the Novel* (New York: Oxford University Press, 1987).

of the middle class or gentry, even if those processes meant reinforcing the division between themselves and other kinds of working women. At the same time, this section provides studies of the ways in which writing is constitutive of professionalisation in other fields, as Janelle Pötzsch and Lana L. Dallley make the case for the ways in which Harriet Taylor Mill and Millicent Garrett Fawcett, as economists, contributed to the expanding field of economic theory. Tim Sommer considers how the Brontës conceptualised the female artist, and sought to excise that identity from sexual impropriety.

The chapters in Part Three address the broader theoretical concerns of *Women, Money and Markets*, focusing on economies shaped by the perceived rationality of the market, which is driven by relentless competition. Within this framework, men were regarded as 'made for conflict, whether the physical conflict of actual war, or … of the competitions of business and ambition', while women were seen as unsuited to such 'rude conflict', owing to their extreme 'sensitiveness'.[2] Such positions as Francis Parkman's aver the exclusion of women from business on the basis of their presumed irrationality and delicacy. In staking a claim for the professional conduct of women, each chapter in this section shows women in the nineteenth century making the case, implicitly or explicitly, for women's fitness for participation in public life – and for their representation in the franchise, based on the fact that there was no easy separation between the public and the private spheres. This final section thus addresses the ways in which women worked as clear-sighted analysts and theorists, who influenced how the market was realised, interpreted and understood, and fashioned professional identities for themselves, whether adopting overt or more covert strategies to do so.

Tim Sommer challenges the long-held association of disrepute and artistic endeavour in his discussion of 'Gendered Professionalism and the Victorian Marketplace: Female Artists as Economic Agents in Anne Brontë's Fiction'. For Sommer, in novels such as *The Tenant of Wildfell Hall* (1848), art provides Brontë's heroines with the opportunity to generate their own income and experience themselves as independent creators. Brontë's approach, therefore, aligns with Lana Dalley and Jill Rappoport's broader observation that women writers crafted economic identities by strategically navigating their public and private roles, in order to question the prevailing ideas about what constituted women's work. Sommer builds on this approach by showing how Brontë's heroines challenged and expanded traditional notions of women's professional and economic contributions. Like Brontë herself, the characters in her novels do not become fully public figures nor do they explicitly advocate for women's legal and economic liberation. The true radicalism of Anne Brontë's career and her works, therefore, lies not in the creation of a new,

[2] Francis Parkman, 'The Woman Question', *The North American Review*, 129:275 (1879), 303–21, esp. pp. 304, 305, 307, www.jstor.org/stable/25100797 (accessed 11 November 2025).

distinctly feminine art, but in the fact that art, as a professional identity, enables women to access economic independence and social involvement.

In her chapter 'Harriet Taylor Mill and the Case for Female Labour Force Participation', Janelle Pötzsch demonstrates the significance and impact of Harriet Taylor Mill's ideas, and how her reputation as a woman and a scholar is unfairly hitched to that of her more famous spouse, John Stuart Mill. Pötzsch reveals the way in which Harriet Taylor Mill saw economic laws operating in the private sphere through her vigorous refutation of the wage-fund doctrine. Pötzsch makes the case that Taylor Mill's essay 'Enfranchisement of Women' (1851) serves as a powerful critique of women's economic dependency, highlighting its adverse impact on their social and political status, and that this dependency becomes even more pronounced when women become mothers. Whether or not Taylor Mill intended her proposal to become law, her suggestion to relinquish maintenance claims underscores the significant economic vulnerability associated with motherhood and the way it restricts women's choices.

In 'Millicent Garrett Fawcett and Popular Political Economy', Lana L. Dalley discusses Garrett Fawcett's didactic writing, particularly *Political Economy for Beginners* (1870) and *Tales in Political Economy* (1874). Dalley considers these texts in relation to the ways in which women contributed to economic theory in a time before their participation was formally sanctioned. By focusing on the work of Millicent Garrett Fawcett, and, to a lesser extent, Jane Marcet and Harriet Martineau, Dalley considers how these women initiated a literary movement in which female writers used their growing influence to integrate political economy into imaginative literature. Within this tradition, women – depicted as characters – are portrayed as operating within, being shaped by, and contributing to capitalist economics, rather than being viewed as outside the economic system, as classical political economists often suggest in response to women's lack of representation in the field.

Rounding out the collection, Camille Stallings adopts a postfeminist perspective in 'Breadwinners and Losers in Annie Thomas's *The Modern Housewife*' through which to consider Annie Thomas, a successful author of sensation fiction. The novel tells the story of a woman who becomes a professional writer, and the tensions it introduces into what she had otherwise expected would be a conventional married and middle-class life. Stallings reveals how Thomas's portrayals of female breadwinners navigate patriarchal constraints, with the work of Thomas contradictorily but profitably acknowledging and simultaneously downplaying the figure of the authoress-as-breadwinner.

Consequently, Thomas's success and life story warrant greater attention for their potential to complicate twentieth-century feminist analyses of women writers' responses to the 'Woman Question'. Thomas's biography illustrates that the strategies enabling a female Victorian author to thrive in the literary world did not always translate into personal financial success, and the representation of women writers did not always reflect the realities of their lives. Thus, while the rhetorical strategies in the work of Thomas may not have always aligned with more radical feminist or emancipatory goals of the period, such as those advocated by suffragist, socialist or anarchist movements, they did contribute to broader efforts to expand women's access to education, careers and economic independence.

By arriving at a postfeminist reading of domestic literature, Stallings brings to a close this wide-reaching study of the ways in which women interacted with markets and managed their money, and the barriers that they encountered in the process. The twelve chapters in this volume have made the case for women's significant contribution to the formation of the modern economy in theory and in praxis. Historically, classical political economists have made little space for women's contributions to the development of economic theory, but a postfeminist reading of women's contributions to financial pedagogy dismantles this assumption. Rather, it is clear that women sought and provided education for themselves and future generations on the matter of money and how to put it to work, which reached broader and more diverse audiences than those coming from inside male-dominated institutions.

From women who announced their participation in the economy volubly, to those who hid behind systems of trusts and pseudonyms; from those who confined themselves to the gestural to those who were outspoken at public annual general meetings and published broadly and popularly on economic topics; from the women who profited from their maintenance of and participation in the economic system as it stood at the time, to those who sought to contest the inequities embedded into it, women have shaped and been shaped by markets that extend far beyond that of marriage.

9

Gendered Professionalism and the Victorian Marketplace: Female Artists as Economic Agents in Anne Brontë's Fiction

Tim Sommer

Professionalisation as Emancipation

At a pivotal point in her posthumously published *Autobiography* (1877), the Victorian novelist and economic theorist Harriet Martineau recalls the failure of her father's textile manufacturing business in the late 1820s. The young Martineau was compelled to support herself and her family through her own writing as a result, but by her own account experienced this change of fortunes as a moment of economic and intellectual emancipation that allowed her 'to feel the blessing of a wholly new freedom'.[1] Whereas previously she 'had been obliged to write … in some private way', she now was at 'liberty to do my own work in my own way'.[2] The pressure to become a professional author, she summarised in retrospect, had rescued her from the narrow confines of the domestic sphere and instead allowed her to 'have worked hard and usefully, won friends, reputation and independence, seen the world abundantly, abroad and at home, and, in short, have truly lived instead of vegetated'.[3] Nineteenth-century fiction offers similar visions of the social and economic dignity of female creative labour. In Mary Brunton's

[1] Harriet Martineau, *Autobiography*, ed. by Maria Weston Chapman, 3 vols (London: Smith, Elder & Co., 1877), vol. 1, p. 142.

[2] Ibid.

[3] Ibid.

novel *Self-Control* (1811), for example, the young heroine Laura Montreville is an amateur painter who mines her talents in response to an economic emergency not unlike that which befell Martineau and her family. Laura's father proves inept at handling the family's finances: after the death of 'the merchant in whose hands he had lately vested his all' the merchant's 'heirs refused to make any payment', leaving the Montrevilles on the brink of bankruptcy.[4] Instead, he comes to rely on his daughter's moral and financial support; a gifted artist, Laura pledges to 'labour night and day, deprive herself of recreation, of rest, even of daily food' in order to make her art yield an income and thereby 'to obtain a subsistence for her father'.[5]

The outlines of Brunton's plot resurface in Anne Brontë's first novel *Agnes Grey* (1847) (*Self-Control* was reprinted several times throughout the Victorian period, most recently in the year Brontë's book was published.). In the opening chapter of *Agnes Grey*, Agnes's mother encourages her other daughter, Mary, to refine her creative abilities as an artist. The aim that Mrs Grey has in mind for Agnes's sister is not the acquisition of a diffuse kind of cultural capital, however, but that of capital in a more literal sense: she wants to sell Mary's drawings to supplement the family's meagre income. A little later in the book, she is anxious to convince her husband that the female members of the household 'can devise a thousand honest ways of making a livelihood'.[6] Here as well as in Brunton and Martineau, the heroic perseverance and morally coded sincerity of such female economic activity – the 'good success' of Mary's drawings, the 'pinching … and scraping' that Agnes practises with her income as a governess – stand in stark contrast to the Victorian venture capitalism that the novel explicitly associates with ill-fated risk-taking as a specifically male practice.[7]

Mrs Grey finds herself forced to turn her daughter into a commercial artist because her husband has fallen victim to a scheme engineered by a merchant friend of his who offered to multiply the family's modest savings but eventually fails to deliver on his promise. As readers learn from Agnes at an early point in her first-person account, Reverend Grey is an incompetent provider for his family. While before his marriage, he 'lived pretty comfortably on the joint income of a small incumbency, and a snug little property of his own', he soon enough begins to live beyond his means:

> Saving was not my father's forte: he would not run in debt, (at least, my mother took good care he should not,) but while he had money, he must spend it; he liked to see his house comfortable, and his wife and daughters

4 Mary Brunton, *Self-Control* (Aberdeen: George Clark and Son, 1847, orig. 1811), p. 27.

5 Ibid., p. 129.

6 Anne Brontë, *Agnes Grey*, ed. by Hilda Marsden and Robert Inglesfield (Oxford: Clarendon Press, 1988, orig. 1847), p. 54.

7 Ibid., p. 53.

> well clothed, and well attended; and besides, he was charitably disposed, and liked to give to the poor, according to his means, or, as some might think, beyond them.[8]

It is this unsustainable management of his own resources that converts Reverend Grey to a belief in the miracles of capitalist asset multiplication. When the merchant vessel into which he has invested the entirety of his savings founders, the family is economically embarrassed and comes to depend on a type of labour that the novel frames as ethically uncompromised and distinctly female.

In *The Tenant of Wildfell Hall* (1848), Brontë's second, and final, novel, female industry and economic prudence ('good care') is similarly contrasted with male profligacy. Whereas the earlier novel realigns a female involvement in the art market with the sphere of the family, *The Tenant of Wildfell Hall* imagines artistic production more radically as an instrument for its protagonist Helen Graham to achieve economic independence from her husband and to sustain herself as a single mother. If art for Mary Grey represents an intermittent occupation, for Helen Graham it becomes a serious professional identity. Having escaped the illusion of the intact domestic sphere, she is left to her own devices and compelled to monetise skills that have previously been little more than private diversions. Like *Agnes Grey*, *The Tenant of Wildfell Hall* consistently contrasts female entrepreneurial acumen with male financial imprudence. A compulsive drinker who gambles away his money, Helen's husband serves as a negative foil for her own moral and financial steadfastness. The novel revolves around a subversive vision of the female artist as an autonomous subject who acquires a social and professional standing of her own in a male-dominated contemporary art market.

What I want to argue here is that Brontë – like Brunton before and Martineau after her – locates the emancipatory power of art not in its potential to furnish an aesthetic expression of female identity but in its ability to provide women with an independent source of income. Whereas scholarship on the representation of female labour in the nineteenth-century novel has tended to focus on domestic or industrial economies, I want to draw attention here to the often neglected role of women as self-employed producers in the creative marketplace, a type of activity that blurs the boundaries between domestic and professional work and between private and public engagement. Brontë's writing emphatically presents nineteenth-century female artists and educators as women of business. In so doing, it pursues an essentially anti-Romantic, materialist argument in the context of which art is associated not with creative self-realisation but with the forces of the market. The female painters and aesthetic instructors in Brontë's fiction leave behind lofty notions of art's social and ideological

[8] Ibid., pp. 3, 5.

autonomy and instead explore their roles as producers of commodities and providers of services, as owners of marketable skills that constitute their working capital. In turning from art as diversion to art as craft, however, the protagonists of the novels come to see economic emancipation as a mixed blessing that involves self-advertisement and aesthetic compromise. Brontë, in other words, juxtaposes artistic vision with commercial production. In what follows, I reconstruct the pervasive presence of this tension in *Agnes Grey* and *The Tenant of Wildfell Hall* but also contextualise it against the background of the careers of Brontë and her sisters as female writers with their own tangible experience of the gendered professionalism of the Victorian cultural market. What emerges from this analysis is a clearer picture of how the Brontës' biographical and fictional explorations of the material realities of female authorship and creative labour illustrate the complex relationship between art, gender and economy in nineteenth-century Britain.

Making (and Losing) Money in *Agnes Grey*

Women, money and markets are at the centre of *Agnes Grey* and its explicitly gendered image of economic activity. Almost without exception, the book's male characters are either idling members of the gentry or reckless investors. If Agnes's father serves as a hapless example of the latter, the former is epitomised by her second employer, the affluent Mr Murray, who is portrayed as 'a blustering, roystering country squire, a devoted fox-hunter, a skilful horse-jockey … and a hearty *bon-vivant*'.[9] Male money-making in *Agnes Grey* takes on a notably disembodied form that capitalises on pre-existing asset ownership and on the work of other people. Reverend Grey's eventually unsuccessful investment scheme appropriately enough relies on a model of international trade that exploits foreign resources and disenfranchised subalterns – a theme that echoes Charlotte Brontë's *Jane Eyre* (1847), in which the morally conflicted Mr Rochester's family fortune has its source in the plantation economy of the West Indies. This thematic strand in *Agnes Grey* and *Jane Eyre* represents something of an implicit commentary on the social and economic position of nineteenth-century women, to the extent that it was customary in the Victorian age to think of the question of women's rights in terms of a comparison with the situation of formerly enslaved people. John Stuart Mill, for example, notes in *The Subjection of Women* (1869) that women's 'position under the common law of England is worse than that of slaves', given that 'the wife … can acquire no property but for [her husband]; the instant it becomes hers … it becomes *ipso facto* his'.[10]

9 Ibid., p. 63.

10 John Stuart Mill, *On Liberty with The Subjection of Women and Chapters on Socialism*, ed. by Stefan Collini (Cambridge: Cambridge University Press, 1989), p. 147.

If male economy in *Agnes Grey* is therefore an expression of modern global capitalism, its female counterpart represents the exact opposite. Mrs Grey's darning, Mary's drawing, and Agnes's teaching are all tied to the restricted sphere of the home and the kind of pre-capitalist forms of manual labour that etymologically point back to the *oikonomia* of the private household. Whereas the male protagonists of the novel are embroiled either in traditional feudal or modern imperialist structures of domination and exploitation, the work of women is characterised as domestic in the double sense of being linked to both the house and the nation.

Brontë gives further nuance to this dichotomy when she describes the markedly different ways in which Agnes's parents respond to the financial calamity that results from Reverend Grey's failed investment. When the family's savings are lost and the Greys are burdened with debt, Agnes's father is paralysed by the events and unable to mitigate their effect on his family. Mrs Grey, by contrast, takes charge of consolidating the family's shaky finances. Brontë gives this moment of female agency an additional edge by making Agnes's mother by birth a member of the landed gentry. Having married beneath her social rank, she was disinherited by her own father as a result, which offers another parallel to the story of Jane Eyre, whose grandfather had similarly 'cut her [mother] off without a shilling' in response to the social disgrace of her marrying 'a poor clergyman'.[11] Reverend Grey's subconscious guilt about having deprived his wife of her former status and privilege is exacerbated by his ill-advised financial choices. Subscribing to a Victorian idealisation of women as passive ornaments rather than as individuals with financial abilities of their own, he is dismayed to find that, thanks to his own mismanagement, his wife – a 'splendid, highly accomplished woman' – has become 'transformed into an active managing housewife, with hands and head continually occupied with household labours and household economy'.[12] Reverend Grey's sentiments illustrate that what Katherine Hallemeier has analysed as the novel's deployment of a 'rhetoric of shame' is not restricted to Brontë's female characters.[13]

In the novel itself, however, this seeming fall from grace – from the idle recreations of the upper-class drawing room to the supposedly menial work involved in making ends meet – is described in distinctly positive terms. Mrs Grey and her daughters manage to pay off the family's debts, to restore its jeopardised reputation, and, in so doing, create a new balance of economic

[11] Charlotte Brontë, *Jane Eyre*, ed. by Jane Jack and Margaret Smith (Oxford: Oxford Clarendon Press, 1969, orig. 1847), p. 26.

[12] Brontë, *Agnes Grey*, p. 8.

[13] While Hallemeier is mostly interested in 'Agnes's embrace of the shame of being both a governess and a woman who writes', Agnes's father experiences shame as an affect related to class and the loss of economic status. Katherine Hallemeier, 'Anne Brontë's Shameful *Agnes Grey*', *Victorian Literature and Culture*, 41:2 (2013), 251–60, at p. 252.

power in the household. The secret behind the female business success of the Greys lies in the fact that they transform the soft socio-cultural capital of female accomplishments – skills such as singing, dancing, drawing and foreign languages – into skills viable beyond the marriage market. The water-colour sketches that Agnes's sister, Mary, produces find ready buyers, and Agnes puts her own abilities to use when she decides to become a governess. To be sure, Mary mostly remains an artist confined to the private sphere and Agnes's profession revolves around a type of care work traditionally coded as female.[14] Yet Brontë revaluates female labour precisely through describing and recognising such activities as genuinely *economic* activities – as work that yields a quantifiable form of payment. My reading of the novel thus challenges Nancy Armstrong's classic claim that nineteenth-century novels like those of the Brontës 'helped to transform the household into what might be called the "counterimage" of the modern marketplace'.[15] In texts such as *Agnes Grey*, *The Tenant of Wildfell Hall* and *Jane Eyre*, the domestic sphere in fact becomes the nucleus for female economic activity.

The mastermind behind the female business ventures that lie at the heart of *Agnes Grey* is Mrs Grey, whose earlier characterisation as an 'accomplished woman' takes on an additional meaning in light of the resourcefulness with which she transforms her daughter's talents into marketable assets. A natural woman of business, she is confident that Mary would only need to be 'doing a few more pictures' and 'trying to dispose of them to some liberal picture-dealer'.[16] What she proposes is a division of labour, with her daughter working as an artist and herself functioning as her agent ('you procure the drawings, and I'll endeavour to find a purchaser').[17] Agnes is likewise guided by her mother's economic advice. When she scouts 'the advertising columns of the newspapers' to find an employer willing to hire her as a governess, it is her mother who makes her 'reject the situations one after another'.[18] Mrs

14 On the social position and occupational realities of nineteenth-century governesses, see Kathryn Hughes, *The Victorian Governess* (London: Hambledon Press, 1993). For an exploration of the function of autobiographical writing in the Victorian governess novel, see Nora Gilbert, 'A Servitude of One's Own: Isolation, Authorship, and the Nineteenth-Century British Governess', *Nineteenth-Century Literature*, 69:4 (2015), 455–80. On the governess theme in *Agnes Grey*, more specifically, see Dara Rossman Regaignon, 'Instructive Sufficiency: Re-Reading the Governess through *Agnes Grey*', *Victorian Literature and Culture*, 29:1 (2001), 85–108; and James R. Simmons Jr, 'Class, Matriarchy, and Power: Contextualizing the Governess in *Agnes Grey*', in *New Approaches to the Literary Art of Anne Brontë*, ed. by Julie Nash and Barbara A. Suess (Aldershot: Ashgate, 2001), pp. 25–43.

15 Nancy Armstrong, *Desire and Domestic Fiction: A Political History of the Novel* (Oxford: Oxford University Press, 1987), p. 48.

16 Brontë, *Agnes Grey*, p. 10.

17 Ibid.

18 Ibid., p. 56.

Grey teaches her daughter to gauge her own market value and not undersell herself, enjoining on her the need to recognise that her 'talents are not such as every poor clergyman's daughter possesses' and that she 'must not throw them away'.[19] She makes Agnes draw up an advertisement herself, listing her 'qualifications', which include 'Music, Singing, Drawing, French, Latin, and German', and thus helping her to find a position that doubles the wages that she had received in her previous employment.[20]

Much of the novel's plot is concerned with the trials and tribulations that follow Agnes's decision to take up the governess profession, with the protagonist suffering at the hands of unruly children and their condescending parents in equal measure. But however arduous the side-effects of the Victorian market for female labour in the education sector turn out to be, Agnes's job nonetheless allows her to send money home and eventually establish herself as an independent entrepreneur of sorts. After her father's death, she joins forces with her mother and the two start a small school of their own, with Agnes no longer 'working as a hireling among strangers' but assuming the role of a self-employed teacher who manages her own finances.[21] Brontë uses Reverend Grey's passing to once again highlight his wife's economic sincerity. When her aged father offers to reinstate her as the legatee of his fortune now that his disdained son-in-law is dead, she turns down the proposal and prefers to honour her husband's memory.

The sudden opportunity to recover a major inheritance points back to the opening of the novel and its critique of the morally questionable and financially unreliable profit margins of capitalist speculation as a distinctly male form of doing business; this position is established in the example of the trade scheme in which Reverend Grey decides to invest in the first chapter, which, he believes, promises to double 'his private property at one stroke; and further increas[e] it ... to an untold amount'.[22] The female Greys consistently refuse to make a quick profit and instead persevere in activities that generate an income out of labour rather than capital. Brontë consistently describes this as an economy that is not only ethically more sincere but also financially more sustainable than the strategies pursued by her male protagonists. The gendered dichotomy between these two types of economy as it surfaces in Brontë's novel illustrates well Mary Poovey's important point that:

> The rhetorical separation of spheres and the image of domesticated, feminized morality were crucial to the consolidation of bourgeois power partly because linking morality to a figure (rhetorically) immune to the self-interest

[19] Ibid.

[20] Ibid.

[21] Ibid., p. 176.

[22] Ibid., p. 5.

> and competition integral to economic success preserved virtue without inhibiting productivity.[23]

Having become a widow, Mrs Grey is close to the poverty line, but she again decides to help herself by drawing on her own resources, as she has 'not forgotten [her] accomplishments'.[24] Declining to be subsidised by her daughter Mary's husband, she develops 'an economical plan' on which to operate her school with Agnes – an arrangement which she is confident will see a steady income 'accrue from our united labours'.[25]

Brontë holds up Mrs Grey as a female role model for her daughters – and for the contemporary readers of the novel – to emulate in her navigation of the male spheres of business and commerce. Agnes and Mary even go so far as to follow the example of their mother when it comes to choosing their partners: both marry clergymen of modest means who depend on the guidance of their wives. The novel ends with Agnes's thumbnail description of her marital union with the country parson Edward Weston, who through her support avoids the pitfalls of living beyond one's means and hence becomes a more reliable provider for his young family than Reverend Grey had been for his. 'Our modest income is amply sufficient for our requirements', she notes by way of concluding her account:

> and by practising the economy we learnt in harder times, and never attempting to imitate our richer neighbours, we manage not only to enjoy comfort and contentment ourselves, but to have every year something to lay by for our children, and something to give to those who need it.[26]

Agnes ekes out a living for her own family through diligently continuing on the path of female economic sincerity and through staying true to the gospel of steady saving that she had learned from observing her mother.

If *Agnes Grey*, in its celebration of the successful strategy of its protagonists in turning social 'accomplishments' into a source of income, offers itself to be read as a text that 'encourages female financial agency and independence', its ending nevertheless sounds a more conservative note.[27] Although the novel favourably contrasts a female business spirit with destructive forms of male risk-taking and debt-making, and although it describes the professional identities of the artist and the teacher as linked to a new sense of female self-empowerment and opportunity, the potential for social autonomy contained

[23] Mary Poovey, *Uneven Developments: The Ideological Work of Gender in Mid-Victorian England* (Chicago IL: University of Chicago Press, 1988), p. 10.

[24] Brontë, *Agnes Grey*, p. 166.

[25] Ibid., p. 167.

[26] Ibid., p. 208.

[27] Joanna Rostek, 'Anne Brontë, *Agnes Grey* (1847)', in *Handbook of the English Novel, 1830–1900*, ed. by Martin Middeke and Monika Pietrzak-Franger (Berlin and Boston MA: De Gruyter, 2020), pp. 237–52, at p. 249.

in such economic activity ultimately remains tied to the domestic sphere. Agnes and her sister Mary end up in wedlock, with husbands who are more considerate in financial matters than Reverend Grey and who in the long run give their wives no occasion, and hence no opportunity, to pursue their own professional development beyond the Victorian household.

Art and Economy in *The Tenant of Wildfell Hall*

In *The Tenant of Wildfell Hall*, published a year after Brontë's first novel, female professionalism poses a more sustained challenge to traditional gender roles. Following her escape from a disastrous marriage and an abusive husband, the book's main character, Helen Graham, turns a former hobby into her chief source of material sustenance. She sells her paintings through an art dealer and uses the money she earns to keep herself and her young son afloat. Helen's precarious status as a working woman and a social outcast serves Brontë as a cautionary tale through which to question the economic principles of nineteenth-century British marriage law, in whose context 'female dependence was constructed and perpetuated'.[28] It was only through a series of Married Women's Property Acts in the latter half of the century that female producers like Helen would come to be entitled to hold and manage their own property. In the 1820s, the period in which the main part of the plot of the novel is set, the doctrine of coverture still granted husbands control over the finances of their wives, and Brontë uses her fiction to draw attention to the predicament that this legal situation created for women whose spouses failed to live up to their social and moral duties. A drunkard, a gambler and a womaniser, Helen's husband, Arthur Huntingdon, disapproves of her work as a painter. When he learns that she has been planning to separate from him, he accuses her of seeking 'to disgrace' him 'by running away and turning artist, and supporting [her]self by the labour of [her] hands'.[29] Seizing on his legally sanctioned authority to prohibit his wife from pursuing a career, he destroys the tools of her trade:

> My painting materials were laid together on the corner table, ready for to-morrow's use, and only covered with a cloth. He soon spied them out, and putting down the candle, deliberately proceeded to cast them into the fire—palette, paints, bladders, pencils, brushes, varnish—I saw them all

[28] Lyn Pykett, 'Women Writing Woman: Nineteenth-Century Representations of Gender and Sexuality', in *Women and Literature in Britain, 1800–1900*, ed. by Joanne Shattock (Cambridge: Cambridge University Press, 2001), pp. 78–98, at p. 84.

[29] Anne Brontë, *The Tenant of Wildfell Hall*, ed. by Herbert Rosengarten (Oxford: Oxford University Press, 2008, orig. 1848), p. 311.

consumed—the palette-knives snapped in two—the oil and turpentine sent hissing and roaring up the chimney.[30]

Huntingdon acts with impunity and his gesture of domination points towards the larger underlying historical reality of male control over Victorian women's means of creative production. Helen realises this as a result of the events and finally manages to break free from Huntingdon, leaving him and setting up her own studio at Wildfell Hall.

Although this represents a more radical vision of female self-sufficiency than the one that features in *Agnes Grey*, critical discussion of *The Tenant of Wildfell Hall* has not always been prepared to acknowledge the subversiveness with which the book describes the art economy and the kind of gendered professionalism it makes possible. In their classic reading of the novel, Sandra M. Gilbert and Susan Gubar mainly describe the text as an allegory of female authorship. *The Tenant of Wildfell Hall*, in this line of argument, is judged according to the degree to which Brontë's protagonist succeeds to give colour and shape to her own, distinctly feminine view of the world. To Gilbert and Gubar, Helen Graham is characterised by an urgent 'need to paint her own condition' and 'to discover a new aesthetic space for herself', an imperative that clashes with the female artist's 'guilt about the impropriety of self-expression'.[31] Seen from this point of view, art is all about the externalisation of gendered identity. Helen is bound to fail, then, because the patriarchal order prevents her from freely expressing her femininity through her creative work.

What such a reading tends to neglect, however, is the emancipatory role that the market plays in the novel. Even where art in *The Tenant of Wildfell Hall* has been described as going beyond the private realm of mere 'self-expression', the crucial economic dimension of the book has remained largely unexplored. Contending that Helen's professional identity allows her to become an active participant in the public sphere, Rachel K. Carnell, for example, has argued that Brontë's protagonist 'challenges the separate gendered spheres by offering herself as one of the rare enlightened women who could claim a voice in public debate'.[32] This grants Brontë's protagonist the kind of public voice that Gilbert and Gubar deny her, but Carnell similarly overstates the importance of immaterial content over material form. What is radical about Helen Graham's paintings is after all not *what* she paints but *that* she paints – and that she manages to paint for a living.

30 Ibid., p. 310.

31 Sandra M. Gilbert and Susan Gubar, *The Madwoman in the Attic: The Woman Writer and the Nineteenth-Century Literary Imagination* (New Haven CT: Yale University Press, 1979), pp. 81–2.

32 Rachel K. Carnell, 'Feminism and the Public Sphere in Anne Brontë's *The Tenant of Wildfell Hall*', *Nineteenth-Century Literature*, 53:1 (1998), 1–24, at p. 11.

Whatever radical dimension that Helen Graham's art may have had before she becomes a professional painter gets watered down once she enters the art world. Her economic independence as a female art professional comes at the cost of having to renounce her creative autonomy. Brontë illustrates this compromise in the middle section of the novel, when it begins to dawn on Helen, who is still trapped in her marriage, that the feasibility of her escape scheme hinges on her commercial success as a selling painter. If painting is to become the means to effect her 'speedy emancipation' from the social and emotional death of her failed marriage, she needs to meet the expectations of a paying audience and accordingly develop a sense of the current fashion, rather than attempting to create daringly innovative art that expresses her precarious status as a woman, as Gilbert and Gubar would have it.[33] Contemplating transatlantic emigration, she writes in her journal:

> I would support myself … by the labour of my hands. The palette and the easel, my darling playmates once, must be my sober toil-fellows now … I must labour hard to improve my talent, and to produce something worth while as a specimen of my powers … Who could tell how long I might have to struggle with the indifference or neglect of others, or my own inexperience or inability to suit their tastes?[34]

That Helen thinks about the United States as a possible refuge from her husband is a striking historical coincidence. In July 1848, a mere month after the appearance of the novel's first English edition, American women's rights activists gathered at Seneca Falls and issued their 'Declaration of Sentiments', one of whose articles denounced the fact that 'he ["man"] has taken from her ["woman"] all right in property, even to the wages she earns'.[35] The Victorian Brontë and her protagonist need to look across the Atlantic to be able to locate an existing liberal feminism on the nineteenth-century cultural and political map.

Helen at this point radically reimagines her previous notion of art as a leisurely activity pursued for the purposes of social diversion. Moving from the drawing room techniques of the pencil sketch and the watercolour to the more ambitious genre of painting in oil, she quite literally gets her hands dirty to maximise her profit margin.[36] Painting for Helen now becomes wage

[33] Brontë, *The Tenant of Wildfell Hall*, p. 307.

[34] Ibid., p. 298.

[35] Elizabeth Cady Stanton, 'Declaration of Sentiments', in *Feminist Writings from Ancient Times to the Modern World: A Global Sourcebook and History*, ed. by Tiffany K. Wayne, 2 vols (Santa Barbara CA: Greenwood, 2011), vol. 1, pp. 208–11, at p. 209.

[36] As Antonia Losano notes, 'the fact that Helen paints in oil rather than watercolor … removes her from the typical female artists of her time, who were more likely to use the supposedly more feminine medium of watercolor than smelly, messy, and expensive oil paint'. Antonia Losano, 'The Professionalization of the Woman Artist in Anne Brontë's *The Tenant of Wildfell Hall*', *Nineteenth-Century Literature*, 58:1 (2003), 1–41, at p. 25.

labour as opposed to creative self-fulfilment: it is 'arduous toil', a factory-like occupation that sees her busy at her canvas 'from daylight till dusk, with very little intermission'.[37] As she tells her suitor Gilbert Markham during his first visit to her studio at Wildfell Hall, she 'cannot afford to paint for [her] own amusement'.[38] Through Helen's young son Arthur, Markham learns that she 'sends all her pictures to London ... and somebody sells them for her there, and sends us the money'.[39]

The juxtaposition between female industry and male wastefulness that Brontë develops in *Agnes Grey* here resurfaces in even more explicit terms. Brontë's two novels preach the Victorian gospel of work, but they give a gendered dimension to the period's celebration of activity over idleness, and its notion of work as both a higher duty and a source of personal dignity. Like the upper-class figures that appear in *Agnes Grey*, Arthur Huntingdon is chronically underemployed. Helen thinks of work as a moral corrective to his many vices: she 'wish[es] he had something to do, some useful trade, or profession, or employment—anything to occupy his head or his hands for a few hours a day, and give him something besides his own pleasure to think about'.[40] Terry Eagleton has argued that both of Brontë's novels are primarily concerned with class rather than gender, depicting 'an opposition between lifestyles' that 'pivot[s] on a ... binary opposition between immoral gentry and righteous protagonist'.[41] While Eagleton provides an intriguing materialist account of the Brontë canon, his sense that 'the essential simplicity of the structural relations' of Anne's novels compares unfavourably with those of her sisters makes him neglect the complex role the art economy plays in her writing.[42] What Brontë does in *The Tenant of Wildfell Hall* is to appropriate the hard-boiled rhetoric of useful work and turn her female protagonist into a paradigmatic example of the doctrine. It is through 'working hard' that Helen gains a sense of her own freedom from male support: 'I shall have so much more pleasure in my labour, my earnings, my frugal fare, and household economy', she says at one point, 'when I know that I am paying my way honestly, and that what little I possess is legitimately all my own'.[43] If work in the nineteenth century was,

37 Brontë, *The Tenant of Wildfell Hall*, p. 299.

38 Ibid., p. 41.

39 Ibid.

40 Ibid., p. 191.

41 Terry Eagleton, *Myths of Power: A Marxist Study of the Brontës* (London: Macmillan, 1975), p. 134. In this context, see also Erin Nyborg, '"A Just and Liberal Landlord": Manliness, Work, and the Landed Gentleman in the Brontës' Novels', *Journal of Victorian Culture*, 22:3 (2017), 362–79, for an analysis of male work and social class in *The Tenant of Wildfell Hall* and other Brontë fiction.

42 Eagleton, *Myths of Power*, p. 134.

43 Brontë, *The Tenant of Wildfell Hall*, p. 333.

as Elaine Showalter suggests, 'in direct conflict with the subordination and repression inherent in the feminine ideal', Brontë seized on its economic effects to make a case for the status benefits of female employment.[44]

In another key respect, however, Brontë departs from the received wisdom of nineteenth-century cultural criticism. Writers like Thomas Carlyle and, after him, Matthew Arnold and John Ruskin, were alarmed by what they perceived as the debasement of art through the industrialisation of culture: an anxiety about a shift from a Romantic ideology of art-as-vocation to the Victorian professionalisation of intellectual and creative labour. Brontë counters such nostalgic praise for restricted production and artisanal manufacture through an emphatic description of Helen Graham's 'arduous toil' at her easel as a well-regulated routine that affects her economic liberation from the bonds of a stifling marriage. It is precisely her self-reinvention as a 'resolutely unromantic' hard-working professional artist that allows Helen to acquire the dignity that had previously been denied to her.[45] Her catering to market demand is not – as in the standard declensionist accounts of Victorian male commentators like Carlyle, Arnold or Ruskin (and, by extension, of modern feminist readers of the novel) – a betrayal of her artistic vision but the very precondition for her material survival.

Brontë does not object to the commercialisation of art so much as she criticises the gendered dynamics of the nineteenth-century creative economy. Helen Graham depends on commercial success to become an autonomous subject, but her financial independence is structurally tied to a modern art market that subjects female producers to the critical scrutiny of male observers and buyers. The novel's depiction of gendered aesthetic judgement is especially pronounced in its characterisation of Markham, who in the first part of the book repeatedly comments on Helen's artwork and emphasises the superiority of his own taste. Writing as an art critic motivated by a sense of male entitlement, he finds Helen's painting of Wildfell Hall 'faithfully drawn', her portrait of Huntingdon 'not badly executed', but at another point claims that he himself, although an amateur at best, 'could make a lovelier sketch than hers'.[46] Having learned to 'suit [the] tastes' of her (male) paying customers, Helen is wise – or, at any rate, disillusioned – enough not to argue with Markham and instead to pretend to follow his advice.

Brontë complements this scathing depiction of male art criticism with a larger exploration of what Antonia Losano has described as the 'sexual

[44] Elaine Showalter, *A Literature of Their Own: British Women Novelists from Brontë to Lessing* (Princeton NJ: Princeton University Press, 1999, orig. 1977), p. 22.

[45] Alexandra K. Wettlaufer, *Portraits of the Artist as a Young Woman: Painting and the Novel in France and Britain, 1800–1860* (Columbus OH: Ohio State University Press, 2011), p. 237.

[46] Brontë, *The Tenant of Wildfell Hall*, pp. 40, 42, 58.

politics of spectatorship' during this period.[47] Both Markham and Huntingdon are voyeurs who pry into Helen's affairs and intrude on the privacy of the creative act. Although at Wildfell Hall she has created for herself a room of her own – a studio that works as a personal sanctuary but at the same time has a distinctly 'professional, business-like appearance' – the boundaries she has set up after all turn out to be permeable.[48] Markham is at liberty to nose around her workspace in her absence and Huntingdon, at the beginning of their courtship, had amused himself with snatching away Helen's drawings and revelling in her creatively expressed admiration of him. If these acts of spectatorial indiscretion revolve around private violations of the intimate sphere of the artist, upon Helen's adoption of the role of the professional artist, privacy ceases to exist as an option altogether. What she produces is, by definition, destined for commercial circulation and public exposure. Over the course of the novel Helen hardens herself against the perceived iniquities of gendered judgement.

In *The Tenant of Wildfell Hall*, Brontë thus develops a more comprehensive vision of female creative labour and its emancipatory potential than she had done in *Agnes Grey*. What both novels share, however, is a socially conservative conclusion. Like Jane Eyre, Helen Graham ends up inheriting a substantial property that relieves her of the need to work for a living but simultaneously deprives her of her economic independence as a gainfully employed middle-class single woman. Like Agnes Grey – and like Jane Eyre, for that matter – she eventually marries, giving up her own income and once again entering into the legal domain of nineteenth-century coverture. Although 'there is no textual evidence that Helen gives up painting after marrying Gilbert', as Losano has pointed out, it seems hard to imagine that she continues painting commercially after becoming first an heiress and then Markham's wife.[49] The gendered economics of Brontë's novel to that

47 Antonia Losano, *The Woman Painter in Victorian Literature* (Columbus OH: Ohio State University Press, 2008), p. 74. On the larger cultural significance of the scenes discussed in the previous paragraph, see Russell Poole, 'Cultural Reformation and Cultural Reproduction in Anne Brontë's *The Tenant of Wildfell Hall*', *Studies in English Literature*, 33:4 (1993), 859–73.

48 Brontë, *The Tenant of Wildfell Hall*, p. 333.

49 Losano, 'The Professionalization of the Woman Artist', p. 21. As Nicole A. Diederich has argued, Brontë in the novel 'constructs [its protagonist's] remarriage as a comparative and competitive practice that restricts Helen's rights and talents'. Nicole A. Diederich, 'The Art of Comparison: Remarriage in Anne Brontë's *The Tenant of Wildfell Hall*', *Rocky Mountain Review of Language and Literature*, 57:2 (2003), 25–41, at p. 25. Other commentators have suggested that Helen's economic status as a wealthy widow troubles conventional gender stereotypes. Elsie B. Michie, for example, draws attention to the fact that it is Helen who proposes to a Markham 'paralyzed by his knowledge' of her financial prowess. Elsie B. Michie, *The Vulgar Question of Money: Heiresses, Materialism, and the Novel of Manners from Jane Austen to Henry James* (Baltimore MD: Johns Hopkins University Press, 2011), p. 14.

extent points towards an authorial stance that is both subversive and conciliatory. As Kate Flint has pointed out, *The Tenant of Wildfell Hall* 'resists assimilation as either a conservative or a radical text in feminist terms'[50]. Faced with financial emergencies that both compel and enable them to transcend the confines of the domestic sphere, Brontë's female protagonists embark on careers as women of business but ultimately forfeit the hard-won autonomy of the professional artist through becoming wives and mothers. There is of course a danger here of reading the conclusions of Brontë's novels simplistically as cancellations of what has come before. As Elsie B. Michie and Jill Galvan have argued in an important revaluation of the Victorian marriage plot, there is a critical tendency to 'privileg[e] conclusion over the path towards it, dismissing that whole path as thematically and discursively subordinate'.[51] My larger point here is that Brontë's endings retroactively normalise and contain the economic radicalism of her plots without erasing it entirely.

The Brontës and the Literary Marketplace

Reversing some of their own prior economic radicalism, the concluding voltas of novels like *Agnes Grey*, *The Tenant of Wildfell Hall* and *Jane Eyre* point to an underlying authorial insecurity about the long-term sustainability of female careers in the nineteenth-century marketplace. If the employed fictional characters of the Brontës throw light on the challenges early Victorian middle-class women faced in the fields of art and education, their own attempts at establishing themselves as successful authors were similarly riddled with anxieties about female professionalism. Like Mrs Grey's daughters and like Helen Graham, the sisters were turning domestic 'accomplishments' into a source of income – working in an environment in which 'literary labour', just like artistic production, could be thought of 'as an extension of a woman's domestic work'.[52] Where their protagonists spend their teenage years learning to draw, sing, and dance, the young Brontës practised their hands at writing. They collaboratively invented stories set in imaginary locales and produced some of these texts

[50] Kate Flint, 'Women Writers, Women's Issues', in *The Cambridge Companion to the Brontës*, ed. by Heather Glen (Cambridge: Cambridge University Press, 2002), pp. 170–91, at p. 178.

[51] Jill Galvan and Elsie Michie, 'Introduction', in *Replotting Marriage in Nineteenth-Century British Literature*, ed. by Jill Galvan and Elsie Michie (Columbus OH: Ohio State University Press, 2018), pp. 1–11, at p. 5.

[52] Linda H. Peterson, *Becoming a Woman of Letters: Myths of Authorship and Facts of the Victorian Market* (Princeton NJ: Princeton University Press, 2009), p. 141.

as miniature manuscript books, whose material form playfully anticipated that of their later published writings.[53]

As they grew older, the sisters turned from these juvenile story worlds to the composition of poetry but also began to feel the power of male prejudice against women's literary activity. When Charlotte Brontë, hoping for advice and encouragement, sent samples of her lyrical efforts to poet laureate Robert Southey in the late 1830s, Southey famously replied that 'literature cannot be the business of a woman's life, and it ought not to be'.[54] Brontë's 'proper duties' as a future housewife and mother would deprive her of the necessary 'leisure' to write and in due course make her 'less eager for celebrity'.[55] Southey's argument that for women literature could never be a 'business' but, at best, 'an accomplishment and a recreation' provides the negative image from which the sisters' later novels depart through illustrating how their female protagonists successfully transform private skills into public commodities, reach an audience, and acquire a reputation.[56] Southey conceded that, by the beginning of Victoria's reign, literature had in fact become a 'business', – he takes pride in 'hav[ing] made literature my profession' – but at the same time sought to discourage women from pursuing careers in the field.[57]

It took Brontë and her sisters another decade to reject Southey's advice and begin to tackle the obstacles on their road towards professional authorship. As Elizabeth Gaskell noted in her *Life of Charlotte Brontë* (1857), 'teaching' for the time being appeared to the sisters 'the only way of earning an independent livelihood'.[58] It was only in the mid-1840s that they set out to get their writing published and to attempt to sustain themselves through the work of their pen. What often tends to be overlooked in the professional biography of the Brontës is that they had already acquired experience in the management of their own financial resources before that point. The sisters put the savings from their teaching income into the burgeoning railway business and fared well with it. Charlotte's description of their cautious investment policies reads like the mirror image of the devastating monetary choices male characters make in her sister's first novel:

53 See Christine Alexander, 'Juvenilia', in *The Brontës in Context*, ed. by Marianne Thormählen (Cambridge: Cambridge University Press, 2012), pp. 98–106 on the early writing of the siblings.

54 Robert Southey, *The Life and Correspondence of Robert Southey*, ed. by Charles Cuthbert Southey, 6 vols (London: Longman, Brown, Green, and Longmans, 1849–50), vol. 6, p. 329.

55 Ibid.

56 Ibid.

57 Ibid., p. 328.

58 Elizabeth Gaskell, *The Life of Charlotte Brontë*, ed. by Alan Shelston (Harmondsworth: Penguin Books, 1975, orig. 1857), p. 184.

> The price of shares varies continually—and any day a small share-holder may find his funds shrunk to their original dimensions—Emily has made herself mistress of the necessary degree of knowledge for conducting the matter, by dint of carefully reading every paragraph & every advertisement in the newspapers that related to rail-roads and as we have abstained from all gambling, all 'mere' speculative buying-in & selling-out—we have got on very decently.[59]

The Brontës thus experimented with the kind of capitalist multiplication of money that in the fictional world of *Agnes Grey* is reserved for men and invariably leads to bankruptcy, but they consciously sought to acquire an economic education and temper the excesses of 'speculative' risk-taking. When the railway bubble was on the brink of bursting in early 1846, Charlotte Brontë told her former teacher and colleague Margaret Wooler that she was 'most anxious' to 'sell our shares ere it be too late—and to secure the proceeds in some safer if, for the present, less profitable—, investment'.[60]

Brontë's letter does not spell out the exact nature of such a potential alternative, but her roughly simultaneous correspondence with London publishers Aylott and Jones shows that she was thinking of writing as a new kind of investment that could yield the sisters a reliable return. She had contacted the firm two days before writing to Wooler, enquiring whether the publishers would be interested in bringing out a collection of poems, a manuscript volume that contained pieces by herself, Emily and Anne. Since the three sisters had not yet published anything, the firm insisted that the volume needed to be printed 'on the Author's account' and thus at their own financial risk.[61] Publishing the book on commission meant that the Brontës were in fact investing capital in themselves, advancing money for the production and advertisement of the volume in the hope of making a long-term profit from sales. Such dreams were quickly shattered: only two out of 1,000 copies of the *Poems* were sold within the first year of publication and the £35 that the sisters had paid appeared to have been lost. It was only at a later point that the sisters made good some of their losses. After the initial success of their novels, Charlotte's publishers Smith, Elder and Co. bought up Aylott and Jones's unsold copies and reissued them in late 1848, with the latter firm transferring to Charlotte the money it had received from Smith.[62]

[59] Charlotte Brontë, *The Letters of Charlotte Brontë: With a Selection of Letters by Family and Friends*, ed. by Margaret Smith, 3 vols (Oxford: Oxford University Press, 1995–2004), vol. 1, p. 390.

[60] Ibid., p. 447. See also Janette Rutterford's contribution on women investors in this volume.

[61] Ibid., p. 445.

[62] See G. D. Hargreaves, 'The Publishing of "Poems by Currer, Ellis and Acton Bell"', *Brontë Society Transactions*, 15:4 (1969), 294–300 for details on the publication history of the volume.

Like Helen Graham, who moves from watercolours to oil painting upon establishing herself as a commercial artist, the Brontës transitioned from the semi-privacy of the lyric to the realist novel, whose market potential by the mid-1840s had outgrown that of poetry. Charlotte, Emily and Anne now turned their full attention to the writing of narrative prose and offered their first novels, including *The Professor*, *Wuthering Heights* and *Agnes Grey*, to a series of – initially hesitant – publishers. Having failed to strike a deal with *The Professor*, Charlotte had more luck with *Jane Eyre*, her second novel. She agreed to an outright sale arrangement with her publishers Smith, Elder and Co., receiving a flat payment of £100 'and another £400 for subsequent editions'.[63] The novel was published in October 1847 and became popular immediately, closely followed by a second and third edition that were printed in early 1848, which launched Charlotte's career as a bread-winning author. Her sisters were struggling harder to achieve similar results. *Wuthering Heights* and *Agnes Grey* were taken up by Thomas Cautley Newby, another London publisher, who made them 'pay £50 in advance, with the promise that the money would be refunded if their novels sold enough copies to cover expenses'.[64] Despite the 'modest commercial success' of the books, Newby never paid back his commission, and Emily and Anne would both be dead within two years.[65] Where in the fiction of the Brontës, female careers are prematurely cut short by the encroaching demands of matrimony and domestic duty, in their own biographies the life of professional authorship ended before it had really begun.

Even where the Brontës managed to make a public impression with the printing of their writings – experiencing at least a taste of the literary 'celebrity' that Southey denied women authors – that impression was limited by the fact that they were working under pseudonyms that concealed their true identity as female producers. Fact and fiction were closely related in this respect, too. Afraid that her abusive husband might use her paintings as a clue to her whereabouts, the protagonist of *The Tenant of Wildfell Hall* is forced to go into hiding and sign her paintings with false initials, which give a misleading impression of who the creator behind the pictures actually is. Although this construct allows Helen Graham to set up a mutually beneficial arrangement with her London art dealer, it simultaneously prevents her

[63] Linda H. Peterson, 'Working With Publishers', in *The Cambridge Companion to Victorian Women's Writing*, ed. by Linda H. Peterson (Cambridge: Cambridge University Press, 2015), pp. 43–58, at p. 44. See also Alexis Easley, 'The Brontës and the Victorian Reading Public, 1846–1860', in *A Companion to the Brontës*, ed. by Diane Long Hoeveler and Deborah Denenholz Morse (Hoboken NJ: Wiley-Blackwell, 2016), pp. 303–17, at pp. 303–8, on Charlotte's management of the publication and reviewing of the sisters' writings.

[64] Peterson, 'Working With Publishers', p. 44.

[65] Ibid. p. 44.

from taking an explicit social or political stance as a woman artist. Her true identity remains a secret to the buyers of her pictures and is only revealed to the readers of Brontë's novel.

The Tenant of Wildfell Hall to that extent reflects the experiences of the Brontës as professional artists who, like Helen Graham, issued their work under assumed names.[66] While their novels were arguably advancing a proto-feminist case for women's economic liberation, the sisters themselves were absent from the mid-nineteenth-century public sphere as female authorial figures. Retrospectively reflecting on their decision to appear before their readers under the guise of Currer, Ellis and Acton Bell, Charlotte Brontë in 1850 explained that their 'own names' had been 'veiled' because the three were profoundly 'averse to personal publicity'.[67] In her preface of July 1848 to the second edition of *The Tenant of Wildfell Hall*, Anne Brontë had used the widespread confusion over the true identity of the Bells to call for something like a gender-blind reception of art. 'If a book is a good one', she suggested, 'it is so whatever the sex of the author may be', since 'all novels are or should be written for both men and women to read'.[68] As progressive as this defence may have been by mid-nineteenth-century standards, it ultimately enabled Brontë to avoid having to solve the pseudonym question and being compelled to speak out as a woman novelist on the Victorian 'woman question'.

Professionalism versus Expressivism

The ambiguous feelings of the Brontës towards their own role as female participants in the literary marketplace in large part stemmed from the absence of the kind of equal critical standards that Anne had described as an aesthetic and social ideal in her 1848 preface. Where 'authoresses', as Charlotte noted, were 'liable to be looked on with prejudice' in a predominantly male climate of public opinion,[69] the male pseudonym became a strategy to gain access to a field whose gatekeepers – figures like Southey – cast doubt

66 The role of pseudonymity in the sisters' navigation of the Victorian literary marketplace is explored in Marrisa Joseph, *Victorian Literary Businesses: The Management and Practices of the British Publishing Industry* (Cham, Switzerland: Palgrave Macmillan, 2019), pp. 60–7. Elaine Showalter speaks of 'the appearance of the male pseudonym' as the key event in what she describes as the 'Feminine phase' in the history of women's writing (the 1840s to the beginning of the 1880s) (Showalter, *A Literature of Their Own*, p. 13).

67 Charlotte Brontë, 'Biographical Notice of Ellis and Acton Bell', in Emily Brontë, *Wuthering Heights*, ed. by Hilda Marsden and Ian Jack (Oxford: Clarendon Press, 1976, orig. 1850), pp. 435–41, at p. 436.

68 Brontë, *The Tenant of Wildfell Hall*, p. 5.

69 Brontë, 'Biographical Notice of Ellis and Acton Bell', p. 436.

on the ability of women to work as artistically independent and economically autonomous agents. At another level, the unease of the sisters with the 'personal publicity' of the successful novelist resulted from an anxiety about having to cater to audience demand, which rose to the surface after their switching from poetry to the more marketable genre of the novel in the wake of the failure of *Poems by Currer, Ellis, and Acton Bell* in 1846. While the sales of *Jane Eyre*, *Wuthering Heights* and *The Tenant of Wildfell Hall* were gradually turning the Brontës into commercial artists, Anne Brontë was intent on emphasising that her aim as a writer was neither 'to amuse the Reader' nor 'to ingratiate [her]self with … the Public'.[70] These, of course, are the very conditions that the protagonists of her two novels ultimately have no choice but to meet. Her fiction served Brontë as a case study to chart exactly this tension between artistic production and market demand. Whereas art in her books becomes merely craft, Brontë sees the novel itself as an art form which can reconcile commercial success with a higher moral calling that transcends commodification.

Conclusion

Both *Agnes Grey* and *The Tenant of Wildfell Hall* showcase the complexity of Brontë's exploration of the connection between gender, aesthetics and economics in mid-nineteenth-century Britain. Highlighting the positive effect of the art world on her female protagonists, Brontë locates the emancipatory power of art in its financial dynamics rather than in its ability to provide a creative expression of feminine identity. In her writings, the modern market for cultural goods appears as an environment that is dominated by anonymous forces and hence leaves women room to deploy strategies of pseudonymity, which bypass gendered obstacles that under different circumstances bar them from becoming women of business. Art allows Brontë's heroines to generate an independent source of income and to experience themselves as autonomous producers. Yet it does not finally turn them into visible participants in the Victorian public. Brontë was thus proceeding cautiously, illustrating Lana L. Dalley and Jill Rappoport's more general observation that, as writers, 'nineteenth-century women … crafted economic identities by carefully mediating between their public and domestic selves' in order to 'challeng[e] popular notions of what constituted women's business'.[71] Like Brontë herself, the protagonists of her novels neither become genuine public

70 Brontë, *The Tenant of Wildfell Hall*, p. 3.

71 Lana L. Dalley and Jill Rappoport, 'Introducing Economic Women', in *Economic Women: Essays on Desire and Dispossession in Nineteenth-Century British Culture*, ed. by Lana L. Dalley and Jill Rappoport (Columbus OH: Ohio State University Press, 2013), pp. 1–21, at p. 16.

figures nor make an explicit case for women's legal and economic emancipation. The true radicalism of Brontë's career as well as her fiction thus manifested itself at a material rather than discursive level – not so much in the fact that she and her characters represent a new kind of distinctly feminine art as in the fact that art, as a professional identity, gives women access to economic agency and social participation.

10

Harriet Taylor Mill and the Case for Female Labour Force Participation

JANELLE PÖTZSCH

Harriet Taylor Mill (1807–58) has long been deemed little more than the unworthy love interest of philosopher and economist John Stuart Mill (1806–73), due to the scandal attached to the start of their relationship.[1] Yet while recent scholars have paid attention to her role as a political philosopher in her own right, Taylor Mill is also noteworthy for her economic analysis of gender inequality.[2] Her seminal essay *Enfranchisement of Women* (1851) details how social structures force women into material dependency on men and how this dependency corrupts gender relations. Taylor Mill thereby challenges contemporary notions about the public and the private sphere and advances the understanding of both the market and the family. Her arguments for women's labour force participation were far ahead of her time. In arguing that women's gainful employment should be encouraged for its effect on the power dynamics within a household rather than for increasing that household's net income, Taylor Mill anticipated the concept of intra-household bargaining that has been developed in the 1990s.[3]

This chapter deals with the feminist economic thought of Harriet Taylor Mill, beginning with an introduction to Harriet Taylor Mill and the reception she has received due to her connection with John Stuart Mill. I then

[1] M. Ashworth, 'The Marriage of John Stuart Mill', *Englishwoman, 30* (1916), 159–72.

[2] Helen McCabe, *Harriet Taylor Mill*, Cambridge Elements: Women in the History of Philosophy Series (Cambridge: Cambridge University Press, 2020).

[3] Nancy Folbre, *Greed, Lust & Gender. A History of Economic Ideas* (Oxford: Oxford University Press, 2009).

proceed with an outline of Taylor Mill's argumentation in her *Enfranchisement*. Finally, I shall focus on Taylor Mill's arguments for women's labour force participation and how they both relate to and advance contemporary economic reasoning.

Reacknowledging Harriet Taylor Mill

Harriet Taylor Mill has only comparatively recently been recognised as a social and political thinker in her own right.[4] This was despite the fact that her second husband, the famous philosopher and economist John Stuart Mill, stated in more than one preface to his works that Taylor Mill 'was the inspirer, and in part the author, of all that is best in my writings'.[5] The significance of Taylor Mill becomes further evident by the fact that J. S. Mill dedicates a whole chapter of his *Autobiography* to her – it has the telling title 'Commencement of the Most Valuable Friendship of My Life'. Moreover, Mill emphasises the fact that his relationship with Taylor was especially an authorial one:

> When two persons have their thoughts and speculations completely in common … it is of little consequence in respect to the question of originality which of them holds the pen; the one who contributes least to the composition may contribute most to the thought; the writings which result are the joint product of both, and it must often be impossible to disentangle their respective parts and affirm that this belongs to one and that to the other. In this wide sense, not only during the years of our married life, but during many of the years of confidential friendship which preceded, all my published writings were as much her work as mine.[6]

Such exuberant praise from a man known for his sobriety and rationality has made many Mill scholars suspicious about the real scope of Taylor

[4] Jo Ellen Jacobs, *The Voice of Harriet Taylor Mill* (Bloomington IN: Indiana University Press, 2002); Helen McCabe, *Harriet Taylor Mill* (Cambridge: Cambridge University Press, 2023), pp. 1–78; Janet A. Seiz and Michèle A. Pujol, 'Harriet Taylor Mill', *The American Economic Review*, 90:2 (2000), 476–9.

[5] John Stuart Mill, *On Liberty and Other Essays* (Oxford: Oxford University Press, 2008), p. 3. Hereafter, John Stuart Mill is J. S. Mill and Harriet Taylor Mill is Taylor Mill to maintain clarity of distinction between husband and wife.

[6] John Stuart Mill, *Autobiography and Literary Essays*, ed. by John M. Robson and Jack Stillinger, with an introduction by Lord Robbins, vol. 1 of *The Collected Works of John Stuart Mill* (Toronto: University of Toronto Press; London: Routledge and Kegan Paul, 1981), p. 251.

Mill's contributions.[7] Some event doubted Taylor's intellectual abilities.[8] Assessments of Taylor Mill's role range from the claim that we are merely dealing with a 'Harriet Taylor Mill Myth'[9] to the suspicion that Mill had a 'lifelong mission to deify Harriet'.[10] Friedrich August von Hayek's introduction to his edited collection of the correspondence between J. S. Mill and Taylor Mill seems to display a more nuanced view: Hayek acknowledges Taylor Mill's influence on J. S. Mill's thought, especially when it comes to politics. However, this concession allows Hayek to trace Mill's socialist sympathies back to Taylor and conclude his study with the somewhat sheepish remark that:

> I believe that a careful study of [J. S. Mill's] later development would show that in some degree he withdrew a little from the more advanced positions which he had taken under her influence and returned to views closer to those he had held in his youth. But this in an impression for which it would be impossible to give here the evidence.[11]

In her introductory essay to her edition of writings by Mill and Taylor Mill on sex equality, Alice Rossi argues that this is a recurrent mechanism of defence among Mill scholars of the early twentieth century: those opposed to socialist ideas highlight Taylor Mill's influence whereas those sympathetic to socialism tend to play it down because they back away from the idea that J. S. Mill's socialist tendencies result from the influence of a woman.[12] Rossi therefore argues that 'one senses in Mill scholars an unwitting desire to reject Harriet Taylor as capable of contributing in any significant way to the vigor of Mill's analysis of political and social issues unless it included some tinge of sentiment or political thought the scholar disapproved of'.[13]

7 See, for instance, Friedrich August von Hayek (ed.), *John Stuart Mill and Harriet Taylor: Their Correspondence and Subsequent Marriage* (Chicago IL: University of Chicago Press, 1951), p. 266; Bruce L. Kinzer, *J. S. Mill Revisited: Biographical and Political Explorations* (New York: Palgrave Macmillan, 2007); Richard Reeves, *John Stuart Mill: Victorian Firebrand* (London: Atlantic Books, 2007), p. 206.

8 For an overview of both contemporary and scholarly criticism of Taylor Mill, see Jo Ellen Jacobs, '"The Lot of Gifted Ladies is Hard": A Study of Harriet Taylor Mill Criticism', *Hypatia*, 9:3 (1994), 132–62; and Alice S. Rossi, 'Sentiment and Intellect: The Story of John Stuart Mill and Harriet Taylor Mill', in *John Stuart Mill and Harriet Taylor Mill: Essays on Sex Equality*, ed. by Alice S. Rossi (Chicago IL: Chicago University Press, 1970), pp. 1–64.

9 H. O. Pappe, *John Stuart Mill and the Harriet Taylor Myth* (Melbourne: Melbourne University Press, 1960).

10 Reeves, *John Stuart Mill*, p. 206.

11 von Hayek (ed.), *John Stuart Mill and Harriet Taylor Mill: Essays on Sex Equality*, p. 266.

12 Rossi, 'Sentiment and Intellect', p. 37. For a topical discussion of J. S. Mill's socialism, see Helen McCabe, *John Stuart Mill, Socialist* (Montreal: McGill-Queen's University Press, 2021).

13 Rossi, 'Sentiment and Intellect', p. 44.

Menaka Philips offers another explanation for the inimical reception of Harriet Taylor Mill. She observes that had J. S. Mill's dedication been slightly more conventional in acknowledging her support rather than her active cooperation, then Harriet Taylor Mill 'might have become the most respected *wife* of the canon. And perhaps this is precisely the problem'.[14] Philips argues that 'the unwillingness to believe in JSM's praise of his wife as an intellectual partner reflects an impoverished understanding of the scope and nature of intellectual collaboration'.[15] Specifically, the exclusive focus on the 'hard currency' of publications *per se* has obscured our view of the emotional and intellectual labour such works, especially collaborative ones, involve. Previous scholarship on J. S. Mill and Taylor Mill therefore offers a highly decontextualised interpretation and has the effect of rendering women's contribution invisible.[16] It is likewise often ignored by Mill scholars that Harriet Taylor's personal experiences had made her acutely aware of gendered expectations, which in turn have made her a more radical social critic than Mill was.[17]

This is especially the case when it comes to the right to divorce and the gendered division of labour.[18] Naturally, feminist and gender issues cannot be regarded separately from economics – and Harriet Taylor Mill has credentials in this area as well. She is currently reacknowledged as the co-author of J. S. Mill's *Principles of Political Economy*.[19] The tendency of J. S. Mill to stress co-authorship, however, forms an obstacle when it comes to acknowledging Taylor Mill as an author in her own right. There are few works that have been published under her name, except for some shorter pieces that appeared in the Unitarian journal *The Monthly Repository*.[20] Like

14 Menaka Philips, 'The "Beloved and Deplored" Memory of Harriet Taylor Mill: Rethinking Gender and Intellectual Labor in the Canon', *Hypatia*, 33:4 (2018), 626–42, at p. 639. Emphasis in the text.

15 Ibid., p. 628.

16 Ibid.

17 Julia Annas, 'Mill and The Subjection of Women', *Philosophy*, 52:200 (1977), 179–94; Mary Ann Dimand, 'The Economics of Charlotte Perkins Gilman', in *Women of Value: Feminist Essays on the History of Women in Economics*, ed. by M. A. Dimand, R. W. Dimand and E. L. Forget (Brookfield VT: Edward Elgar, 1995), pp. 124–49; Michèle A. Pujol, 'The Feminist Economic Thought of Harriet Taylor Mill (1807–1858)', in *Women of Value*, pp. 82–102.

18 Susan Mendus, 'John Stuart Mill and Harriet Taylor on Women and Marriage', *Utilitas*, 6:2 (1994), 287–99.

19 Ronald G. Bodkin, 'Women's Agency in Classical Economic Thought: Adam Smith, Harriet Taylor Mill, and J. S. Mill', *Feminist Economics*, 5:1 (1999), 45–60; Friedrich August von Hayek (ed.), *John Stuart Mill and Harriet Taylor: Their Correspondence and Subsequent Marriage* (Chicago IL: Chicago University Press, 1951); Pujol, 'The Feminist Economic Thought of Harriet Taylor Mill', pp. 82–102.

20 Francis Edward Mineka, *The Dissidence of Dissent: The Monthly Repository, 1806–1838* (Chapel Hill NC: University of North Carolina Press, 1944).

the *Principles*, also the rigorous newspaper articles on domestic violence have been co-authored with J. S. Mill.[21] The same goes for *On Liberty*; even though J. S. Mill acknowledges Taylor Mill's influence in its foreword.[22] In this instance, technological developments have helped to cast a new light on Taylor Mill's role as an author: by using digital humanities techniques, Christoph Schmidt-Petri, Michael Schefczyk and Lilly Osburg have demonstrated 'that Harriet Taylor Mill's contribution to *On Liberty* is sufficiently substantial for her to count as co-author'.[23]

The authorship puzzle has been less enigmatic regarding the essay 'The Enfranchisement of Women', given that J. S. Mill himself called the essay 'hers'. In her own words, Taylor Mill describes her role in the writing partnership in a modest yet revealing manner: 'In a peculiar sense, my share in it being little more than that of an editor and amanuensis.'[24] Published in the *Westminster Review* in 1851, Taylor Mill's essay is 'partly a review of recent events regarding the campaign for women's suffrage in America, and partly a series of arguments for giving votes to British women'.[25] It is noteworthy because her essay gives material reasons for gender inequality. Taylor Mill argues that 'numbers of women are wives and mothers only because there is no other career open to them, no other occupation for their feelings or their activities'.[26] According to Taylor Mill, women are compelled to marry and become mothers simply because social structures prevent them from becoming financially independent.

Material Girls

In a departure from the gender essentialism of the nineteenth century that was both prevalent and frequently pathologised, and that thus tended to differentiate between men and women and their roles in society on such grounds as emotionality and, of course, hysteria, Harriet Taylor Mill makes

[21] Rita Manning, 'The Tyranny of Bodily Strength: Harriet Taylor Mill and John Stuart Mill on Domestic Violence', in *Analyzing Violence Against Women*, ed. by Wanda Teays (Cham: Springer, 2019), pp. 151–65.

[22] Mill, *On Liberty and Other Essays*, p. 3.

[23] Christoph Schmidt-Petri, Michael Schefczyk and Lilly Osburg, 'Who Authored *On Liberty*? Stylometric Evidence on Harriet Taylor Mill's Contribution', *Utilitas*, 34 (2022), 120–38, at p. 138.

[24] Quoted in Evelyn L. Pugh, 'John Stuart Mill, Harriet Taylor, and Women's Rights in America, 1850–1873', *Canadian Journal of History*, 13:3 (1978), 423–42, at p. 425.

[25] Helen McCabe, *Harriet Taylor Mill* (Cambridge: Cambridge University Press, 2023), p. 34.

[26] Harriet Taylor Mill, 'Enfranchisement of Women', in *John Stuart Mill and Harriet Taylor Mill: Essays on Sex Equality*, ed. by Alice S. Rossi (Chicago IL: Chicago University Press, 1970), pp. 89–121, at p. 104.

a striking case for an early form of social constructivism.[27] Taylor Mill identifies an intersection between biological differences and social construction where gender relations are concerned. She holds that the division between public and private spheres for men and women are rooted in prehistoric custom, hypothesising that 'in the beginning, and among tribes that are still in a primitive condition, women were and are the slaves of men for the purposes of toil'.[28] Such a division of labour was possible because of the superior bodily strength of men, who might physically subjugate women, which eventually found expression in legislation: in other words, the difference in physical strength between men and women is mirrored in their different legal status – and women, being 'the physically weaker' 'have been made legally inferior'.[29] As society became more refined, so did male control over women: women ceased to be 'the slaves of men for purposes of toil' and became 'the slaves of men for purposes of sensuality' instead.[30]

Nineteenth-century Europe, according to Taylor Mill, displays 'a third and milder dominion' because it secures its influence 'by sedulous inculcation of the mind',[31] which makes women embrace 'feminine' virtues like submissiveness, selflessness and domesticity. In this, she is very much the daughter of Wollstonecraft. Moreover, this credo has carried the logic of separate spheres for men and women to its extremes. As a result, 'the lives of the two persons were apart. The wife was part of the furniture of home – of the resting-place to which the man returned from business or pleasure'.[32] Taylor Mill argues that the private sphere is a far cry from women's actual inclinations, claiming that the concept of the private sphere was established to cater to male preferences:

> We ask why the existence of one-half the species should be merely ancillary to that of the other—why each woman should be a mere appendage to a man, allowed to have no interests of her own, that there may be nothing to compete in her mind with *his* interests and *his* pleasure; the only reason which can be given is, that men like it.[33]

Women's ideological confinement to the private sphere not only reduces them to 'slaves of men for purposes of sensuality', it also implies prohibiting

[27] On nineteenth-century gender essentialism, see Stephanie A. Shields, 'Passionate Men, Emotional Women: Psychology Constructs Gender Difference in the Late Nineteenth Century', *History of Psychology*, 10:2 (May 2007), 92–110; Yael S. Feldman, 'From Essentialism to Constructivism? The Gender of Peace and War – Gilman, Woolf, Freud', *Partial Answers: Journal of Literature and the History of Ideas*, 2:1 (2004), 113–45.

[28] Taylor Mill, 'Enfranchisement', p. 108.

[29] Ibid., p. 99.

[30] Ibid., p. 108.

[31] Ibid.

[32] Ibid., p. 109.

[33] Ibid., 107. Emphasis added.

women from opportunities to make a living.[34] Taylor Mill points out that all activities that 'task the higher faculties in an important field, which leads to distinction, riches or even pecuniary independence, are fenced round as the exclusive domain of the predominant section': in other words, men.[35] Consequently, for Taylor Mill, the superior physical strength and legal status of men ultimately translate into financial power over women. Taylor Mill is thus convinced that current social structures and cultural norms express nothing but the vested interests of men.

Taylor Mill argues that once 'the reasons alleged for excluding women from active life … are stripped of their garb of declamatory phrases, and reduced to the simple expression of meaning, they seem to be mainly three'.[36] To substantiate her thesis that society is adapted to male preferences, Taylor Mill engages with three arguments against female wage labour. Her aim is to show that these arguments are either fallacious or proceed from unjustified hypotheses. She begins with the so-called 'maternity argument' according to which women are disqualified for gainful employment by motherhood.[37] Taylor Mill challenges the validity of this 'maternity argument' by pointing out that it is unjustly applied to single women as well: 'The maternity argument deserts its supporters in the case of single women, a large and increasing class of the population.'[38]

Yet the greatest injustice of the maternity argument consists in its limiting women's outlooks and confining them solely to the role of the mother, which amounts 'to make imperative on women that they shall be either mothers or nothing'.[39] Taylor Mill highlights the absurdity and injustice of this idea by observing that 'no one proposes to exclude the male sex from Parliament because a man may be a soldier or sailor in active service, or a merchant whose business requires all his time and energies'.[40] So even though some occupations are indeed more demanding and time-consuming than others, people who practise them are still free to *choose* to confine themselves to it in case their occupation leaves them little room for anything else: in other words, the merchant might indeed focus on his business and the stock exchange rather than engage in politics as well.

This is why Taylor Mill holds that 'where incompatibility is real, it will take care of itself'.[41] It is not, then, necessary to establish by law who may engage to which extent in which field. The people concerned are suited best

34 Ibid., p. 108.

35 Ibid., p. 97.

36 Taylor Mill, 'Enfranchisement', p. 103.

37 Ibid.

38 Ibid.

39 Ibid.

40 Ibid.

41 Ibid.

to assess their time budget. Since 'neither women nor men need any law to exclude them from an occupation, if they have undertaken another which is incompatible with it', it is a 'gross injustice in making the incompatibility a pretence for the exclusion of those in whose case it does not exist'.[42] Taylor Mill considers such legislation too detailed and therefore unnecessary; however, when it comes to women, such reasoning is not only unnecessary but also harmful since it restricts women's options. Again Taylor Mill argues that 'numbers of women are wives and mothers only because there is no other career open to them, no other occupation for their feelings or their activities'.[43] She emphasises the fact that the maternity argument harbours a naturalistic fallacy since the restriction of women's options are passed off as 'natural', or essentialist, and even God-given: 'To say that women must be excluded from active life because maternity disqualifies them for it, is in fact to say, that every other career should be forbidden them in order that maternity be their only resource.'[44]

The second argument against 'the admission of women to political or professional life', which Taylor Mill seeks to refute, states that the public sphere has a 'hardening effect on the character'.[45] Following this logic, women should be spared the corrupting influences of business and politics in order to offer men an alternate, even correcting, model; or, as Taylor Mill phrases it:

> There are still, however, persons who say that the world and its avocations render men selfish and unfeeling; that the struggles, rivalries, and collisions of business and politics make them harsh and unamiable; that if half the species must unavoidably be given up to these things, it is the more necessary that the other half should be kept free from them; that to preserve women from the bad influences of the world, is the only chance of preventing men from being wholly given up to them.[46]

Taylor Mill argues that this assumption has lost all validity, and that social and civil advancement has rendered physical violence nearly non-existent, at least in the professional sphere – both Taylor Mill and J. S. Mill were well aware that violence, both physical and psychological, was still prevalent especially in the private sphere. In the 1850s, they published numerous journal articles in which they discuss recent (court) cases of domestic violence and offer possible remedies.[47] It is therefore dubious to hold that women need protection by banning them from the public sphere. As for

[42] Ibid.
[43] Ibid., p. 104.
[44] Ibid.
[45] Ibid., pp. 106; 103.
[46] Ibid., p. 106.
[47] See Manning, 'The Tyranny of Bodily Strength'.

the alleged beneficial moral influence of (confined) women on (public) men, Taylor Mill challenges the very idea of the ideology of separate spheres by pointing out its degrading effects on both sexes: 'There is hardly any situation more unfavourable to the maintenance of elevation of character or force of intellect, than to live in the society, and seek by preference the sympathy, of inferiors in mental endowments.'[48] Taylor Mill is convinced that men become worse because of the female company they keep: The poor education granted to women make them inappropriate companions because they have 'no knowledge and no care about the great ideas and purposes which dignify life'.[49] Nevertheless, Taylor Mill emphasises that this degrading effect has nothing to do with the mental or moral abilities of women per se. It stems rather from their lack of training: 'It is from nothing in the faculties themselves, but from the petty subjects and interests on which alone they are exercised, that the companionship of women, such as their present circumstances make them, so often exercises a dissolvent influence on high faculties and aspirations in men.'[50] Taylor Mill establishes the idea that patriarchal society is not only harmful and unjust to women as it indoctrinates them and constrains their options; it is equally corrupting for men, who forfeit the chance of true companionship and mutual growth. Ironically, the society men have devised to serve their own comfort eventually debases them. Taylor Mill highlights that men and women need to unite to experience true moral and intellectual development: 'In the present closeness of association between the sexes, men cannot retain manliness unless women acquire it.'[51]

Competing for Funds

Taylor Mill summarises the third and final argument against women's gainful employment as follows: '[I]t is urged, that to give the same freedom of occupation to women as to men, would be an injurious addition to the crowd of competitors, by whom the avenues to almost all kinds of employment

48 Taylor Mill, 'Enfranchisement', p. 110.

49 Ibid., p. 111.

50 Ibid.

51 Ibid., p. 110. Incidentally, Charles Dickens, like Taylor Mill, associated with the South Place Chapel Circle of radical Unitarians, and entertained similar ideas. His novels are full of women who fully meet the usual criteria of conventional femininity and prove fatal, or at least burdensome, to their husbands and partners, like Dora from David Copperfield. See Kathryn Gleadle, *The Early Feminists: Radical Unitarians and the Emergence of the Women's Rights Movement* (Basingstoke: Macmillan, 1998), 59f. I would suggest that Jane Austen's Lady Bertram from *Mansfield Park* (1814) fits into this category of a conventionally 'feminine' and hence essentially useless, or even harmful, woman.

are choked up, and its remuneration depressed.'[52] The reasoning behind this argument builds on the so-called wages-fund theory, an important element of the orthodox political economy of the nineteenth century.[53] According to the wages-fund theory, 'the level of wages is determined by dividing the funds available for wage payment by the number of labourers'.[54]

The basic tenets of the wages-fund doctrine were already established by Adam Smith in his *Wealth of Nations* (1776), whose groundwork was developed further in David Ricardo's *Principles of Political Economy* (1817). According to Smith, the division of labour is both the cause and effect of economic growth; yet although economic growth is *initiated* by the division of labour, it is sustained solely by capital accumulation. The more capital is accumulated, the greater the amount available for wages. This, in turn, makes possible a further division of labour: an increasing wages-fund allows for the employment of more workers. Essentially, 'wages are a part of the capital of the employer advanced to the worker as wages to maintain him during production'.[55] The wages-fund doctrine is hence 'two things at once: a theory of wages and of capital'.[56] David Ricardo explicitly states that wages are paid from capital and are moreover fixed. Other names usually associated with the wages-fund theory are James Mill and John Stuart Mill, with debate persisting on whether J. S. Mill did 'recant' the wages-fund doctrine.[57] The latter provides the following understanding of the wages-fund in his *Principles of Political Economy*:

> Wages, then, depend mainly upon the demand and supply for labour; or as it is often expressed, on the proportion between population and capital. By population is here meant the number only of the labouring class, or rather those work for hire; and by capital only circulating capital, and not even the whole of that, but the part which is expended in the direct purchase of labour... With these limitations of the terms, wages ... cannot rise, but by an increase of the aggregate funds employed in hiring labourers, or a diminution in the number of the competitors for hire.[58]

[52] Taylor Mill, 'Enfranchisement', p. 104.

[53] James Clark Sherburne, *John Ruskin or the Ambiguities of Abundance: A Study in Social and Economic Criticism* (Cambridge MA: Harvard University Press, 1972), p. 156.

[54] Ibid.

[55] Russel McKenzie and John Levendies, 'What Recantation? The Wages Fund Doctrines of J.S. Mill in Light of Smith, and Ricardo', *Humanomics*, 24:4 (2008), 293–305, at p. 295.

[56] Ibid., p. 293.

[57] Engaging in this discussion would be well beyond the scope of this paper. Interested readers may wish to consult Mark Donoghue, 'Mill's Affirmation of the Classical Wage Fund Doctrine', *Scottish Journal of Political Economy*, 44:1 (1997), 82–99; McKenzie and Levendis, 'What Recantation?'; and Kevin Vallier, 'Production, Distribution, and J.S. Mill', *Utilitas*, 22:2 (2010), 103–25.

[58] John Stuart Mill, *Principles of Political Economy, with Some of Their Applications to Social Philosophy: Collected Works II* (Toronto: University of Toronto Press; London: Routledge and Kegan Paul, 1965), 337f.

Even though the capital available for wages increases with the progress of wealth, it is still somewhat predetermined. J. S. Mill therefore holds that '[m]ore than that amount … the wages-receiving class cannot possibly divide among them … the sum be divided being fixed the wages of each depend solely on the divisor, the number of participants'.[59] According to this principle, the only way to increase wages is to reduce the number of workers. Therefore, based on this idea, to include women 'one-half the species', in the workforce, would diminish wages to a hitherto unimagined degree. The proponents of separate spheres could then argue that such separation is not only 'natural', but also sensible from an economic point of view.

Taylor Mill is quick to point out that such economic reasoning 'does not reach the political question'; in other words, it offers no sufficient argument for withholding women 'the rights of citizenship',[60] including the right to vote. Nevertheless, she leaves this aspect aside and summarises the alleged economic effect of women's inclusion in the labour market as follows: '[T]hat, if women competed with men [for employment], a man and a woman could not together earn more than is now earned by the man alone.'[61] Taylor Mill remarks that she considers such a scenario would be the 'worst ever asserted, much worse than is at all likely to be realized', thereby casting doubt on an economic forecast that appears far from objective.[62] In his classic study of John Ruskin's criticism of contemporary economic thinking, James Clark Sherburne stresses 'the usefulness of the doctrine [of the wages fund] in its more rigid form to opponents of the labour movement. They could declare that the fixed nature of the fund made wage increases 'scientifically' impossible'.[63] Such vested interests were not lost on Taylor Mill, who compared women uncritical of the status quo to 'tenants or labourers who vote against their own political interests to please their landlords or employers'.[64] Taylor Mill induced J. S. Mill to include a chapter 'On the Futurity of the Labouring Classes' in their *Principles of Political Economy*, as J. S. Mill states in his *Autobiography* that this chapter was 'entirely due to her: in the first draft of the book, that chapter did not exist. She pointed out the need of such a chapter, and the extreme imperfection of the book without it: 'she was the cause of my writing it; and the more general part of the chapter … was wholly an exposition of her thoughts, often in words taken from her own lips.'[65] Her observation quoted above that '[n]umbers of women are

59 Ibid., p. 992.

60 Taylor Mill, 'Enfranchisement', p. 104.

61 Ibid.

62 Ibid.

63 Sherburne, *Ambiguities of Abundance*, p. 157. Emphasis in the text.

64 Taylor Mill, 'Enfranchisement', p. 118.

65 John Stuart Mill, *Autobiography and Literary Essays: Collected Works I* (Toronto: University of Toronto Press, 1981), p. 255.

wives and mothers only because there is no other career open to them, no other occupation for their feelings or their activities' alerts her readers to the fact that the economic and the social sphere, as well as the public and private one, are mutually dependent.[66] Predictions on the allegedly harmful effects of reforms that threaten the status quo should therefore be taken with a pinch of salt. Indeed, her qualifying sentence that she considers the scenario painted by opponents of women's gainful employment 'much worse than is at all likely to be realized'.[67]

Still, Taylor Mill takes this objection seriously enough to apply it rigorously. If employers and labourers, tenants and landlords, and even labourers among themselves, all compete for funds and bargaining power, why should it be different when it comes to men and women? What, then, were the effects if 'the joint income [of husband and wife] would be the same as before'? Taylor Mill claims that 'the woman would be raised from the position of a servant to that of a partner'[68] – a fascinating break from the traditional view of husband and wife as 'one person'! Taylor Mill's argument for women's gainful employment calls attention to the individuality of wives, whose personalities do not consist only of their husbands.

We now also see how this economic argument fits into Taylor Mill's essay, which is about the *Enfranchisement of Women*. Demonstrating how entrenched anti-enfranchisement positions were, James Mill, John Stuart Mill's own father, had once famously argued that women do not need the vote because they are being represented by their male relatives.[69] This argument has been renounced most forcefully by William Thompson and Anna Wheeler and Harriet Martineau in their *Appeal of One-Half the Human Race* (1825) and *Society in America* (1837), respectively.[70] Importantly and in a similar vein, Taylor Mill stresses that equating married women's *economic* interests with those of her husbands is equally presumptuous. Both partners need to be financially independent to establish a relationship at eye-level: '[A] woman who contributes materially to the support of the family, cannot be treated in the same contemptuously tyrannical manner as one who, however she may toil as a domestic drudge, is a dependent on the man for subsistence.'[71]

For Taylor Mill, women's gainful employment is not so much about increasing the income of an individual household. Rather, it should be encour-

66 Taylor Mill, 'Enfranchisement', p. 104.

67 Ibid.

68 Ibid.

69 See 'Article on Government', which was published in the *Encyclopaedia Britannica* in 1819 and is reprinted in Susan Groag Bell and Karen M. Offen (eds), *Women, the Family and Freedom: 1880–1950* (Stanford CA: Stanford University Press 1983). Quoted in Folbre, *Greed, Lust and Gender* (2009), p. 165.

70 For details, see Folbre, *Greed, Lust and Gender*, pp. 78, 165.

71 Taylor Mill, 'Enfranchisement', p. 105.

aged for its effects on the power relations within that household. Taylor Mill is presently being discussed under the term of intra-household bargaining, an achievement of the feminist turn in economics of the 1990s. This turn was a response to New Home Economics instigated by the work of economist Gary Becker, as the first to bring 'household decision-making into the purview of economic analysis'.[72] In his *Treatise of the Family* (1991), Becker applies economic principles to analyse the decision-making processes in households, yet, despite breaking new ground, Becker's model of the household rests on several major assumptions, 'the criticism of which has been the jumping-off place for the development of intra-household economics'.[73]

The most notable feature of Becker's model is the assumption of altruism on part of the household head, who rules like a 'benevolent dictator' over 'his' family.[74] Elizabeth Katz has argued that 'while there are good reasons to believe that family members care about one another's welfare, there are more compelling ways of representing inter-dependent utility functions than subsuming them all under one decision-maker who keeps everybody's best interest in mind'.[75] Finally, feminist economist Julie A. Nelson has pointed out that the household head can be altruistic simply and precisely because of his control over household resources.[76] In sum, Becker 'never examines the contractual asymmetries criticised by feminists since the mid-nineteenth century – legal provisions that accord more legal authority and control over household resources to husbands than to wives'.[77]

We have seen that Taylor Mill considers men's absolute control over resources as the root cause of the persistence of gender inequality. Moreover, she highlights that this economic power entails also political power: 'The most insignificant of men, the man who can obtain influence or consideration nowhere else, finds one place where he is chief and head … He is judge, magistrate, ruler over their [the family's] joint concern; arbiter of all differences between them.'[78] A benevolent dictator is still a dictator; and strangely, a family is considered a 'unit' despite its lack of checks and balances. The unitary model envisaged by Gary Becker (and that apparently was also the common notion against which Taylor Mill wrote) fails

[72] Folbre, *Greed, Lust and Gender*, p. 299.

[73] Elizabeth Katz, 'The Intra-Household Economics of Voice and Exit', *Feminist Economics*, 3:3 (1997), 25–46, at p. 27.

[74] Gary S. Becker, 'Altruism in the Family and Selfishness in the Market Place', *Economica*, 48:1 (1981), 1–15.

[75] Katz, 'Intra-Household Economics', p. 27.

[76] Julie A. Nelson, 'Economic Theory and Feminist Theory: Comments on Chapters by Polachek, Ott, and Levin', in *Out of the Margin: Feminist Perspectives on Economics*, ed. by E. Kuiper and J. Sap (London and New York: Routledge, 1995), pp. 120–5.

[77] Folbre, *Greed, Lust and Gender*, p. 300.

[78] Taylor Mill, 'Enfranchisement', p. 113.

'to recognize systematic, gender (and age) -based power relations which structure household resource allocation'.[79] Taylor Mill was among the first to draw attention to such power relations within the family and how they affect its economic decisions surrounding the division of labour, consumption, inheritance and even fertility. Today's intra-household economics conceptualise the household as 'an institution infused with historical and psychological meanings which significantly impinge upon its economic decision-making'.[80]

Taylor Mill's arguments suggest that the wages-fund doctrine offers a reductive view of economics and economic mechanisms. However, this is not meant to suggest that Taylor Mill was unique in possessing this view, and in fact the wages-fund doctrine met broad and severe criticism.[81] Still, most critics of the wages-fund doctrine wrote in the late 1860s, whereas Taylor Mill's essay was published in 1851, so that it seems fair to say that she was among the first to call attention to the limited view that this theory offered. Furthermore, even J. S. Mill recanted the wages-fund doctrine as late as 1869. Her statement that a married woman who earns her own money 'would be raised from the position of a servant to that of a partner' implies that economic laws apply also in the private sphere.[82] As she had made clear in her initial analysis of the possible causes for gender inequality, the social, legal and economic status of a person are interrelated and affect each other, which is why men's superior physical strength has translated into a higher social position and eventually into economic power over women.

Taylor Mill stresses that the only way to increase women's low status is their inclusion in the labour market. In a footnote to her *Enfranchisement*, she refers to the wide-spread domestic abuse women suffer at the hands of their partners and declares: 'Wretches unfit to have the smallest authority over any living thing, have a helpless woman for their household slave. These excesses could not exist if women both earned, and had the right to possess, a part of the income of the family.'[83] A woman needs to be economically independent to acquire standing both in the eyes of her husband and of society; what is more, women were only able to leave abusive relationships if they had the ready means to do so. Taylor Mill demystifies gender relations by showing that the inequality between men and women has little if anything to do with biology or romanticism. Rather, it has its roots in women's economic dependency on men.

79 Katz, 'Intra-Household Economics', p. 29.

80 Ibid.

81 See Sherburne, *Ambiguities of Abundance*, p. 156.

82 Taylor Mill, 'Enfranchisement', p. 104f.

83 Taylor Mill, 'Enfranchisement', p. 105.

Regulation Reconsidered

Although Taylor Mill welcomes female wage labour, she does dwell on its possible consequences of generally decreasing wages in the long run. She optimistically declares that 'remedies will be found for it in time' and suggests that some '[p]alliatives might be applied immediately'.[84] One such palliative to offset the negative side-effects of women's inclusion in the labour market might be the exclusion of another group who currently competes in the labour market. Specifically, Taylor Mill demands 'a more rigid exclusion of children from industrial employment' and argues that this should be the case especially 'during the years in which [children] ought to be working only to strengthen their bodies and minds for after-life'.[85] The way that Taylor Mill differentiates between women's employment and that of children is interesting, as it reveals a great deal about her social and political vision: 'Children are necessarily dependent, and under the power of others; and their labour, being not for themselves but for the gain of their parents, is a proper subject for legislative regulation.'[86] Unlike women, children are *necessarily* dependent because of their lack of bodily strength and education. Furthermore, Taylor Mill emphasises that children do not work for their own gain but for the gain of their families. Apart from a minimum of physical and intellectual maturity, an individual needs some initial independence to ensure that he or she is able to reap the benefits of his or her labour and does not have to hand the remuneration over to another party, be it parents or husbands. Taylor Mill stresses that people should have reached 'the age of self-government' before they sell their labour. Once this is the case, everyone has 'an equal claim to be permitted to sell whatever kind of useful labour they are capable of, for the price which it will bring' (ibid.). The age restriction thus seems the only kind of regulation that the state should enact. Taylor Mill forewords the notion that anything else amounts to despotism: 'so long as competition is the general law of human life, it is tyranny to shut out one-half of the competitors.'[87]

[84] Ibid.

[85] Ibid. Note that Taylor Mill's *Enfranchisement* was published just four years after the Ten Hours Act (1847), which restricted the working hours of both women and children in textile factories. See Asa Briggs, *A Social History of England* (London: Penguin Books, 1994), p. 220.

[86] Taylor Mill, 'Enfranchisement', p. 105.

[87] Ibid.

Working Mothers

Taylor Mill urges women to obtain employment regardless of their marital status to ensure they enter and maintain more equal marital relationships. In Taylor Mill's philosophy, if gender inequality has economic roots, it can be done away with only by reducing women's material dependency on men. However, this might be feasible only as long as a couple has no children. In his *Subjection of Women* (1869), J. S. Mill remarks that he considers 'the common arrangement, by which the man earns the income and the wife superintends the domestic expenditure ... in general the most suitable division of labour'.[88] He argues that the task of applying 'the husband's earnings to the general comfort of the family', plus the 'physical suffering' surrounding pregnancy and childbirth as well as women's exclusive responsibility for their children during their early infancy already constitute the lion's share of both physical and mental labour typical of family life. J. S. Mill therefore holds that it is 'not ... a desirable custom, that the wife should contribute by her labour to the income of the family'.[89]

Taylor Mill, mother of three and unhappily married, takes her demand for women's economic independence one step further.[90] She suggests that 'all laws whatever relating to marriage' should be abolished.[91] She explicitly includes a woman's maintenance claims for her children: 'if a woman had children she must take charge of them, women could not then have children without considering how to maintain them'.[92] Taylor Mill thereby makes clear that women become vulnerable not only because of romantic attachments but especially because of family ties. Moreover, she laments that women 'use' children to make husbands commit and thereby secure their living – another fatal attitude women have adopted because society

88 Mill, *On Liberty and Other Essays*, p. 522.

89 Ibid. Julia Annas, Susan M. Okin and Gail Tulloch have argued that this position of Mill is inconsistent with his feminism, see Julia Annas, 'Mill and The Subjection of Women', *Philosophy*, 52:200 (1977), 179–94; Susan M. Okin, 'John Stuart Mill, Liberal Feminist', in *Women in Western Political Thought*, ed. by Susan M. Okin (Princeton NJ: Princeton University Press, 1979), pp. 197–232; Gail Tulloch, *Mill and Sexual Equality* (Hertfordshire: Harvester Wheatsheaf, 1989). Helen McCabe, on the other hand, has suggested that Mill simply anticipates the notorious 'double shift' of working mothers, see Helen McCabe, '"Good Housekeeping"? Re-assessing John Stuart Mill's Position on the Gendered Division of Labour', *History of Political Thought*, 39:1 (2018), 135–55.

90 Although her first husband, John Taylor, was politically interested like her and introduced her to radical Unitarian circles, she eventually confided to the Reverend of this congregation, William J. Fox, about her unhappy marriage and her 'want of intellectual companionship'. It was Fox who introduced her to J. S. Mill (see Mineka, *Dissidence of Dissent*, p. 273).

91 Taylor Mill, 'Enfranchisement', p. 86.

92 Ibid.

allows them no other occupation than that of wife and mother: '[N]ow it is thought to be the woman's interest to have children as so many ties to a man who feeds her.'[93]

One might argue that the ability to leverage children in marital disputes would be feasible only for relatively affluent women, or women who have an established and successful career, which would enable them to act as sole provider for their children. Was Taylor Mill, who had been born into an upper-middle-class family and whose first husband was a pharmaceuticals wholesaler, class blind and hence unaware of the living conditions of women of lower social status? Penelope Deutscher observes a form of classism in Taylor Mill that meant that Taylor Mill 'associated the lower class, the poor, or the working class with the worst instances of abuse of women'.[94] Deutscher thus concludes that Taylor Mill's:

> Feminism was concurrently co-opted in consolidation of hierarchy. Rather than tell us that the ignorant poor, like all humans, should be in a position of so-called perfect equality (which was, of course, also her position) Taylor Mill wrote that the elevation of women to perfect equality would refine and elevate the lower classes.[95]

Given Taylor Mill's broad political interests, especially regarding the situation of the working class, and her social commitment to abolish domestic abuse, however, it is doubtful that she lacked awareness. Still, Taylor Mill's suggestion that mothers forfeit maintenance claims harbours a certain Malthusian bent, as few women would be able to afford to raise children alone.

Her proposal seems less outlandish once we link it to some arguments made in *Principles of Political Economy*. In Book IV, Mill and Taylor Mill envision a so-called 'stationary state', in other words a society with little if any economic growth and a low population rate. Mill and Taylor Mill determine that a small population preserves natural resources and leads to higher wages for the working classes. Apparently, Taylor Mill discerns a similar economic mechanism at play in the family: the more children a woman has, the greater her financial dependence on her husband. According to Taylor Mill, mothers 'barter person for bread'.[96] The dependency of women can be precluded only if women are able to provide on their own for their children.

It might seem extreme to make children the sole responsibility of their mothers and exempt men from their paternal duties. However, Taylor Mill's whole *Enfranchisement* is a forceful indictment of women's economic dependency, which negatively affects their social and political status, and

[93] Ibid.

[94] Penelope Deutscher, 'When Feminism Is "High" and Ignorance Is "Low": Harriet Taylor Mill on the Progress of the Species', *Hypatia*, 21:3 (2006), 136–50, at p. 139.

[95] Ibid., p. 146.

[96] Taylor Mill, 'Enfranchisement', p. 86.

this dependency only deepens once women become mothers. Regardless of whether Taylor Mill wished her proposal legislated, her suggestion to forfeit maintenance claims draws attention to the extent of economic vulnerability motherhood involves and how it limits women's options.

Conclusion

In this chapter, I have made the case that Harriet Taylor Mill offers a bold argument for the benefits of women participating in the labour force that runs counter to the dominant position at the time, the wages-fund doctrine. Taylor Mill bases her position on the urgent need to address women's financial dependency on men, as, in her view, this was both cause and effect of gender inequality. Furthermore, it was a problem that exacerbated other deep-rooted social issues; as Janette Rutterford has demonstrated elsewhere in the present volume, it was an issue that was only intensifying as the number of 'surplus women' increased across the century.

By arguing that this systemic inequality emerged through the redundant organising principle of the superior physical strength of men, which then, in Taylor Mill's study, translated into men's higher social position and economic power over women, she offers a lively account of the ways in which the social, legal and economic status of a person, and especially women, was closely interrelated. Furthermore, Taylor Mill explores the ways in which the individual was both product of and contributor to the evolution and maintenance of the structures that govern economic relations, of which the wages-fund doctrine was but one. Her work provides a stepping stone to the possibility for legislative change that could meaningfully alter the condition of women and children, as well as drawing attention to the dangers of retaining entrenched ideological positions.

Harriet Taylor Mill's objection to the wages-fund doctrine anticipates central theses of today's intra-household economics. In paying attention to the way in which the private sphere is affected by laws governing the economy, Taylor Mill challenges contemporary notions about gender roles, family hierarchies and the market. Her work provides solid evidence that the 'separate spheres' ideology that continues to dominate modern, popular perceptions of the nineteenth century was just that – a doctrine – and one that was not universally accepted at the time. Taylor Mill thus brings home the forceful message that women in general and mothers in particular need to become materially independent in order to increase their status, and to inure themselves against exploitation, neglect or abandonment. Her work points to the need of women to intervene on matters of economic discourse rather than to accept or perpetuate the status quo, which, as Harriet Taylor Mill suggests, was so often rooted in the archaic and the obsolete.

11

Millicent Garrett Fawcett and Popular Political Economy

Lana L. Dalley

On 2 February 2018, the *New York Times* published an article titled 'Why Women's Voices are Scarce in Economics'. The author, Justin Wolfers, summarised a new report that 'shows that since the turn of the [twenty-first] century, there has been no increase in the share of women entering the pipeline to become professional economists'.[1] Wolfers cites many of the typical barriers for women entering male-dominated professional fields: inadequate parental-leave policies; uneven gendered work standards; and biased teaching evaluations, just to name a few. 'The result', Wolfers states 'is that women's voices are underrepresented' in the field of economics and this gender imbalance shapes the field in meaningful ways:

> Women economists tend to focus on different topics than men. While men dominate macroeconomics, women are more visible among those studying labour markets, health and education. The only majority-female economics conference I've ever attended was on the economics of children, a field focused on schooling, family structure and child well-being. If there were more female economists, more attention would surely be paid to these issues.[2]

Of course, the dearth of female economists is not new. Women have been woefully underrepresented in modern economics since its inception. In the eighteenth and nineteenth centuries – the historical subject of this collection – women were not taken seriously as economists or economic thinkers; when women wrote about economics, their voices remained marginal and they were frequently denigrated as mere popularisers of the science.

[1] Justin Wolfers, 'Why Women's Voices are Scarce in Economics', *New York Times*, 2 February 2018.

[2] Ibid.

As Wolfers acknowledges, this absence of female economists has another profound effect on the history of economic thought: women are scarcely represented as economic actors within economic theory, and the 'feminine' sphere of home and the family is equally scarce. Although the scope of classical political economy was quite broad – encompassing moral philosophy and dealing with many aspects of everyday life – its scope did not extend to women, who are virtually absent within early economic theory, and rarely did it extend to the domestic sphere where women were ideologically, and often literally, seated in the nineteenth century.

In Victorian studies, scholars have long been thinking and writing about women's economic roles in the period, beginning with the early historical accounts of Victorian women and work by Wanda Neff and Lee Holcombe.[3] More recently, Deanna Kreisel has shown how Hardy and Eliot's fictional representations of women embodied contemporary economic ideology.[4] Krista Lysack and Erika Rappaport have carefully examined women shoppers, in fiction and in real life, respectively.[5] Nancy Henry's work shows that women were not just contributing to the economy by shopping, but also by investing, and Jill Rappoport examines how alternative economies – like gift exchange – functioned as a source of economic agency for women in the period.[6] Focusing on women's writing at the *Fin de Siècle*, Brooke Cameron examines the economic dimensions of feminist cooperation.[7] *Economic Women: Essays on Desire and Dispossession in Nineteenth-Century British Culture*, an essay collection that I co-edited with Jill Rappoport, is the first to consider the multiple and varied economic roles that women occupied in the period – covering business, political economy, the family, and the ethics of exchange. While much interesting work has been done on women and economics in the nineteenth century, comparatively little work has been done on women writers and political economy. Put more bluntly, the invisibility of women within the discipline of economics has long been

[3] See Wanda Fraiken Neff, *Victorian Working Women: An Historical and Literary Study of Women in British Industries and Professions, 1832–1850* (New York: Columbia University Press, 1929); and Jeff Holcombe, *Victorian Ladies at Work: Middle-Class Working Women in England and Wales, 1850–1914* (Hamden CT: Archon Books, 1973).

[4] Deanna Kreisel, *Economic Woman: Demand, Gender, and Narrative Closure in Eliot and Hardy* (Toronto: University of Toronto Press, 2012).

[5] Krista Lysack, *Come Buy, Come Buy: Shopping and the Culture of Consumption in Victorian Women's Writing* (Columbus OH: Ohio University Press, 2008); Erika Rappaport, *Shopping for Pleasure: Women in the Making of London's West End* (Princeton NJ: Princeton University Press, 2000).

[6] Nancy Henry, *Women, Literature, and Finance in Victorian Britain: Cultures of Investment* (New York: Palgrave Macmillan, 2018); Jill Rappoport, *Giving Women: Alliance and Exchange in Victorian Culture* (Oxford: Oxford University Press, 2012).

[7] S. Brooke Cameron, *Critical Alliances: Economics and Feminism in English Women's Writing, 1880–1914* (Toronto: University of Toronto Press, 2020).

replicated in Victorian studies, and is only beginning to be remedied by scholarship such as that contained within this edited volume.

Club, College and Corpus

Despite the increased number of women writers and advances in women's education over the course of the nineteenth century, for most of the period there were no recognised female political economists and women's participation in formal economic writing was not sanctioned. At the inaugural meeting of the Political Economy Club in 1821, for example, twenty-nine men were present and no women. Members of the club met once a month and discussed a single economic question posed by a member; even a cursory glance at the list of questions reveals that women were not only absent as club members, but also as subjects worthy of consideration. Women were certainly writing about economics, but their writing remained outside the political economy canon.

In the early nineteenth century, Jane Marcet and Harriet Martineau initiated a literary trend in which women writers used their emerging literary authority to merge political economy with imaginative literature; within this tradition women, as characters in the stories, are imagined as functioning within, being shaped by, and contributing to capitalist economics, rather than imagined as functioning outside the economic system, as classical political economists most often imply they do through non-representation. The fact that these stories were written by women also nods to the possibility of women becoming economists and contributing to the growing corpus of economic writing. Around the mid-nineteenth century, a number of women essayists began writing about economics from a feminist perspective; Barbara Leigh Smith Bodichon, Emily Davies and Clara Collet, to name a few, actively generated a feminist economic discourse predicated on notions of self-dependence and usefulness and conceptualised in the language of political economy. At the same time, journals such as the *English Woman's Journal*, the *Victoria Magazine* and *Woman and Work* regularly disseminated commentary on the subject. In the final decades of the period, more women began formally participating in the discipline of economics: in the late 1870s, Mary Paley Marshall co-wrote a textbook, *The Economics of Industry*, with her husband and became the first female economics lecturer at Cambridge University; in 1895, Beatrix Potter Webb, along with four others, founded the London School of Economics; and, when the Royal Economic Society was founded in 1890, Clara Collet and six other women were present at the inaugural meeting. The visibility of women within economics clearly increased over the course of the nineteenth century.

Millicent Garrett Fawcett, who was a lecturer on political economy at Queen's College, London, and was a member of the British Economic

Association, was among the most visible of these early women economists. She was an advocate for women's economic education, eventually co-founding Newnham College and creating curriculum for women there; she also occasionally lectured at the King's College Department for Ladies, the College for Working Women, and the Working Men's College.[8] Her impressive 'services to education' were recognised when she was awarded an honorary doctorate of law at the University of St Andrews in 1899.[9] For Garrett Fawcett, it was important for women to learn about economics for their intellectual and personal betterment and she devoted much of her professional career to expanding women's access to the economic curriculum, through both formal instruction and didactic writing. She wrote widely about economics, including textbooks, stories, periodical essays and encyclopaedic entries. Her work and legacy are the subject of this chapter; more broadly, though, I am interested in reflecting on the tradition of women's didactic economic writing in the nineteenth century and reconceiving its importance to the discipline of economics. Historically, women's didactic economic writing has often been dismissed as derivative and inferior; such claims have typically been the reason women writers are precluded from being considered as economists in the period. They are not regarded as practitioners, but merely popularisers. However, this attitude fails to acknowledge the disciplinary expertise required to write a didactic text and the widespread impact of such work.

Without question, the didactic work of women writers like Jane Marcet, Harriet Martineau and Millicent Garrett Fawcett was much more widely read than the work of the period's male economists. Their work was not only popular, but profitable and influential; their work was not unoriginal and imitative but, in its conception, focus and selection, offered an original contribution to the field. This edited volume showcases a variety of economic activity from women across the eighteenth and nineteenth centuries; this chapter contributes to this showcase by exploring the role of Millicent Garrett Fawcett and her female predecessors in contributing to political economy, through the publication of popular didactic texts, at a time before women's participation within the field was formally sanctioned.

In 1847, Garrett Fawcett was born into a large wealthy family in Aldeburgh. Her father, Newson Garrett, got his start as a pawnbroker before saving and inheriting enough money to purchase a corn and coal warehouse. The Garretts had six daughters and four sons; three of their six daughters, including Millicent, would go on to be pioneers in the women's rights movement. Her older sister Elizabeth was the first British woman doctor and perhaps remains the most well-known member of the family. Another

8 David Rubinstein, *A Different World for Women: The Life of Millicent Garrett Fawcett* (Columbus OH: Ohio State University Press, 1991), p. 106.

9 Ibid.

older sister, Agnes, made her name as one of the first professional woman house decorators. Garrett Fawcett was formally educated until just before her sixteenth birthday, when she had to leave school because of what she describes in her memoirs as a 'sudden … financial crisis at home'.[10] It is worth mentioning here that Harriet Martineau was similarly prompted to begin writing for payment when her father suffered serious economic losses in the 1820s; it is, perhaps, no coincidence that Martineau and Garrett Fawcett were personally affected by economic losses before they began writing economic texts. In their lived experience, they were intimately aware of how economic contingencies could come to bear on women's lives.

When Garrett Fawcett was twenty-two, she received an offer of marriage from Henry Fawcett, a liberal Member of Parliament to whom she was introduced by John Stuart Mill. Earlier in his life, Henry had been blinded in a shooting accident and Millicent spent much of their married life aiding him in his work. In her memoir *What I Remember*, she writes fondly of her marriage, stating, 'My political education was just beginning; naturally I had to read and write for my husband. I grappled with newspapers and blue books, and learned more or less to convey their import to him'.[11] It was this aspect of their relationship that made her claim: 'My marriage naturally made an enormous difference in my life, an even greater difference than is usual in the normal cases of the passage from girlhood to wife and motherhood.'[12] By all accounts, their marriage was rather egalitarian, with Henry routinely encouraging her to pursue outside employment. The couple had only one child, Phillipa; during Phillipa's childhood, there was a 'degree of malicious gossip' about Garrett Fawcett's neglect of her daughter, with press coverage painting her as 'a neglectful mother'; this slander undoubtedly sprung from Garrett Fawcett's work in the women's rights movement and the assumption that, because of that work, she was necessarily neglecting her maternal duties.[13] For example, a letter from a family friend warned Henry about 'slanderous imputations on Mrs. Fawcett's character and good sense', including a rumour that Phillipa was boarded out 'because Mrs. Fawcett … refused to undertake her early education'; the rumour was so entrenched that the friend 'could not get anyone' to believe the truth.[14] After Henry's death in 1884, Garrett Fawcett notably never sought to remarry but instead dedicated her life to her work for women,

[10] Millicent Garrett Fawcett, *What I Remember* (London: T. Fisher Unwin Ltd, 1924), p. 32.

[11] Ibid., p. 42.

[12] Ibid., p. 36.

[13] Rubinstein, *A Different World for Women*, p. 20; and see Melissa Terras and Elizabeth Crawford, *Millicent Garrett Fawcett: Selected Writings* (London: UCL Press, 2022), p. 4.

[14] Ray Strachey, *Millicent Garrett Fawcett* (London: John Murray, 1931), p. 62.

most visibly by leading the National Union of Women's Suffrage Societies from 1897–1919.

During this period, Garrett Fawcett dedicated herself almost exclusively to the women's rights movement. In the years immediately following the granting of women's suffrage, many women left full-time feminist activism behind and joined the ranks of professional paid labour. Garrett Fawcett, though, continued to write and speak on various subjects, including her opposition to the 'new feminism' exemplified by Eleanor Rathbone's 'family allowance' proposal, which was a socialist plan that proposed the government give families a cash payment to support their children; her support for extending British feminism to other countries; and her belief that women's suffrage should be expanded to young women aged twenty-one to thirty years old. Despite the *Woman's Leader* declaring, six years before the death of Garrett Fawcett, that 'the professional feminist has now almost disappeared', Garrett Fawcett remained a 'professional feminist' for her entire life.[15]

Throughout the course of her life, Garrett Fawcett was also a remarkably prolific writer. She published her first article, titled 'The education of women of the middle and upper classes' in *Macmillan's Magazine* in April 1868. She earned £7 for it and promptly donated her earnings to Mill's campaign for re-election. Garrett Fawcett would go on to publish twelve books, including one novel, *Janet Doncaster*, nineteen pamphlets, and more than 300 articles in publications such as *Common Cause*, *The Englishwoman*, *Woman's Leader*, *Fortnightly Review*, *Contemporary Review* and the *Economic Journal*. As Barbara Caine explains, Millicent Garrett Fawcett 'exemplifies Victorian bourgeois or liberal feminism, in her outlook, her attitudes and her approach … Her ideas on the woman question are almost invariably seen as an extension of the liberal ideas on political economy which she shared with her husband, Henry Fawcett' (197). The epistemological relationship between political economy and early liberal feminism was strong; Victorian feminism relied on the *laissez-faire* politics and liberal notions of the self that are pervasive in political economy, so it is not surprising to see the period's most prominent feminists meaningfully engage with economic theory.

Tales in Political Economy

While the legacy of Garrett Fawcett in the Suffrage movement has historically been more visible than her work within the field of economics, her contributions to the history of economics deserve more attention. In addition to her textbook, essays and encyclopaedic entries, Garrett Fawcett also published a set of four didactic economic stories titled *Tales in Political*

[15] Rubinstein, *A Different World for Women*, p. 265.

Economy (1874). In the preface to the stories, she acknowledges that she is part of a tradition of didactic economic writing that emerged earlier in the period, cheekily apologising for 'plagiarising' Martineau's *Illustrations*:

> It is hoped that these little tales may be of some use to those who are trying to teach Political Economy. I cannot let them go to press without a word of apology to Miss Martineau for my plagiarism of the idea, which she made so popular thirty years ago, of hiding the powder, Political Economy, in the raspberry jam of the story. ('Preface')

Garrett Fawcett here acknowledges the perceived separation of scientific and novelistic discourses and argues that the delights of fiction will help readers to better understand and profit from political economy. Her conception of economics as at odds with the pleasures inherent in fiction is not surprising given the popular reputation of political economy in the nineteenth century. Referred to by Carlyle as the 'dismal science' and regarded, by the popular mind, as in conflict with the language of emotional morality because it – economics – represented the secular language of facts, it is indeed noteworthy that Garrett Fawcett, and Martineau before her, conceived of the two discourses as compatible.[16]

In the nineteenth century, novels were conceived as the domain of pleasure and emotions, while more 'serious' works – on such topics as history, politics or economics – were conceived as serving a higher intellectual purpose that contributed to the greater good in ways that fiction did – and could – not. Nancy Armstrong notes that authors like Austen 'had helped to establish the woman's authority over a specific domain of knowledge—that of the emotions'.[17] As a consequence, their domain of influence and accepted knowledge – and, consequently, their domain of writing – was seriously circumscribed by the cultural attitudes regarding what was proper and useful reading material. As is demonstrated with writers like Garrett Fawcett and Martineau, women might be regarded as teachers and popularisers, but not original economic thinkers. Debates about the novel during this period were fuelled, in large part, by its perceived separation from other types of writing by a principally male authorship, such as works on the subject of political economy; such writing represented authority over empirical and scientific knowledge, rather than emotional knowledge, and emphasised the abstract rather than the personal. The gendered implications of this argument were quite far reaching. Women writers were generally excluded from those types of writing that fell outside novel writing, except, of course, didactic domestic literature like conduct books and household manuals – a

[16] Thomas Carlyle, 'Occasional Discourse on the Negro Question', *Fraser's Magazine for Town and Country*, 40 (1849), pp. 670–9, esp. p. 672.

[17] Nancy Armstrong, *Desire and Domestic Fiction* (Oxford: Oxford University Press, 1987), p. 43.

literary segregation that aligned with contemporary gender ideologies and with beliefs about gendered domains of knowledge. To write beyond these boundaries could be, in itself, an act of feminist resistance. I argue that for Garrett Fawcett it certainly was.

Victorian Women Writers and the Pedagogical Imperative

Beginning in the early decades of the century, writers like Jane Marcet and Harriet Martineau wrote didactic books about political economy to educate readers, including women, about a subject to which they were typically barred access. As Natasha Glaisyer and Sara Pennell explain, didactic books 'made their claims to educate and inspire from the outset, and were constructed both textually and physically, to achieve these goals'.[18] Glaisyer and Pennell further note that, within scholarship, 'didactic texts and their uses have often been marginalised, if not overlooked'.[19] Throughout the nineteenth century, women's writing about political economy was predominantly pedagogical; if didactic texts are dismissed as derivative and insignificant, then women's early contributions to the field of economics are rendered invisible. As Glaisyer and Pennell explain:

> In looking at didactic texts historically, as a medium of knowledge construction and knowledge communication, we come up against the enduring debates over hierarchies of, and access to, knowledge. Any expansion in popular education, or demotic access to 'more' knowledge (whatever that knowledge is), is often accompanied by fears that established hierarchies are at risk.[20]

Adam Smith's *On the Wealth of Nations*, published in 1776, established the field of political economy, which steadily gained cultural clout from that point onwards. Smith's work, and the work of political economists more generally, was considered scientific rather than didactic and, thus, resided at the top of the established hierarchy of economic 'knowledge construction and communication', while women's didactic writing rested firmly below.

However, I argue that women's didactic writing about political economy constituted a radical move towards 'wider information dissemination'.[21] For example, Marcet's *Conversations on Political Economy* was published in 1816 and offered readers a didactic conversation about economics between the older Mrs B and the younger Caroline; the fact that the text centred

[18] Natasha Glaisyer and Sara Pennell, *Didactic Literature in England, 1500–1800* (London: Routledge, 2003), p. 3.

[19] Ibid., p. 2.

[20] Ibid., p. 7.

[21] Glaisyer and Pennell, *Didactic Literature in England,* p. 11.

on a conversation between two women makes an implicit argument about the relevance of economics to women's everyday lives. Martineau's *Illustrations of Political Economy* was published sixteen years later, in 1832, and offered readers twenty-five fictional stories that illustrated specific economic principles. Martineau wrote *Illustrations* at a pivotal moment in the history of women's writing, as more women were writing than ever before and fiction was becoming an increasingly popular genre; the confluence of these circumstances laid the groundwork for *Illustrations*' popularity, which was profound. As Elaine Freedgood notes, 'By 1834 the monthly sales of the series had reached 10,000, several times that of many of Dickens's novels, which at 2,000 or 3,000 per month were considered highly successful' (213).

In the preface to her tales, Martineau describes that she thought that 'the principles which regulate society should … be made more clear and interesting … by pictures of what those principles are actually doing in communities'.[22] In her *Autobiography*, though, she expresses regret that so few people understood that her purpose was 'exhibiting' the principles of political economy 'in their natural workings in selected passages of social life' rather than 'smothering them up in a story'.[23] When Martineau's publishers initially wanted to leave the term political economy out of her series' title, she refused, later stating, 'I knew that science could not be smuggled in anonymously'.[24] Martineau envisioned political economy not as a science artificially 'smuggled' into fictional tales, but rather as a science whose principles were so natural and far-reaching – and, as such, tied to human feeling, morality and lived experience – that they were ideal fictional material, shaping domestic and familial relations and, therefore, relevant to the representation thereof. This is reinforced by Martineau's theory that 'every perfect plot in fiction is taken bodily from real life' because it is beyond human ability to create an admirable plot that is not anchored in reality.[25] This is the juncture where Martineau's notions about political economy and fiction merge – fiction is capable of illustrating the principles of political economy because those principles, according to Martineau, are natural and unchanging – the characters in the story are mere actors following a script that is already, and always, determined by those principles. In the preface to *Illustrations*, she writes that the 'reason why we choose the form of narrative is, that we really think it the best in which Political Economy can be taught, as we might say of nearly every kind of moral science'.[26] For writers like Marcet, Martineau and Garrett Fawcett, their pedagogical work was

22 Harriet Martineau, *Illustrations of Political Economy* (London: Charles Fox, 1834), p. xiii.

23 Harriet Martineau, *Autobiography* (London: James R. Osgood & Co, 1877), p. 105.

24 Ibid., p. 124.

25 Ibid., p. 179.

26 Martineau, *Illustrations*, p. xiii.

driven by a belief that economic knowledge was best conveyed representationally, rather than abstractly, an ethos that aligned their work with what was considered the feminine discourse of fiction rather than the masculine discourse of economics. While many critics have dismissed nineteenth-century women's didactic economic writing as unoriginal, derivative, and problematically orthodox, I claim that such writing contributed to a feminist economics that prioritised lived experience over theoretical knowledge.

The possibility of readerly identification fundamentally motivates these pedagogical texts. In *Conversations*, Marcet justifies the use of the colloquial form to teach political economy because she says that the questions of the young Caroline are 'such as would be likely to arise in the mind of an intelligent young person, fluctuating between the *impulse of her heart* and the *progress of her reason*, and naturally imbued with all the prejudices and popular feelings of *uninformed benevolence*' (ix, emphasis added). Here Marcet draws attention to the competing discourses of emotion and rationality, as they are relevant to popular conceptions of political economy, anchors them both to the morality of an 'uninformed benevolence' and, in so doing, suggests that economic knowledge encompasses both the 'impulses of [the] heart' and the 'progress of … reason'. She assigns her audience (whom she presumes to be comprised of intelligent, young people) 'all the prejudices and popular feelings of uniformed benevolence' and, in so doing, creates a bond of readerly identification between the reader and Caroline. This sympathetic bond is constructed as a means of converting the reader into an avid student of political economy via Caroline's own conversion and, thus, converting 'uniformed benevolence' into informed benevolence. Caroline initially expresses an 'antipathy to political economy' that is transformed in the course of her *conversations* with Mrs B. into both a genuine understanding of the principles and an appreciation of her newfound knowledge.[27]

Similarly, Martineau also believed that once readers encountered the principles of political economy illustrated in a fictional form capable of engendering readerly identification, they would not only understand the operation of those principles but also realise that moral stability is dependent on proper economic behaviour, as determined by those principles. In the preface to *Illustrations*, she writes:

> There is no doubt that all that is true and important about any virtue,—integrity, for instance,—may be said in the form of a lecture, or written in a chapter of moral philosophy; but the faithful history of an upright man, his sayings and doings, his trials, his sorrows, his triumphs and rewards, teaches the same truths in a more effectual as well as more popular form. (xiii)

[27] Jane Marcet, *Conversations on Political Economy: In which the Elements of that Science are Familiarly Explained* (London: Bowles & Dearborn, 1817), p. 15.

Martineau clearly does not believe that the texts of political economy are capable of engendering readerly identification. Instead, she contends that it is fiction's ability to do so – by conveying to the reader the 'faithful history of an upright man' – that makes fiction a proper genre for illustrating economic principles. In her book *Intellectual Women and Victorian Patriarchy*, Deirdre David characterises Harriet Martineau as a 'dutiful intellectual daughter, repeating … the words of her intellectual fathers'.[28] While Martineau was one of the foremost feminist thinkers of the nineteenth century, much of the critical response to Martineau, and especially to her economic writing, has described her in terms similar to David's and her work as been characterised as unoriginal and uninspired. Martineau's *Illustrations* was, though, deeply influential to many, including Garrett Fawcett who drew on them in her conception of her *Tales in Political Economy*. For both writers, fiction allowed them to expand the representational scope and relevance of political economy. The popularity of these efforts led one anonymous reviewer of Martineau's *Illustrations* in *Tait's Edinburgh Magazine* to declare, 'The ladies seem determined to make the science of Political Economy their own'.[29] Although political economy was often characterised as solely the domain of men, this reviewer accurately points out that women writers had a lot to say on the subject. The fact that women's contributions to political economy have been routinely ignored or dismissed means that nineteenth-century political economy continues to be referred to and thought of as solely the sphere of men. And, conversely, when political economy is thought of as the domain of men it is easy to overlook women's contributions to the field.

Garrett Fawcett's significant work within the suffrage movement has also overshadowed her work as an economist. Garrett Fawcett's legacy is complicated by her marriage to a prominent economist, not least because her economic contributions have often been subsumed into the legacy of her husband. Within the limited scope of scholarship on her life and work, the vast majority explores her role as an activist who fought for women's expanded rights in the workplace, the home and the state. Indeed, within her own collection of memoirs, most of her recollections are of her time as a leader in the suffragist movement. While that work certainly occupied much of Garrett Fawcett's later life, her early adulthood was spent making a name for herself in political economy. In his biography, Rubinstein divides her life into four parts: youth and marriage 1847–84; the middle years 1884–1905; the suffrage at last 1906–18; and the final years 1918–29. Within this framework, Garrett Fawcett's economic work comes in the first

[28] Deirdre David, *Intellectual Women and Victorian Patriarchy* (London: Palgrave Macmillan, 1987), p. 35.

[29] 'Review of Illustrations of Political Economy', *Tait's Edinburgh Magazine*, August 1832, pp. 612–17, at p. 612.

fifth of her life, laying the groundwork for the feminist activism that would come to define her legacy.

Thus, critically examining Garrett Fawcett's contribution to economic thought not only helps to illuminate how Garrett Fawcett's feminism shaped nineteenth century economics, but also points to the ways in which economic thinking shaped Garrett Fawcett's feminism; Garrett Fawcett was a fervent supporter of *laissez-faire* policies and her faith in free market capitalism was the foundation of her support for women's expanded rights and opportunities.[30] Most importantly, though, examining the economic work of writers like Garrett Fawcett demonstrates how discourse – economic and literary – both produces culture and reflects it. Recent work in the field of narrative economics has persuasively shown how the 'viral spread of popular narratives' can affect 'economic behaviour', giving scholars good reason to look at how dominant narratives of the nineteenth century – including popular stories, and the recurring motifs therein, written by women – may have shaped economic behaviour and understanding, and the field of economics itself.[31] Because fiction was an increasingly accessible form throughout the nineteenth century, it was a site for widespread analysis, and for deployment of economic theory by those who were excluded from participating in formal economic debate. The nineteenth-century literary imagination was conditioned and shaped by the discourse of political economy; imaginative literature was thus dialogically interconnected with popular understandings of what was meant by political economy. In this way, scholars can look at imaginative literature in the period as circulating a narrative economics that had far more reach than political economy itself; to use Shiller's terms, such stories had the ability to go 'viral' and shape the economic landscape. Women writers' economic fiction created popular narratives about economics and implicitly made the case that economics was best understood through lived experience rather than abstract principle. These texts also aimed to make political economy – a discipline perceived as exclusionary and difficult – more accessible to the general public.

Political Economy for Beginners

In 1870, Millicent Garrett Fawcett published an economics textbook titled *Political Economy for Beginners* in the hopes that it would help encourage

30 See 'The Education of Middle and Upper Classes, 1868', 'Women and Representative Government, 1883', 'Introduction to Wollstonecraft's *A Vindication of the Rights of Woman*, 1891' and 'The White Slave Trade: Its Causes, and the Best Means of Preventing It, 1899', in Terras and Crawford, *Millicent Garrett Fawcett: Selected Writings*.

31 Robert J. Shiller, *Narrative Economics: How Stories Go Viral & Drive Major Economic Events* (Princeton NJ: Princeton University Press, 2019), p. 3.

teachers to incorporate political economy into their curriculum. The idea for the book arose a year before when she was assisting her husband, Henry Fawcett, with the third edition of his economics textbook, *Manual of Political Economy*. In the context of this chapter, it is worth noting that Garrett Fawcett was not formally cited as a contributor to her husband's textbook even though she helped with its composition and continued updating subsequent editions after his death.[32] In the preface to the first edition of *Political Economy for Beginners*, she writes:

> When I was helping my husband to prepare a third edition of his *Manual of Political Economy*, it occurred to us both that a small book, explaining as briefly as possible the most important principles of the science, would be useful to beginners, and would perhaps be an assistance to those who are desirous of introducing the study of Political Economy into schools. It is mainly with the hope that a short and elementary book might help to make Political Economy a more popular study in boys' and girls' schools that the following pages have been written. ('Preface')

Garrett Fawcett wrote a textbook in the hopes that a curriculum would follow. While *Manual of Political Economy* was written for advanced students of economics, Garrett Fawcett believed that there was a need for a more elementary version, specifically one for schoolchildren. The textbook was a tremendous success, 'published in ten editions', translated into multiple languages, and used as a 'set book in political economy in the first prospectus of the University College of Bristol in 1876'.[33] It is worth noting that, at the time, political economy was still becoming established as a legitimate area of study and, thus, the economics curriculum was still fairly rudimentary. By expanding the political economy curriculum into the primary school classroom, Garrett Fawcett's *Political Economy for Beginners* made an important contribution to the field. In subsequent editions, Garrett Fawcett added additional pedagogical tools, including questions, puzzles and an index, in the hope that they would be value to teachers and students would make the textbook more likely to be adopted. In 1874, when she published the fourth edition of the textbook, she also published her *Tales in Political Economy*. In the preface to the fourth edition of *Political Economy for Beginners*, she notes that she published it in the hopes that it 'may be useful to those young students who find that some of the puzzles carry them out of their depth'.[34] In other words, the *Tales* are meant as a companion to the textbook because they help reader comprehend some of the more difficult economic theories through fictional illustration.

[32] Rubinstein, *A Different World for Women*, p. 32.

[33] Ibid. p. 28.

[34] Millicent Garrett Fawcett, *Political Economy for Beginners*, p. vii.

Despite the success of *Political Economy for Beginners*, Henry Fawcett repeatedly, and condescendingly, called it 'my wife's little book' when writing to her publisher, a description clearly designed to minimise its significance.[35] Garrett Fawcett's biographer, David Rubinstein, points out that Henry used this patronising language even as he 'attempted to secure a large new edition at an increased royalty', a rhetorical move that, at first glance, seems paradoxical.[36] In order to make an argument for a new edition and increased royalty, one might imagine that Henry would aggrandise his wife's work; instead, he refers to it as 'little' – a modifier that diminishes its importance. A modern reader cannot help but imagine a sort of condescending 'wink, wink, nod, nod' in the exchange between Garrett Fawcett's publisher and husband as they minimise her contributions to the field. This example illustrates the epistemic discrimination faced by women economists in the nineteenth century. I use the term *epistemic discrimination* to describe the bias against women as economists at that time; within the field of economics, epistemic discrimination most often materialised as a distrust of women's *production* of economic knowledge. While women were often believed to be capable of *teaching* economics, they were not thought to be capable of contributing meaningfully to the field. Although Garrett Fawcett's *Tales in Political Economy* and *Political Economy for Beginners* are derivations of existing material, it is important to note that her larger body of work does evidence original economic thought. This is most notable, perhaps, in her entry on 'Communism' for the ninth edition of the *Encyclopaedia Britannica* (1877), a text that Rubinstein calls her 'principal economics publication in the period' because it demonstrates a 'detailed knowledge of the theory and history of attempts to abolish the institution of private property' and offers a measured evaluation of Communism's advantages and disadvantages.[37]

Conclusion

In her contributions to economics, Garrett Fawcett emphasises access to knowledge; both *Political Economy for Beginners* and *Tales in Political Economy* were written to expand the understanding of political economy in British society. Garrett Fawcett's acknowledgement that fictional tales could evoke sympathy and understanding in a way that the 'powder' of economic theory could not is not only a reflection of the cultural attitudes about fiction and science so prevalent in the nineteenth century, it is also

[35] Rubinstein, *A Different World for Women*, p. 29.

[36] Ibid.

[37] Rubinstein, *A Different World for Women*, p. 52.

a feminist critique of the exclusive nature of a science that, in Garrett Fawcett's view, affects deeply the well-being of every member of British society. Her critique rests on an acknowledgement that lived experience is registered, but not fully explored, in formal economic theory; the moral and emotional contingencies of economics can be better conveyed by shifting economic discourse into the mode of fiction, which allows readers to better understand how economic theory comes to bear on their lives. While women's didactic economic writing has often been dismissed within the history of economics, the supposition that the field of political economy should be accessible to everyone was an important contribution to the discipline and the cultural moment. Women economists like Garrett Fawcett would have acutely felt the exclusionary nature of the discipline and the gendered nature of Victorian economics more generally. For Garrett Fawcett this is perhaps best illustrated in the fact that, despite the financial success of her economic textbook, she was subject to the married women's property laws of the time and, therefore, the book and its profits were not her property, but her husband's, a fact that further casts a shadow over his reference to it as his 'wife's little book'. According to Rubinstein:

> In a speech [Garrett Fawcett] made in 1880 she referred with greater accuracy to the fact that one of her books, which must have been *Political Economy for Beginners* (1870), was not her own property, so that when Harry had made his will he had to bequeath her the copyright of her own book.[38]

Despite her accomplishments in the field of economics, Garrett Fawcett was denied formal sanction as an economist during her lifetime. This is most clearly seen by the fact that John Stuart Mill refused to nominate her for inclusion in the Political Economy Club, despite being prompted to do so by a close mutual friend; according to Rubinstein, in 1871 Sir Charles Dilke wrote to Mill 'to recommend her election to the club'.[39] The Political Economy Club was a highly prestigious group; membership was strictly limited to thirty and new members had to be nominated by an existing member, debated on the club floor, and then voted in. The exclusivity of the Political Economy is notable because, at the time, it was the forum to debate and settle questions within the discipline. When Dilke recommended that Mill nominate Garrett Fawcett for membership, he cited her 'little book' (*Political Economy for Beginners*), as well as many articles 'both signed and anonymous'; Dilke pointed out that he was too junior a member to propose her and suggested that Mill 'might be willing to do so'.[40] Unfortunately, he was not. Because she was a woman, Mill refused to nominate her, claiming that his support would be suspect given that he was

[38] Rubinstein, *A Different World for Women*, p. 53

[39] Ibid., p. 30.

[40] Ibid., pp. 30–1.

a supporter of women's rights. According to Garrett Fawcett's biographer, Mill was bothered by her independence, and he distrusted her 'doctrinaire economic views'.[41] The Political Economy Club did not elect its first woman member until 1920, a fact that underscores the discipline's inhospitability to women and its deliberately maintained exclusivity, facts that punctuate the significance of Garrett Fawcett's work to democratise the discipline.

Women's absence within the political economy canon means that they have also often been overlooked in academic studies of nineteenth-century economic thought. Indeed, the first book about female economics, *Adam Smith's Daughters*, by Bette Polkinghorn and Dorothy Thomson, was not published until 1973 and identifies only eight female economists in nearly a 200-year time span. Garrett Fawcett was one of those economists. After the publication of *Adam Smith's Daughters*, it was nearly twenty years before the subject was engaged more thoroughly. In the 1990s, the publication of books like Michele Pujol's *Feminism and Anti-Feminism in Early Economic Thought* (1992) and essay collections like *Beyond Economic Man: Feminist Theory and Economics* (1993), *Feminism and Political Economy in Victorian England* (1994) and *Out of the Margin: Feminist Perspectives on Economics* (1995), drew attention to the ways in which women have traditionally been excluded from economic history. More recently, trade books like Katrine Marçal's *Who Cooked Adam Smith's Dinner: A Story of Women and Economics* (2016) and Victoria Bateman's *The Sex Factor: How Women Made the West Rich* (2019) continue to uncover women's economic contributions and make an argument for a more inclusive economic praxis. And, of course, the #MeToo movement drew widespread public attention to the ways in which women's participation in the market and the workplace is often stymied by sexual harassment and assault. All this has got people seriously rethinking what they thought they knew about the relationship between women and economics.

At a time when no women were considered 'economists', Garrett Fawcett came dangerously close. She wrote bestselling books on the subject, lectured on the discipline at university, and had the audacity to suppose women could be economic actors. Because of the didactic nature of her work, though, scholars have been reticent to take it seriously, regarding it instead as merely popularising the work of men and ignoring the fact that her economic writing was read much more widely than any of the male political economists of the time. Given women's ongoing marginalisation within economics, both as practitioners and subjects, the contributions of Garrett Fawcett to the field certainly merit more attention and respect, as does the broader tradition of women's didactic writing of which she was a part.

41 Ibid., p. 46.

12

Breadwinners and Losers in Annie Thomas's *The Modern Housewife*

Camille Stallings

> So with idle gentlewomen in London who have nothing to do but to wish for remunerative employment, and who come and discuss their wishes with you to a length that compels you to leave your own work [of professional authorship] undone, or to "scumble" it in a way that robs it of half its value … Confess now! doesn't this feminine habit of "dropping-in" upon you in the morning upset your plans, destroy your concentration, and generally mar your work?
>
> *The Modern Housewife, or, How We Live Now*, p. 148.[1]

Death and Destitution

On 6 September 1911, Annie Thomas, a writer of sensation novels, who was well-known in Britain and the United States, applied for emergency funding from the Royal Literary Fund (RLF). Despite a forty-year-long literary career and immense popularity, she was ageing into financial precarity. Included with her application to the RLF was a letter: 'My dear husband died suddenly yesterday', she writes, 'I am left in very straightened circumstances'.[2] She must raise funds immediately, Thomas explains, but cannot auction off her belongings for another three to four weeks. In the 'meantime', she adds, 'I hardly know which way to [turn]'. Because her husband

1 Annie Thomas, *The Modern Housewife, or, How We Live Now* (London: Ward, Lock and Co., 1883), p. 148.

2 Mrs Annie Hall Pender Cudlip, 'Annie Thomas', MS 2750, Archives of the Royal Literary Fund, World Microfilms, *Nineteenth Century Collections Online*, https://link.gale.com/apps/doc/AIUDQK801660925/NCCO?u=oxford&sid=NCCO&xid=b89b09fb (accessed 3 July 2020).

has died without leaving a will, Thomas points out that, 'by law', she is only entitled to one-third of the family possessions.[3] Despite her advanced years (as she was by then seventy-five), recent bereavement and ailing health, she offers to write a 'series of papers … for a weekly' publication in return for funding. Thomas could little afford to mourn. She had to get back to work.

Annie Thomas: A Biography

Annie Thomas began her literary career in 1862 with 'A Stroll in the Park', for the inaugural issue of *London Society: An Illustrated Magazine of Light and Amusing Literature for the Hours of Relaxation* (1862–98). She was, at the time, only twenty-three years old but had already become the breadwinner for her and her mother. Her father, Lieutenant George Thomas, had died a few years earlier, in 1856, leaving Thomas and her mother nearly penniless.[4] With her first publication, Thomas earned 12 guineas (approximately £12, 12s.).[5] As the American journalist, author and war correspondent Franc B. Wilkie writes of Thomas's initial encounter with literary success, this was indeed a 'munificent sum' for her.[6] Thomas next published a short serial, 'The House in Piccadilly', also in *London Society*, which ran from March through to June 1862. Thomas sold the manuscript of her first novel, *Cross of Honour* (1863), shortly thereafter to John Maxwell (1820–95) for £5. Maxwell is perhaps better known as Mary Elizabeth Braddon's husband, but, in the early 1860s, he had already made a name for himself publishing cheap, often sensational, fiction, with Braddon working alongside him in an editorial capacity.[7] According to Wilkie, when Maxwell offered Thomas £10 for a different manuscript, Thomas took her manuscript elsewhere and secured the substantial sum of £300 for it, reflecting Thomas's capacity to negotiate more favourable terms for her work.[8]

[3] Annie Thomas, Letter to the RLF, 22 September 1911, MS 2750, Archives of the Royal Literary Fund.

[4] Megan A. Stephan, 'Thomas [married name Cudlip], Annie Hall (1838–1918)', *ODNB*, 23 September 2004.

[5] Franc B. Wilkie, *Sketches Beyond the Sea*, 2nd edn (Chicago IL: Hazlitt and Reed, 1879), p. 157.

[6] Wilkie, *Sketches Beyond the Sea*, p. 157.

[7] Katherine Mullim, 'Braddon [married name Maxwell], Mary Elizabeth (1835–1915)', *ODNB*, 23 September 2004; John Sutherland, *The Longman Companion to Victorian Fiction* (New York: Routledge, 2014), p. 428.

[8] Wilkie, *Sketches Beyond the Sea*, p. 157. Per Thomas's own accounting, this second novel would have been *Lady Lorme*, published by Ward and Lock in 1863. Nonetheless, Thomas maintained a strong professional relationship with Maxwell, as he also published Thomas's third novel *Sir Victor's Choice*, in 1864 and her sixth, *Barry O'Bourne*, in 1865.

Thomas's business acumen and literary skill ensured her sustained success for more than fifty years: as she continued to write and publish both widely and consistently, she increasingly garnered better compensation for her writing. At the height of Anthony Trollope's career, when he was editor of *Saint Paul's Magazine*, Trollope paid Thomas £13 for contributing to the journal.[9] According to one study, Trollope also increased the rate he offered Thomas between her first and second stories, and by a substantial amount: '7s 9d per page'.[10] The notable increase, Malcom argues, indicates that Trollope's regard for Thomas's work grew from one manuscript to the next. In negotiations with Frank Leslie, an Englishman who ran an extensive and successful publishing business in the United States, Thomas secured an agreement for supplying one monthly instalment of 1,000 words each, for £7 each, totalling £84 for that year. True to Leslie's reputation for 'unashamedly' supplying 'sensation … murders, prizefights, and disasters', Leslie tells Thomas that her pieces 'can scarcely be too sensational'.[11]

As late as the 1890s, Thomas could still command respectable remuneration for her work. According to one contract she signed with Digby, Long and Company for the one-volume *False Pretences* (1895), Thomas initially earned £50, alongside provisions for additional royalties in future.[12] According to Mary Elizabeth Braddon (1835–1915), managing both familial and professional life did, however, strain Thomas's earning potential. In a letter supporting Thomas for an earlier RLF application, Braddon, a friend of Thomas and a fellow sensation novelist, writes: 'She might no doubt have done better for herself had she not been obliged to be the bread-winner as well as the woman of letters.'[13] In yet another letter written to the RLF on behalf of Thomas, Braddon discloses that Thomas 'had to bring up and educate her brother's sons as well as her own children'.[14] On the one hand, Braddon's insight into and defence of the complexity of Thomas's circumstances reflect a tension between women's professional labour and what is required of them within their own household. On the other hand, nineteenth-century female authors were shrewd about how they represented

9 'Cudlip, Annie Hall (Thomas), 1838–1918', The Wellesley Index. Accessed 24 Feb. 2021.

10 Judith Wittosch Malcom, 'Trollope's *Saint Pauls Magazine*' (PhD dissertation, University of Michigan, 1984), p. 90.

11 Letter from Frank Leslie to Annie Thomas. Box 1, folder 23, UCLA special collections archives. Date illegible.

12 Signed contract between Annie Thomas Cudlip and Digby, Long and Co., 30 June 1895, box 1, folder 40, UCLA special collections archives.

13 Mary Elizabeth Braddon, letter to the RLF, 4 April 1907. MS Archives of the Royal Literary Fund: Archives of the Royal Literary Fund 2750.

14 Letter to RLF, 26 June 1908. MS Archives of the Royal Literary Fund: Archives of the Royal Literary Fund 2750.

themselves.[15] In this particular case, Braddon's inclusion of such detail would have carried persuasive weight: by depicting Thomas as dedicated to her familial 'duties', she would more likely be seen as worthy of receiving the RLF grant.

By the late Victorian and Edwardian period, women representing female authors had an established tradition. The professional success of women authors was typically carefully balanced, and at times underweighted, with performing their domestic roles. Among the most well-known examples of this rhetorical strategy is Elizabeth Gaskell's intervention into the discourse surrounding the life of Charlotte Brontë as a daughter, sister and author. In *The Life of Charlotte Brontë*, Gaskell emphasises Brontë's faithful service to her father and sickly sisters, who died young. With such a crafted representation, Gaskell could therefore attempt to quell anxieties about women writers abandoning their 'natural' duties.

In her lifetime, Brontë's domestic loyalties were questioned and criticised, for instance, in reviews of *Jane Eyre*.[16] Notably, however, Gaskell does not oversimplify the matter, but instead scripts a duality of roles and, to an extent, personhoods. On the publication of *Jane Eyre*, Gaskell writes, '[h]enceforward Charlotte Brontë's existence becomes divided into two parallel currents—her life as Currer Bell [Brontë's pen name], the author; her life as Charlotte Brontë, the woman. There were separate duties belonging to each character—not opposing each other; not impossible, but difficult to be reconciled'.[17] As an act of friendship and solidarity, Gaskell thus drafted a story that would argue on behalf of Brontë's decision to pursue her fiction writing and preserve – and partially establish – her reputation.[18]

Linda H. Peterson argues that Gaskell's model of representing the woman writer dominated the discourse in mid-Victorian England. Furthermore, Peterson contends that the conversation depended on a bifurcated identity, that is, one divided between 'the author' and 'the woman'.[19] Peterson rightly calls this framework a myth; she notes that Gaskell's biography did not always align with facts and timelines. After all, Gaskell's aim was first to protect Brontë's reputation and ensure it for posterity. Second to that, Gaskell adhered to facts when they supported the primary goal. However, this strategy performed, whether intentionally or not, an invaluable act of

[15] See Pauline Nestor, 'Introduction', in *Female Friendship and Communities: Charlotte Brontë, George Eliot, and Elizabeth Gaskell* (Oxford: Clarendon, 1985).

[16] Linda H. Peterson, *Becoming a Woman of Letters: Myths of Authorship and Facts of the Victorian Market* (Princeton NJ: Princeton University Press, 2009), p. 134.

[17] Elizabeth Gaskell, *The Life of Charlotte Brontë* (London: Penguin, [1857] 1997), p. 258.

[18] 'The biography itself is a testimony to Gaskell's sense of communality. In one sense it is simply an act of friendship, a fervent desire to create 'A right understanding of the life of my dear friend': Nestor, *Female Friendship and Communities*, p. 32.

[19] Peterson, *Becoming a Woman of Letters*, p. 132.

service to protect a nascent community of women authors.[20] By rendering the female author less threatening to the social system and patriarchal authority, the woman writer could do her public-facing work in the world. Nevertheless, Gaskell's approach was not without possible downsides: 'it [did] not present a model for the sustained achievement of the woman writer; [instead] it separate[d] the artistic life from the domestic and rea[d] them oppositionally (or sequentially)'.[21] This mythology of the woman writer doing it all – maintaining the same degree of loyalty towards unpaid housework and caring responsibilities as towards paid intellectual labour – persisted well into Thomas's life and professional work.

***The Modern Housewife*, a Case Study**

Thomas's *Modern Housewife* contributes to the same mythologising of the successful woman writer. It is also a text that inserts itself into an established discourse on the male breadwinner family model, which by the 1880s had become the idealised form of family organisation for both the middle- and working-classes.[22] The protagonist, Edith, is fully dedicated to running the household and takes pride in doing so. Moreover, the text itself is dominated by this narrative; generically, it overtly instructs the female sex on the 'virtues' of domestic duty and household economy. Yet towards the end of the serialised story, one finds out that Thomas's heroine is not only a mother and a wife, but also an author who is so successful that *she* is the family breadwinner. In downplaying Edith's independent stream of income – which, as Carol Dyhouse's work attests, may have brought shame to the male economic 'head' of the household – Thomas preserves the 'parallel streams' model that Elizabeth Gaskell promulgated in *The Life of Charlotte Brontë*.[23]

Their family income is no pittance: at one point, Edith mentions their family income, which is 'a thousand a year'.[24] According to Margaret Beetham, an income of £1,000 annually would have placed Edith and Arthur at the very top of the middle class. Beetham writes that one contemporary article, 'Marriages Frugal and Otherwise', published in *Englishwoman's*

[20] For more on female writer communities, see Nestor, *Female Friendship and Communities*, p. 32.

[21] Peterson, *Becoming a Woman of Letters*, p. 134.

[22] Wally Seccombe, 'Patriarchy Stabilized: The Construction of the Male Breadwinner Wage Norm in Nineteenth-Century Britain', *Social History*, 11:1 (January 1986): 54.

[23] Carol Dyhouse, *Girls Growing up in Late Victorian and Edwardian England* (London and New York: Routledge, 2013); Peterson, *Becoming a Woman of Letters*, p. 7. See also John Tosh, *A Man's Place: Masculinity and the Middle-Class Home in Victorian England* (New Haven CT: Yale University Press, [1999], 2008), pp. 14, 25.

[24] Thomas, *Modern Housewife*, p. 30.

Domestic Magazine, 'dealt with budgets from £60–£70 to £500–£1,000—from the respectable lower middle class to the very wealthy indeed'.[25] On the one hand, Edith is in an enviable financial situation, indicating *Modern Housewife*'s aspirational elements. On the other hand, Thomas's work operates against the dominant ideology and practice of the day, namely, that 'respectable' middle-class women ought not to work or earn an income.

To reinforce the notion that domestic duties are primary, Edith lives in a suburb, 'a small prettily-appointed villa, standing symmetrically in the middle of its own grounds, about an hour south of London'.[26] Recalling Dyhouse's research on the geographical separation between the feminine and masculine spheres, Thomas situates her heroine within her 'proper' ambit. In *Modern Housewife*, the daily commuter train is also an important structural element of the narrative. From the beginning of their marriage, Edith accompanies her husband to the railway station to see him off for his daily commute into the city for work. When Edith returns home, she enters a fully domestic and separate world: one that will not be interrupted by a male presence (save children, servants or doctors) until evening. Thomas thus demarcates a geographic and moral zone that is fully feminine and defined by her economy, household duties, and labour.

Modern Housewife's narrative begins with the young and naive Edith, newly married, and filled with aspirations of idealised middle-class married life and motherhood. In Edith's words, 'I took my seat upon my throne … and the day after my coronation prepared to reign beneficently and discreetly over my kingdom'.[27] Despite her queenly self-conception, she was at the service of her husband's comfort and timetable: the 'onus', Thomas's heroine says, is on her to her husband and guests brings 'in[to] our married home', and ensuring that her husband feels no 'shame' in doing so.[28] Appearing to align with the idealisations of the likes of the distinctly unfeminist Ruskin and Baldwin, Thomas seemingly presents the wife as responsible for her husband's domestic happiness.

A Postfeminist Approach

In this chapter, I examine the interdependent relationship among the economic lives of Victorian women writers, mythologies (to borrow Linda H. Peterson's word) about female authorship, and feminist disruptions to the male breadwinner discourse. I also contend that scholars of women's history

25 Margaret Beetham, *A Magazine of Her Own? Domesticity and Desire in the Woman's Magazine, 1800–1914* (London: Routledge, 1966), p. 60.

26 Thomas, *Modern Housewife*, p. 1.

27 Ibid.

28 Ibid.

and literature must reevaluate Annie Thomas's contribution to the 'Woman Question' in tandem with her long and successful literary career. As such, this chapter participates in postfeminist discourse in that it enters 'critical debates on the state of contemporary feminism and the work of the feminist cultural critic'.[29] As Stéphanie Grenz and Benjamin A. Brabon argue, the concept of postfeminism is contested; it is rife with 'definitional ambiguity' and rendered at times complex and at other times incoherent from 'oppositional understandings and appropriations'.[30] For Jane Kalbfleisch, postfeminism has two broad delineations: for some, largely for the French critic, it is antithetical to feminism; for others, namely those in the Anglo-American context, it continues the work of postmodernism. Regarding the latter, this vein 'emerged in the eighties as many academic feminists were seduced by the rhetoric of poststructuralism, striv[ing] to escape the binary logic of the first [position] through a tolerance of difference'.[31] Some critics, including Yvonne Tasker and Diane Negra, consider the *post* in *postfeminism* as denoting 'the "pastness" of feminism, whether that supposed pastness is merely noted, mourned, or celebrated'.[32] More recently, Emma Roche situates her postfeminist critique alongside critical evaluations of neoliberalism. Moreover, Roche writes that she 'use[s] the term "postfeminism" to denote that "double engagement" of feminist with antifeminist rhetoric'.[33] Productively, yet clearly, aligning more with the position that Kalbfleisch identifies, Roche examines contemporary narratives in film and literature that present feminism as 'no longer needed'.[34]

Akin to Genz and Brabon, this chapter takes its stance in critical debates by affirming that postfeminism comprises all of these frameworks. As Grenz and Brabon explain, postfeminism is both 'a descriptive popular category and … an academic theoretical tendency'.[35] More importantly, especially for this chapter's aims, postfeminism itself does not need to be coherent; rather, a plurality of postfeminist critiques strengthens the scholarly corpus on representations of women, both contemporary narratives and those emerging in earlier centuries. Multiplicity does not, however,

[29] Stéphanie Genz and Benjamin A. Brabon, *Postfeminism: Cultural Texts and Theories*, 2nd edn (Edinburgh: Edinburgh University Press, 2009, 2018), p. 4.

[30] Benjamin A. Brabon and Stéphane Genz (eds), *Postfeminist Gothic: Critical Interventions in Contemporary Culture* (Basingstoke: Palgrave Macmillan, 2017), p. 2.

[31] Jane Kalbfleisch, 'When Feminism Met Postfeminism: The Rhetoric of a Relationship', in *Generations: Academic Feminists in Dialogue*, ed. by Devoney Looser and E. Ann Kaplan (Minneapolis MN: University of Minnesota Press, 1997), p. 250.

[32] Yvonne Tasker and Diane Negra (eds), *Interrogating Postfeminism: Gender and the Politics of Popular Culture* (Durham NC: Duke University Press, 2007), p. 1.

[33] Emma Roche, *Women, Violence and Postmillennial Romance Fiction* (Abingdon: Routledge, 2023), p. 2.

[34] Ibid., p. 13.

[35] Brabon and Genz, *Postfeminist Gothic*, p. 4.

negate a throughline in postfeminist work. Rather, postfeminism is a reassessment, either implicitly or explicitly, of second-wave feminism, both revaluating it and augmenting scholarship conducted in the latter part of the twentieth century. In this chapter, I take up Annie Thomas as a case study to continue feminist recovery work, which began in earnest in the 1970s, and – importantly – to recover women's narratives passed over by earlier generations of feminist critics due to these authors' apparent incongruity with a feminist agenda.

In selecting Thomas as a case study, this chapter also takes inspiration and direction from Linda H. Peterson's *Becoming a Woman of Letters: Myths of Authorship and Facts of the Victorian Market* (2009). Peterson's research likewise engages with lesser-known female authors, including Mary Howitt, Charlotte Ridell and Marcy Cholmondeley, although she also covers 'canonised' writers such as Harriet Martineau and Elizabeth Gaskell. Placing attention on Thomas serves two ends: first, doing so redresses the omission of Thomas from the 'canon' of successful women writers in nineteenth-century Britain; second, it broadens the scope of the work of Peterson and others by attending to authoress–breadwinner narratives. Importantly, this chapter challenges existing research on the discourse of the male provider within a traditional family structure, arguing that Thomas's *Modern Housewife* sought to disrupt the gendered cultural hegemony of the term *breadwinner*.[36] As such, Thomas's writing might gain currency in postfeminist scholarship, as today's feminist academics continue the project of writing feminisms and rendering the work of women visible and normative.

Moreover, Thomas's popularity and success, combined with her biography, deserve greater attention for their capacity to complicate twentieth-century feminist work on literary responses by women writers to the 'Woman Question'. As Thomas's life attests, the strategies that made a female Victorian author successful in the literary economy did not necessarily translate into personal economic success, George Eliot being one of the outstanding exceptions. Nor did the mythologies in representation align with real-world conditions. This does not mean, however, that they were wholly bereft of supporting women's wider access to education, professions, and economic agency. For example, *The Modern Housewife*'s protagonist is the family's financial provider. Nevertheless, rhetorically, Thomas represents this mother–wife–breadwinner character non-threateningly, thereby preserving traditional domestic and gender roles. Simultaneously, women are didactically exhorted

[36] Angélique Janssens (ed.), *The Rise and Decline of the Male Breadwinner Family?* (Cambridge: Cambridge University Press, 1998), p. 11–12, 21; Emma Griffin, *Bread Winner: An Intimate History of the Victorian Economy* (New Haven CT: Yale University Press, 2020), p. 104; Colin Creighton, 'The Rise and Decline of the "Male Breadwinner Family" in Britain', *Cambridge Journal of Economics*, 23:5, Special Issue On the Family (September 1999), 519–41.

not to surrender to the social expectations of their sex of 'paying calls', which Carol Dyhouse points out was a prescribed female 'duty' among the middle classes.[37] Thus, *Modern Housewife*'s relationship to the 'Woman Question' is complex, addressing women running the home economically as earners and being heads of their homes in daily life. To complicate such narratives even further, part of what makes Thomas's life and work particularly salient to women's history is how her styling of the married 'authoress' as breadwinner diverged from Thomas's real-world experiences and economic conditions. Placing attention on this disparity makes more visible the work of postfeminist scholars in retrieving heretofore 'lost' nineteenth-century narratives and offers strategies for promoting a widening female ambit.

Domestic Literature

While postfeminism is not necessarily historicist, bringing this approach to Thomas's fiction as it relates to the 'Woman Question' is nonetheless productive. As Talia Schaffer argues, if the historian is always 'trying to fill gaps in a linear historical record', then scholarship may not be alive to 'alternative modes of organization, nor the kinds of possibilities, texts, and feminisms that an atemporal, nonlinear arrangement might support. Victorian feminist criticism is increasingly exploring such new temporalities'.[38] To consider Thomas's text generically, *Modern Housewife* fulfils many of the predictable elements of conduct literature: the division of labour being determined by one's sex and the underlying structural drive to reform society via 'stabilising' the family unit. Leonore Davidoff places the genesis of such domestic writing in the eighteenth century, with William Cowper and Hannah More, who 'se[t] the terms for the characterisation of domesticity and sexual difference'.[39] From the outset, women writers have participated actively in the discourse; many 'explored the contradictions between the claims for women's [moral] superiority and their social subordination, a tension which could not be resolved within early Victorian society'.[40] Moreover, this tradition has its roots in eighteenth- and nineteenth-century Christian teachings, and to some degree Evangelicalism.[41]

[37] Dyhouse, *Girls Growing Up*, p. 24.

[38] Talia Schaffer, 'Victorian Feminist Criticism: Recovery Work and the Care Community', *Victorian Literature and Culture*, 47:1 (2018), 67.

[39] Leonore Davidoff, *Family Fortunes: Men and Women of the English Middle Class 1780–1850* (Boca Raton FL: Routledge, 2018), p. 149.

[40] Ibid.

[41] 'Cowper offered a serious critique of many aspects of aristocratic and gentry life and, like so many Evangelicals, sought a regeneration of the social and political world': Davidoff, *Family Fortunes*, p. 162.

The link between conduct literature and ideologies of sexual difference, domesticity and politics is clear: the first pages of Hannah More's novel, *Coelebs in Search of a Wife, Comprehending Observations of Domestic Habits and Manners, Religion and Morals* (1807), addresses women's education, social roles, and the purposes behind female education. Notably, More's work was published within twenty years of Mary Wollstonecraft's *A Vindication of the Rights of Woman* (1792). Here, Wollstonecraft argues that women's emancipation will come from cultivating her intellect and defining herself in terms of active citizenship in the polity first, then as a mother: 'speaking of women at large, their first duty is to themselves as rational creatures, and the next, in point of importance, as citizens, is that, which includes so many, of a mother.'[42] Harriet Martineau, writing much later but in reference to her youth in the 1810s and 1820s, frames her own drive to gain independence through intellectual work by juxtaposing her ambitions with societal expectations. In her autobiography, she writes:

> When I was young, it was not thought proper for young ladies to study very conspicuously; and especially with pen in hand. Young ladies (at least in provincial towns) were expected to sit down in the parlour to sew,—during which reading aloud was permitted,—or to practice their music; but so as to be fit to receive callers, without any signs of blue-stockingism which could be reported abroad … and thus my first studies in philosophy were carried on with great care and reserve.[43]

Intervening in these contemporary debates, More's novel responds to Wollstonecraft's interpretation of women's nature and their roles while imbricating both Rousseau and Milton – all on the first page. Though the two women's publishers were geographically proximate, they occupied different ideological and literary positions. Their readerships did likewise, with the 'Clapham Sect' (which included one of More's supporters, William Wilberforce) opposing what they saw as Wollstonecraft's dangerous ideas. More herself labelled Wollstonecraft's *Vindication of the Rights of Woman* 'absurd'.[44] In this exchange, however, it is clear that she is inserting herself into public discourse, even if it is to disavow a woman's public role. In the introductory paragraph, Coeleb claims surprise that the women with whom he speaks often take offense to Milton's Eve. He, however, admires her greatly: 'I confess that as the Sophia of Rousseau had her young

[42] Mary Wollstonecraft, *A Vindication of the Rights of Woman* (New York and London: Norton, 2009 [1792]), p. 154.

[43] Harriet Martineau, *Harriet Martineau's Autobiography*, vol. 1, ed. by Maria Weston Chapman (Cambridge: Cambridge University Press, 2010 [1877]), pp. 100–1.

[44] Hannah More, Letter to Horatio Walpole, Earl of Orford, 7 February 1793, in *The Letters of Horace Walpole, Earl of Orford*, ed. by Peter Cunningham et al., 20 vols (London: Richard Bentley, 1857–61), vol. 4, p. 374.

imagination captivated by the character of Fenelon's Telemachus, so I early became enamoured of that of Milton's Eve.'[45] In fact, for him, the Adam–Eve duo of *Paradise Lost* 'formed an idea of conjugal happiness'.[46] Milton's Eve, whom Wollstonecraft notes originates from 'Moses's poetical story', may be easier for a man to admire because Eve's character demonstrates 'that woman was created for man' and that 'the whole creation was only created for his convenience and or pleasure'.[47] Contra Milton, Wollstonecraft writes:

> Milton describes our first frail mother, though when he tells us that women are formed for softness and sweet attractive grace … he meant to deprive us of souls [rationality], and insinuate that we were beings only designed [for] sweet attractive grace … to gratify the sense of man.[48]

More, already a household name and well-known for her didactic tracts and conduct writing, published this one and only novel – and it is more of 'a treatise on female manners and education than … a work of fiction'.[49] This, too, is pervasive within the genre: fictive narratives, plots, and characters all serve the ends of 'educating' young women into their proper roles in the family and society.

By the mid-Victorian period, idealising the domestic sphere was ubiquitous, although certainly not uncontested. Among the most well-known proponents of a sexual division of labour, and one that served the male's needs at home, is John Ruskin. In *Sesame and Lilies* (1865), he writes: 'This is the true nature of home—it is the place of Peace; the shelter, not only from all injury, but from all terror, doubt, and division. In so far as it is not this, it is not home.'[50] Writing just a few years later, Baldwin Brown, a controversial minister but an outspoken social reformer, claimed that a man is 'world-weary' and, as such, the women in his house must 'pray, think, strive to make a home something like a bright, serene, restful, joyful nook of heaven in an unheavenly world'.[51]

[45] Hannah More, *Coelebs in Search of a Wife, Comprehending Observations Of Domestic Habits and Manners, Religion and Morals*, vol. 1 (London: T. Cadell and W. Davies, 1808), p. 1.

[46] Ibid.

[47] Wollstonecraft, *A Vindication of the Rights of Woman*, p. 29.

[48] Ibid., p. 22.

[49] Davidoff, *Family Fortunes*, p. 155; J. Skedd, *Oxford Dictionary of National Biography*, s.v. 'More, Hannah', last updated 25 September 2014, https://doi.org/10.1093/ref:odnb/19179.

[50] John Ruskin, 'Of Queens' Gardens', in *The Works of John Ruskin*, vol. 18, ed. by E. T. Cook and A. D. O. Wedderbern (London: George Allen, 1903), sec. 68, 122. Qtd in Walter E. Houghton, *The Victorian Frame of Mind: 1830–1870* (New Haven CT and London: Yale University Press, 1957 [1958?]), p. 343.

[51] Quoted in R. Tudor Jones, *ODNB*, sv., 'Brown, James Baldwin, the younger', last updated 30 May 2013, https://doi.org/10.1093/ref:odnb/3616; Baldwin Brown, *Young*

Towards the end of the century, the gendered division between the public and the domestic spheres was more than literary idealisation or moralised sermon; it was an observable fact among middle-class households. Carol Dyhouse notes that, with the rise of commuter railways, middle-class suburbs would have nearly no men, save perhaps a gardener, during the day. She writes that 'urban growth had taken a distinct form which emphasised the sexual division of labour'.[52] By then, middle-class families had moved 'to leafy residential suburbs … Daily[,] [men] travelled into work on commuter trains, leaving their women-folk and children stranded in suburbia'.[53] Developing an ethnographic social history of the suburbs, Dyhouse includes the testimony of women residing there between 1870 and 1914, who described the suburbs as being bereft of men during working hours; or, as John Tosh referred to these absent men, they comprised 'the invisible breadwinner'.[54]

Economically, it was vital to preserve dignity among middle-class male breadwinners by not having the women of the family earning an income. Dyhouse makes clear that the popular perception among suburban communities was that no woman 'had "a career or a paid job of her own, either a married woman or a spinster. A paid job for one of this [*sic*] womenfolk would have cast an unbearable reflection of incompetence upon the money-getting male"'.[55] Against this social history of popular opinion, then, Thomas's *Modern Housewife* departs on the subject of paid labour. However, Thomas does so while performing the genre's traditional work of conservative didacticism. In scripting a mother–wife–breadwinner protagonist, Thomas's narrative has a boldness to it; certainly, it worked against the grain of some prescriptions of feminine conduct when negotiating between work and home. Annie Thomas was, it seems, more the daughter of Wollstonecraft than a descendant of More; this is an important distinction and, perhaps, a surprising one for a writer of a conduct manual of household management.

Historicising the Breadwinner

Thomas's decision to create a breadwinning heroine challenged the dominant practice and ideology of her time. Recent work produced by economic

Men and Maidens: A Pastoral for the Times (London: Hodder & Stoughton, 1871), pp. 38–9. Qtd in Houghton, *The Victorian Frame of Mind*, p. 345.

52 Dyhouse, *Girls Growing Up*, p. 4.

53 Ibid.

54 Katherine Chorley, *Manchester Made Them* (London: Faber & Faber, 1950), p. 149, quoted in Dyhouse, *Girls Growing Up*, p. 4; Tosh, *A Man's Place*, p.195.

55 Chorley, *Manchester Made Them*, p. 150. Qtd in Dyhouse, *Girls Growing Up*, p. 6.

and social historians on the breadwinner demonstrates that by the mid-nineteenth century, the male breadwinner family model had become both an aspiration and an ideology beset with unreconcilable contradictions. Comparing data against idealisations, scholars regularly noted that the male breadwinner model was either unattainable (except for a privileged few) or created poverty and dependence for women and children.[56] Annie Thomas's *Modern Housewife* contributes to the nineteenth-century discourse on breadwinning. More importantly, it speaks to the changing identity of the breadwinner, shifting the definitional ambit from working class to middle class, and from male to female – much earlier than scholars had previously contended. John Tosh argues that the term 'breadwinner' was new in the Victorian era, although more nuance is needed here and will be addressed more in-depth later in this chapter.[57] Either way, the novel semantic movement during the early and mid-Victorian era is clear: it linked the word and concept to the male gender. Thus, in *Modern Housewife*, Thomas's descriptive shift of the breadwinner in terms of both gender and class suggests that Thomas's position on women as economic agents is radical – despite *Modern Housewife*'s framing adhering to traditional conventions of domestic duty and household management.

By the mid-nineteenth century, the male breadwinner family model had become the ideal, despite it being difficult to achieve and precarious for women and children. Wally Seccombe, a sociologist, writes that in 'the nineteenth century, only the uppermost stratum of working men in the skilled trades were able to win high enough wages and sufficiently steady year-round employment to be their families' sole money-makers'.[58] Horrell and Humphries note that women and children working in factories may

[56] See Seccombe, 'Patriarchy Stabilized'; Sara Horrell and Jane Humphries, 'The Origins and Expansion of the male Breadwinner Family: The Case of Nineteenth-Century Britain', *International Review of Social History*, 42 (1997): 23–67; Creighton, 'The Rise and Decline of the "Male Breadwinner Family" in Britain'; Janssens, *The Rise and Decline of the Male Breadwinner Family*. More recently, Griffin's *Bread Winner* gives voice to working-class women's unpaid domestic labour by unearthing their autobiographies (using the Burnett Archive of Working-Class Autobiography). Among Griffin's important findings is that working-class women's autobiographies consistently documented that they 'only indicated a preference for working inside the home when they were already shouldering a double burden of paid work outside the home and unpaid work within it' (34). This double-shift model, Griffin argues, emerged in tandem with the ideology of the male breadwinner; notably, because boys and men could earn more than their female counterparts, families strategised to garner the most income possible for the unit. This often meant using female family members to perform unpaid domestic labour and sending the boys and men to earn higher wages than girls and women could command.

[57] Oxford English Dictionary, s.v. 'breadwinner (n)', July 2023, https://doi.org/10.1093/OED/1148507142.

[58] Seccombe 'Patriarchy Stabilized', p. 54.

have been unique among the working classes in that their contributions to family income were more stable until the latter part of the Victorian period (although Horrell and Humphries remain essentially silent concerning factories overworking and abusing children).[59] Seccombe's research demonstrates, moreover, that female dependence on men was '*not* a foreordained consequence of capitalist growth, but rather was the outcome of struggle in which an increasingly conservative labour movement' reacted by curtailing the access of women to employment to push up male wages.[60] In turn, this pitted middle- and working-class women's interests against one another, as the former sought to strengthen their male-heads-of-household's wages at the expense of cross-class solidarity with working women, something that is borne out in Thomas's story. As Seccombe notes:

> Instead of reaching out to organize women workers, and fighting to equalize their pay by strengthening their bargaining power, most unions attempted to defend their own narrow corporate interests by means of legislative regulation, exclusion and often intimidation and harassment of unorganized women workers. In doing so, they made the male breadwinner norm their ideological armament ... fostering a breach between an increasingly middle-class feminist movement, preoccupied with raising the wages of their members, overwhelmingly men.[61]

Even among Marxist social historians, like Eric Hobsbawm, the argument persisted that scholars could 'ignore' nineteenth-century women's and children's economic contributions, as their waged 'rate was normally fixed in relation to the male wage'.[62] Among the most striking finding that challenges Hobsbawm's and others' assumptions is that, in the English context, working women contributed significantly to family budgets.[63] In the later decades of the twentieth century and the early twenty-first, scholars have demonstrated that women's paid labour and economic contribution to the family unit are, in fact, 'the historical norm', not a 'breakdown in traditional

[59] Horrell and Humphries, 'Origins and Expansion'; for additional non-British contexts, see Beatrice Moring, *Women in the Factory, 1880–1930* (London: Boydell and Brewer, 2024).

[60] Seccombe, 'Patriarchy Stabilized', pp. 54–5. Emphasis original. See Janelle Pötzsche's chapter in this volume on the problem of the wages–fund doctrine.

[61] As Seccombe points out, 'more than a century later, the Left still pays a very great price for this division' (74).

[62] Seccombe, 'Patriarchy Stabilized', p. 53. Seccombe quotes Eric Hobsbawm, *Labouring Men* (Weidenfeld and Nicolson, 1964).

[63] Horrell and Humphries, 'Origins and Expansion'; Janssens, *Rise and Decline*; Joyce Burnette, 'How not to Measure the Standard of Living: Male Wages, Non-Market Production and Household Income in Nineteenth-Century Europe', *Economic History Review,* 78:1 (2025), 87–112; Moring, *Women in the Factory*. This list includes references to both the British and Continental European contexts.

ways of family organization'.[64] In fact, until the nineteenth century, as Joyce Burnette argues, the pecuniary worth of women's work was both visible and acknowledged. Burnette writes: 'an English observer from 1785 … notes … that a male labourer might contribute only half of [the] family income: "I have known instances of the wife's management of the live stock, together with the earnings of herself and her children in haytime, and harvest, etc., produce nearly as much money in the course of the year, as her husband by all his labour during the same time."'[65] Academics now argue that women's post-Second World War economic visibility is a return to the norm, not an erosion of traditional family values (if one defines 'traditional' as female economic dependency).[66] Jane Humphries's research contends that before parliamentary enclosure, rural women's work was more visible; both their non-market and market production were often included in family budgets.[67] Humphries notes that the economic value of a woman's gleaning could equal up to double what her husband could earn in wages.[68] By historicising working-women's relationship to labour and income, one sees that the *in*visibility of women's work under industrial conditions is contingent. The same holds for assumptions and practices of women's financial dependence on an adult male earner. Social and economic historians of the twentieth century have found that, in the mid to late-nineteenth century, the term 'breadwinner' was gendered as male. However, earlier in the nineteenth century, 'bread-winner' was used in connection with both working-class men and women. In 1841, the article 'Rustic Controversies', in *Fraser's Magazine*, a fiddler's fiddle is called 'his bread-winner'.[69] Earlier, in 1832, *Tait's Edinburgh Magazine* published 'The Howdie; An Autobiography', in which an old woman was said to have 'made her bread by distilling peppermint'.[70] The *Oxford English Dictionary* notes a 1721 usage, which connects the 'breadwinner' concept with a woman and the instrument by which she earns her living: 'An aged woman, who has but the distaff for

[64] Janssens (ed.), 'Introduction', in *The Rise and Decline of the Male Breadwinner Family*, pp. 7–8. Janssens refers to and paraphrases Seccombe's argument in *Weathering the Storm: Working Class Families from the Industrial Revolution to the Fertility Decline* (London: Verso, 1993). See also Burnette, 'How Not to Measure'.

[65] Burnette, 'How Not to Measure', p. 21. Quoting Ivy Pinchbeck, *Women Workers*.

[66] Regarding women's work and the changes wrought by the two world wars, see Seccombe, 'Patriarchy Stabilized', p. 54; and Creighton, 'Rise and Decline', p. 524.

[67] Jane Humphries, 'Enclosures, Common Rights, and Women: The Proletarianization of Families in the Late Eighteenth and Early Nineteenth Centuries', *Journal of Economic History*, 50:1 (March 1990), 17–42.

[68] Regarding family budgets, see Horrell and Humphries, 'Origins and Expansion'; Burnette, 'How Not to Measure'; Griffin, 'Introduction', in *Bread Winner*.

[69] 'Rustic Controversies, No. V. The Penny Wedding', *Fraser's Magazine*, 23:136 (April 1841), 453.

[70] 'Howdie; An Autobiography', *Tait's Edinburgh Magazine*, 1:6 (September 1832), 708.

her bread-winner.'[71] By the time of the publication of *Modern Housewife*, however, the male breadwinner model had become established as the ideal that best aligns with each sex's 'nature'. Annie Thomas's Edith is important within women's literary history because she charts a path forward *from* female dependence *to* female interdependence.

Wally Seccombe notes that the mid-point of the nineteenth century is when the male breadwinner model 'was consolidated as the dominant working-class family ideal'.[72] Seccombe's attention homes in on the transition from the family wage model, within which the whole family is assumed to be vital economic contributors, to the individual wage model, a prerequisite for the male breadwinner framework. Seccombe writes: 'There was nothing natural (that is, biologically necessary or socially immutable) about the particular family division of labour which became the proletarian norm in the Victorain era.'[73] The 'nature', or 'biology', argument has long been weaponised to institutionalise female financial, legal and other forms of dependency on a male head. Angélique Janssens calls the pecuniary results of this 'feminized poverty'.[74]

Despite their dependency (and thus their precarity), women still worked – and worked hard. They just often did not get paid for it. Emma Griffin reminds her readership that in Victorian and Edwardian households, housework was gruelling; furthermore, households 'could not function without water, fuel and food, and obtaining these things involved hard, physical work and took many hours daily'.[75] Industrialisation, the emergence of the factory system, and rural enclosure were not the only social and economic constructs that produced female poverty. Seccombe's research adds another factor: unions and organised labour efforts fought, often successfully, to deny women's right to employment. '[O]nly if women's and children's employment were legally *curtailed*, or banned outright', Seccombe writes, 'would men's wages ever rise to the level of a living wage, and their families be properly supported. This was the argument which legitimated the drive to restrict women's employment in the second half of the nineteenth century'.[76] With a higher, liveable wage, the contention went, men's wives and children could live out their natural and biological teleology. That is, their 'wives could remain at home and become good homemakers (just like your

[71] *Oxford English Dictionary*, s.v. 'breadwinner (n), meaning and use 1'.

[72] Seccombe, 'Patriarchy Stabilized', p. 54.

[73] Seccombe, 'Patriarchy Stabilized', p. 62. Seccombe, like Horrell and Humphries, carefully details that ideals and practised norms varied by industry, although in the mid-nineteenth century, the male breadwinner family model had attained an idealised status. Seccombe notes that achieving that ideal was another matter entirely (54).

[74] Janssens, 'Introduction', Rise and Deline, p. 39.

[75] Griffin, *Bread Winner*, p. 87.

[76] Seccombe, 'Patriarchy Stabilized', p. 55.

wives), and our children could stay at school and get a good education (like your children)'.[77] Attempts to mitigate the ills of an unregulated, or a 'free', labour market still devalued women's work and rendered their economic contributions to their households invisible and uncompensated. Moreover, such devaluation underscored the centrality of a male breadwinner among the unskilled and skilled working classes.

However, middle-class women's dependence on the male wage also matters. Mabel Atkinson, who had been active in the women's suffrage movement and a Fabian, referred to this class of women as being forced into a parasitic relationship with male heads of households. In contrast to the 'ruthless exploitation' of working-class women, middle-class women were deprived of meaningful work.[78] Atkinson writes: 'Dusting, arranging flowers, and paying calls were the important duties of their existence.' In Thomas's *Modern Housewife*, Edith works against this ideology by being a career woman, self-identifying as the family's 'breadwinner'. Edith, Thomas's spokeswoman, achieves it all: she maintains her career and excels in motherhood and performing gendered duties. This fiction, nevertheless, comes with a more realistic cost, as Edith's suburban isolation circumscribes 'her contact with the social world' beyond.[79]

Annie Thomas Rethinks the Breadwinner

The didactic tone of Thomas's narrative is notable for its departure from domestic concerns such as recipes and which articles of clothing are appropriate for boys and girls at different life stages. Now, the teaching identifies an ideal reader: Edith, as the first-person narrator, claims that it is two 'classes of women' to whom she 'appeal[s]'.[80] The first encompasses 'women whose husbands' incomes vary from three hundred to a thousand a year, and who (being portionless) have to go to their husbands for every five-pound note or shilling they require for household and other expenses'. As for the 'second class', this is 'composed of women who are situated precisely as I am myself—of women who are professional authors or artists—at any rate who are "bread-winners" in some walk of life'.[81] Structurally, the traditional hierarchy is retained; economically dependent wives are named first, with the second possibility of womanhood trailing.

77 Seccombe, 'Patriarchy Stabilized', p. 55.

78 Mabel Atkinson, 'The Economic Foundations of the Women's Movement', *Women's Economic Writing in the Nineteenth Century*, ed. by Lana L. Dalley (London and New York: Routledge, 2023), p. 89.

79 Atkinson, 'Economic Foundations', p. 89.

80 Thomas, *Modern Housewife*, p. 43.

81 Ibid.

The framing, however, is important. The phrasing attending the first cohort of wives emphasises their dependence; when Thomas's modern, upper-middle-class housewife refers to these women as 'portionless', the diction is strikingly engaged with discourses around the women's movement, emerging New Woman narratives, and the 'Woman Question'. The second group is anything but 'portionless' or economically dependent on a male breadwinner because she is herself a 'bread-winne[r]'. Regarding Edith's character, being the breadwinner is not only a possibility but also bestows greater dignity than being 'portionless'. Despite the narrative framing of domestic duty, Edith's breadwinning status underlines Thomas's more radical position concerning women as active economic participants.

Race, Class and Crime

Yet *Modern Housewife* is not simply conduct literature; it also follows key conventions of the *Bildungsroman*. Despite her best attempts to live this middle-class ideal, the first time her husband brings home dinner guests, Edith grossly overspends, and the meal itself is a tepid experience. Edith's moral growth, central to the *Bildungsroman*, comes from acquiring both economic acumen and 'worldly' wisdom. Although such skills are developed strictly within the domestic sphere, Thomas's work is inserting itself into public discourse in important and valuable ways for middle-class women.

Nevertheless, Thomas's focaliser, Edith, practices a problematic form of feminine agency. As part of her education, Edith must learn – and then reinforce and police – the racist and classist ideologies of late Victorian Britain. Edith is not seen acting in solidarity with other women, whether in her own class or otherwise, but in service of herself, her family, and, by extension, the nation. In the main, her interactions with her employees are framed by her failure to notice and correct the criminal behaviour of her cook and groom. Together, this pair has been embezzling money through exaggerated orders for household food and oats for the horses; their plan is to marry and use these funds to establish a household of their own.[82] The cook is a Black woman, against whom Edith uses a racial slur. Her cook 'confessed (for a certain sum) that William [the groom] and herself had arranged to marry when they should between them have robbed us of enough to set up house for themselves comfortably'.[83] Rather than considering the struggle of working people to achieve a modicum of domestic security that might compel them to siphon off a portion for their own survival, the episode characterises the working-class woman of colour in

[82] Ibid., p. 40.

[83] Ibid.

the text unsympathetically as a thief, a sexual profligate, and open to selling truth for cash.[84]

Consequently, the lesson that propels Edith's *Bildung* forwards reinforces the notion that female economic and moral agency are middle-class domains and aspirations that are unavailable to non-white, non-middle-class women. This aspect of the text entrenches the breach within the women's movement, that of middle-class women working to expand their rights at the expense of working-women's rights to earn a liveable wage themselves.[85] For Thomas, the Victorian housewife performs a much more significant economic *and* political function in her exercise, or failure to exercise, class management and, especially, the active management of class power.[86] Readers receive instruction on managing and disciplining employed labour. The fiscal and political lesson is clear: Edith must stop being distracted by sociality, shopping and other activities, and acquire more sophisticated management tools. Thus, her maturation narrative commences by learning to discipline the servant class.

Thomas continues in the tradition of Thackery and Trollope in critiquing consumerism and household mismanagement; however, where Thackery and Trollope explore the strain of masculine ambition, Thomas reframes mismanagement from the female position.[87] Aptly, Edith becomes an autodidact in household management, studying 'Mrs. Beeton's admirable *Book of Household Management*'.[88] This is a notable moment of meta-intertextuality, as *Modern Housewife* was published serially in the *Englishwoman's Domestic Magazine*, which had been jointly run by Mrs Beeton and her husband, Samuel Beeton, before the former passed away in 1865.[89] The text acts as embedded advertisement that serves to profit the publisher and, by extension, the author. Thomas, however, adds another element to the traditional conduct manual. Her heroine, it is divulged, also works *outside* the ambit of domesticity. She is an 'authoress'. Suddenly, the reader learns that frivolity and naivety are not the only causes of household neglect; Edith has allowed her work as a writer to lessen her domestic efficacy. Because overseeing the household's economy must now become 'my chief consideration', she

[84] Ibid.

[85] See Seccombe, 'Patriarchy Stabilized', p. 74. The pitting of middle-class women against their working-class counterparts is discussed in greater depth later in this chapter.

[86] Elizabeth Langland, *Nobody's Angels: Middle-Class Women and Domestic Ideology in Victorian Culture* (Ithaca NY: Cornell University Press, 1995), p. 8.

[87] Anthony Trollope, *The Way We Live Now* [1875], ed. by Frank Kermode (London: Penguin, 1994); William Makepeace Thackeray, *Vanity Fair: A Novel without a Hero* [1847–8], ed. by John Sutherland (Oxford: Oxford University Press, 1998).

[88] Thomas, *Modern Housewife*, p. 47.

[89] Janette Ryan, 'Beeton [*née* Mayson]. Isabella Mary (1836–1865)', *ODNB*, 23 September 2004. https://doi.org/10.1093/ref:odnb/37172. According to Ryan, this woman's magazine, begun in 1852, 'pioneered the middle-class woman's magazine'.

bemoans, 'my writing (I had just begun to use my pen professionally) fell into arrears'.[90] This prioritisation of 'selves' (the author, the mother, the wife) aligns with the tradition of representing female authors' 'parallel lives'. It also reinforces the 'proper' order of things: the duties of wife and mother override authorship. The word *arrears* reminds readers of the weight of unmet obligations and the financial cost of neglecting to write. Alongside re-encountering this hierarchy of female selves and duties, the reader also receives vital knowledge about Edith: she is in the early stages of a literary career, and she may even have professional ambition. Thomas thus weaves together two strains of feminine identity: the first is conservative or traditional; the second comprises intellectual labour and economic agency.

Such representations are not wholly new. What is notable is Edith's professional growth in tandem with her 'ethical' maturation. Eventually, the reader learns that Edith has become the breadwinner of the family; this process, however, unlike her maturation as a household manager, has been nearly entirely elided from the plot. Nonetheless, in the background of rising successfully to the challenge of household management, Edith surpasses her husband's income, which he earns from working as 'a young partner in an old firm' in the city.[91] In content as well as form, then, *Modern Housewife* preserves the hierarchy of female roles while teaching a female readership that they could want and have more than the family hearth.

Hiding Behind Her Rhetoric

In her carefully constructed text, Thomas creates space to argue that a middle-class white women's dignity and agency come from owning their own 'portion'. Downplaying a wife's and mother's capacity to earn her own income, however, is not the same as denying or condemning it. Rather, one sees Thomas promoting very modern ideas of womanhood while skilfully embedding them within larger narratives of traditional female roles. Edith's character may not be a 'Girton Girl' or a 'Lady Doctor' – the less-acknowledged peers of the 'New Woman' – but she, like them, is a 'discursive interjection[n] into Victorian debates over the future of the educated working woman'.[92] Thus, Edith may appear throughout most of *Modern Housewife* to follow the conventions of Victorian wifely duties; in reality, she is disseminating dangerously modern ideas. Even her husband is notably 'modern'. At one point, when moralising about female afternoon visiting

90 Thomas, *Modern Housewife*, p. 31.

91 Ibid., p. 2.

92 Rachel Carr, *The 'Girton Girl' and 'Lady Doctor': Women, Higher Education and Medicine in Popular Victorian Fiction by Women* (PhD thesis, King's College London, 1998). Quotation from the abstract.

hours, he contrasts Edith with the 'idle gentlewomen in London who have nothing to do but *wish* for remunerative employment'.[93] Moreover, these women 'mar' Edith's work 'in a way that robs it of half its value'.[94] Unlike men who would be ashamed to have their wives earning an income, Arthur characterises Edith's work as important and valuable. In this passage, he is also represented as a husband supportive towards and protective of his wife's non-domestic roles and labour. Seen from this perspective, Thomas's narrative possesses qualities that feminist scholars may have overlooked. Undeniably, Edith's character is, at the very least, an 'attemp[t] to negotiate' female economic agency within a specific set of cultural constructs.[95]

As a strategic participant in the wider discourse on the 'Woman Question', towards the end of *Modern Housewife*, Thomas addresses the structural barriers to women finding work and commanding adequate wages. Referring to the infamous problem of the surplus woman described in Janette Rutterford's chapter, Edith asks:

> Where is the root of this evil? Why are these women, some of them in the full prime of their powers, cast out as "superfluous" from our prosperous population? I hear that there are governess' institutions and "needy ladies' high-art needlework societies," but neither one nor the other seems to meet these cases or supply their needs.[96]

As for being an authoress, Thomas's narrator points to systemic challenges: 'but it is also grievous that we—women like myself … should have to convert ourselves into agents for the disposal of these articles.'[97] 'I feel the times are crooked indeed,' she laments, 'which do not afford adequate support to cultured gentlewomen, amply qualified to impart her cultivation to others'.[98] As for the national economy, Edith bemoans: 'too well we know that "all the markets overflow." But there must be a demand for this over-supply somewhere?'[99] Supply and demand, that perennial topic of capitalist discourse, garners the attention of Edith and thus Thomas's readership. In a narrative that is largely concerned with domestic economy, this turn to the national economy rounds out the work of a modern 'authoress'; it portrays women actively shaping economic discourse and, more importantly, seeing women's economic lives as an integral part of that dialogue. This discursive

93 Thomas, *Modern Housewife*, p. 148. Emphasis added.

94 Ibid.

95 Carr, *The 'Girton Girl' and 'Lady Doctor'*. Quotation from the abstract.

96 Ibid., p. 150. In this, it picks up both Rutterford's and Vosper's observations on the significance of the 'surplus' women problem for the economy; see Vosper in this volume, especially pp. 72–4.

97 Ibid., p. 151.

98 Ibid., pp. 151–2.

99 Ibid., p. 152.

turn makes explicit – indeed, visible – the relationship between the condition of women and the broader workings of a gendered economy.

Conclusion

In this chapter, I have argued for a postfeminist reading of Annie Thomas's *Modern Housewife*. Alongside a close reading of this text as a case study, I have pointed to discrepancies between fictional narratives about women's authorship and Thomas's own biography. Such divergences between representations of professional women and their real-world experience deserve attention, as these are opportunities to distinguish more carefully between what might be read as prescriptive and what might be seen as descriptive in the nineteenth century.[100] For women authors from the mid-Victorian through to the Edwardian periods, the tradition of 'parallel lives' was one among many survival strategies in the professionalisation of women's writing. Thomas provides an uncomfortable reminder of middle-class white women's complicity in the maintenance of racist and classist positions, even as they provide ways for these women to advance their own position. It is clear through the interventions that writers such as Thomas made into public discourse that middle-class women were impacting ideological shifts that altered the way in which labour was described and understood in both class and gender terms. Interventions like Thomas's also emphasise the significant role that women held in class discipline. In narrating Edith's *Bildung* such that it includes identifying and responding to servants' criminal behaviour, and by reclassifying the breadwinner as being middle class and female, Thomas contributes to the shifting vertical order; namely, Thomas's text externalises the ruling class's dominance while forging space for middle-class women's participation in the hierarchical ranking of wages, classes and behaviour – criminal or otherwise. In this way, studying such texts adds nuance and complexity to scholarly understandings of women's socio-economic history.

Postfeminism thus offers a framework to complicate Edith's breadwinning status. On the one hand, Edith is a literary touchstone. When readers encountered this character, Edith could strike against gendered assumptions and conventions and show literate women how to win financial independence whilst maintaining familial interdependence. Significantly, though, Thomas's narrative places the onus on Edith, and only on Edith, to achieve her breadwinner role. The text's portrayal of relentless self-improvement; internalised moral reprimands against idleness, shopping, and poor household management skills; and pulling continuous double-shifts, is not

[100] See Hannah Barker and Elaine Chalus, 'Introduction', in *Gender in Eighteenth-Century England: Roles, Representations and Responsibilities*, ed. by Hannah Barker and Elaine Chalus (London: Routledge, 1997), pp. 1–28.

interrogated. Edith's unpaid domestic labour sustains her husband's earning capacity, and her financially uncompensated management of the children produces the next generation of workers. After, or amid, giving her time and energy to the family unit's success as a whole, she pivots to her paid work. One of the persistent paradoxes of feminism that relies on women's self-improvement has been its inability to resolve women's progress with capitalism's demand for free female domestic labour. Women, both in the nineteenth century and today, face systemic barriers during childbearing and child-rearing years. Furthermore, those socialised as women can be conditioned to eschew the risks associated with breaking out of traditional roles. All too familiarly, for instance, women in the public eye or working in political or civic roles are judged according to perceptions of their performances as mothers or caregivers, or for choosing to be childfree, much like Charlotte Brontë experienced as a daughter and sister. The labour of postfeminists, then, is to read some of these narratives, such as Thomas's, less as descriptive or prescriptive – as in the vein of Barker and Chalus's reassessment of conduct literature – and more for the rhetorical intervention that make to women's changing position. This is especially true when working with texts that might appear more modest in their ambitions and less forthright than those written by women who have been historically claimed as feminist or proto-feminist.[101]

[101] See Atkinson, 'The Economic Foundations of the Women's Movement', pp. 93–6.

Bibliography

Primary Sources

Manuscript and Archival Collections

Derby, Local Studies Library
Derbyshire Deeds, 11103
National Library of Israel Digital Collections, https://dlp.nli.org.il
Jewish Colonial Trust, Memorandum and Articles of Association, 20 March 1899
Jewish Colonial Trust, Geschäftsbericht nebst Bilanz und Gewinn- und Verlustrechnung für die Jahre 1899–1922
Jewish Colonial Trust Share Clubs, Statuten des Jewish Colonial Trust Share Clubs, 1900
Kew, The National Archives (TNA)
PROB 11/1213
PROB 11/810/343
PROB 11/1409/46
Matlock, Derbyshire Record Office (DRO)
D176M, Box 22 M
D255 M/F 1
D255 M/F 5
D255 M/T 66
Royal Literary Fund
MS 2750
Sheffield City Archive
LD 2189
Stafford, Staffordshire Record Office (SRO)
B/C 11
UCLA Special Collections Archives
Box 1, Folder 23
Box 1, Folder 40
The Baring Archive
HC1.153. BAR
Other
Memorial inscription, St Martin's Church, Alfreton, Derbyshire

Printed Primary Sources

Contemporary Books and Articles

A 'Banker's Daughter', *Guide to the Unprotected in Everyday Matters Relating to Property and Income*, 1st edn (London: Macmillan & Co., 1863).

A 'Banker's Daughter', *Guide to the Unprotected in Everyday Matters Relating to Property and Income*, 7th edn (London: Macmillan & Co., 1900).

Anonymous, *The Corinna of England, and a Heroine in the Shade: A Modern Romance. By the Author of 'The Winter in Bath', 'The Banks of the Wye', 'The Woman of Colour', 'Light and Shade', &c. &c.*, vol. II (London: Printed for J. Ginger, 1809).

Anonymous, *The Woman of Colour: A Tale*, ed. by Lyndon J. Dominique (Peterborough ON: Broadview Press, 2008 [1808]).

Barbauld, Anna Laetitia, *The British Novelists; with an Essay, and Prefaces Biographical and Critical, by Mrs. Barbauld*, 50 vols. (London: Printed for F. C. and J. Rivington; W. Otridge and Son; A. Strahan; T. Payne; G. Robinson; W. Lowndes; Wilkie and Robinson; Scatcherd and Letterman; J. Walker; J. Cuthell; Vernor, Hood, and Sharpe; R. Lea; J. Nunn; Lackington and Co.; Clarke and Son; C. Law; Longman, Hurst, Rees, and Orme; Cadell and Davies; E. Jeffery; J. K. Newman; Crosby and Co.; J. Carpenter; S. Bagster; T. Booth; J. Mobray; J. and J. Richardson; Black, Parry, and Kingsbury; J. Harding; R. Phillips; J. Mawman; J. Booker; J. Asperne; R. Baldwin; Mathews and Leigh; J. Faulder; Johnson and Co.; Sherwood and Co.; J. Miller; W. Creech, Edinburgh; and Wilson and Son, York, 1810).

Barrett Browning, Elizabeth, *Aurora Leigh*, ed. by Kerry McSweeney (Oxford: Oxford University Press, 1993 [1857]).

Beeton, Samuel, *Beeton's Guide to Investing Money with Safety and Profit, Etc.* (London: Ward, Lock & Co., 1870).

Brontë, Anne, *Agnes Grey*, ed. by Hilda Marsden and Robert Inglesfield (Oxford: Oxford University Press, 1988 [1847]).

—*The Tenant of Wildfell Hall*, ed. by Herbert Rosengarten (Oxford: Oxford University Press, 2008 [1848]).

Brontë, Charlotte, *Jane Eyre*, ed. by Jane Jack and Margaret Smith (Oxford: Oxford University Press, 1969 [1847]).

—*The Letters of Charlotte Brontë: With a Selection of Letters by Family and Friends*, ed. by Margaret Smith, 3 vols (Oxford: Clarendon Press, 1995–2004).

Brontë, Emily, *Wuthering Heights*, ed. by Hilda Marsden and Ian Jack (Oxford: Clarendon Press, 1976 [1847]).

Brown, Baldwin, *Young Men and Maidens: A Pastoral for the Times* (London: Hodder & Stoughton, 1871).

Brunton, Mary, *Self-Control* (Aberdeen: George Clark and Son, 1847 [1811]).

Burke, Edmund, *The Works of the Right Honourable Edmund Burke*, 12 vols (London: Rivington, 1812).

Burney, Fanny, *The Wanderer; or, Female Difficulties*, ed. by Margaret Anne Doody, Robert L. Mack and Peter Sabor (New York: Oxford University Press, 1991 [1814]).

Clarke, Richard, *The Nabob; or, Asiatic Plunderers. A Satyrical Poem, in a Dialogue Between a Friend and the Author. To Which Are Annexed, a Few Fugitive Pieces of Poetry* (London: Printed for the author; and sold, 1773).

Cotton, William, *Everybody's Guide to Money Matters. With a description of the various investments chiefly dealt in on the Stock Exchange, etc.* (London: Frederick Warne & Co, 1898).

Craik, Dinah M. M., *About Money and Other Things: A Gift-Book* (London: MacMillan & Co, 1886).

Craik, Dinah M. M., *John Halifax, Gentleman* (London: Hurst and Blackett, 1856)

Cunningham, Peter (ed.), *The Letters of Horace Walpole, Earl of Orford*, 20 vols (London: Richard Bentley, 1857–61).

Dickens, Charles, *Great Expectations*, ed. by Angus Calder (London: Airmont Publishing, 1965 [1861]).

Duncan, William Wallace, *Investment and Speculation in Stocks and Shares* (London: Effingham Wilson, 1894; 3rd edn, 1895).

East, Edward Hyde, *Reports of Cases Argued and Determined in the Court of King's Bench* (London: J. Butterworth and Son, 1807).

Edwards, Bryan, *The History, Civil and Commercial, of the British Colonies in the West Indies* (London: John Stockdale, 1801).

Engels, Friedrich, *The Condition of the Working Class in England*, ed. by Victor Kiernan (London: Penguin Classics, 2009 [1845]).

Farey, John, *A General View of the Agriculture and Minerals of Derbyshire*, 3 vols (London: G. & W. Nicol, 1811–17).

Garrett Fawcett, Millicent, *Janet Doncaster* (London: Smith, Elder, & Co., 1875).

—*Political Economy for Beginners* (London: Macmillan and Co., 1876).

—*Tales in Political Economy* (London: Macmillan and Co., 1874).

—*What I Remember* (London: T. Fisher Unwin Ltd, 1924).

Gaskell, Elizabeth, *Cranford*, ed. by Elizabeth Porges Watson (Oxford: Oxford University Press, 2011).

—*Mary Barton*, ed. by Thomas Recchio (New York and London: W. W. Norton & Co., 2008).

—*North and South*, ed. by Angus Easson (Oxford: Oxford University Press, 2008).

—*The Letters of Mrs Gaskell*, ed. by J. A. V. Chapple and Arthur Pollard (Manchester: Manchester University Press, 1997).

—*The Life of Charlotte Brontë* (London: Penguin Books, 1997 [1857]).

—*The Life of Charlotte Brontë*, ed. by Alan Shelston (Harmondsworth: Penguin Books, 1975 [1857]).

Gissing, George, *The Odd Women* (London: Lawrence & Bullen, 1893).

Grand, Sarah, 'The New Aspect of the Woman Question', *North American Review*, 158:448 (March 1894), 270–6.

Howe, Julia Ward, Lucy Stone, Thomas Wentworth Higginson, Elizabeth Cady Stanton and Wendell Phillips, 'The Other Side of the Woman Question, *North American Review*, 129:276 (November 1879), 413–46.

Hume, David, *A Treatise of Human Nature*, ed. by L. A. Selby-Bigge and P. H. Nidditch (Oxford: Clarendon Press, 1978 [1739–40)].

—*Essays: Moral, Political, and Literary*, ed. by T. H. Green and T. H. Grose (London: Longmans, Green, 1882 [1758]).

Johnson, Samuel, *A Dictionary of the English Language* (London: W. Strahan, for J. and P. Knapton; T. and T. Longman; C. Hitch and L. Hawes; A. Millar; and R. and J. Dodsley, 1755).

Layman, William, *The Pioneer, or Strictures on Maritime Strength and Economy: To Which is Added an Exposé of a Discovery for Preparing Forest Trees for Immediate Service* (London: E. Bridgewater, 1821).

—*Outline of a Plan for the Better Cultivation, Security & Defence, of the British West Indies; Being the Original Suggestion for Providing an Effectual Substitute for the African Slave Trade, and Preventing the Dependence of Those Colonies on America for Supplies* (London: Printed for and sold by Black, Parry, and Kingsbury, 1807).

Mandeville, Bernard, *The Fable of the Bees: or, Private Vices, Public Benefits*, 2 vols (London: T. Ostell, 1806 [1714]).

Marcet, Jane, *Conversations on Political Economy: in which the elements of that science are familiarly explained* (Boston: Bowles & Dearborn, 1817).

Martineau, Harriet, *Autobiography*, ed. by Maria Weston Chapman, 3 vols (Boston and London: J. R. Osgood, 1877).

—*Illustrations of Political Economy* (London: Charles Fox, 1834).

Mill, John Stuart, *Autobiography and Literary Essays*, ed. by John M. Robson and Jack Stillinger, with an introduction by Lord Robbins, vol. 1, *The Collected Works of John Stuart Mill* (Toronto: University of Toronto Press; London: Routledge and Kegan Paul, 1981).

—*On Liberty and Other Essays* (Oxford: Oxford University Press, 2008 [1859]).

—*On Liberty with The Subjection of Women and Chapters on Socialism*, ed. by Stefan Collini (Cambridge: Cambridge University Press, 1989 [1859]).

—*Principles of Political Economy, with Some of Their Applications to Social Philosophy, Collected Works II* (Toronto and Buffalo: University of Toronto Press, 1965 [1848]).

Milton, John, *Paradise Lost*, ed. by Stephen Orgel and Jonathan Goldberg (Oxford: Oxford University Press, 2008), VIII.465–9.

More, Hannah, *Coelebs in Search of a Wife, Comprehending Observations of Domestic Habits and Manners, Religion and Morals*, vol. 1 (London: T. Cadell and W. Davies, 1808).

Mortimer, Thomas, *A General Dictionary of Commerce, Trade, and Manufactures: Exhibiting Their Present State in Every Part of the World: and Carefully Compiled from the Latest and Best Authorities* (United Kingdom: Phillips, 1810).

Ouida (Maria Louisa Ramé), 'The New Woman', *North American Review*, 158:450 (May 1894), 610–19.

Parkes, Bessie Rayner, *Remarks on the Education of Girls, with Reference to the Social, Legal, and Industrial Position of Women in the Present Day* (London: John Chapman, 1856).

Parkman, Francis, 'The Woman Question', *North American Review*, 129:275 (October 1879), 303–21.

—'The Woman Question Again', *North American Review*, 130:278 (January 1880), 16–30.

Pimenoff, Lydia Lvovna, 'Science and the Woman's Question', *North American Review*, 156:435 (February 1893), 248–51.

Ruskin, John, *The Works of John Ruskin*, vol. 18, ed. by E. T. Cook and A. D. O. Wedderburn (London: George Allen, 1903).

Seacole, Mary, *Wonderful Adventures of Mrs. Seacole in Many Lands*, ed. by Sara Salih (London: Penguin Books, 2005 [1857]).

'Senex', *Counsel to Ladies and Easy-Going Men on Their Business Investments: And Cautions against the Lures of Wily Financiers & Unprincipled Promoters* (London: Effingham Wilson, 1892).

Smiles, Samuel, *Self-Help: With Illustrations of Character and Conduct* (London: Murray, 1859).

Smith, Adam, *An Inquiry into the Nature and Causes of the Wealth of Nations*, ed. by Kathryn Sutherland (Oxford: Oxford University Press, 2008; first published 1776).

—*An Inquiry into the Nature and Causes of the Wealth of Nations*, ed. by R. H. Campbell and A. S. Skinner (Oxford: Clarendon Press, 1976 [1776]).

—*The Theory of Moral Sentiments*, ed. by Ryan Patrick Hanley (London: Penguin Classics, 2009 [1759]).

—*The Theory of Moral Sentiments*, ed. by D. D. Raphael and A. L. Macfie (Oxford: Clarendon Press, 1976 [1759]).

Southey, Robert, *The Life and Correspondence of Robert Southey*, ed. by Charles Cuthbert Southey, 6 vols (London: Longman, Brown, Green & Longmans, 1849–50).

Stewart, Bertrand, *Outlines of Business Knowledge Requisite for Women: Four Lectures … Delivered to the Home Education Society* (London: Hatchard, 1896).

Taylor, Charles (ed.), *The Literary Panorama* (London: C. Taylor, 1807).

Thackeray, William Makepeace, *The History of Pendennis* (London: Penguin Books, 1986 [1850]).

Thomas, Annie, *The Modern Housewife, or, How We Live Now* (London: Ward, Lock and Co., 1883).

W B., *Women as Investors* (Birmingham: Cornish Bros, 1908).

Walpole, Horace, *The Letters of Horace Walpole*, vol. 8, ed. by P. Toynbee (Oxford: Oxford University Press, 1905).

Wharton, Edith, *A Backward Glance* (London: Constable, 1972 [1934]).

—*The House of Mirth* (New York: Viking Penguin, 1985 [1905]).

Wilkes, Wettenhall, *A Letter of Genteel Moral Advice to a Young Lady*, 4th edn (London: Printed for R. Dodsley, 1746).

Wilkie, Franc B., *Sketches Beyond the Sea*, 2nd edn (Chicago: Hazlitt and Reed, 1879).

Wilson, A. J., *Practical Hints to Investors: And Some Words to Speculators* (London: C. Wilson, 1897).

Wollstonecraft, Mary, *The Works of Mary Wollstonecraft*, ed. by Janet Todd and Marilyn Butler, 7 vols (London: Pickering & Chatto, 1989 [1794]).

—*A Vindication of the Rights of Woman* (New York; London: W. W. Norton, 2009 [1792]).

—*Original Stories from Real Life; with Conversations Calculated to Regulate the Affections, and Form the Mind to Truth and Goodness* (London: J. Johnson, 1796).

—*Mary and The Wrongs of Woman*, ed. by Gary Kelly (Oxford: Oxford University Press, 1988 [1798]).

Yates, Lucy Helen, *The Management of Money: A Handbook of Finance for Women* (London: Horace Cox, 1903).

Official Documents and Publications

India Office Records

Miscellaneous Bonds, Nos 1–2945, 1814–1821, IOR Z/O/1/8, 6 March 1816.

Parliamentary Papers

Parliamentary Papers (London: H. M. Stationery Office, Session 24 November 1812 to 22 July 1813), vols 3 and 8.

Newspapers and Periodicals

The Derby Mercury

Derby Mercury, 14 February 1793.

Derby Mercury, 22 March 1792.

Derby Mercury, 28 March 1793.

Derby Mercury, 9 August 1810.

Derby Mercury, 20 July 1825.

The Economist

Economist, 14 March 1903.

The Examiner

Examiner, 4 November 1848.

The Financial Times

Financial Times, 17 March 1891.

Financial Times, 17 June 1891.

Financial Times, 13 January 1904.

Financial Times, 2 March 1911.

Financial Times, 5 April 1916.

Financial Times, 19 September 1925.

Financial Times, 26 February 1926.

Financial Times, 27 March 1926.

Fraser's Magazine for Town and Country

Fraser's Magazine, April 1849.

The Gentleman's Magazine

Gentleman's Magazine, 71 (1792).

London Evening Post

London Evening Post, 4–6 June 1741.

London Evening Post, 4–6 June 1741.

The London Gazette

London Gazette, 5 February 1793.

London Gazette, 3 March 1812.

Punch Magazine

Punch Magazine, 30 May 1857.

Punch Magazine, 3 December 1856.
Tait's Edinburgh Magazine
Tait's Edinburgh Magazine, August 1832.
The Cornhill Magazine
Cornhill Magazine, 1863.
The Prospective Review
Prospective Review, 5:17 (January 1849).
The Times
Times, 15 September 1854.
Times, 31 October 1872.
Women's Penny Paper
Women's Penny Paper, 21 June 1890.
The Review
Defoe, Daniel, *Review*, no. 5, 10 January 1706.
—*Review*, nos 55, 57, 59, 1, 5 and 10 August 1710.
—*Review*, no. 116, 21 December 1710.
Tatler
Addison, Joseph, *Tatler*, no. 116, 5 January 1710.
The Spectator
Addison, Joseph, *Spectator*, no. 3, 3 March 1711.
—*Spectator*, no. 10, 12 March 1711.
—*Spectator*, no. 69, 9 May 1711.
Steele, Richard, *Spectator*, no. 218, 9 November 1711.

Artworks

Gillray, James, *The Leadenhall Volunteer, Drest in his Shawl*, hand-coloured etching, published by Hannah Humphrey, 8 March 1797, The British Museum, London.

Wright, Joseph, *Thomas Staniforth of Darnall*, Co. York, oil on canvas, 1769, Tate Britain, London, accession number T00794.

Secondary Sources

Ablow, Rachel, *The Marriage of Minds: Reading Sympathy in the Victorian Marriage Plot* (Stanford CA: Stanford University Press, 2007).

Acheson, G., G. Campbell and J. D. Turner, 'Active Controllers or Wealthy Rentiers? Large Shareholders in Victorian Public Companies', *Business History Review*, 89:4 (2015), 661–91.

Acheson, Graeme G., Gareth Campbell, Áine Gallagher and John D. Turner. 'Independent Women: Investing in British Railways, 1870–1922', *Economic History Review*, 74:2 (May 2021), 471–95.

Acheson, Graeme G., Gareth Campbell and John D. Turner, 'Who Financed the Expansion of the Equity Market? Shareholder Clienteles in Victorian Britain', *Business History*, 59:4 (2017), 607–37.

Adelman, Richard, and Catherine Packham (eds), *Political Economy, Literature & the Formation of Knowledge, 1720–1850* (New York and Abingdon, 2018).

Annas, Julia, 'Mill and The Subjection of Women', *Philosophy*, 52:200 (1977), 179–94.

Armstrong, Nancy, *Desire and Domestic Fiction: A Political History of the Novel* (New York: Oxford University Press, 1987).

Arrow, Kenneth J., *Essays in the Theory of Risk-Bearing* (Amsterdam: North-Holland, 1971).

Ashworth, M. 'The Marriage of John Stuart Mill', *Englishwoman*, 30 (1916), 159–72.

Aston, Jennifer, 'Female Business Ownership in Birmingham 1849–1901', *Midland History*, 37:2 (2012), 187–206.

Atkinson, Mabel, 'The Economic Foundations of the Women's Movement', in *Women's Economic Writing in the Nineteenth Century*, ed. by Lana L. Dalley (London and New York: Routledge, 2023).

Austin, J. L., *How to do Things with Words* (Cambridge MA: Harvard University Press), 1975.

Backscheider, Paula R., 'Defoe's Lady Credit', *Huntington Library Quarterly*, 44:2 (Spring 1981), 89–100.

Bailey, Joanne, 'Favoured or Oppressed? Married Women, Property and "Covertur" in England, 1660–1800', *Continuity and Change*, 17:3 (2002), 351–72

Balkun, Mary McAleer, and Susan C. Imbarrato (eds), *Women's Narratives of the Early Americas and the Formation of Empire* (New York: Palgrave Macmillan, 2016).

Barber, B. M., and T. Odean, 'Boys Will Be Boys: Gender, Overconfidence, and Common Stock Investment', *Quarterly Journal of Economics*, 116:1 (2001), 262–92.

Barker, Hannah, and Elaine Chalus, *Gender in Eighteenth-Century England: Roles, Representations and Responsibilities* (London: Routledge, 1997).

Barker, Theodore, and John Harris, *A Merseyside Town in the Industrial Revolution: St. Helens 1750–1900* (London: Frank Cass, 1954).

Barnes, Alan, and Stephen Leach, 'The Painter, the Patron, the Wife and her Lover: The Portraits by Joseph Wright of Derby (1734–1787) of the Revd Henry Case and Mrs Ellen Morewood (1782)', *British Art Journal*, 22 (2021).

Barringer, Tim, and Wayne Modest (eds), *Victorian Jamaica* (Durham NC: Duke University Press, 2018).

Basset, Karine, and Michèle Baussant, 'Utopia, Nostalgia: Intersections', *Conserveries mémorielles* [*En ligne*], no. 22, 9 July 2018, http://journals.openedition.org/cm/3048.

Bastiat, Frédéric, *Economic Harmonies* (Paris: Guillaumin, 1850).

Basu, Kaushik, *Beyond the Invisible Hand: Groundwork for a New Economics* (Princeton NJ: Princeton University Press, 2010).

Bataille, Georges, *La Part Maudite* (Paris: Éditions de minuit, 1967).

Bateman, Thomas, *A Descriptive and Historical Account of Alfreton* (printed privately, 1812).

Bateman, Victoria, *The Sex Factor: How Women Made the West Rich* (Cambridge: Polity Press, 2019).

Becker, Gary S., 'Altruism in the Family and Selfishness in the Market Place', *Economica*, 48:1 (1981), 1–15.

Becker, Gary S., *A Treatise on the Family* (Cambridge MA: Harvard University Press, 1991).

Beckett, J. V., 'Elizabeth Montagu: Bluestocking Turned Landlady', *Huntington Library Quarterly*, 49:2 (1986), 149–64.

Beer, Gillian, 'The Reader's Wager: Lots, Sorts and Futures', *Essays in Criticism*, 40 (1990), 99–123.

Beetham, Margaret, *A Magazine of Her Own? Domesticity and Desire in the* Woman's Magazine, *1800–1914* (London: Routledge, 1966).

Bell, Amy E., 'How Women May Keep Their Money 1', *Englishwoman's Review: A Journal of Woman's Work*, 15 April 1892.

Bell, Millicent (ed.), *The Cambridge Companion to Wharton* (Cambridge: Cambridge University Press, 1995).

Berg, Maxine, and Pat Hudson, *Slavery, Capitalism and the Industrial Revolution* (Cambridge: Polity Press, 2023).

Berlant, Lauren, and Michael Warner, 'Sex in Public', *Critical Inquiry*, 24:2 (1998), 547–66.

Bloch, Ernst, *The Principle of Hope*, trans. by Neville Plaice, Stephen Plaice and Paul Knight (Cambridge MA: MIT Press, 1959; repr. 1995).

Bodkin, Ronald G., 'Women's Agency in Classical Economic Thought: Adam Smith, Harriet Taylor Mill, and J.S. Mill', *Feminist Economics*, 5:1 (1999), 45–60.

Bose, Sugata, *A Hundred Horizons: The Indian Ocean in the Age of Global Empire* (Cambridge MA: Harvard University Press, 2006).

Bossaerts, Peter, 'What Can Neurobiology Teach us about Emotion and Rationality in Financial Decision-Making?', *Frontiers in Psychology*, 12 (2021): 667541, https://doi.org/10.3389/fpsyg.2021.667541.

Bowen, H. V., *Revenue and Reform: The Indian Problem in British Politics 1757–1773* (Cambridge: Cambridge University Press, 1991).

Boyington, Amy, *Hidden Patrons: Women and Architectural Patronage in Georgian Britain* (London: Bloomsbury Visual Arts, 2023)

Brabon, Benjamin A., and Stéphane Genz (eds), *Postfeminist Gothic: Critical Interventions in Contemporary Culture* (Basingstoke: Palgrave Macmillan, 2017).

Brass, Tom, 'Capitalist Unfree Labour: A Contradiction?', *Critical Sociology*, 35:6 (2009), 743–65.

Briggs, Asa, *A Social History of England* (London: Penguin, 1994).

Britton, Jeanne, *Vicarious Narratives: A Literary History of Sympathy, 1750–1850* (Oxford: Oxford University Press, 2019).

Bronfen, Elisabeth, *Over Her Dead Body: Death, Femininity and the Aesthetic* (New York: Routledge, 1992).

Budish, Eric, Peter Cramton and John Shim, 'The High-Frequency Trading Arms Race: Frequent Batch Auctions as a Market Design Response', *Quarterly Journal of Economics*, 130:4 (2015), 1547–621.

Butler, Judith, *Bodies that Matter: On the Discursive Limits of Sex* (New York: Routledge, 1993).

Calpern, Amanda L., Briony McDonagh and Jennifer Aston (eds), *Women and the Land, 1500–1900* (Woodbridge: Boydell Press, 2019).

Cameron, S. Brooke, *Critical Alliances: Economics and Feminism in English Women's Writing, 1880–1914* (Toronto: Toronto University Press, 2020).

Campt, Tina M., *Listening to Images* (Durham NC: Duke University Press, 2017).

Capuano, Peter, and Sue Zemka (eds), *Victorian Hands: The Manual Turn in Nineteenth-Century Body Studies* (Columbus OH: Ohio State University Press, 2000).

Carnell, Rachel K., 'Feminism and the Public Sphere in Anne Brontë's *The Tenant of Wildfell Hall*', *Nineteenth-Century Literature*, 53:1 (1998), 1–24.

Carr, Rachel, *The 'Girton Girl' and 'Lady Doctor': Women, Higher Education and Medicine in Popular Victorian Fiction by Women* (London: King's College London Press, 1998).

Cass, Youssef, *City Bankers, 1890–1914* (Cambridge: Cambridge University Press, 1994).

Chase, Malcolm, and Christopher Shaw (eds), *The Imagined Past: History and Nostalgia* (New York: Manchester University Press, 1989).

Checkland, S. G., *The Rise of the Industrial Society in England, 1815–1885* (London: Longman, 1964).

Cheffins, Brian R., *Corporate Ownership and Control* (Oxford: Oxford University Press, 2008).

Choma, Anne, *Gentleman Jack: The Real Anne Lister* (London: BBC Books, 2019).

Chorley, Katherine, *Manchester Made Them* (London: Faber & Faber, 1950).

Colley, Linda, *Britons: Forging the Nation, 1707–1817* (New Haven CT: Yale University Press, 1991).

Collinge, Peter, 'Morewood [née Goodwin] (bap. 1741, d. 1824) of Alfreton, Derbyshire, Colliery Owner and Ironstone Extractor', *Oxford Dictionary of National Biography* (2016) https://doi.org/10.1093/ref:odnb/109611.

Condorelli, Stefano, and Daniel Menning (eds), *Boom, Bust and Beyond: New Perspectives on the 1720 Stock Market Bubble* (Berlin: De Gruyter Oldenbourg, 2019).

Cookson, John Earnest, 'British Society and the French Wars, 1793–1815', *Australian Journal of Politics and History*, 31 (1985), 192–203.

Cookson, John Earnest, 'Political Arithmetic and War in Britain, 1793–1815', *War and Society*, 1:2 (1983), 37–60.

Cottrell, Philip L., *Industrial Finance, 1830–1914: The Finance and Organization of English Manufacturing Industry* (London: Methuen, 1979).

Courtemanche, Eleanor, *The 'Invisible Hand' and British Fiction, 1818–1860: Adam Smith, Political Economy, and the Genre of Realism* (Basingstoke: Palgrave Macmillan, 2011).

Craven, Maxwell, and Michael Stanley, *The Derbyshire Country House* (Derby: Breedon Books Publishing Co., 1991).

Creighton, Colin, 'The Rise and Decline of the "Male Breadwinner Family" in Britain', *Cambridge Journal of Economics*, 23:5 (1999), 519–41.

Creighton, Louise Hume, *Oxford Dictionary of National Biography*, https://doi.org/10.1093/ref:odnb/38640.

Creighton, Louise, 'Women and Finance', *Financial Review of Reviews*, September 1910, no. 59.

Crellin, Rachel J., *Change and Archaeology* (London: Routledge, 2020)

Crosthwaite, Paul, Peter Knight, Nicky Marsh, Helen Paul and James Taylor, *Invested: How Three Centuries of Stock Market Advice Reshaped Our Money, Markets, and Minds* (Chicago IL: University of Chicago Press, 2022).

Cudlip, Annie Hall (Thomas), *1838–1918, The Wellesley Index.*

Culler, Jonathan, 'Philosophy and Literature: The Fortunes of the Performative', *Poetics Today*, 24 (2002), 48–64.

D'Agostino, Peter, *The European Counterculture, 1968–1980* (New York: Routledge, 2003).

Dalley, Lana L., and Jill Rappoport, *Economic Women: Essays on Desire and Dispossession in Nineteenth-Century British Culture* (Columbus OH: Ohio University Press, 2014).

Dalley, Lana L. (ed.), *Women's Economic Writing in the Nineteenth Century* (London and New York: Routledge, 2023).

Dalrymple, William, *The Anarchy: The Relentless Rise of the East India Company* (London: Bloomsbury Publishing, 2019).

Daniels, Stephen, *Joseph Wright* (London: Tate Publishing, 1999).

Davidoff, Leonore, *Family Fortunes: Men and Women of the English Middle Class 1780–1850* (Boca Raton FL: Routledge, 2018).

Derrida, Jacques, *Writing and Difference. Translated by Alan Bass* (Chicago IL: University of Chicago Press, 1978).

Deutscher, Penelope, 'When Feminism is "High" and Ignorance is "Low": Harriet Taylor Mill on the Progress of the Species', *Hypatia*, 21:3 (2006), 136–50.

Diederich, Nicole A., 'The Art of Comparison: Remarriage in Anne Brontë's *The Tenant of Wildfell Hall*', *Rocky Mountain Review of Language and Literature*, 57:2 (2003), 25–41.

Dimand, M. A., R. W. Dimand and E. L. Forget (eds), *Women of Value: Feminist Essays on the History of Women in Economics* (Brookfield VT: Edward Elgar, 1995).

Dimcock, Wai-Chee, 'Debasing Exchange: Edith Wharton's *The House of Mirth*', *PMLA*, 100 (1985) 783–91.

Donoghue, Mark, 'Mill's Affirmation of the Classical Wage Fund Doctrine', *Scottish Journal of Political Economy*, 44:1 (1997), 82–99.

Dooley, Terry, and Christopher Ridgway (eds), *Visitors to the Country House in Ireland and Britain: Welcome and Unwelcome* (Dublin: Four Courts, 2023)

Drescher, Seymour, *The Mighty Experiment: Free Labor Versus Slavery in British Emancipation* (Oxford: Oxford University Press, 2004).

Dyhouse, Carol, *Girls Growing up in Late Victorian and Edwardian England* (London and New York: Routledge, 2013).

Eagleton, Terry, *Myths of Power: A Marxist Study of the Brontës* (London: Routledge, 1975).

Edwardes, Michael, *The Nabobs at Home* (London: Constable, 1991).

Edwards, Amy, *Are We Rich Yet? The Rise of Mass Investment Culture in Contemporary Britain* (Berkely CA: University of California Press, 2022).

Egerton, Judy, *Wright of Derby* (London: Tate, 1990).

Elliott, Kamilla, 'The Romance of Politics and the Politics of Romance in Elizabeth Gaskell's Mary Barton', *Gaskell Society Journal*, 21 (2007), 21–37.

Engels, Friedrich, *The Condition of the Working Class in England*, ed. by Victor Kiernan (London: Penguin Books, 1987).

Erickson, Amy Louise, 'Coverture and Capitalism', *History Workshop Journal*, 59 (2005), 1–16.

Esch, Deborah (ed.), *New Essays on The House of Mirth* (Cambridge: Cambridge University Press, 2001).

Esposito, Elena, *Artificial Communication: How Algorithms Produce Social Intelligence* (Cambridge MA: MIT Press, 2022).

Farey, John, *A General View of the Agriculture and Minerals of Derbyshire* (3 vols, 1811–17).

Fama, Eugene F., 'Efficient Capital Markets: A Review of Theory and Empirical Work', *Journal of Finance,* 25:2 (1970), 383–417.

Feldman, Paula R., *British Women Poets of the Romantic Era: An Anthology* (Baltimore MD: Johns Hopkins University Press, 2001).

Ferber, Marianne, and Julie A. Nelson (eds), *Beyond Economic Man: Feminist Theory and Economics* (Chicago IL: University of Chicago Press, 1983).

Ferguson, Niall, *The World's Banker: A History of the House of Rothschild* (London: Weidenfeld & Nicolson, 1998).

Folbre, Nancy, *Greed, Lust & Gender: A History of Economic Ideas* (Oxford: Oxford University Press, 2009).

Foucault, Michel, *Discipline and Punish: The Birth of the Prison*, trans. by Alan Sheridan (New York: Vintage Books, 1977).

Ford, Trevor, and J. H. Rieuwerts (eds), *Lead Mining in the Peak District* (Bakewell: Peak Park Joint Planning Board, 1968).

Forrest, Derek William, *Francis Galton: The Life and Work of a Victorian Genius* (London: Paul Elek, 1974).

Fox, Celina, *The Arts of Industry in the Age of Enlightenment* (New Haven CT: Yale University Press, 2010).

Freedgood, Elaine, *The Ideas in Things: Fugitive Meaning in the Victorian Novel* (Chicago IL and London: University of Chicago Press, 2006).

Friedman, Milton, *Capitalism and Freedom* (Chicago IL: University of Chicago Press, 1962)

Furlough, E., *Consumer Cooperation in France: The Politics of Consumption, 1834–1930* (Ithaca NY: Cornell University Press, 1991).

Gallagher, Catherine, *The Industrial Reformation of English Fiction: Social Discourse and Narrative Form, 1832–1867* (Chicago IL: University of Chicago Press, 1985).

Galvan, Jill, and Elsie Michie (eds), *Replotting Marriage in Nineteenth-Century British Literature* (Columbus OH: Ohio State University Press, 2018).

Geggus, David, 'The Enigma of Jamaica in the 1790s: New Light on the Causes of Slave Rebellions', *William and Mary Quarterly,* 44:2 (1987), 274–99.

Genovese, Michael, *The Problem of Profit: Finance and Feeling in Eighteenth-Century British Literature* (Charlottesville VA: University of Virginia Press, 2019).

Genz, Stéphanie, and Benjamin A. Brabon, *Postfeminism: Cultural Texts and Theories,* 2nd edn (Edinburgh: Edinburgh University Press, 2009, 2018).

Gerber, David J., 'II Freedom, Law, and Competition: The Nineteenth Century as Prelude', in *Law and Competition in Twentieth-Century Europe: Protecting Prometheus* (Oxford: Oxford University Press, 2001).

Gerrard, Teresa. 'New Methods in the History of Reading: "Answers to Correspondents" in the Family Herald, 1860–1900', *Publishing History,* 43 (1998), 53–69.

Gilbert, Nora, 'A Servitude of One's Own: Isolation, Authorship, and the Nineteenth-Century British Governess', *Nineteenth-Century Literature*, 69:4 (2015), 455–80.

Gilbert, Sandra M., and Susan Gubar, *The Madwoman in the Attic: The Woman Writer and the Nineteenth-Century Literary Imagination* (New Haven CT: Yale University Press, 1979).

Glaisyer, Natasha, and Sara Pennell (eds), *Didactic Literature in England, 1500–1800: Expertise Constructed* (London: Routledge, 2003).

Gleadle, Kathryn, 'Revisiting Family Fortunes: Reflections on the Twentieth Anniversary of the Publication of L. Davidoff and C. Hall's Family Fortunes: Men and Women of the English Middle Class, 1780–1850', *Women's History Review*, 16:5 (2007), 773–82.

—*The Early Feminists: Radical Unitarians and the Emergence of the Women's Rights Movement, 1831–51* (London: Palgrave Macmillan, 1998).

Glen, Heather (ed.), *The Cambridge Companion to the Brontës* (Cambridge: Cambridge University Press, 2002).

Godden, Judith F. 'Creighton, Louise Hume (1850–1936)', *Oxford Dictionary of National Biography*, September 2004, https://doi.org/10.1093/ref:odnb/38640.

Goede, Marieke de, 'Mastering "Lady Credit": Discourses of Financial Crisis in Historical Perspective', *International Feminist Journal of Politics*, 2:1 (Spring 2000), 58–81.

Goodman, Elise (ed.), *Art and Culture in the Eighteenth Century: New Dimensions and Multiple Perspectives* (Newark DE: University of Delaware Press, 2001).

Götz, Norbert, 'Moral Economy: Its Conceptual History and Analytical Prospects', *Journal of Global Ethics*, 11:2 (2015), 147–62.

Graciano, Andrew, 'The Book of Nature is Open to All Men', *Huntington Library Quarterly*, 68:4 (2005), 583–600.

—*Joseph Wright, Esq. Painter and Gentleman* (Newcastle-upon-Tyne: Cambridge Scholars Publishing, 2012).

Greiner, Rae, *Sympathetic Realism in Nineteenth-Century British Fiction* (Baltimore MD: Johns Hopkins University Press, 2012).

Griffin, Emma, *Bread Winner An Intimate History of the Victorian Economy* (New Haven CT: Yale University Press, 2020).

Groenewegen, Peter (ed.), *Feminism and Political Economy in Victorian England* (Aldershot and Brookfield VT: Edward Elgar, 1994).

Guest, Harriet, *Small Change: Women, Learning, Patriotism, 1750–1810* (Chicago IL: University of Chicago Press, 2000).

—*Unbounded Attachment: Sentiment and Politics in the Age of the French Revolution* (Oxford: Oxford University Press, 2013).

Hahn, Daniel, *The Tower Menagerie* (London: Simon and Schuster, 2003).

Hallemeier, Katherine, 'Anne Brontë's Shameful *Agnes Grey*', *Victorian Literature and Culture*, 41:2 (2013), 251–60.

Hargreaves, G. D., 'The Publishing of "Poems by Currer, Ellis and Acton Bell"', *Brontë Society Transactions*, 15:4 (1969), 294–300.

Harrington, Dana, 'Gender, Commerce, and the Transformation of Virtue in Eighteenth-Century Britain', *Rhetoric Society Quarterly*, 31:3 (2001), 33–52.

Harris, Jose, *Private Lives, Public Spirit: Britain, 1870–1914* (London: Penguin Books, 1994).

Harris, Stanley A., 'Sarah Clayton's Letter and John Wood of Bath', *Transactions of the Historic Society of Lancashire and Cheshire*, 100 (1948).

Harrison, Mary-Catherine, 'How Narrative Relationships Overcome Empathic Bias: Elizabeth Gaskell's Empathy across Social Difference', *Poetics Today*, 32:2 (2011), 255–88.

Hartman, Saidiya, 'Venus in Two Acts', *Small Axe*, 12:2 (2008), 1–14.

—*Scenes of Subjection: Terror, Slavery, and Self-Making in Nineteenth-Century America* (New York: Oxford University Press, 1997).

—*Wayward Lives, Beautiful Experiments: Intimate Histories of Social Upheaval* (New York: W.W. Norton & Company, 2019).

Hayden, Ruth, *Mrs. Delany: Her Life and Her Flowers* (London: British Museum Press, 2000).

Hayek, Friedrich August von (ed.), *John Stuart Mill and Harriet Taylor: Their Correspondence and Subsequent Marriage* (Chicago IL: University of Chicago Press, 1951).

Hayes, Adam, 'Enacting a Rational Actor: Roboadvisors and the Algorithmic Performance of Ideal Types', *Economy and Society*, 49:4 (2020), 562–95.

Henry, Nancy, and Cannon Schmitt (eds), *Victorian Investments: New Perspectives on Finance and Culture* (Bloomington IN: Indiana University Press, 2009)

Henry, Nancy, Women, *Literature and Finance in Victorian Britain* (Cham: Palgrave Macmillan, 2018).

Helsinger, Elizabeth K., and William Veeder, *The Woman Question: Society and Literature in Britain and America, 1837–83* (Chicago IL: University of Chicago Press, 1983).

Hewitt, Martin, *The Dawn of the Cheap Press in Victorian Britain: The End of the 'Taxes on Knowledge', 1849–1869* (London: Bloomsbury Publishing, 2013).

Hobbs, Andrew, *A Fleet Street in Every Town: The Provincial Press in England, 1855–1900* (Cambridge: Open Book Publishers, 2018).

Hobson, John A., and Thorstein Veblen, *Veblen and the Theory of the Leisure Class* (London: Routledge/Thoemmes Press, 1994).

Hoeller, Hildegard, *Edith Wharton's Dialogue with Realism and Sentimental Fiction* (Gainesville FL: University of Florida Press, 2000).

Hoeveler, Diane Long, and Deborah Denenholz Morse (eds.), *A Companion to the Brontës* (Hoboken, NJ: Wiley-Blackwell, 2016).

Holcombe, Lee, *Wives and Property: Reform of the Married Women's Property Law in Nineteenth-Century England* (London: Wiley-Blackwell, 1985)

—*Victorian Ladies at Work: Middle-Class Working Women in England and Wales, 1850–1914* (Hamden CT: Archon Books, 1973).

Holman, P., 'Ann Ford Revisited', *Eighteenth Century Music*, 1:2 (2004), 157–81.

Holt, Thomas C., *The Problem of Freedom: Race, Labor, and Politics in Jamaica and Britain, 1832–1938* (Baltimore MD and London: Johns Hopkins University Press, 1999).

Holzman, James Mayer, *The Nabobs in England: A Study of the Returned Anglo-Indian, 1760–1785* (New York: Columbia University Press, 1926).

Hoppit, Julian, 'Financial Crises in Eighteenth-Century England', *Economic History Review*, 39:1 (1986), 39–58.

Horn, Gerd-Rainer, *The Spirit of '68: Rebellion in Western Europe and North America, 1956–1976* (Oxford: Oxford University Press, 2007).

Horrell, Sara, and Jane Humphries, 'The Origins and Expansion of The Male Breadwinner Family: The Case of Nineteenth Century Britain', *International Review of Social History*, 42, Supplement S5 (1997), 25–64.

Houghton, Walter E., *The Victorian Frame of Mind: 1830–1870* (New Haven CT and London: Yale University Press, 1957).

Howe, Irving (ed.), *Edith Wharton: A Collection of Critical Essays* (Englewood Cliffs NJ: Prentice Hall, 1962).

Huang, Kristina, '"Ameliorating the Situation" of Empire: Slavery and Abolition in The Woman of Colour', *Eighteenth-Century Fiction*, 34:2 (Winter 2022), 167–86.

Huggins, Sofia Prado, 'Reading Slantwise: Dido in *The Woman of Colour* (1808)', *Eighteenth-Century Fiction*, 35:1 (2023), 27–42.

Hughes, Kathryn, *The Victorian Governess* (London: Hambledon Press, 1993).

Humphries, Jane, 'Enclosures, Common Rights, and Women: The Proletarianization of Families in the Late Eighteenth and Early Nineteenth Centuries', *Journal of Economic History*, 50:1 (March 1990), 17–42.

Hunt, Tamara L., and Michal Jan Rozbicki (eds), *Speculative Enterprise: Public Theaters and Financial Markets in London and Paris, 1688–1763* (Columbus OH: Ohio State University Press, 2011).

Ibbett, Katherine, 'When I do, I Call it Affect', *Paragraph*, 40:2 (2017), 244–53.

Ince, Onur Ulas, 'Not a Partnership in Pepper, Coffee, Callico, or Tobacco: Edmund Burke and the Vicissitudes of Colonial Capitalism', *Polity*, 44:3 (2012), 340–72.

Jacobs, Jo Ellen, '"The Lot of Gifted Ladies is Hard": A Study of Harriet Taylor Mill Criticism', *Hypatia*, 9:3 (1994), 132–62.

—*The Voice of Harriet Taylor Mill* (Bloomington IN: Indiana University Press, 2002).

Jaffe, Audrey, *Scenes of Sympathy: Identity and Representation in Victorian Fiction* (Ithaca NY: Cornell University Press, 2000).

James, Henry, and Edith Wharton, *Henry James and Edith Wharton: Letters, 1900–1915*, ed. by Lyall H. Powers (New York: Charles Scribner's Sons, 1990).

Jameson, Friedrich, *Marxism and Form: Twentieth-Century Dialectical Theories of Literature* (Princeton NJ: Princeton University Press, 1971).

Jamieson, Anna, '"Comforts in Her Calamity": Shopping and Consumption in the Late Eighteenth-Century Private Madhouse', *Eighteenth-Century Studies*, 55:1 (2021), 83–102.

Janssens, Angelique (ed.), *The Rise and Decline of the Male Breadwinner Family?* (Cambridge: Cambridge University Press, 1998).

Johnson, Claudia L., *Equivocal Beings: Politics, Gender and Sentimentality in the 1790s* (Chicago IL: University of Chicago Press, 1995).

Johnson, Reginald, *A History of Alfreton* (Ripley: R. Johnson, 1968).

Jones, Geoffrey, *British Multinational Banking, 1830–1990* (Oxford: Clarendon Press, 1993).

Jones, R. Tudor, *Oxford Dictionary of National Biography*, s.v. 'Brown, James Baldwin, the Younger', last updated 30 May 2013, https://doi.org/10.1093/ref:odnb/3616.

Joseph, Marrisa, *Victorian Literary Businesses: The Management and Practices of the British Publishing Industry* (Cham, Switzerland: Palgrave Macmillan, 2019).

Looser, Devoney, and E. Ann Kaplan (eds), *Generations: Academic Feminists in Dialogue* (Minneapolis MN: University of Minnesota Press, 1997).

Kamm, Josephine, *John Stuart Mill in Love* (London: Faber & Faber, 1977).

Katsiaficas, George, *The Imagination of the New Left: A Global Analysis of 1968* (Boston MA: South End Press, 1987).

Katz, Elizabeth, 'The Intra-Household Economics of Voice and Exit', *Feminist Economics*, 3:3 (1997), 25–46.

Kavanagh, Thomas M., *Enlightenment and the Shadows of Chance: The Novel and the Culture of Gambling in Eighteenth-Century France* (Baltimore MD: Johns Hopkins University Press, 1993).

Keay, John, *The Honourable Company: A History of the English East India Company* (London: HarperCollins, 1993).

Keynes, John Maynard, *The General Theory of Employment, Interest, and Money* (London: Macmillan, 1936).

Kinzer, Bruce L., *J. S. Mill Revisited: Biographical and Political Explorations* (New York: Palgrave Macmillan, 2007).

Knezevic, Borislav, 'An Ethnography of the Provincial: The Social Geography of Gentility in Elizabeth Gaskell's *Cranford*', *Victorian Studies*, 41:3 (1998), 405–26.

Kniper, Edith, and Jolande Sap, (eds) *Out of the Margin: Feminist Perspectives on Economics* (London: Routledge, 1995).

Kowaleski-Wallace, Elizabeth, *Consuming Subjects: Women, Shopping, and Business in the Eighteenth Century* (New York: Columbia University Press, 1997).

Kreisel, Deanna, *Economic Woman: Demand, Gender, and Narrative Closure in Eliot and Hardy* (Toronto: University of Toronto Press, 2012).

Kynaston, David, *The Financial Times: A Centenary History* (London: Viking, 1988).

Langton, John, 'Clayton, Sarah (1712–1779)', *Oxford Dictionary of National Biography* https://doi.org/10.1093/ref:odnb/48911.

Langland, Elizabeth, *Nobody's Angels: Middle-Class Women and Domestic Ideology in Victorian Culture* (Ithaca NY: Cornell University Press, 1995).

Laurence, Anne, Josephine Maltby and Janette Rutterford (eds), *Women and Their Money 1700 to 1950: Essays on Women and Finance* (London: Routledge, 2009).

Lawson, Philip, *The East India Company: A History* (London: Routledge, 1993).

Lee, Alan J., *The Origins of the Popular Press in England, 1855–1914* (London: Croom Helm, 1976).

Levine, Philippa, *Victorian Feminism, 1850–1900* (London: Hutchinson Education, 1987).

Levitan, Kathrin, 'Redundancy, the "Surplus Woman" Problem, and the British Census, 1851–1861', *Women's History Review*, 17:3 (2008), 359–76.

Lewis, Cherry, 'David Mushet, John Farey and William Smith: Geologising in the Forest of Dean', *Earth Sciences History*, 35:1 (2016), 167–96.

Liddington, Jill, *Female Fortune: Land, Gender and Authority: The Anne Lister Diaries and Other Writings, 1833–36* (London: Rivers Oram Press, 1998).

Lindsay, Jean, 'The Butterley Coal and Iron Works 1792–1826', *Derbyshire Archaeological Journal*, 85 (1965), 25–43.

Livesay, Daniel, *Children of Uncertain Fortune: Mixed-Race Jamaicans in Britain and the Atlantic Family, 1733–1833* (Williamsburg VA: Omohundro Institute of Early American History and Culture; Chapel Hill NC: University of North Carolina Press, 2018).

Lo, Andrew W., *Adaptive Markets: Financial Evolution at the Speed of Thought* (Princeton NJ: Princeton University Press, 2017).

Looser, Devoney, and E. Ann Kaplan (eds), *Generations: Academic Feminists in Dialogue* (Minneapolis MN: University of Minnesota Press, 1997).

Losano, Antonia, 'The Professionalization of the Woman Artist in Anne Brontë's *The Tenant of Wildfell Hall*', *Nineteenth-Century Literature*, 58:1 (2003), 1–41.

—*The Woman Painter in Victorian Literature* (Columbus OH: Ohio State University Press, 2008).

Lotmann, Yuri M., 'Theme and Plot: The Theme of Cards and the Card Game in Russian Literature of the Nineteenth Century', *PTL*, 3 (1978), 455–92.

Lowe, Lisa, *The Intimacies of Four Continents* (Durham NC: Duke University Press, 2015).

Lowenfeld, H., *Financial Review of Reviews*, no. 25 (November 1907), 15–25.

Lysack, Krista, *Come Buy, Come Buy: Shopping and the Culture of Consumption in Victorian Women's Writing* (Basingstoke: Palgrave Macmillan, 2018).

Maclaran, Pauline, 'Marketing and Feminism in Historic Perspective', *Journal of Historical Research in Marketing*, 4:3 (2012), 462–76.

MacLure, Jennifer, 'Diagnosing Capitalism: Vital Economics and the Structure of Sympathy in Gaskell's Industrial Novels', *Nineteenth-Century Contexts*, 38:5 (2016), 343–52.

MacKenzie, Donald, *Trading at the Speed of Light: How Ultrafast Algorithms Are Transforming Financial Markets* (Princeton NJ: Princeton University Press, 2021).

Magee, Gary B., and Andrew S. Thompson, *Empire and Globalisation: Networks of People, Goods and Capital in the British World, c. 1850–1914* (Cambridge: Cambridge University Press, 2010).

Maltby, Josephine, and Janette Rutterford, '"She Possessed Her Own Fortune": Women Investors from the Late Nineteenth Century to the Early Twentieth Century', *Business History*, 48:2 (2006), 220–53.

Marçal, Katrine, *Who Cooked Adam Smith's Dinner? A Story of Women and Economics* (New York: Pegasus Books, 2016).

Marshall, Alfred, *Principles of Economics*, 8th edn (London: Macmillan, 1920).

Marshall, John, *Royal Naval Biography, or, Memoirs of the Services of All the Flag-Officers, Superannuated Rear-Admirals, Retired-Captains, Post-Captains and Commanders [microform]* (London: Longman, Rees, Orme, Brown, and Green, 1832), vol. 3, part 2.

Marshall, Peter James, *Edmund Burke and the British Empire in the West Indies: Wealth, Power, and Slavery* (Oxford: Oxford University Press, 2019).

—*The Making and Unmaking of Empires: Britain, India, and America c.1750–1783* (Oxford: Oxford University Press, 2005).

Maxted, Ian, *The London Book Trades 1775–1800: A Preliminary Checklist of Members* (Folkestone: Dawson, 1977).

McCabe, Helen, '"Good Housekeeping"? Re-Assessing John Stuart Mill's Position on the Gendered Division of Labour', *History of Political Thought*, 39:1 (2018), 135–55.

—'Harriet Taylor Mill', in *Cambridge Elements: Women in the History of Philosophy* (Cambridge: Cambridge University Press, 2020).

—*Harriet Taylor Mill* (Cambridge: Cambridge University Press, 2023).

—*John Stuart Mill, Socialist* (Montreal: McGill-Queen's University Press, 2021).

McDonagh, Briony, *Elite Women and the Agricultural Landscape, 1700–1830* (London: Routledge, 2018).

McDonald, Lynn, 'Florence Nightingale and Mary Seacole on Nursing and Health Care', *Journal of Advanced Nursing*, 70:6 (2014), 1436–45.

McDowell, Margaret B., *Edith Wharton* (Boston MA: Twayne Publishers, 1976).

McKenzie, Russel, and John Levendies, 'What Recantation? The Wages Fund Doctrines of J.S. Mill in Light of Smith, and Ricardo', *Humanomics*, 24:4 (2008), 293–305.

McKeon, Michael, 'Pastoral Revolution', in *Refiguring Revolutions: Aesthetics and Politics from the English Revolution to the Romantic Revolution, ed. by* Kevin Sharpe and Stephen N. Zwicker (Berkeley CA: University of California Press, 1998), pp. 241–66.

—*The Origins of the English Novel, 1600–1740*, 15th anniversary edn (Baltimore MD: Johns Hopkins University Press, 2002).

Mellor, Anne K., 'Righting the Wrongs of Woman: Mary Wollstonecraft's Maria', *Nineteenth-Century Contexts*, 19:4 (1996), 413–24.

Mendus, Susan, 'John Stuart Mill and Harriet Taylor on Women and Marriage', *Utilitas*, 6:2 (1994), 287–99.

Michie, Elsie B., *The Vulgar Question of Money: Heiresses, Materialism, and the Novel of Manners from Jane Austen to Henry James* (Baltimore MD: Johns Hopkins University Press, 2011).

Michie, Ranald, *The City of London: Continuity and Change, 1850–1990* (London: Macmillan, 1992).

Middeke, Martin, and Monika Pietrzak-Franger (eds), *Handbook of the English Novel, 1830–1900* (Berlin: De Gruyter, 2020).

Miller, D. A., *Bringing Out Roland Barthes* (Berkeley CA: University of California Press, 1992).

—*Jane Austen, or the Secret of Style* (Princeton NJ and Oxford: Princeton University Press, 2005).

Mineka, Francis Edward, *The Dissidence of Dissent: The Monthly Repository, 1806–1838* (Chapel Hill NC: University of North Carolina Press, 1944).

Mitchell, B. R., and H. G. Jones, *Second Abstract of British Historical Statistics* (Cambridge: Cambridge University Press, 1971).

Morewood, Thomas Christmas, *Notes on the Family of Morewood (1938)*, ed. by Frank Morewood and Jenny Morewood (Oakville CA: Morewood Family Publications, 1992).

Moring, Beatrice, *Women in the Factory, 1880–1930* (London: Boydell and Brewer, 2024).

Mossner, Ernest Campbell, *The Life of David Hume* (Oxford: Clarendon Press; New York: Oxford University Press, 1980).

Morgan, Jennifer L., *Reckoning with Slavery: Gender, Kinship, and Capitalism in the Early Black Atlantic* (Durham NC: Duke University Press, 2021).

Morgan, Kenneth, 'Slave Women and Reproduction in Jamaica, c.1776–1834', *History*, 91:2 (2006), 231–53.

Mossner, Ernest Campbell, *The Life of David Hume* (Oxford: Oxford University Press, 1980).

Mullim, Katherine, 'Braddon [married name Maxwell], Mary Elizabeth (1835–1915)', *Oxford Dictionary of National Biography*, 23 September 2004.

Murphy, Anne L., *The Origins of English Financial Markets: Investment and Speculation before the South Sea Bubble* (Cambridge: Cambridge University Press, 2009).

Mushet, George, *The Diary of George Mushet, 1805–13*, ed. by R. M. Healey (Chesterfield: Derbyshire Archaeological Society, 1982).

Mussell, 'Repetition: Or, "In Our Last"', *Victorian Periodical Review*, 48:3 (Autumn 2015), 343–58.

Nader, Laura (ed.), *Kroeber Anthropological Society Papers: Essays on Controlling Processes*, no. 77 (1994), 65–102.

Nash, Julie, and Barbara A. Suess (eds), *New Approaches to the Literary Art of Anne Brontë* (Aldershot: Ashgate, 2001).

Nechtman, Tillman, *Nabobs: Empire and Identity in Eighteenth-Century Britain* (Cambridge: Cambridge University Press, 2010; this edn 2013).

Neff, Wanda Fraiken, *Victorian Working Women: An Historical and Literary Study of Women in British Industries and Professions, 1832–1850* (Columbia NY: Columbia University Press, 1929).

Nestor, Pauline, *Female Friendship and Communities: Charlotte Brontë, George Eliot, and Elizabeth Gaskell* (Oxford: Clarendon, 1985).

Norden, Bess, 'The Suffrage at Selfridge's', *New Statesman & Society*, 5:220 (1992), 34–5.

Norris, Siân, *Bodies Under Siege: How the Far-Right Attack on Reproductive Rights Went Global* (London: Verso, 2023).

Nyborg, Erin, '"A Just and Liberal Landlord": Manliness, Work, and the Landed Gentleman in the Brontës' Novels', *Journal of Victorian Culture*, 22:3 (2017), 362–79.

O'Gorman, Francis (ed.), *Victorian Literature and Finance* (Oxford: Oxford University Press, 2007).

Okin, Susan M. (ed.), *Women in Western Political Thought* (Princeton NJ: Princeton University Press, 1979).

Packham, Catherine, *Mary Wollstonecraft and Political Economy: The Feminist Critique of Commercial Modernity* (Cambridge: Cambridge University Press, 2024).

Pappe, H. O., *John Stuart Mill and the Harriet Taylor Myth* (Melbourne: Melbourne University Press, 1960).

Parlett, David, *A History of Card Games* (Oxford: Oxford University Press, 1991).

Paul, Helen J., *The South Sea Bubble: An Economic History of its Origins and Consequences* (London: Routledge, 2011).

Pedersen, Sarah, 'What's in a Name? The Revealing Use of Noms de Plume in Women's Correspondence to Daily Newspapers in Edwardian Scotland', *Media History*, 10:3 (2004), 175–85.

Peterson, Linda H. (ed.), *The Cambridge Companion to Victorian Women's Writing* (Cambridge: Cambridge University Press, 2015), pp. 43–58.

—*Becoming a Woman of Letters: Myths of Authorship and Facts of the Victorian Market* (Princeton NJ: Princeton University Press, 2009).

Petley, Christer, 'Slaveholders and Revolution: The Jamaican Planter Class, British Imperial Politics, and the Ending of the Slave Trade, 1775–1807', *Slavery & Abolition*, 39:1 (2017), 53–79.

Philips, Menaka, 'The "Beloved and Deplored" Memory of Harriet Taylor Mill: Rethinking Gender and Intellectual Labor in the Canon', *Hypatia*, 33:4 (2018), 626–42.

Pinch, Adela, *Strange Fits of Passion: Epistemologies of Emotion, Hume to Austen* (Stanford CA: Stanford University Press, 1996).

Pinto, Samantha, '"The Right Woman in the Right Place": Mary Seacole and Corrective Histories of Empire', *Ariel: A Review of International English Literature*, 50:2 (2019), 1–31.

Poole, Russell, 'Cultural Reformation and Cultural Reproduction in Anne Brontë's *The Tenant of Wildfell Hall*', *Studies in English Literature*, 33:4 (1993), 859–73.

Poovey, Mary (ed.), *The Financial System in Nineteenth-Century Britain* (New York: Oxford University Press, 2003).

—*Genres of the Credit Economy: Mediating Value in Eighteenth- and Nineteenth-Century Britain* (Chicago IL: University of Chicago Press, 2008).

—*Uneven Developments: The Ideological Work of Gender in Mid-Victorian England* (Chicago IL: University of Chicago Press, 1988).

Porter, Dilwyn, '"A Trusted Guide of the Investing Public": Harry Marks and the Financial News 1884–1916', *Business History*, 28:1 (1986), 1–17.

Potter, Hugh, and Philip Riden (eds), *Minutes of the Meetings of the Cromford Canal Co., 1789–1799*, Derbyshire Record Society, 39 (Chesterfield, 2015).

Preda, Alex, 'The Rise of the Popular Investor: Financial Knowledge and Investing in England and France, 1840–1880', *Sociological Quarterly*, 42:2 (2001), 205–31.

Pugh, Evelyn L., 'John Stuart Mill, Harriet Taylor, and Women's Rights in America, 1850–1873', *Canadian Journal of History*, 13:3 (1978), 423–42.

Pujol, Michèle A., *Feminism and Anti-Feminism in Early Economic Thought* (Aldershot and Brookfield VT: Edward Elgar, 1992).

Purcell, Emma, 'Inheritance and Influence: Heiresses and the Montagu Property Network, c.1749–1827', *Journal for Eighteenth-Century Studies*, 44:4 (2021), 439–52.

Raistrick, Arthur, and Bernard Jennings, *A History of Lead Mining in the Pennines* (London: Longmans, 1965).

Rappaport, Erika, *Shopping for Pleasure: Women and the Making of London's West End* (Princeton NJ: Princeton University Press, 2001).

Rappaport, Helen, *In Search of Mary Seacole: The Making of a Cultural Icon* (London: Simon & Schuster, 2022).

Rappoport, Jill, *Giving Women: Alliance and Exchange in Victorian Culture* (Oxford: Oxford University Press, 2012).

Reeves, Richard, *John Stuart Mill: Victorian Firebrand* (London: Atlantic Books, 2007).

Reid, Anthony, 'Sugar, Slavery, and Productivity in Jamaica, 1750–1807', *Slavery & Abolition*, 37:1 (2015), 159–82.

Ricoeur, Paul, *Time and Narrative*, vol. 2 (Chicago IL: University of Chicago Press, 1984).

Riden, Philip, *The Butterley Company 1790–1830*, Derbyshire Record Society, 16 (Chesterfield, 1990).

Robb, George, *Ladies of the Ticker: Women and Wall Street from the Gilded Age to the Great Depression* (Urbana IL: University of Illinois Press, 2017).

Robinson, Joan, *Economic Philosophy* (Harmondsworth: Penguin, 1962).

Robson, K. J. R., 'Schools of Industry: Their Part in the Development of Technical Education in Hull', *The Vocational Aspect of Secondary and Further Education*, 5:10 (1953).

Roche, Emma, *Women, Violence and Postmillennial Romance Fiction* (London: Routledge, 2023).

Rosenthal, Laura J., *Infamous Commerce: Prostitution in Eighteenth-Century British Literature and Culture* (Ithaca NY: Cornell University Press, 2006).

Rossi, Alice S. (ed.), *John Stuart Mill and Harriet Taylor Mill: Essays on Sex Equality* (Chicago IL: University of Chicago Press, 1970).

Rossman Regaignon, Dara, 'Instructive Sufficiency: Re-Reading the Governess through *Agnes Grey*', *Victorian Literature and Culture*, 29:1 (2001), 85–108.

Rubinstein, David, *A Different World for Women: The Life of Millicent Garrett Fawcett* (Columbus OH: Ohio State University Press, 1991).

Rutterford, Janette, 'Votes for Women: The Role of Women Shareholders in the Campaign for Women's Suffrage in Edwardian Britain', *Entreprises et Histoire*, 107:2 (2022), 90–109.

—'The Rise of the Small Investor in the United States and United Kingdom, 1895 to 1970', *Enterprise & Society*, 18:3 (2017), 485–535.

Rutterford, Janette, David R. Green, Josephine Maltby and Alastair Owens, 'Who Comprised the Nation of Shareholders? Gender and Investment in Great Britain, c. 1870–1935', *Economic History Review*, 64:1 (2011), 157–87.

—'Researching Shareholding and Investment in England and Wales: Approaches, Sources and Methods', *Accounting History*, 3 (2011), 269–92.

Rutterford, Janette, and Josephine Maltby, '"The Widow, the Clergyman and the Reckless": Women Investors in England, 1830–1914', *Feminist Economics*, 12:1/2 (2006), 111–38.

Rutterford, Janette, and Dimitris P. Sotiropoulos, 'Financial Diversification before Modern Portfolio Theory: UK Financial Advice Documents in the Late Nineteenth and the Beginning of the Twentieth Century', *European Journal of the History of Economic Thought*, 23:6 (2016), 919–45.

Ryan, Janette, 'Beeton [née Mayson]. Isabella Mary (1836–1865)', *Oxford Dictionary of National Biography*, 23 September 2004, https://doi.org/10.1093/ref:odnb/3717.

Ryden, David, *West Indian Slavery and British Abolition, 1783–1807* (New York: Cambridge University Press, 2009).

Said, Edward W., *Orientalism* (London: Routledge & Kegan Paul, 1978; repr. 1980).

Salah, Leila, *The Impossibility of Aid: Governing Development in an Age of Emergency* (London: Duke University Press, 2016).

Salih, Sarah, *Introduction to Wonderful Adventures of Mrs. Seacole in Many Lands* (London: Penguin Books, 2005).

Samuelson, Paul A., *Economics: An Introductory Analysis*, 1st edn (New York: McGraw-Hill, 1948).

Schaffer, Talia, 'Victorian Feminist Criticism: Recovery Work and the Care Community', *Victorian Literature and Culture*, 47:1 (2018).

—*Communities of Care: The Social Ethics of Victorian Fiction* (Princeton NJ and Oxford: Princeton University Press, 2021).

Schifferes, Steve, and Richard Roberts (eds), *The Media and Financial Crises: Comparative and Historical Perspectives* (London: Routledge, 2015).

Schmidt-Petri, Christoph, Michael Schefczyk and Lilly Osburg, 'Who Authored *On Liberty*? Stylometric Evidence on Harriet Taylor Mill's Contribution', *Utilitas*, 34 (2022), 120–38.

Schofield, R. B., *Benjamin Outram 1764–1805: An Engineering Biography* (Cardiff: Merton Priory Press, 2000).

Seccombe, Wally, 'Patriarchy Stabilized: The Construction of the Male Breadwinner Wage Norm in Nineteenth-Century Britain', *Social History*, 11:1 (January 1986), 53–76.

Seiz, Janet A., and Michèle A. Pujol, 'Harriet Taylor Mill', *American Economic Review*, 90:2 (2000), 476–79.

Shattock, Joanne (ed.), *Women and Literature in Britain, 1800–1900* (Cambridge: Cambridge University Press, 2001).

Shepherd, Verene, Bridget Brereton and Barbara Bailey (eds), *Engendering History: Caribbean Women in Historical Perspective* (New York: St Martin's Press, 1995).

Sherburne, James Clark, *John Ruskin or the Ambiguities of Abundance: A Study in Social and Economic Criticism* (Cambridge MA: Harvard University Press, 1972).

Shiller, Robert J., *Narrative Economics: How Stories Go Viral & Drive Major Economic Events* (Princeton NJ: Princeton University Press, 2019).

Showalter, Elaine, *A Literature of Their Own: British Women Novelists from Brontë to Lessing* (Princeton NJ: Princeton University Press, 1999; orig. 1977).

Siskin, Clifford, *The Work of Writing: Literature and Social Change in Britain, 1700–1830* (Baltimore MD: Johns Hopkins University Press, 1999).

Skedd, J., *Oxford Dictionary of National Biography*, s.v. 'More, Hannah', last updated 25 September 2014, https://doi.org/10.1093/ref:odnb/19179.

Spear, Percival, *The Nabobs: A Study of the Social Life of the English in Eighteenth-Century India* (London: Curzon Press, 1932).

Stebbings, Chantal, *The Private Trustee in Victorian England* (Cambridge: Cambridge University Press, 2002).

Stephan, Megan A., 'Thomas [married name Cudlip], Annie Hall (1838–1918)', *Oxford Dictionary of National Biography*, 23 September 2004.

Stiglitz, Joseph E., *Whither Socialism?* (Cambridge MA: MIT Press, 1994).

Stobart, Jon, and Alastair Owens (eds), *Urban Fortunes: Property and Inheritance in the Town, 1700–1900* (Aldershot: Ashgate, 2000).

Stone, Lawrence, and Jeanne C. Fawtier Stone, *An Open Elite? England 1540–1880* (Oxford: Clarendon Press, 1986).

Strachey, Ray, *Millicent Garrett Fawcett* (London: John Murray, 1931).

Summers, Anne, 'Pride and Prejudice: Ladies and Nurses in the Crimean War', *History Workshop Journal,* 16:1 (1983), 33–56.

Sutherland, John, *The Longman Companion to Victorian Fiction* (London: Routledge, 2014).

Tasker, Yvonne, and Diane Negra (eds), *Interrogating Postfeminism: Gender and the Politics of Popular Culture* (Durham NC: Duke University Press, 2007).

Taylor, Barbara, *Mary Wollstonecraft and the Feminist Imagination* (Cambridge: Cambridge University Press, 2003).

Taylor, James, '"Distrust All Advice … and Make No Exception in Favour of Our Advice": Financial Knowledge and Knowingness in Late Victorian Britain', *English Historical Review,* 136:580 (2021), 619–50.

Taylor, James, 'Inside and Outside the London Stock Exchange: Stockbrokers and Speculation in Late Victorian Britain', *Enterprise & Society,* 22:3 (2021), 842–77.

Taylor, James, 'Trust, Friends, and Investments in Late Victorian England', *Historical Journal,* 64:5 (2021), 1311–31.

Teay, Wandas (ed.), *Analyzing Violence Against Women* (Cham: Springer, 2019).

Terras, Melissa, and Elizabeth Crawford, *Millicent Garrett Fawcett: Selected Writings* (London: UCL Press, 2022).

Thompson, Edward Palmer, 'The Moral Economy of the English Crowd in the Eighteenth Century', *Past & Present,* 50 (1971), 76–136.

—*The Making of the English Working Class* (London: Victor Gollancz Ltd, 1963).

Thompson, Nicola Diane, *Victorian Women Writers and the Woman Question* (United Kingdom, Cambridge University Press, 1999).

Thomson, Dorothy Lampen, *Adam Smith's Daughters* (New York: Exposition Press, 1973).

Thormählen, Marianne (ed.), *The Brontës in Context* (Cambridge: Cambridge University Press, 2012).

Tilley, Joseph, *The Old Halls, Manors and Families of Derbyshire: The Scarsdale Hundred,* 4 vols (London: Simpkin, Marshall, Hamilton, Kent and Co., 1889).

Tillman, Lynne, *Love for Sale: Essays on Art, Literature, and Politics* (New York: Scribner, 2006).

Tobias, Sarah, and Arlene Stein (eds), *The Perils of Populism* (New Brunswick NJ: Rutgers University Press, 2022).

Tosh, John, *A Man's Place: Masculinity and the Middle-Class Home in Victorian England* (New Haven CT: Yale University Press, 1999).

Tulloch, Gail, *Mill and Sexual Equality* (Hertfordshire: Harvester Wheatsheaf, 1989).

Vallier, Kevin, 'Production, Distribution, and J.S. Mill', *Utilitas,* 22:2 (2010), 103–25.

Vann, Michael G., *The Great Hanoi Rat Hunt: Empire, Disease, and Modernity in French Colonial Vietnam* (Oxford: Oxford University Press, 2018).

Vercelli, Alessandro, *Crisis and Sustainability: The Delusion of Free Markets* (London: Palgrave Macmillan, 2017).

—*Finance and Democracy: Towards a Sustainable Financial System* (Cham: Palgrave Macmillan, 2019).

Wager, Susan M., 'Review of Benedict Leca, Aileen Ribeiro and Amber Ludwig, Thomas Gainsborough and the Modern Woman', *Enfilade,* (24 June 2011).

Wallis, Jane, *Joseph Wright of Derby, 1734–1797* (Derby: Derby Museum & Art Gallery, 1997).

Wayne, Tiffany K. (ed.). *Feminist Writings from Ancient Times to the Modern World: A Global Sourcebook and History*, 2 vols (Santa Barbara CA: Greenwood, 2011).

Webster, Anthony, *The Twilight of the East India Company: The Evolution of Anglo-Asian Commerce and Politics, 1790–1860* (Woodbridge: Boydell & Brewer, 2009).

Weingast, Barry R., 'Persistent Inefficiency: Adam Smith's Theory of Slavery and Its Abolition in Western Europe', in *The Adam Smith Review*, vol. 12 (London: Routledge, 2020), pp. 290–310.

Wettlaufer, Alexandra K., *Portraits of the Artist as a Young Woman: Painting and the Novel in France and Britain, 1800–1860* (Columbus OH: Ohio State University Press, 2011).

Williams, Eric, *Capitalism and Slavery* (Chapel Hill NC: University of North Carolina Press, 1944).

Williams, Raymond, *Culture and Society 1780–1950* (London: Chatto & Windus, 1967, orig. 1958).

Wolfers, Justin, 'Why Women's Voices are Scarce in Economics', *New York Times*, 2 February 2018.

Woodmansee, Martha, and Mark Osteen (eds), *The New Economic Criticism: Studies at the Intersection of Literature and Economics* (London: Routledge, 1999).

Worsnop, Judith, 'A Re-evaluation of "the Problem of Surplus Women" in Nineteenth-Century England: The Case of the 1851 Census', *Women's Studies International Forum*, 13:1 (1990), 21–31.

Wright, Amina, *Joseph Wright of Derby: Bath and Beyond* (Bath: Philip Wilson Publishers, 2014).

Unpublished Theses and Conference Papers

Collinge, Peter, 'Female Enterprise in Georgian Derbyshire, 1780–1840' (PhD thesis, Keele University, 2015).

—'"With force and arms", Ellen Morewood (1741–1824), Rebel Queen of Alfreton', paper delivered at the British Society for Eighteenth-Century Studies, St Hugh's College, University of Oxford, 8 January 2015.

Evans, Shaun, 'The Account Book of Eliza Gifford of Nerquis, Flintshire', paper delivered at the Power and Patriarchy Conference, University of Liverpool, 25 January 2022.

Fisher, William, 'Queer Money', unpublished paper presented at New Economic Criticism. Case Western Reserve University, Cleveland, Ohio. 22 October 1994.

Malcom, Judith Wittosch, 'Trollope's *Saint Paul's Magazine*' (PhD thesis, University of Michigan, 1984).

McKinnon Dick, Malcolm, 'English Conservatives and Schools for the Poor c.1780–1833: A Study of the Sunday School, School of Industry and the Philanthropic Society's School for Vagrant and Criminal Children' (PhD thesis, University of Leicester, 1979).

Nestler, Gerald, 'The Derivative Condition: A Present Inquiry into the History of Futures' (PhD thesis, Goldsmiths, University of London, 2017).

Walker, Melissa, 'On Their Own: The Single Woman, Feminism, and Self-Help in British Women's Print Culture (1850–1900)' (PhD thesis, University of Guelph, 2012).

Wosnitzer, Robert, 'Desk, Firm, God, Country: Proprietary Trading and the Speculative Ethos of Financialism' (PhD thesis, New York University, 2014).

Web-based Sources

International Monetary Fund (IMF), 'Artificial Intelligence Can Make Markets More Efficient – and More Volatile', *IMF Blog*, 15 October 2024, www.imf.org/en/Blogs/Articles/2024/10/15/artificial-intelligence-can-make-markets-more-efficient-and-more-volatile.

National Archives, 'Access to Archives (A2A)', The National Archives, www.nationalarchives.gov.uk/a2a.

National Gas Archive, 'Welcome to National Gas Archive', National Gas Archive, https://gasarchive.nationalgas.com/.

Rappaport, Helen, 'Sarah Forbes Bonetta: The Captive African Princess Gifted to Queen Victoria', *HelenRappaport.com.*

Sharren, Kandice, 'By the Author of …', *Women's Print History Project*, https://womensprinthistoryproject.com/blog/post/108.

Vision of Britain, 'History of the Census of Population', *Vision of Britain*, www.visionofbritain.org.uk/census/.

Walters, Guy, 'The Black Florence Nightingale and the Making of a PC Myth', *Daily Mail Online*, 31 December 2012, www.dailymail.co.uk/news/article-2255095/The-black-Florence-Nightingale-making-PC-myth-One-historian-explains-Mary-Seacoles-story-stood-up.html.

Index

Printed and bound by CPI Group (UK) Ltd, Croydon, CR0 4YY

13/09/2026

14961005-0007